D1604506

UNIX® SYSTEM V
RELEASE 4

Programmer's Guide:
Networking Interfaces

UNIX Software Operation

Published by Prentice-Hall, Inc.
A Division of Simon & Schuster
Englewood Cliffs, New Jersey 07632

10 9 8 7 6 5 4 3 2 1

ISBN   0-13-947078-6

UNIX
PRESS
A Prentice Hall Title

P R E N T I C E   H A L L

ORDERING INFORMATION

UNIX® SYSTEM V, RELEASE 4 DOCUMENTATION

To order single copies of UNIX® SYSTEM V, Release 4 documentation, please call (201) 767-5937.

ATTENTION DOCUMENTATION MANAGERS AND TRAINING DIRECTORS:
For bulk purchases in excess of 30 copies please write to:
Corporate Sales
Prentice Hall
Englewood Cliffs, N.J. 07632.
Or call: (201) 592-2498.

ATTENTION GOVERNMENT CUSTOMERS: For GSA and other pricing
information please call (201) 767-5994.

Prentice-Hall International (UK) Limited, *London*
Prentice-Hall of Australia Pty. Limited, *Sydney*
Prentice-Hall Canada Inc., *Toronto*
Prentice-Hall Hispanoamericana, S.A., *Mexico*
Prentice-Hall of India Private Limited, *New Delhi*
Prentice-Hall of Japan, Inc., *Tokyo*
Simon & Schuster Asia Pte. Ltd., *Singapore*
Editora Prentice-Hall do Brasil, Ltda., *Rio de Janeiro*

AT&T UNIX® System V Release 4

General Use and System Administration

UNIX® System V Release 4 Network User's and Administrator's Guide
UNIX® System V Release 4 Product Overview and Master Index
UNIX® System V Release 4 System Administrator's Guide
UNIX® System V Release 4 System Administrator's Reference Manual
UNIX® System V Release 4 User's Guide
UNIX® System V Release 4 User's Reference Manual

General Programmer's Series

UNIX® System V Release 4 Programmer's Guide: ANSI C
    and Programming Support Tools
UNIX® System V Release 4 Programmer's Guide: Character User Interface
    (FMLI and ETI)
UNIX® System V Release 4 Programmer's Guide: Networking Interfaces
UNIX® System V Release 4 Programmer's Guide: POSIX Conformance
UNIX® System V Release 4 Programmer's Guide: System Services
    and Application Packaging Tools
UNIX® System V Release 4 Programmer's Reference Manual

System Programmer's Series

UNIX® System V Release 4 ANSI C Transition Guide
UNIX® System V Release 4 BSD / XENIX® Compatibility Guide
UNIX® System V Release 4 Device Driver Interface / Driver−Kernel
    Interface (DDI / DKI) Reference Manual
UNIX® System V Release 4 Migration Guide
UNIX® System V Release 4 Programmer's Guide: STREAMS

Available from Prentice Hall

Contents of Volume

TLI and Sockets Programming
Introduction
Transport Interface Programming
The Sockets Interface
Sockets Migration and Sockets-to-TLI Conversion
Index: TLI and Sockets Programming

Remote Procedure Calls
Introduction to Remote Procedure Calls
rpcgen Programming Guide
Remote Procedure Call Programming Guide
External Data Representation Standard: Protocol
    Specification
Remote Procedure Calls: Protocol Specification
RPC Administration
The YP Service
Index: Remote Procedure Calls

Network Selection and Name-to-Address Mappping
Network Selection and Name-to-Address Mapping
Index: Network Selection and Name-to-Address Mapping

Writing a Port Monitor for the Service Access Facility

Appendix A: Manual Pages

Contents

Programmer's Guide: Networking Interfaces

Figures and Tables

Table of Contents _____

1 Introduction

Introduction

The AT&T Transport Interface (TLI) was introduced in UNIX System V Release 3 as a standard transport-independent programming interface. The Network Selection and Name-to-Address Mapping facilities have been added to Release 4.0 to provide a means of guaranteeing media and protocol independence for transport applications. Network Selection and Name-to-Address Mapping allow programmers to get transport-specific information to network applications in a transport-independent way.

As part of the unification of UNIX System V and Berkeley UNIX, the sockets interface and support for the DARPA protocols (the TCP/IP Internet Package) have also been added to System V Release 4.0.

Both TLI and sockets provide a programming interface to the transport layer. In System V Release 4.0, both are implemented within the STREAMS framework. They differ in the following ways:

- TLI is media- and protocol-independent. It allows applications to run over any transport protocol that supports the TLI interface.

- The sockets interface has historically been tied to the Internet protocol suite, TCP/IP and UDP/IP.

It is expected that new applications will take advantage of TLI's protocol independence and that the socket interface will be used primarily in expanding and maintaining existing sockets-based applications.

Organization of the Document

The document contains this Introduction and three major chapters. Chapter 2, "Transport Interface Programming," describes the UNIX System Transport Interface (TLI).

Chapter 3, "The Sockets Interface," describes the socket-based interface to the transport layer.

Chapter 4, "Sockets Migration and Sockets-to-TLI Conversion," describes the differences between the TLI and sockets interfaces and shows how BSD sockets applications can be adapted to System V Release 4, and how sockets applications, whether Berkeley- or System V-based, can be modified to run under TLI. The chapter includes parallel code examples and tables of equivalent sockets and TLI functions.

Network Selection and Name-to-Address Mapping

TLI applications require an understanding of the Network Selection and Name-to-Address Mapping facilities provided with this release if they are to run as media- and protocol-independent applications. Network Selection provides a standard interface to the networks available in any current environment. Name-to-Address Mapping allows applications to translate transport-specific addresses. The following material is available:

- *Programmer's Guide: Networking Interfaces.* Chapter 8, "Network Selection and Name-to-Address Mapping." This chapter provides comprehensive coverage of these facilities.

- *System Administrator's Guide.* Chapter 10, "Network Services." The description of the Network Selection and Name-to-Address Mapping facilities is intended for administrators and does not include complete descriptions of the library routines.

- *Programmer's Guide: Networking Interfaces.* The following manual pages are included at the end of the Network Selection and Name-to-Address Mapping chapter:

  □ getnetconfig(3N). Describes the Network Selection library routines that manipulate the network configuration administrative file, netconfig.

  □ getnetpath(3N). Describes the routines that manipulate the NETPATH variable. The NETPATH environment variable allows programmers to choose the networks in the netconfig file that an application is to try.

  □ netconfig(4). Describes the network configuration database file.

  □ environ(5). Describes the NETPATH environment variable.

  □ netdir(3N). Contains descriptions of the Name-to-Address Mapping library functions.

2   Transport Interface Programming

Introduction

This chapter provides detailed information, with various examples, on the UNIX system Transport Interface. This interface is intended to supersede the socket-based interprocess communications mechanisms as the standard means of gaining direct access to transport services.

The following discussion assumes a working knowledge of UNIX system and C language programming and data communication concepts. Familiarity with the Reference Model of Open Systems Interconnection (OSI) is required as well.

Background

To place the Transport Interface in perspective, a discussion of the OSI Reference Model is first presented. The Reference Model partitions networking functions into seven layers, as depicted in Figure 2-1.

Figure 2-1: OSI Reference Model

Layer 7	application
Layer 6	presentation
Layer 5	session
Layer 4	transport
Layer 3	network
Layer 2	data link
Layer 1	physical

Layer 1   The physical layer is responsible for the transmission of raw data over a communication medium.

Layer 2   The data link layer provides the exchange of data between network layer entities. It detects and corrects any errors that may occur in the physical layer transmission.

Layer 3   The network layer manages the operation of the network. In particular, it is responsible for the routing and management of data exchange between transport layer entities within the network.

Layer 4   The transport layer provides transparent data transfer services between session layer entities by relieving them from concerns of how reliable and cost-effective transfer of data is achieved.

Layer 5   The session layer provides the services needed by presentation layer entities that enable them to organize and synchronize their dialogue and manage their data exchange.

Layer 6   The presentation layer manages the representation of information that application layer entities either communicate or reference in their communication.

Layer 7   The application layer serves as the window between corresponding application processes that are exchanging information.

A basic principle of the Reference Model is that each layer provides services needed by the next higher layer in a way that frees the upper layer from concern about how these services are provided. This approach simplifies the design of each particular layer.

Industry standards either have been or are being defined at each layer of the Reference Model. Two standards are defined at each layer: one that specifies an interface to the services of the layer, and one that defines the protocol by which services are provided. A service interface standard at any layer frees users of the service from details of how that layer's protocol is implemented, or even which protocol is used to provide the service.

The transport layer is important because it is the lowest layer in the Reference Model that provides the basic service of reliable, end-to-end data transfer needed by applications and higher layer protocols. In doing so, this layer hides the topology and characteristics of the underlying network from its users. More important, however, the transport layer defines a set of services common to layers of many contemporary protocol suites, including the International Standards Organization (ISO) protocols, the Transmission Control Protocol and Internet Protocol (TCP/IP) of the ARPANET, Xerox Network Systems (XNS), and the Systems Network Architecture (SNA).

A transport service interface, then, enables applications and higher layer protocols to be implemented without knowledge of the underlying protocol suite. That is a principle goal of the UNIX system Transport Interface. Also, because an inherent characteristic of the transport layer is that it hides details of the physical medium being used, the Transport Interface offers both protocol and medium independence to networking applications and higher layer protocols.

The UNIX system Transport Interface was modeled after the industry standard ISO Transport Service Definition (ISO 8072). As such, it is intended for those applications and protocols that require transport services. Because the Transport Interface provides reliable data transfer, and because its services are common to several protocol suites, many networking applications will find these services useful.

The Transport Interface is implemented as a user library using the STREAMS input/output mechanism. Therefore, many services available to STREAMS applications are also available to users of the Transport Interface. These services will be highlighted throughout this guide. For detailed information about STREAMS, see the *DDI Driver-Kernel Interface (DDI/DKI) Reference Manual* or the *Programmer's Guide: STREAMS*.

Document Organization

This chapter is organized as follows:

- "Overview of the Transport Interface," a summary of the basic services available to Transport Interface users and a presentation of the background information needed for the remainder of the section.

- "Introduction to Connection-Mode Service," a description of the services associated with connection-based (or virtual circuit) communication.

- "Introduction to Connectionless-Mode Service," a description of the services associated with connectionless (or datagram) communication.

- "A Read/Write Interface," a description of how users can use the services of read(2) and write(2) to communicate over a transport connection.

- "Advanced Topics," a discussion of important concepts not covered in earlier sections. These include asynchronous event handling and processing of multiple, simultaneous connect requests.

- "State Transitions," which defines the allowable state transitions associated with the Transport Interface.

- "Guidelines for Protocol Independence," which establishes necessary guidelines for developing software that can be run without change over any transport protocol developed for the Transport Interface.

- "Examples," which presents the full listing of each programming example used throughout the guide.

- "Glossary," a definition of the Transport Interface terms and acronyms used in this section.

This section describes the more important and common facilities of the Transport Interface, but is not meant to be exhaustive. Appendix A of this document contains manual pages giving complete descriptions of each Transport Interface routine.

Overview of the Transport Interface

This section presents a high level overview of the services of the Transport Interface, which supports the transfer of data between two user processes. Figure 2-2 illustrates the Transport Interface.

Figure 2-2: Transport Interface

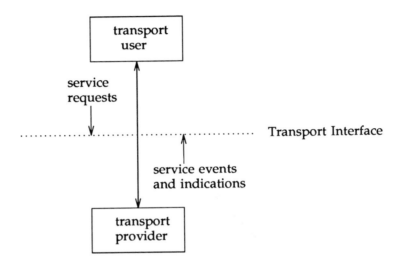

The transport provider is the entity that provides the services of the Transport Interface, and the transport user is the entity that requires these services. An example of a transport provider is the ISO transport protocol, while a transport user may be a networking application or session layer protocol.

The transport user accesses the services of the transport provider by issuing the appropriate service requests. One example is a request to transfer data over a connection. Similarly, the transport provider notifies the user of various events, such as the arrival of data on a connection.

The Network Services Library of UNIX System V includes a set of functions that support the services of the Transport Interface for user processes (see intro(3)). These functions enable a user to make requests to the provider and process incoming events. Programs using the Transport Interface can link the appropriate routines as follows:

```
cc prog.c -lnsl
```

Modes of Service

The Transport Interface provides two modes of service:

- connection-mode
- connectionless-mode

Connection-mode is circuit-oriented and enables the transmission of data over an established connection in a reliable, sequenced manner. It also provides an identification procedure that avoids the overhead of address resolution and transmission during the data transfer phase. This service is attractive for applications that require relatively long-lived, datastream-oriented interactions.

Connectionless-mode, by contrast, is message-oriented and supports data transfer in self-contained units with no logical relationship required among multiple units. This service requires only a preexisting association between the peer users involved, which determines the characteristics of the data to be transmitted. All the information required to deliver a unit of data (for example, the destination address) is presented to the transport provider, together with the data to be transmitted, in one service access (which need not relate to any other service access). Each unit of data transmitted is entirely self-contained. Connectionless-mode service is attractive for applications that:

- involve short-term request/response interactions
- exhibit a high level of redundancy
- are dynamically reconfigurable
- do not require guaranteed, in-sequence delivery of data

Connection-Mode Service

The connection-mode transport service is characterized by four phases:

- local management
- connection establishment
- data transfer
- connection release

Local Management

The local management phase defines local operations between a transport user and a transport provider. For example, a user must establish a channel of communication with the transport provider, as illustrated in Figure 2-3. Each channel between a transport user and transport provider is a unique endpoint of communication, and will be called the transport endpoint. The t_open(3N) routine enables a user to choose a particular transport provider that will supply the connection-mode services, and establishes the transport endpoint.

Figure 2-3: Channel Between User and Provider

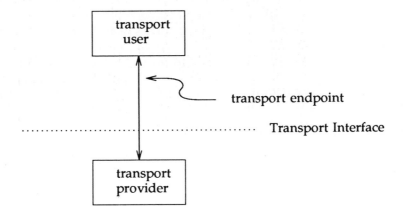

Another necessary local function for each user is to establish an identity with the transport provider. Each user is identified by a transport address. More accurately, a transport address is associated with each transport endpoint, and one user process may manage several transport endpoints. In connection-mode service, one user requests a connection to another user by specifying that user's address. The structure of a transport address is defined by the address space of the transport provider. An address may be as simple as a random character string (for example, "file_server"), or as complex as an encoded bit pattern that specifies all information needed to route data through a network. Each transport provider defines its own mechanism for identifying users. Addresses may be assigned to each transport endpoint by t_bind(3N).

In addition to t_open and t_bind, several routines are available to support local operations. Table 2-1 summarizes all local management routines of the Transport Interface.

Table 2-1: Local Management Routines of the Transport Interface

Command	Description
t_alloc	Allocates Transport Interface data structures.
t_bind	Binds a transport address to a transport endpoint.
t_close	Closes a transport endpoint.
t_error	Prints a Transport Interface error message.
t_free	Frees structures allocated using t_alloc.
t_getinfo	Returns a set of parameters associated with a particular transport provider.
t_getstate	Returns the state of a transport endpoint.

Table 2-1: Local Management Routines of the Transport Interface (continued)

Command	Description
t_look	Returns the current event on a transport endpoint.
t_open	Establishes a transport endpoint connected to a chosen transport provider.
t_optmgmt	Negotiates protocol-specific options with the transport provider.
t_sync	Synchronizes a transport endpoint with the transport provider.
t_unbind	Unbinds a transport address from a transport endpoint.

Connection Establishment

The connection establishment phase enables two users to create a connection, or virtual circuit, between them, as demonstrated in Figure 2-4.

Figure 2-4: Transport Connection

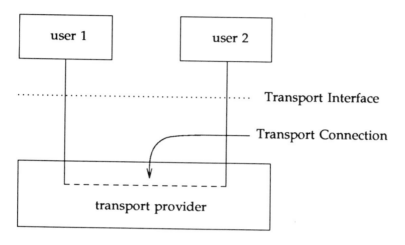

This phase is illustrated by a client-server relationship between two transport users. One user, the server, typically advertises some service to a group of users, and then listens for requests from those users. As each client requires the service, it attempts to connect itself to the server using the server's advertised transport address. The t_connect(3N) routine initiates the connect request. One argument to t_connect, the transport address, identifies the server the client wishes to access. The server is notified of each incoming request using t_listen(3N), and may call t_accept(3N) to accept the client's request for access to the service. If the request is accepted, the transport connection is established.

Table 2-2 summarizes all routines available for establishing a transport connection.

Table 2-2: Routines for Establishing a Transport Connection

Command	Description
t_accept	Accepts a request for a transport connection.
t_connect	Establishes a connection with the transport user at a specified destination.
t_listen	Retrieves an indication of a connect request from another transport user.
t_rcvconnect	Completes connection establishment if t_connect was called in asynchronous mode (see the section "Advanced Topics").

Data Transfer

The data transfer phase enables users to transfer data in both directions over an established connection. Two routines, t_snd(3N) and t_rcv(3N), send and receive data over this connection. All data sent by a user is guaranteed to be delivered to the user on the other end of the connection in the order in which it was sent. Table 2-3 summarizes the connection mode data transfer routines.

Table 2-3: Connection Mode Data Transfer Routines

Command	Description
t_rcv	Retrieves data that has arrived over a transport connection.
t_snd	Sends data over an established transport connection.

Connection Release

The connection release phase allows you to break an established connection. When you decide that a conversation should end, you can request that the provider release the transport connection. Two types of connection release are supported by the Transport Interface. The first is an abortive release, which directs the transport provider to release the connection immediately. Any previously sent data that has not yet reached the other transport user may be discarded by the transport provider. The t_snddis(3N) routine initiates this abortive disconnect, and t_rcvdis(3N) processes the incoming indication for an abortive disconnect.

All transport providers must support the abortive release procedure. In addition, some transport providers may also support an orderly release facility that enables users to terminate communication gracefully with no data loss. The functions t_sndrel(3N) and t_rcvrel(3N) support this capability. Table 2-4 summarizes the connection release routines.

Table 2-4: Connection Release Routines

Command	Description
t_rcvdis	Returns an indication of an aborted connection, including a reason code and user data.
t_rcvrel	Returns an indication that the remote user has requested an orderly release of a connection.
t_snddis	Aborts a connection or rejects a connect request.
t_sndrel	Requests the orderly release of a connection.

Connectionless-Mode Service

The connectionless-mode transport service is characterized by two phases: local management and data transfer. The local management phase defines the same local operations described above for the connection-mode service.

The data transfer phase enables a user to transfer data units (sometimes called datagrams) to the specified peer user. Each data unit must be accompanied by the transport address of the destination user. Two routines, t_sndudata(3N) and t_rcvudata(3N), support this message-based data transfer facility. Table 2-5 summarizes all routines associated with connectionless-mode data transfer.

Table 2-5: Routines for Connectionless-Mode Data Transfer

Command	Description
t_rcvudata	Retrieves a message sent by another transport user.
t_rcvuderr	Retrieves error information associated with a previously sent message.
t_sndudata	Sends a message to the specified destination user.

State Transitions

The Transport Interface has two components:

- the library routines that provide the transport services to users

- the state transition rules that define the sequence in which the transport routines may be invoked

The state transition rules can be found later in this chapter in the state tables in the section "State Transitions." The state tables define the legal sequence of library calls based on state information and the handling of events. These events include user-generated library calls, as well as provider-generated event indications.

Any user of the Transport Interface must completely understand all possible state transitions before writing software using the interface.

Introduction to Connection-Mode Service

This section describes the connection-mode service of the Transport Interface. As discussed in the previous section, the connection-mode service can be illustrated using a client-server paradigm. The important concepts of connection-mode service will be presented using two programming examples. The examples are related: the first example illustrates how a client establishes a connection to a server and then communicates with it; the second example shows the server's side of the interaction. All examples discussed in this chapter are presented complete later in the section "Some Examples."

In the examples, the client establishes a connection with a server process. The server then transfers a file to the client. The client, in turn, receives the data from the server and writes it to its standard output file.

Local Management

Before the client and server can establish a transport connection, each must first establish a local channel (the transport endpoint) to the transport provider using t_open, and establish its identity (or address) using t_bind.

The set of services supported by the Transport Interface may not be implemented by all transport protocols. Each transport provider has a set of characteristics associated with it that determines the services it offers and the limits associated with those services. This information is returned to the user by t_open, and consists of the following:

addr   maximum size of a transport address

options   maximum bytes of protocol-specific options that may be passed
            between the transport user and transport provider

tsdu   maximum message size that may be transmitted in either
            connection-mode or connectionless-mode

etsdu   maximum expedited data message size that may be sent over a
            transport connection

connect   maximum number of bytes of user data that may be passed
            between users during connection establishment

discon   maximum bytes of user data that may be passed between users during the abortive release of a connection

servtype   the type of service supported by the transport provider

The three service types defined by the Transport Interface are:

T_COTS   The transport provider supports connection-mode service but does not provide the optional orderly release facility.

T_COTS_ORD The transport provider supports connection-mode service with the optional orderly release facility.

T_CLTS   The transport provider supports connectionless-mode service. Only one such service can be associated with the transport provider identified by t_open.

NOTE t_open returns the default provider characteristics associated with a transport endpoint. However, some characteristics may change after an endpoint has been opened. This will occur if the characteristics are associated with negotiated options (option negotiation is described later in this section). For example, if the support of expedited data transfer is a negotiated option, the value of this characteristic may change. t_getinfo may be called to retrieve the current characteristics of a transport endpoint.

Once a user establishes a transport endpoint with the chosen transport provider, it must establish its identity. As mentioned earlier, t_bind does this by binding a transport address to the transport endpoint. In addition, for servers, this routine informs the transport provider that the endpoint will be used to listen for incoming connect indications, also called connect requests.

An optional facility, t_optmgmt(3N), is also available during the local management phase. It enables a user to negotiate the values of protocol options with the transport provider. Each transport protocol is expected to define its own set of negotiable protocol options, which may include such information as Quality-of-Service parameters. Because of the protocol-specific nature of options, only applications written for a particular protocol environment are expected to use this facility.

The Client

The local management requirements of the example client and server are used to discuss details of these facilities. The following are the definitions needed by the client program, followed by its necessary local management steps.

```
#include <stdio.h>
#include <tiuser.h>
#include <fcntl.h>

#define SRV_ADDR   1        /* server's well known address */

main()
{
        int fd;
        int nbytes;
        int flags = 0;
        char buf[1024];
        struct t_call *sndcall;
        extern int t_errno;

        if ((fd = t_open("/dev/tivc", O_RDWR, NULL)) < 0) {
                t_error("t_open failed");
                exit(1);
        }

        if (t_bind(fd, NULL, NULL) < 0) {
                t_error("t_bind failed");
                exit(2);
        }
```

The first argument to t_open is the pathname of a file system node that identifies the transport protocol that will supply the transport service. In this example, /dev/tivc is a STREAMS clone device node that identifies a generic, connection-based transport protocol (see clone(4)). The clone device finds an available minor device of the transport provider for the user. It is opened for both reading and writing, as specified by the O_RDWR open flag. The third argument may be used to return the service characteristics of the transport provider to the user. This information is useful when writing protocol-independent software (discussed in the section "Guidelines for Protocol Independence," below). For simplicity, the client and server in this example ignore this information and assume the transport provider has the following characteristics:

- The transport address is an integer value that uniquely identifies each user.

- The transport provider supports the T_COTS_ORD service type, and the example will use the orderly release facility to release the connection.

- User data may not be passed between users during either connection establishment or abortive release.

- The transport provider does not support protocol-specific options.

Because these characteristics are not needed by the user, NULL is specified in the third argument to t_open. If the user needed a service other than T_COTS_ORD, another transport provider would be opened. An example of the T_CLTS service invocation is presented in the section "Introduction to Connectionless-Mode Service."

The return value of t_open is an identifier for the transport endpoint that will be used by all subsequent Transport Interface function calls. This identifier is actually a file descriptor obtained by opening the transport protocol file (see open(2)). The significance of this fact is highlighted in the section "A Read/Write Interface."

After the transport endpoint is created, the client calls t_bind to assign an address to the endpoint. The first argument identifies the transport endpoint. The second argument describes the address the user would like to bind to the endpoint, and the third argument is set on return from t_bind to specify the address that the provider bound.

The address associated with a server's transport endpoint is important, because that is the address used by all clients to access the server. However, the typical client does not care what its own address is, because no other process will try to access it. That is the case in this example, where the second and third arguments to t_bind are set to NULL. A NULL second argument directs the transport provider to choose an address for the user. A NULL third argument specifies that the user does not care what address was assigned to the endpoint.

If either t_open or t_bind fail, the program will call t_error(3N) to print an appropriate error message to stderr. If any Transport Interface routine fails, the global integer t_errno will be assigned a transport error value. A set of error values has been defined (in <tiuser.h>) for the Transport Interface, and t_error will print an error message corresponding to the value in t_errno. This routine is analogous to perror(3), which prints an error message based on the value of errno. If the error associated with a transport function is a system error, t_errno will be set to TSYSERR, and errno will be set to the appropriate value.

The Server

The server in this example must take similar local management steps before communication can begin. The server must establish a transport endpoint through which it will listen for connect indications. The necessary definitions and local management steps are shown below:

```
#include <tiuser.h>
#include <stropts.h>
#include <fcntl.h>
#include <stdio.h>
#include <signal.h>

#define DISCONNECT -1
#define SRV_ADDR   1          /* server's well known address */

int conn_fd;                          /* connection established here */
extern int t_errno;

main()
{
        int listen_fd;            /* listening transport endpoint */
        struct t_bind *bind;
        struct t_call *call;

        if ((listen_fd = t_open("/dev/tivc",
          O_RDWR, NULL)) < 0) {
                t_error("t_open failed for listen_fd");
                exit(1);
        }

        /*
         * By assuming that the address is an integer value,
         * this program may not run over another protocol.
         */

        if ((bind = (struct t_bind *)t_alloc(listen_fd,
          T_BIND, T_ALL)) == NULL) {
                t_error("t_alloc of t_bind structure failed");
```

(continued on next page)

```
            exit(2);
    }

    bind->qlen = 1;
    bind->addr.len = sizeof(int);
    *(int *)bind->addr.buf = SRV_ADDR;

    if (t_bind(listen_fd, bind, bind) < 0) {
            t_error("t_bind failed for listen_fd");
            exit(3);
    }

    /*
     * Was the correct address bound?
     */
    if (*(int *)bind->addr.buf != SRV_ADDR) {
            fprintf(stderr, "t_bind bound wrong address\n");
            exit(4);
    }
```

As with the client, the first step is to call t_open to establish a transport end-point with the desired transport provider. This endpoint, listen_fd, will be used to listen for connect indications. Next, the server must bind its well-known address to the endpoint. This address is used by each client to access the server. The second argument to t_bind requests that a particular address be bound to the transport endpoint. This argument points to a t_bind structure with the following format:

```
struct t_bind {
        struct netbuf addr;
        unsigned qlen;
}
```

where addr describes the address to be bound, and qlen specifies the maximum outstanding connect indications that may arrive at this endpoint. All Transport Interface structure and constant definitions are found in <tiuser.h>.

The address is specified using a `netbuf` structure that contains the following
members:

```
struct netbuf {
        unsigned int maxlen;
        unsigned int len;
        char *buf;
}
```

where `buf` points to a buffer containing the data, `len` specifies the bytes of data
in the buffer, and `maxlen` specifies the maximum bytes the buffer can hold (and
need only be set when data is returned to the user by a Transport Interface routine). For the `t_bind` structure, the data pointed to by `buf` identifies a transport address. It is expected that the structure of addresses will vary among
each protocol implementation under the Transport Interface. The `netbuf` structure is intended to support any address structure.

If the value of `qlen` is greater than 0, the transport endpoint may be used to
listen for connect indications. In such cases, `t_bind` directs the transport provider to begin queueing connect indications destined for the bound address
immediately. Furthermore, the value of `qlen` specifies the maximum outstanding connect indications the server wishes to process. The server must respond
to each connect indication, either accepting or rejecting the request for connection. An outstanding connect indication is one to which the server has not yet
responded. Often, a server will fully process a single connect indication and
respond to it before receiving the next indication. When this occurs, a value of
1 is appropriate for `qlen`. However, some servers may wish to retrieve several
connect indications before responding to any of them. In such cases, `qlen`
specifies the maximum number of outstanding indications the server will process. An example of a server that manages multiple outstanding connect indications is presented in the section "Advanced Topics."

`t_alloc`(3N) is called to allocate the `t_bind` structure needed by `t_bind`.
`t_alloc` takes three arguments. The first is a file descriptor that references a
transport endpoint. This is used to access the characteristics of the transport
provider (see `t_open`(3N)). The second argument identifies the appropriate
Transport Interface structure to be allocated. The third argument specifies
which, if any, `netbuf` buffers should be allocated for that structure. `T_ALL`
specifies that all `netbuf` buffers associated with the structure should be

allocated, and causes the addr buffer to be allocated in this example. The size of this buffer is determined from the transport provider characteristic that defines the maximum address size. The maxlen field of this netbuf structure will be set to the size of the newly allocated buffer by t_alloc. The use of t_alloc helps ensure the compatibility of user programs with future releases of the Transport Interface.

The server in this example processes connect indications one at a time, so qlen is set to 1. The address information is then assigned to the newly allocated t_bind structure. This t_bind structure passes information to t_bind in the second argument and returns information to the user in the third argument.

On return, the t_bind structure contains the address that was bound to the transport endpoint. If the provider could not bind the requested address (perhaps because it had been bound to another transport endpoint), it will choose another appropriate address.

NOTE Each transport provider manages its address space differently. Some transport providers may allow a single transport address to be bound to several transport endpoints, while others may require a unique address per endpoint. The Transport Interface supports either choice. Based on its address management rules, a provider will determine if it can bind the requested address. If not, it will choose another valid address from its address space and bind it to the transport endpoint.

The server must check the bound address to ensure that it is the one previously advertised to clients. Otherwise, the clients will be unable to reach the server.

If t_bind succeeds, the provider will begin queueing connect indications. entering the next phase of communication, connection establishment.

Connection Establishment

The connection establishment procedures highlight the distinction between clients and servers. The Transport Interface imposes a different set of procedures in this phase for each type of transport user. The client starts the connection establishment procedure by requesting a connection to a particular server using t_connect(3N). The server is then notified of the client's request by calling t_listen(3N). The server may either accept or reject the client's request. It will call t_accept(3N) to establish the connection, or call t_snddis(3N) to reject the request. The client will be notified of the server's decision when t_connect completes.

The Transport Interface supports two facilities during connection establishment that may not be supported by all transport providers:

■ The ability to transfer data between the client and server when establishing the connection.

 The client may send data to the server when it requests a connection. This data will be passed to the server by t_listen. Similarly, the server can send data to the client when it accepts or rejects the connection. The connect characteristic returned by t_open determines how much data, if any, two users may transfer during connect establishment.

■ The negotiation of protocol options.

 The client may specify protocol options that it would like the transport provider and/or the remote user to support. The Transport Interface supports both local and remote option negotiation. As discussed earlier, option negotiation is inherently a protocol-specific function. Use of this facility is discouraged if protocol independent software is a goal (see the section "Guidelines for Protocol Independence").

The Client

Continuing with the client/server example, the steps needed by the client to establish a connection are shown next:

```
/* By assuming that the address is an integer value,
 * this program may not run over another protocol.
 */
if ((sndcall = (struct t_call *)t_alloc(fd, T_CALL, T_ADDR)) == NULL) {
        t_error("t_alloc failed");
        exit(3);
}
sndcall->addr.len = sizeof(int);
*(int *)sndcall->addr.buf = SRV_ADDR;

if (t_connect(fd, sndcall, NULL) < 0) {
        t_error("t_connect failed for fd");
        exit(4);
}
```

The t_connect call establishes the connection with the server. The first argument to t_connect identifies the transport endpoint through which the connection is established, and the second argument identifies the destination server. This argument is a pointer to a t_call structure with the following format:

```
struct t_call {
        struct netbuf addr;
        struct netbuf opt;
        struct netbuf udata;
        int sequence;
}
```

addr identifies the address of the server, opt may be used to specify protocol-specific options that the client would like to associate with the connection, and udata identifies user data that may be sent with the connect request to the server. The sequence field has no meaning for t_connect.

t_alloc is called above to allocate the t_call structure dynamically. Once allocated, the appropriate values are assigned. In this example, no options or user data are associated with the t_connect call, but the server's address must be set. The third argument to t_alloc is set to T_ADDR to specify that an appropriate netbuf buffer should be allocated for the address. The server's address is then assigned to buf, and len is set accordingly.

The third argument to t_connect can be used to return information about the newly established connection to the user, and may retrieve any user data sent by the server in its response to the connect request. It is set to NULL by the client here to indicate that this information is not needed. The connection will be established on successful return of t_connect. If the server rejects the connect request, t_connect will fail and set t_errno to TLOOK.

Event Handling

The TLOOK error has special significance in the Transport Interface. TLOOK notifies the user if a Transport Interface routine is interrupted by an unexpected asynchronous transport event on the given transport endpoint. As such, TLOOK does not report an error with a Transport Interface routine, but the normal processing of that routine will not be done because of the pending event. The events defined by the Transport Interface are listed here:

T_LISTEN	A request for a connection, called a connect indication, has arrived at the transport endpoint.
T_CONNECT	The confirmation of a previously sent connect request, called a connect confirmation, has arrived at the transport endpoint. The confirmation is generated when a server accepts a connect request.
T_DATA	User data has arrived at the transport endpoint.
T_EXDATA	Expedited user data has arrived at the transport endpoint. Expedited data will be discussed later in this section.
T_DISCONNECT	A notification that the connection was aborted or that the server rejected a connect request, called a disconnect indication, has arrived at the transport endpoint.
T_ORDREL	A request for the orderly release of a connection, called an orderly release indication, has arrived at the transport endpoint.
T_UDERR	The notification of an error in a previously sent datagram, called a unitdata error indication, has arrived at the transport endpoint (see the section "Introduction to Connectionless-Mode Service").

It is possible in some states to receive one of several asynchronous events, as described in the state tables of the section "State Transitions." The t_look(3N) routine enables a user to determine what event has occurred if a TLOOK error is returned. The user can then process that event accordingly. In the example, if a connect request is rejected, the event passed to the client will be a disconnect indication. The client will exit if its request is rejected.

The Server

Returning to the example, when the client calls t_connect, a connect indication will be generated on the server's listening transport endpoint. The steps required by the server to process the event are discussed below. For each client, the server accepts the connect request and spawns a server process to manage the connection.

```
if ((call = (struct t_call *)t_alloc(listen_fd, T_CALL, T_ALL)) == NULL) {
        t_error("t_alloc of t_call structure failed");
        exit(5);
}

while (1) {
        if (t_listen(listen_fd, call) < 0) {
                t_error("t_listen failed for listen_fd");
                exit(6);
        }

        if ((conn_fd = accept_call(listen_fd, call)) != DISCONNECT)
                run_server(listen_fd);
}
```

The server will loop forever, processing each connect indication. First, the server calls t_listen to retrieve the next connect indication. When one arrives, the server calls accept_call to accept the connect request. accept_call accepts the connection on an alternate transport endpoint (as discussed below) and returns the value of that endpoint. conn_fd is a global variable that identifies the transport endpoint where the connection is established. Because the connection is accepted on an alternate endpoint, the server may continue listening for connect indications on the endpoint that was bound for listening. If the call is accepted without error, run_server will spawn a process to manage the connection.

The server allocates a t_call structure to be used by t_listen. The third argument to t_alloc, T_ALL, specifies that all necessary buffers should be allocated for retrieving the caller's address, options, and user data. As mentioned earlier, the transport provider in this example does not support the transfer of user data during connection establishment, and also does not support any protocol options. Therefore, t_alloc will not allocate buffers for the user data and options. It must, however, allocate a buffer large enough to store the address of the caller. t_alloc determines the buffer size from the addr characteristic returned by t_open. The maxlen field of each netbuf structure will be set to the size of the newly allocated buffer by t_alloc (maxlen is 0 for the user data and options buffers).

Using the t_call structure, the server calls t_listen to retrieve the next connect indication. If one is currently available, it is returned to the server immediately. Otherwise, t_listen will block until a connect indication arrives.

The Transport Interface supports an asynchronous mode for these routines, which prevents a process from blocking. This feature is discussed in the section "Advanced Topics."

When a connect indication arrives, the server calls accept_call to accept the client's request, as follows:

```
accept_call(listen_fd, call)
int listen_fd;
struct t_call *call;
{
        int resfd;

        if ((resfd = t_open("/dev/tivc", O_RDWR, NULL)) < 0) {
                t_error("t_open for responding fd failed");
                exit(7);
        }

        if (t_bind(resfd, NULL, NULL) < 0) {
                t_error("t_bind for responding fd failed");
                exit(8);
        }

        if (t_accept(listen_fd, resfd, call) < 0) {
                if (t_errno == TLOOK) {  /* must be a disconnect */
                        if (t_rcvdis(listen_fd, NULL) < 0) {
                                t_error("t_rcvdis failed for listen_fd");
                                exit(9);
                        }
                        if (t_close(resfd) < 0) {
                                t_error("t_close failed for responding fd");
                                exit(10);
                        }
                        /* go back up and listen for other calls */
                        return(DISCONNECT);
                }
                t_error("t_accept failed");
                exit(11);
        }
        return(resfd);
}
```

accept_call takes two arguments.

■ listen_fd identifies the transport endpoint where the connect indication arrived

■ call is a pointer to a t_call structure that contains all information associated with the connect indication.

The server first establishes another transport endpoint by opening the clone device node of the transport provider and binding an address. As with the client, a NULL value is passed to t_bind to specify that the user does not care what address is bound by the provider. The newly established transport endpoint, resfd, is used to accept the client's connect request.

The first two arguments of t_accept specify the listening transport endpoint and the endpoint where the connection will be accepted, respectively. A connection may be accepted on the listening endpoint, but this prevents other clients from accessing the server for the duration of the connection.

The third argument of t_accept points to the t_call structure associated with the connect indication. This structure should contain the address of the calling user and the sequence number returned by t_listen. The value of sequence is significant if the server manages multiple outstanding connect indications. The "Advanced Topics" section presents an example of this situation. Also, the t_call structure should identify protocol options the user would like to specify, and user data that may be passed to the client. Because the transport provider in this example does not support protocol options or the transfer of user data during connection establishment, the t_call structure returned by t_listen may be passed without change to t_accept.

For simplicity in the example, the server will exit if either the t_open or t_bind call fails. exit(2) will close the transport endpoint associated with listen_fd, causing the transport provider to pass a disconnect indication to the client that requested the connection. This disconnect indication notifies the client that the connection was not established; t_connect will fail, setting t_errno to TLOOK.

t_accept may fail if an asynchronous event has occurred on the listening transport endpoint before the connection is accepted, and t_errno will be set to TLOOK. The state transition table in the "State Transitions" section shows that the only event that may occur in this state with only one outstanding connect indication is a disconnect indication. This event may occur if the client decides to undo the connect request it had previously sent. If a disconnect indication arrives, the server must retrieve the disconnect indication using t_rcvdis. This routine takes a pointer to a t_discon structure as an argument, which is used to retrieve information associated with a disconnect indication. In this example, however, the server does not care to retrieve this information, so it sets the argument to NULL. After receiving the disconnect indication,

`accept_call` closes the responding transport endpoint and returns DISCON-
NECT, which informs the server that the connection was disconnected by the
client. The server then listens for further connect indications.

Figure 2-5 illustrates how the server establishes connections.

Figure 2-5: Listening and Responding Transport Endpoints

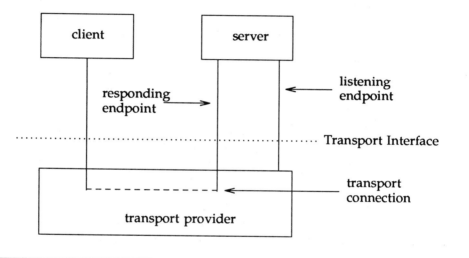

The transport connection is established on the newly created responding endpoint, and the listening endpoint is freed to retrieve further connect indications.

Data Transfer

Once the connection has been established, both the client and server may begin
transferring data over the connection using t_snd and t_rcv. The Transport
Interface does not differentiate the client from the server from this point on.
Either user may send and receive data, or release the connection. The Transport
Interface guarantees reliable, sequenced delivery of data over an existing con-
nection.

Two classes of data may be transferred over a transport connection:

- normal data
- expedited data

Expedited data is typically associated with urgent information. The exact semantics of expedited data are subject to the interpretations of the transport provider. Furthermore, not all transport protocols support the notion of an expedited data class (see t_open(3N)).

All transport protocols support the transfer of data in byte stream mode, where "byte stream" implies no concept of message boundaries on data that are transferred over a connection. However, some transport protocols support the preservation of message boundaries over a transport connection. This service is supported by the Transport Interface, but protocol-independent software must not rely on its existence.

The message interface for data transfer is supported by a special flag of t_snd and t_rcv called T_MORE. The messages, called Transport Service Data Units (TSDU), may be transferred between two transport users as distinct units. The maximum size of a TSDU is a characteristic of the underlying transport protocol. This information is available to the user from t_open and t_getinfo. Because the maximum TSDU size can be large (possibly unlimited), the Transport Interface allows a user to transmit a message in multiple units.

To send a message in multiple units over a transport connection, the user must set the T_MORE flag on every t_snd call except the last. This flag specifies that the user will send more data associated with the message in a subsequent call to t_snd. The last message unit should be transmitted with T_MORE turned off to specify that this is the end of the TSDU.

Similarly, a TSDU may be passed in multiple units to the receiving user. Again, if t_rcv returns with the T_MORE flag set, the user should continue calling t_rcv to retrieve the remainder of the message. The last unit in the message will be identified by a call to t_rcv that does not set T_MORE.

The T_MORE flag implies nothing about how the data may be packaged below the Transport Interface or how the data may be delivered to the remote user. Each transport protocol, and each implementation of that protocol, may package and deliver the data differently.

For example, if a user sends a complete message in a single call to t_snd, there is no guarantee that the transport provider will deliver the data in a single unit to the remote transport user. Similarly, a TSDU transmitted in two message units may be delivered in a single unit to the remote transport user. The message boundaries may only be preserved by noting the value of the T_MORE flag on t_snd and t_rcv. This will guarantee that the receiving user will see a message with the same contents and message boundaries as was sent by the remote user.

The Client

Continuing with the client/server example, the server will transfer a log file to the client over the transport connection. The client receives this data and writes it to its standard output file. A byte stream interface is used by the client and server, where message boundaries (that is, the T_MORE flag) are ignored. The client receives data using the following instructions:

```
while ((nbytes - t_rcv(fd, buf, 1024, &flags)) !- -1) {
        if (fwrite(buf, 1, nbytes, stdout) < 0) {
                fprintf(stderr, "fwrite failed\n");
                exit(5);
        }
}
```

The client continuously calls t_rcv to process incoming data. If no data is currently available, t_rcv blocks until data arrives. t_rcv retrieves the available data up to 1024 bytes, which is the size of the client's input buffer, and returns the number of bytes received. The client then writes this data to standard output and continues. The data transfer phase will complete when t_rcv fails. t_rcv will fail if an orderly release or disconnect indication arrives, as discussed later in this section. If the fwrite(3S) call fails for any reason, the client will exit, closing the transport endpoint. If the transport endpoint is closed (either by exit or t_close) during the data transfer phase, the connection will be aborted and the remote user will receive a disconnect indication.

The Server

Looking now at the other side of the connection, the server manages its data transfer by spawning a child process to send the data to the client. The parent process then loops back to listen for further connect indications. `run_server` is called by the server to spawn this child process as follows:

```
connrelease()
{
        /* conn_fd is global because needed here */
        if (t_look(conn_fd) == T_DISCONNECT) {
                fprintf(stderr, "connection aborted\n");
                exit(12);
        }
        /* else orderly release indication - normal exit */
        exit(0);
}

run_server(listen_fd)
int listen_fd;
{
        int nbytes;
        FILE *logfp;                    /* file pointer to log file */
        char buf[1024];

        switch (fork()) {

        case -1:
                perror("fork failed");
                exit(20);

        default: /* parent */

                /* close conn_fd and then go up and listen again */
                if (t_close(conn_fd) < 0) {
                        t_error("t_close failed for conn_fd");
                        exit(21);
                }
                return;

        case 0:         /* child */

                /* close listen_fd and do service */
                if (t_close(listen_fd) < 0) {
                        t_error("t_close failed for listen_fd");
```

(continued on next page)

```
                    exit(22);
        }
        if ((logfp = fopen("logfile", "r")) == NULL) {
                    perror("cannot open logfile");
                    exit(23);
        }

        signal(SIGPOLL, connrelease);
        if (ioctl(conn_fd, I_SETSIG, S_INPUT) < 0) {
                    perror("ioctl I_SETSIG failed");
                    exit(24);
        }
        if (t_look(conn_fd) != 0) {  /* was disconnect there? */
                    fprintf(stderr, "t_look: unexpected event\n");
                    exit(25);
        }

        while ((nbytes = fread(buf, 1, 1024, logfp)) > 0)
                    if (t_snd(conn_fd, buf, nbytes, 0) < 0) {
                                t_error("t_snd failed");
                                exit(26);
                    }
```

After the fork, the parent process returns to the main processing loop and listens for further connect indications. Meanwhile, the child process will manage the newly established transport connection. If the fork call fails, exit closes the transport endpoint associated with listen_fd, sending a disconnect indication to the client, and the client's t_connect call will fail.

The server process reads 1024 bytes of the log file at a time and sends that data to the client using t_snd. buf points to the start of the data buffer, and nbytes specifies the number of bytes to be transmitted. The fourth argument can contain one of the two optional flags below:

■ T_EXPEDITED specifies that the data is expedited

■ T_MORE defines message boundaries when transmitting messages over a connection.

Neither flag is set by the server in this example.

If the user floods the transport provider with data, the provider may exert back pressure to provide flow control. In such cases, t_snd will block until the flow control is relieved, and will then resume its operation. t_snd will not complete until nbyte bytes have been passed to the transport provider.

The t_snd routine does not look for a disconnect indication (showing that the connection was broken) before passing data to the provider. Also, because the data traffic flows in one direction, the user will never look for incoming events. If the connection is aborted, the user should be notified since data may be lost. The user can invoke t_look, which checks for incoming events before each t_snd call. A more efficient solution is presented in the example. The STREAMS I_SETSIG ioctl enables a user to request a signal when a given event occurs (see streamio(5) and signal(2)). S_INPUT causes a signal to be sent to the user if any input arrives on the Stream referenced by conn_fd. If a disconnect indication arrives, the signal catching routine (connrelease) prints an error message and then exits.

If the data traffic flowed in both directions in this example, the user would not have to monitor the connection for disconnects. If the client alternated t_snd and t_rcv calls, it could rely on t_rcv to recognize an incoming disconnect indication.

Connection Release

At any point during data transfer, either user may release the transport connection and end the conversation. As mentioned earlier, two forms of connection release are supported by the Transport Interface:

- Abortive release breaks a connection immediately and may result in the loss of any data that has not yet reached the destination user.

  Either user may call t_snddis to generate an abortive release. Also, the transport provider may abort a connection if a problem occurs below the Transport Interface. t_snddis enables a user to send data to the remote user when aborting a connection. Although the abortive release is supported by all transport providers, the ability to send data when aborting a connection is not.

  When the remote user is notified of the aborted connection, t_rcvdis must be called to retrieve the disconnect indication. This call returns a reason code that identifies why the connection was aborted, and returns any user data that may have accompanied the disconnect indication (if the abortive release was initiated by the remote user). This reason code is specific to the underlying transport protocol, and should not be interpreted by protocol-independent software.

■ Orderly release gracefully terminates a connection and guarantees that no data will be lost.

All transport providers must support the abortive release procedure, but orderly release is an optional facility that is not supported by all transport protocols.

The Server

The client-server example in this section assumes that the transport provider supports the orderly release of a connection. When all the data has been transferred by the server, the connection may be released as follows:

```
            if (t_sndrel(conn_fd) < 0) {
                    t_error("t_sndrel failed");
                    exit(27);
            }
            pause(); /* until orderly release indication arrives */
    }
}
```

The orderly release procedure consists of two steps by each user. The first user to complete data transfer may initiate a release using t_sndrel, as illustrated in the example. This routine informs the client that no more data will be sent by the server. When the client receives this indication, it may continue sending data back to the server if desired. When all data have been transferred, however, the client must also call t_sndrel to indicate that it is ready to release the connection. The connection is released only after both users have requested an orderly release and received the corresponding indication from the other user.

In this example, data is transferred in one direction from the server to the client, so the server does not expect to receive data from the client after it has initiated the release procedure. Thus, the server simply calls pause(2) after initiating the release. Eventually, the remote user responds with its orderly release request, which generates a signal that will be caught by connrelease. Remember that the server earlier issued an I_SETSIG ioctl call to generate a signal on any

incoming event. Since the only possible Transport Interface events that can
occur in this situation are a disconnect indication or orderly release indication,
connrelease terminates normally when the orderly release indication arrives.
The exit call in connrelease will close the transport endpoint, freeing the
bound address for another user. If a user process wants to close a transport
endpoint without exiting, it may call t_close.

The Client

The client's view of connection release is similar to that of the server. As mentioned earlier, the client continues to process incoming data until t_rcv fails. If
the server releases the connection (using either t_snddis or t_sndrel),
t_rcv will fail and set t_errno to TLOOK. The client then processes the connection release as follows:

```
if ((t_errno == TLOOK) && (t_look(fd) == T_ORDREL)) {
        if (t_rcvrel(fd) < 0) {
                t_error("t_rcvrel failed");
                exit(6);
        }
        if (t_sndrel(fd) < 0) {
                t_error("t_sndrel failed");
                exit(7);
        }
        exit(0);
}
t_error("t_rcv failed");
exit(8);
}
```

When an event occurs on the client's transport endpoint, the client checks
whether the expected orderly release indication has arrived. If so, it proceeds
with the release procedures by calling t_rcvrel to process the indication and
t_sndrel to inform the server that it is also ready to release the connection.
At this point the client exits, closing its transport endpoint.

Because not all transport providers support the orderly release facility just
described, users may have to use the abortive release facility provided by
t_snddis and t_rcvdis. However, steps must be taken by each user to
prevent data loss. For example, a special byte pattern may be inserted in the

data stream to indicate the end of a conversation. There are many possible routines for preventing data loss. Each application and high level protocol must choose an appropriate routine given the target protocol environment and requirements.

Introduction to Connectionless-Mode Service

This section describes the connectionless-mode service of the Transport Interface. Connectionless-mode service is appropriate for short-term request/response interactions, such as transaction processing applications. Data are transferred in self-contained units with no logical relationship required among multiple units.

The connectionless-mode services will be described using a transaction server as an example. This server waits for incoming transaction queries, and processes and responds to each query.

Local Management

Just as with connection-mode service, the transport users must do appropriate local management steps before transferring data. A user must choose the appropriate connectionless service provider using t_open and establish its identity using t_bind.

t_optmgmt may be used to negotiate protocol options associated with the transfer of each data unit. As with the connection-mode service, each transport provider specifies the options, if any, that it supports. Option negotiation is therefore a protocol-specific activity.

In the example, the definitions and local management calls needed by the transaction server are as follows:

```
#include <stdio.h>
#include <fcntl.h>
#include <tiuser.h>

#define SRV_ADDR   2                    /* server's well known address */

main()
{
        int fd;
        int flags;

        struct t_bind *bind;
        struct t_unitdata *ud;
        struct t_uderr *uderr;

        extern int t_errno;

        if ((fd = t_open("/dev/tidg", O_RDWR, NULL)) < 0) {
                t_error("unable to open /dev/provider");
                exit(1);
        }

        if ((bind = (struct t_bind *)t_alloc(fd,
          T_BIND, T_ADDR)) == NULL) {
                t_error("t_alloc of t_bind structure failed");
                exit(2);
        }

        bind->addr.len = sizeof(int);
        *(int *)bind->addr.buf = SRV_ADDR;
        bind->qlen = 0;

        if (t_bind(fd, bind, bind) < 0) {
                t_error("t_bind failed");
                exit(3);
        }

        /*
         * is the bound address correct?
         */

        if (*(int *)bind->addr.buf != SRV_ADDR) {
                fprintf(stderr, "t_bind bound wrong address\n");
                exit(4);
        }
```

The local management steps should look familiar by now. The server establishes a transport endpoint with the desired transport provider using t_open. Each provider has an associated service type, so the user may choose a particular service by opening the appropriate transport provider file. This connectionless-mode server ignores the characteristics of the provider returned by t_open in the same way as the users in the connection-mode example, by setting the third argument to NULL. For simplicity, the transaction server assumes the transport provider has the following characteristics:

- The transport address is an integer value that uniquely identifies each user.

- The transport provider supports the T_CLTS service type (connectionless transport service, or datagram).

- The transport provider does not support any protocol-specific options.

The connectionless server also binds a transport address to the endpoint so that potential clients may identify and access the server. A t_bind structure is allocated using t_alloc and the buf and len fields of the address are set accordingly.

One important difference between the connection-mode server and this connectionless-mode server is that the qlen field of the t_bind structure has no meaning for connectionless-mode service, since all users are capable of receiving datagrams once they have bound an address. The Transport Interface defines an inherent client-server relationship between two users while establishing a transport connection in the connection-mode service. However, no such relationship exists in the connectionless-mode service. It is the context of this example, not the Transport Interface, that defines one user as a server and another as a client.

Because the address of the server is known by all potential clients, the server checks the bound address returned by t_bind to ensure it is correct.

Data Transfer

Once a user has bound an address to the transport endpoint, datagrams may be sent or received over that endpoint. Each outgoing message is accompanied by the address of the destination user. In addition, the Transport Interface enables a user to specify protocol options that should be associated with the transfer of the data unit (for example, transit delay). As discussed earlier, each transport provider defines the set of options, if any, that may accompany a datagram. When the datagram is passed to the destination user, the associated protocol options may be returned as well.

The following sequence of calls illustrates the data transfer phase of the connectionless-mode server:

```
if ((ud = (struct t_unitdata *)t_alloc(fd,
  T_UNITDATA, T_ALL)) == NULL) {
        t_error("t_alloc of t_unitdata structure failed");
        exit(5);
}

if ((uderr = (struct t_uderr *)t_alloc(fd,
  T_UDERROR, T_ALL)) == NULL) {
        t_error("t_alloc of t_uderr structure failed");
        exit(6);
}

while (1) {
        if (t_rcvudata(fd, ud, &flags) < 0) {
                if (t_errno == TLOOK) {

                        /*
                         * Error on previously sent datagram
                         */

                        if (t_rcvuderr(fd, uderr) < 0) {
                                exit(7);
                        }

                        fprintf(stderr, "bad datagram, error = %d\n",
                                uderr->error);
                        continue;
                }
                t_error("t_rcvudata failed");
```

(continued on next page)

```
                    exit(8);
        }

        /*
         * Query() processes the request and places the
         * response in ud->udata.buf, setting ud->udata.len
         */

        query(ud);

        if (t_sndudata(fd, ud, 0) < 0) {
                t_error("t_sndudata failed");
                exit(9);
        }
    }
}

query()
{
        /* Merely a stub for simplicity */

}
```

The server must first allocate a t_unitdata structure for storing datagrams, which has the following format:

```
struct t_unitdata {
        struct netbuf addr;
        struct netbuf opt;
        struct netbuf udata;
}
```

addr holds the source address of incoming datagrams and the destination address of outgoing datagrams, opt identifies any protocol options associated with the transfer of the datagram, and udata holds the data itself. The addr, opt, and udata fields must all be allocated with buffers large enough to hold any possible incoming values. As described in the previous section, the T_ALL argument to t_alloc will ensure this and will set the maxlen field of each netbuf structure accordingly. Because the provider does not support protocol options in this example, no options buffer will be allocated, and maxlen will be

Programmer's Guide: Networking Interfaces

set to zero in the netbuf structure for options. The server also allocates a t_uderr structure for processing any datagram errors, as discussed later in this section.

The transaction server loops forever, receiving queries, processing the queries, and responding to the clients. It first calls t_rcvudata to receive the next query. t_rcvudata will retrieve the next available incoming datagram. If none is currently available, t_rcvudata will block, waiting for a datagram to arrive. The second argument of t_rcvudata identifies the t_unitdata structure in which the datagram should be stored.

The third argument, flags , must point to an integer variable and may be set to T_MORE on return from t_rcvudata to specify that the user's udata buffer was not large enough to store the full datagram. In this case, subsequent calls to t_rcvudata will retrieve the remainder of the datagram. Because t_alloc allocates a udata buffer large enough to store the maximum datagram size, the transaction server does not have to check the value of flags.

If a datagram is received successfully, the transaction server calls the query routine to process the request. This routine will store the response in the structure pointed to by ud, and will set ud->udata.len to specify the number of bytes in the response. The source address returned by t_rcvudata in ud->addr will be used as the destination address by t_sndudata.

When the response is ready, t_sndudata is called to return the response to the client. The Transport Interface prevents a user from flooding the transport provider with datagrams using the same flow control mechanism described for the connection-mode service. In such cases, t_sndudata will block until the flow control is relieved, and will then resume its operation.

Datagram Errors

If the transport provider cannot process a datagram that was passed to it by t_sndudata, it will return a unit data error event, T_UDERR, to the user. This event includes the destination address and options associated with the datagram, plus a protocol-specific error value that describes what may be wrong with the datagram. The reason a datagram could not be processed is protocol-specific. One reason may be that the transport provider could not interpret the destination address or options. Each transport protocol is expected to specify all reasons why it is unable to process a datagram.

The unit data error indication is not necessarily intended to indicate success or failure in delivering the datagram to the specified destination. The transport protocol decides how the indication will be used. Remember, the connectionless service does not guarantee reliable delivery of data.

The transaction server will be notified of this error event when it attempts to receive another datagram. In this case, t_rcvudata will fail, setting t_errno to TLOOK. If TLOOK is set, the only possible event is T_UDERR, so the server calls t_rcvuderr to retrieve the event. The second argument to t_rcvuderr is the t_uderr structure that was allocated earlier. This structure is filled in by t_rcvuderr and has the following format:

```
struct t_uderr {
        struct netbuf addr;
        struct netbuf opt;
        long error;
}
```

where addr and opt identify the destination address and protocol options as specified in the bad datagram, and error is a protocol-specific error code that specifies why the provider could not process the datagram. The transaction server prints the error code and then continues by entering the processing loop again.

A Read/Write Interface

A user may wish to establish a transport connection and then exec(2) an existing user program such as cat(1) to process the data as it arrives over the connection. However, existing programs use read(2) and write(2) for their input/output needs. The Transport Interface does not directly support a read/write interface to a transport provider, but one is available with UNIX System V. This interface enables a user to issue read and write calls over a transport connection that is in the data transfer phase. This section describes the read/write interface to the connection-mode service of the Transport Interface. This interface is not available with the connectionless-mode service.

The read/write interface is presented using the client example of the "Introduction to Connection-Mode Service" section with some minor modifications. The clients are identical until the data transfer phase is reached. At that point, this client will use the read/write interface and cat(1) to process incoming data. cat can be run without change over the transport connection. Only the differences between this client and that of the example in the "Introduction to Connection-Mode Service" section are shown below.

```
#include <stropts.h>
    .
    .                /*
    .                 * Same local management and connection
    .                 * establishment steps.
    .                 */
    .

    if (ioctl(fd, I_PUSH, "tirdwr") < 0) {
            perror("I_PUSH of tirdwr failed");
            exit(5);
    }

    close(0);
    dup(fd);
    execl("/usr/bin/cat", "/usr/bin/cat", 0);
    perror("execl of /usr/bin/cat failed");
    exit(6);
}
```

The client invokes the read/write interface by pushing the tirdwr(7) module onto the Stream associated with the transport endpoint where the connection was established (see I_PUSH in streamio(5)). This module converts the Transport Interface above the transport provider into a pure read/write interface.

With the module in place, the client calls close(2) and dup(2) to establish the transport endpoint as its standard input file, and uses /usr/bin/cat to process the input. Because the transport endpoint identifier is a file descriptor, the facility for duping the endpoint is available to users.

Because the Transport Interface uses STREAMS, the facilities of this character input/output mechanism can be used to provide enhanced user services. By pushing the tirdwr module above the transport provider, the user's interface is effectively changed. The semantics of read and write must be followed, and message boundaries will not be preserved.

 The tirdwr module may only be pushed onto a Stream when the transport endpoint is in the data transfer phase. Once the module is pushed, the user may not call any Transport Interface routines. If a Transport Interface routine is invoked, tirdwr will generate a fatal protocol error, EPROTO, on that Stream, rendering it unusable. Furthermore, if the user pops the tirdwr module off the Stream (see I_POP in streamio(5)), the transport connection will be aborted.

The exact semantics of write, read, and close using tirdwr are described below. To summarize, tirdwr enables a user to send and receive data over a transport connection using read and write. This module will translate all Transport Interface indications into the appropriate actions. The connection can be released with the close system call.

write

The user may transmit data over the transport connection using write. The tirdwr module will pass data through to the transport provider. However, if a user attempts to send a zero-length data packet, which the STREAMS mechanism allows, tirdwr will discard the message. If the transport connection is aborted (for example, because the remote user aborts the connection using t_snddis), a STREAMS hangup condition will be generated on that Stream, and further write calls will fail and set errno to ENXIO. The user can still retrieve any available data after a hangup.

read

read may be used to retrieve data that has arrived over the transport connection. The tirdwr module will pass data through to the user from the transport provider. However, any other event or indication passed to the user from the provider will be processed by tirdwr as follows:

- read cannot process expedited data because it cannot distinguish expedited data from normal data for the user. If an expedited data indication is received, tirdwr will generate a fatal protocol error, EPROTO, on that Stream. This error causes further system calls to fail. You should therefore not communicate with a process that is sending expedited data.

- If an abortive disconnect indication is received, tirdwr will discard it and generate a STREAMS hangup condition on that Stream. Subsequent read calls will retrieve any remaining data, and then read will return zero for all further calls (indicating end-of-file).

- If an orderly release indication is received, tirdwr will discard the indication and deliver a zero-length STREAMS message to the user. As described in read(2), this notifies the user of end-of-file by returning 0.

- If any other Transport Interface indication is received, tirdwr generates a fatal protocol error, EPROTO, on that Stream. This causes further system calls to fail. If a user pushes tirdwr onto a Stream after the connection has been established, no indication will be generated.

close

With tirdwr on a Stream, the user can send and receive data over a transport connection for the duration of that connection. Either user may terminate the connection by closing the file descriptor associated with the transport endpoint or by popping the tirdwr module off the Stream. In either case, tirdwr will take the following actions:

- If an orderly release indication was previously received by tirdwr, an orderly release request will be passed to the transport provider to complete the orderly release of the connection. The remote user who initiated the orderly release procedure will receive the expected indication when data transfer completes.

- If a disconnect indication was previously received by `tirdwr`, no special action is taken.

- If neither an orderly release indication nor disconnect indication previously received by `tirdwr`, a disconnect request will be passed to the transport provider to abort the connection.

- If an error previously occurred on the Stream and a disconnect indication has not been received by `tirdwr`, a disconnect request will be passed to the transport provider.

A process may not initiate an orderly release after `tirdwr` is pushed onto a Stream, but `tirdwr` will handle an orderly release properly if it is initiated by the user on the other side of a transport connection. If the client in this section is communicating with the server program in the "Introduction to Connection-Mode Service" section, that server will terminate the transfer of data with an orderly release request. The server then waits for the corresponding indication from the client. At that point, the client exits and the transport endpoint is closed. As explained in the first list item above, when the file descriptor is closed, `tirdwr` will initiate the orderly release request from the client's side of the connection. This will generate the indication that the server is expecting, and the connection will be released properly.

Advanced Topics

This section presents the following important concepts of the Transport Interface that have not been covered in the previous section:

- an optional non-blocking (asynchronous) mode for some library calls

- an advanced programming example that defines a server supporting multiple outstanding connect indications and operating in an event driven manner

Asynchronous Execution Mode

Many Transport Interface library routines may block waiting for an incoming event or the relaxation of flow control. However, some time-critical applications should not block for any reason. Similarly, an application may wish to do local processing while waiting for some asynchronous transport interface event.

Support for asynchronous processing of Transport Interface events is available to applications using a combination of the STREAMS asynchronous features and the non-blocking mode of the Transport Interface library routines. Earlier examples in this guide have illustrated the use of the poll system call and the I_SETSIG ioctl command for processing events asynchronously.

In addition, each Transport Interface routines that may block waiting for some event can be run in a special non-blocking mode. For example, t_listen will normally block, waiting for a connect indication. However, a server can periodically poll a transport endpoint for existing connect indications by calling t_listen in the non-blocking (or asynchronous) mode. The asynchronous mode is enabled by setting O_NDELAY or O_NONBLOCK on the file descriptor. These can be set as a flag on t_open, or by calling fcntl(2) before calling the Transport Interface routine. fcntl can be used to enable or disable this mode at any time. All programming examples in this chapter use the default synchronous processing mode.

O_NDELAY or O_NONBLOCK affect each Transport Interface routine differently. To determine the exact semantics of O_NDELAY or O_NONBLOCK for a particular routine, see the relevant pages in Appendix A of this document.

Advanced Programming Example

The following example demonstrates two important concepts. The first is a server's ability to manage multiple outstanding connect indications. The second is an illustration of the ability to write event-driven software using the Transport Interface and the STREAMS system call interface.

The server example in the "Introduction to Connection-Mode Service" section is capable of supporting only one outstanding connect indication, but the Transport Interface supports the ability to manage multiple outstanding connect indications. One reason a server might wish to receive several simultaneous connect indications is to impose a priority scheme on each client. A server may retrieve several connect indications, and then accept them in an order based on a priority associated with each client. A second reason for handling several outstanding connect indications is that the single-threaded scheme has some limitations. Depending on the implementation of the transport provider, it is possible that while the server is processing the current connect indication, other clients will find it busy. If, however, multiple connect indications can be processed simultaneously, the server will be found to be busy only if the maximum allowed number of clients attempt to call the server simultaneously.

The server example is event-driven: the process polls a transport endpoint for incoming Transport Interface events, and then takes the appropriate actions for the current event. The example demonstrates the ability to poll multiple transport endpoints for incoming events.

The definitions and local management functions needed by this example are similar to those of the server example in the section "Introduction to Connectionless-Mode Service."

```
#include <tiuser.h>
#include <fcntl.h>
#include <stdio.h>
#include <poll.h>
#include <stropts.h>
#include <signal.h>

#define NUM_FDS        1
#define MAX_CONN_IND   4
#define SRV_ADDR       1      /* server's well known address */

int conn_fd;                  /* server connection here */
extern int t_errno;

/* holds connect indications */
struct t_call *calls[NUM_FDS][MAX_CONN_IND];

main()
{
        struct pollfd pollfds[NUM_FDS];
        struct t_bind *bind;
        int i;

        /*
         * Only opening and binding one transport endpoint,
         * but more could be supported
         */
        if ((pollfds[0].fd = t_open("/dev/tivc",
          O_RDWR, NULL)) < 0) {
                t_error("t_open failed");
                exit(1);
        }

        if ((bind = (struct t_bind *)t_alloc(pollfds[0].fd,
          T_BIND, T_ALL)) == NULL) {
                t_error("t_alloc of t_bind structure failed");
                exit(2);
        }
        bind->qlen = MAX_CONN_IND;
        bind->addr.len = sizeof(int);
        *(int *)bind->addr.buf = SRV_ADDR;

        if (t_bind(pollfds[0].fd, bind, bind) < 0) {
                t_error("t_bind failed");
                exit(3);
        }
```

(continued on next page)

```
/*
 * Was the correct address bound?
 */

if (*(int *)bind->addr.buf != SRV_ADDR) {
        fprintf(stderr, "t_bind bound wrong address\n");
        exit(4);
}
```

The file descriptor returned by t_open is stored in a pollfd structure (see poll(2)) that polls the transport endpoint for incoming data. Notice that only one transport endpoint is established in this example. However, the remainder of the example is written to manage multiple transport endpoints. Several endpoints could be supported with minor changes to the above code.

An important aspect of this server is that it sets qlen to a value greater than 1 for t_bind. This specifies that the server is willing to handle multiple outstanding connect indications. Remember that the earlier examples single-threaded the connect indications and responses. The server would accept the current connect indication before retrieving additional connect indications. This example, however, can retrieve up to MAX_CONN_IND connect indications at one time before responding to any of them. The transport provider may negotiate the value of qlen downward if it cannot support MAX_CONN_IND outstanding connect indications.

Once the server has bound its address and is ready to process incoming connect requests, it does the following:

```
        pollfds[0].events - POLLIN;
    while (1) {
            if (poll(pollfds, NUM_FDS, -1) < 0) {
                    perror("poll failed");
                    exit(5);
            }
            for (i - 0; i < NUM_FDS; i++) {

                    switch (pollfds[i].revents) {

                    default:
                            perror("poll returned error event");
                            exit(6);

                    case 0:
                            continue;

                    case POLLIN:
                            do_event(i, pollfds[i].fd);
                            service_conn_ind(i, pollfds[i].fd);
                    }
            }
    }
}
```

The events field of the pollfd structure is set to POLLIN, which will notify the server of any incoming Transport Interface events. The server then enters an infinite loop, in which it polls the transport endpoint(s) for events, and then processes those events as they occur.

The poll call will block indefinitely, waiting for an incoming event. On return, each entry (corresponding to each transport endpoint) is checked for an existing event. If revents is set to 0, no event has occurred on that endpoint. In this case, the server continues to the next transport endpoint. If revents is set to POLLIN, an event does exist on the endpoint. In this case, do_event is called to process the event. If revents contains any other value, an error must have occurred on the transport endpoint, and the server will exit.

For each iteration of the loop, if any event is found on the transport endpoint, service_conn_ind is called to process any outstanding connect indications. However, if another connect indication is pending, service_conn_ind will save the current connect indication and respond to it later. This routine will be explained shortly.

If an incoming event is discovered, the following routine is called to process it:

```
do_event(slot, fd)
{
        struct t_discon *discon;
        int i;

        switch (t_look(fd)) {

        default:
                fprintf(stderr,"t_look: unexpected event\n");
                exit(7);

        case T_ERROR:
                fprintf(stderr,"t_look returned T_ERROR event\n");
                exit(8);

        case -1:
                t_error("t_look failed");
                exit(9);

        case 0:
                /* since POLLIN returned, this should not happen */
                fprintf(stderr,"t_look returned no event\n");
                exit(10);

        case T_LISTEN:
                /*
                 * find free element in calls array
                 */
                for (i = 0; i < MAX_CONN_IND; i++) {
                        if (calls[slot][i] == NULL)
                                break;
                }

                if ((calls[slot][i] = (struct t_call *)t_alloc(fd,
                  T_CALL, T_ALL)) == NULL) {
                        t_error("t_alloc of t_call structure failed");
                        exit(11);
                }

                if (t_listen(fd, calls[slot][i]) < 0) {
                        t_error("t_listen failed");
                        exit(12);
                }
                break;
```

(continued on next page)

```
case T_DISCONNECT:
        discon = (struct t_discon *)t_alloc(fd,
          T_DIS, T_ALL);

        if (t_rcvdis(fd, discon) < 0) {
                t_error("t_rcvdis failed");
                exit(13);
        }
        /*
         * find call ind in array and delete it
         */
        for (i = 0; i < MAX_CONN_IND; i++) {
                if (discon->sequence ==
                  calls[slot][i]->sequence) {
                        t_free(calls[slot][i], T_CALL);
                        calls[slot][i] = NULL;
                }
        }
        t_free(discon, T_DIS);
        break;
    }
}
```

This routine takes a number, slot, and a file descriptor, fd, as arguments.
slot is used as an index into the global array calls. This array contains an
entry for each polled transport endpoint, where each entry consists of an array
of t_call structures that hold incoming connect indications for that transport
endpoint. The value of slot is used to identify the transport endpoint.

do_event calls t_look to determine the Transport Interface event that has
occurred on the transport endpoint specified by fd. If a connect indication
(T_LISTEN event) or disconnect indication (T_DISCONNECT event) has arrived,
the event is processed. Otherwise, the server prints an appropriate error message and exits.

For connect indications, do_event scans the array of outstanding connect indications looking for the first free entry. A t_call structure is then allocated for
that entry, and the connect indication is retrieved using t_listen. There must
always be at least one free entry in the connect indication array, because the
array is large enough to hold the maximum number of outstanding connect
indications as negotiated by t_bind. The processing of the connect indication
is deferred until later.

If a disconnect indication arrives, it must correspond to a previously received connect indication. This occurs if a client attempts to undo a previous connect request. In this case, do_event allocates a t_discon structure to retrieve the relevant disconnect information. This structure has the following members:

```
struct t_discon {
        struct netbuf udata;
        int reason;
        int sequence;
}
```

where udata identifies any user data that might have been sent with the disconnect indication, reason contains a protocol-specific disconnect reason code, and sequence identifies the outstanding connect indication that matches this disconnect indication.

Next, t_rcvdis is called to retrieve the disconnect indication. The array of connect indications for slot is then scanned for one that contains a sequence number that matches the sequence number in the disconnect indication. When the connect indication is found, it is freed and the corresponding entry is set to NULL.

As mentioned earlier, if any event is found on a transport endpoint, service_conn_ind is called to process all currently outstanding connect indications associated with that endpoint as follows:

```
service_conn_ind(slot, fd)
{
        int i;

        for (i = 0; i < MAX_CONN_IND; i++) {
                if (calls[slot][i] == NULL)
                        continue;

                if ((conn_fd = t_open("/dev/tivc", O_RDWR, NULL))
                    < 0) {
                                t_error("open failed");
                                exit(14);
                }
                if (t_bind(conn_fd, NULL, NULL) < 0) {
                        t_error("t_bind failed");
                        exit(15);
                }

                if (t_accept(fd, conn_fd, calls[slot][i]) < 0) {
                        if (t_errno == TLOOK) {
                                t_close(conn_fd);
                                return;
                        }
                        t_error("t_accept failed");
                        exit(16);
                }
                t_free(calls[slot][i], T_CALL);
                calls[slot][i] = NULL;

                run_server(fd);
        }
}
```

For the given slot (the transport endpoint), the array of outstanding connect indications is scanned. For each indication, the server will open a responding transport endpoint, bind an address to the endpoint, and then accept the connection on that endpoint. If another event (connect indication or disconnect indication) arrives before the current indication is accepted, t_accept will fail and set t_errno to TLOOK.

NOTE The user cannot accept an outstanding connect indication if any pending connect indication events or disconnect indication events exist on that transport endpoint.

If this error occurs, the responding transport endpoint is closed and service_conn_ind will return immediately (saving the current connect indication for later processing). This causes the server's main processing loop to be entered, and the new event will be discovered by the next call to poll. In this way, multiple connect indications may be queued by the user.

Eventually, all events will be processed, and service_conn_ind will be able to accept each connect indication in turn. Once the connection has been established, the run_server routine used by the server in the "Introduction to Connection-Mode Service" section is called to manage the data transfer.

State Transitions

These tables describe all state transitions associated with the Transport Interface. First, however, the states and events will be described.

Transport Interface States

Table 2-6 defines the states used to describe the Transport Interface state transitions.

Table 2-6: States Describing Transport Interface State Transitions

State	Description	Service Type
T_UNINIT	uninitialized – initial and final state of interface	T_COTS, T_COTS_ORD, T_CLTS
T_UNBND	initialized but not bound	T_COTS, T_COTS_ORD, T_CLTS
T_IDLE	no connection established	T_COTS, T_COTS_ORD, T_CLTS
T_OUTCON	outgoing connection pending for client	T_COTS, T_COTS_ORD
T_INCON	incoming connection pending for server	T_COTS, T_COTS_ORD
T_DATAXFER	data transfer	T_COTS, T_COTS_ORD
T_OUTREL	outgoing orderly release (waiting for orderly release indication)	T_COTS_ORD
T_INREL	incoming orderly release (waiting to send orderly release request)	T_COTS_ORD

Outgoing Events

The outgoing events described in Table 2-7 correspond to the return of the
specified transport routines, where these routines send a request or response to
the transport provider.

In the table, some events (such as acceptN) are distinguished by the context in
which they occur. The context is based on the values of the following variables:

ocnt   count of outstanding connect indications

fd   file descriptor of the current transport endpoint

resfd   file descriptor of the transport endpoint where a connection will
be accepted

Table 2-7: Outgoing Events

Event	Description	Service Type
opened	successful return of t_open	T_COTS, T_COTS_ORD, T_CLTS
bind	successful return of t_bind	T_COTS, T_COTS_ORD, T_CLTS
optmgmt	successful return of t_optmgmt	T_COTS, T_COTS_ORD, T_CLTS
unbind	successful return of t_unbind	T_COTS, T_COTS_ORD, T_CLTS
closed	successful return of t_close	T_COTS, T_COTS_ORD, T_CLTS
connect1	successful return of t_connect in synchronous mode	T_COTS, T_COTS_ORD

Table 2-7: Outgoing Events (continued)

Event	Description	Service Type
connect2	TNODATA error on t_connect in asynchronous mode, or TLOOK error due to a disconnect indication arriving on the transport endpoint	T_COTS, T_COTS_ORD
accept1	successful return of t_accept with ocnt == 1, fd == resfd	T_COTS, T_COTS_ORD
accept2	successful return of t_accept with ocnt == 1, fd != resfd	T_COTS, T_COTS_ORD
accept3	successful return of t_accept with ocnt > 1	T_COTS, T_COTS_ORD
snd	successful return of t_snd	T_COTS, T_COTS_ORD
snddis1	successful return of t_snddis with ocnt <= 1	T_COTS, T_COTS_ORD
snddis2	successful return of t_snddis with ocnt > 1	T_COTS, T_COTS_ORD
sndrel	successful return of t_sndrel	T_COTS_ORD
sndudata	successful return of t_sndudata	T_CLTS

Incoming Events

The incoming events correspond to the successful return of the specified routines, where these routines retrieve data or event information from the transport provider. The only incoming event not associated directly with the return of a routine is pass_conn, which occurs when a user transfers a connection to another transport endpoint. This event occurs on the endpoint that is being passed the connection, despite the fact that no Transport Interface routine is issued on that endpoint. pass_conn is included in the state tables to describe the behavior when a user accepts a connection on another transport endpoint.

In Table 2-8, the rcvdis events are distinguished by the context in which they occur. The context is based on the value of ocnt, which is the count of outstanding connect indications on the transport endpoint.

Table 2-8: Incoming Events

Incoming Event	Description	Service Type
listen	successful return of t_listen	T_COTS, T_COTS_ORD
rcvconnect	successful return of t_rcvconnect	T_COTS, T_COTS_ORD
rcv	successful return of t_rcv	T_COTS, T_COTS_ORD
rcvdis1	successful return of t_rcvdis with ocnt <= 0	T_COTS, T_COTS_ORD
rcvdis2	successful return of t_rcvdis with ocnt == 1	T_COTS, T_COTS_ORD
rcvdis3	successful return of t_rcvdis with ocnt > 1	T_COTS, T_COTS_ORD
rcvrel	successful return of t_rcvrel	T_COTS_ORD

Table 2-8: Incoming Events (continued)

Incoming Event	Description	Service Type
rcvudata	successful return of t_rcvudata	T_CLTS
rcvuderr	successful return of t_rcvuderr	T_CLTS
pass_conn	receive a passed connection	T_COTS, T_COTS_ORD

Transport User Actions

In the state tables that follow, some state transitions are accompanied by a list of actions the transport user must take. These actions are represented by the notation [n], where n is the number of the specific action as described below.

[1]   Set the count of outstanding connect indications to zero.

[2]   Increment the count of outstanding connect indications.

[3]   Decrement the count of outstanding connect indications.

[4]   Pass a connection to another transport endpoint as indicated in t_accept.

State Tables

The following tables describe the Transport Interface state transitions. Given a current state and an event, the transition to the next state is shown, as well as any actions that must be taken by the transport user (indicated by [n]). The state is that of the transport provider as seen by the transport user.

The contents of each box represent the next state, given the current state (column) and the current incoming or outgoing event (row). An empty box represents a state/event combination that is invalid. Along with the next state, each box may include an action list (as specified in the previous section). The transport user must take the specific actions in the order specified in the state table.

The following should be understood when studying the state tables:

■ The t_close routine is referenced in the state tables (see closed event in Table 2-9), but may be called from any state to close a transport endpoint. If t_close is called when a transport address is bound to an endpoint, the address will be unbound. Also, if t_close is called when the transport connection is still active, the connection will be aborted.

■ If a transport user issues a routine out of sequence, the transport provider will recognize this and the routine will fail, setting t_errno to TOUT-STATE. The state will not change.

■ If any other transport error occurs, the state will not change unless explicitly stated on the manual page for that routine. The exception to this is a TLOOK or TNODATA error on t_connect, as described in Table 2-1. The state tables assume correct use of the Transport Interface.

■ The support routines t_getinfo, t_getstate, t_alloc, t_free, t_sync, t_look, and t_error are excluded from the state tables because they do not affect the state.

A separate table is shown for common local management steps, data transfer in connectionless-mode, and connection-establishment/connection-release/data-transfer in connection-mode.

Table 2-9: Common Local Management State Table

event \ state	T_UNINIT	T_UNBND	T_IDLE
opened	T_UNBND		
bind		T_IDLE [1]	
optmgmt			T_IDLE
unbind			T_UNBND
closed		T_UNINIT	

Table 2-10: Connectionless-Mode State Table

event \ state	T_IDLE
sndudata	T_IDLE
rcvudata	T_IDLE
rcvuderr	T_IDLE

Table 2-11: Connection-Mode State Table

state / event	T_IDLE	T_OUTCON	T_INCON	T_DATAXFER	T_OUTREL	T_INREL
connect1	T_DATAXFER					
connect2	T_OUTCON					
rcvconnect		T_DATAXFER				
listen	T_INCON [2]		T_INCON [2]			
accept1			T_DATAXFER[3]			
accept2			T_IDLE [3][4]			
accept3			T_INCON [3][4]			
snd				T_DATAXFER		T_INREL
rcv				T_DATAXFER	T_OUTREL	
snddis1		T_IDLE	T_IDLE [3]	T_IDLE	T_IDLE	T_IDLE
snddis2			T_INCON [3]			
rcvdis1		T_IDLE		T_IDLE	T_IDLE	T_IDLE
rcvdis2			T_IDLE [3]			
rcvdis3			T_INCON [3]			
sndrel				T_OUTREL		T_IDLE
rcvrel				T_INREL	T_IDLE	
pass_conn	T_DATAXFER					

Guidelines for Protocol Independence

By defining a set of services common to many transport protocols, the Transport Interface offers protocol independence for user software. However, not all transport protocols support the services supported by the Transport Interface. If software must be run in a variety of protocol environments, only the common services should be accessed. The following guidelines highlight services that may not be common to all transport protocols.

- In the connection-mode service, the concept of a transport service data unit (TSDU) may not be supported by all transport providers. The user should make no assumptions about the preservation of logical data boundaries across a connection. If messages must be transferred over a connection, a protocol should be implemented above the Transport Interface to support message boundaries.

- Protocol and implementation specific service limits are returned by the t_open and t_getinfo routines. These limits are useful when allocating buffers to store protocol-specific transport addresses and options. It is the responsibility of the user to access these limits and then adhere to the limits throughout the communication process.

- User data should not be transmitted with connect requests or disconnect requests (see t_connect(3N) and t_snddis(3N)). Not all transport protocols support this capability.

- The buffers in the t_call structure used for t_listen must be large enough to hold any information passed by the client during connection establishment. The server should use the T_ALL argument to t_alloc, which determines the maximum buffer sizes needed to store the address, options, and user data for the current transport provider.

- The user program should not look at or change options that are associated with any Transport Interface routine. These options are specific to the underlying transport protocol. The user should not pass options with t_connect or t_sndudata. In such cases, the transport provider will use default values. Also, a server should use the options returned by t_listen when accepting a connection.

- Protocol-specific addressing issues should be hidden from the user program. A client should not specify any protocol address on t_bind, but instead should allow the transport provider to assign an appropriate address to the transport endpoint. Similarly, a server should retrieve its address for t_bind in such a way that it does not require knowledge of the transport provider's address space. Such addresses should not be hard-coded into a program. A name server procedure could be useful in this situation, but the details for providing this service are outside the scope of the Transport Interface. Detailed information about Network Selection and Name-to-Address Mapping can be found in the "Network Selection and Name-to-Address Mapping" chapter.

■ The reason codes associated with t_rcvdis are protocol-dependent. The user should not interpret this information if protocol-independence is important.

■ The error codes associated with t_rcvuderr are protocol-dependent. The user should not interpret this information if protocol-independence is a concern.

■ The names of devices should not be hard-coded into programs, because the device node identifies a particular transport provider, and is not protocol independent.

■ The optional orderly release facility of the connection-mode service (provided by t_sndrel and t_rcvrel) should not be used by programs targeted for multiple protocol environments. This facility is not supported by all connection-based transport protocols. In particular, its use will prevent programs from successfully communicating with ISO open systems.

Some Examples

The examples presented throughout this guide are shown in their entirety in this section.

Connection-Mode Client

The following code represents the connection-mode client program described in the section "Introduction to Connection-Mode Service." This client establishes a transport connection with a server, and then receives data from the server and writes it to its standard output. The connection is released using the orderly release facility of the Transport Interface. This client communicates with each of the connection-mode servers presented in the guide.

```
#include <stdio.h>
#include <tiuser.h>
#include <fcntl.h>

#define SRV_ADDR    1          /* server's well known address */

main()
{
        int fd;
        int nbytes;
        int flags = 0;
        char buf[1024];
        struct t_call *sndcall;
        extern int t_errno;

        if ((fd = t_open("/dev/tivc", O_RDWR, NULL)) < 0) {
                t_error("t_open failed");
                exit(1);
        }

        if (t_bind(fd, NULL, NULL) < 0) {
                t_error("t_bind failed");
                exit(2);
        }

        /*
         * By assuming that the address is an integer value,
         * this program may not run over another protocol.
         */
```

(continued on next page)

```
        if ((sndcall = (struct t_call *)t_alloc(fd,
          T_CALL, T_ADDR)) == NULL) {
                t_error("t_alloc failed");
                exit(3);
        }
        sndcall->addr.len = sizeof(int);
        *(int *)sndcall->addr.buf = SRV_ADDR;

        if (t_connect(fd, sndcall, NULL) < 0) {
                t_error("t_connect failed for fd");
                exit(4);
        }

        while ((nbytes = t_rcv(fd, buf, 1024, &flags)) != -1) {
                if (fwrite(buf, 1, nbytes, stdout) < 0) {
                        fprintf(stderr, "fwrite failed\n");
                        exit(5);
                }
        }

        if ((t_errno == TLOOK) && (t_look(fd) == T_ORDREL)) {
                if (t_rcvrel(fd) < 0) {
                        t_error("t_rcvrel failed");
                        exit(6);
                }
                if (t_sndrel(fd) < 0) {
                        t_error("t_sndrel failed");
                        exit(7);
                }
                exit(0);
        }
        t_error("t_rcv failed");
        exit(8);
}
```

Connection-Mode Server

The following code represents the connection-mode server program described in the "Introduction to Connection-Mode Service" section. This server establishes a transport connection with a client, and then transfers a log file to the client on the other side of the connection. The connection is released using the orderly release facility of the Transport Interface. The connection-mode client presented earlier will communicate with this server.

```c
#include <tiuser.h>
#include <stropts.h>
#include <fcntl.h>
#include <stdio.h>
#include <signal.h>

#define DISCONNECT -1
#define SRV_ADDR    1          /* server's well known address */

int conn_fd;                            /* connection established here */
extern int t_errno;

main()
{
        int listen_fd;                  /* listening transport endpoint */
        struct t_bind *bind;
        struct t_call *call;

        if ((listen_fd = t_open("/dev/tivc", O_RDWR, NULL))
          < 0) {
                t_error("t_open failed for listen_fd");
                exit(1);
        }
        /*
         * By assuming that the address is an integer value,
         * this program may not run over another protocol.
         */
        if ((bind = (struct t_bind *)t_alloc(listen_fd,
          T_BIND, T_ALL)) == NULL) {
                t_error("t_alloc of t_bind structure failed");
                exit(2);
        }
        bind->qlen = 1;
        bind->addr.len = sizeof(int);
        *(int *)bind->addr.buf = SRV_ADDR;

        if (t_bind(listen_fd, bind, bind) < 0) {
```

(continued on next page)

```
                    t_error("t_bind failed for listen_fd");
                    exit(3);
        }
        /*
         * Was the correct address bound?
         */
        if (*(int *)bind->addr.buf != SRV_ADDR) {
                    fprintf(stderr, "t_bind bound wrong address\n");
                    exit(4);
        }
        if ((call = (struct t_call *)t_alloc(listen_fd,
          T_CALL, T_ALL)) == NULL) {
                    t_error("t_alloc of t_call structure failed");
                    exit(5);
        }
        while (1) {
                    if (t_listen(listen_fd, call) < 0) {
                             t_error("t_listen failed for listen_fd");
                             exit(6);
                    }
                    if ((conn_fd = accept_call(listen_fd, call))
                      != DISCONNECT)
                             run_server(listen_fd);
        }
}
accept_call(listen_fd, call)
int listen_fd;
struct t_call *call;
{
        int resfd;
        if ((resfd = t_open("/dev/tivc", O_RDWR, NULL)) < 0) {
                    t_error("t_open for responding fd failed");
                    exit(7);
        }
        if (t_bind(resfd, NULL, NULL) < 0) {
                    t_error("t_bind for responding fd failed");
                    exit(8);
        }
        if (t_accept(listen_fd, resfd, call) < 0) {
                    if (t_errno == TLOOK) {   /* must be a disconnect */
                             if (t_rcvdis(listen_fd, NULL) < 0) {
                                      t_error("t_rcvdis failed for listen_fd");
```

(continued on next page)

```
                                        exit(9);
                                }
                                if (t_close(resfd) < 0) {
                                        t_error("t_close failed for responding fd");
                                        exit(10);
                                }
                                /* go back up and listen for other calls */
                                return(DISCONNECT);
                        }
                        t_error("t_accept failed");
                        exit(11);
                }
        return(resfd);
}

connrelease()
{
        /* conn_fd is global because needed here */
        if (t_look(conn_fd) == T_DISCONNECT) {
                fprintf(stderr, "connection aborted\n");
                exit(12);
        }

        /* else orderly release indication - normal exit */
        exit(0);
}

run_server(listen_fd)
int listen_fd;
{
        int nbytes;
        FILE *logfp;                    /* file pointer to log file */
        char buf[1024];

        switch (fork()) {

        case -1:
                perror("fork failed");
                exit(20);

        default: /* parent */

                /* close conn_fd and then go up and listen again */
                if (t_close(conn_fd) < 0) {
                        t_error("t_close failed for conn_fd");
                        exit(21);
                }
                return;

        case 0:                 /* child */
```

(continued on next page)

```
                /* close listen_fd and do service */
                if (t_close(listen_fd) < 0) {
                        t_error("t_close failed for listen_fd");
                        exit(22);
                }
                if ((logfp = fopen("logfile", "r")) == NULL) {
                        perror("cannot open logfile");
                        exit(23);
                }
                signal(SIGPOLL, connrelease);
                if (ioctl(conn_fd, I_SETSIG, S_INPUT) < 0) {
                        perror("ioctl I_SETSIG failed");
                        exit(24);
                }
                if (t_look(conn_fd) != 0) { /* was disconnect there? */
                        fprintf(stderr, "t_look: unexpected event\n");
                        exit(25);
                }

                while ((nbytes = fread(buf, 1, 1024, logfp)) > 0)
                        if (t_snd(conn_fd, buf, nbytes, 0) < 0) {
                                t_error("t_snd failed");
                                exit(26);
                        }

                if (t_sndrel(conn_fd) < 0) {
                        t_error("t_sndrel failed");
                        exit(27);
                }
                pause(); /* until orderly release indication arrives */
        }
}
```

Connectionless-Mode Transaction Server

The following code represents the connectionless-mode transaction server program described in the section "Introduction to Connectionless-Mode Service."
This server waits for incoming datagram queries, and then processes each query
and sends a response.

```
#include <stdio.h>
#include <fcntl.h>
#include <tiuser.h>

#define SRV_ADDR    2                    /* server's well known address */

main()
{
        int fd;
        int flags;
        struct t_bind *bind;
        struct t_unitdata *ud;
        struct t_uderr *uderr;
        extern int t_errno;


        if ((fd = t_open("/dev/tidg", O_RDWR, NULL)) < 0) {
                t_error("unable to open /dev/provider");
                exit(1);
        }

        if ((bind = (struct t_bind *)t_alloc(fd,
          T_BIND, T_ADDR)) == NULL) {
                t_error("t_alloc of t_bind structure failed");
                exit(2);
        }
        bind->addr.len = sizeof(int);
        *(int *)bind->addr.buf = SRV_ADDR;
        bind->qlen = 0;

        if (t_bind(fd, bind, bind) < 0) {
                t_error("t_bind failed");
                exit(3);
        }

        /*
         * is the bound address correct?
         */
```

(continued on next page)

```
if (*(int *)bind->addr.buf != SRV_ADDR) {
        fprintf(stderr, "t_bind bound wrong address\n");
        exit(4);
}

if ((ud = (struct t_unitdata *)t_alloc(fd,
  T_UNITDATA, T_ALL)) == NULL) {
        t_error("t_alloc of t_unitdata structure failed");
        exit(5);
}
if ((uderr = (struct t_uderr *)t_alloc(fd,
  T_UDERROR, T_ALL)) == NULL) {
        t_error("t_alloc of t_uderr structure failed");
        exit(6);
}

while (1) {
        if (t_rcvudata(fd, ud, &flags) < 0) {
                if (t_errno == TLOOK) {
                        /*
                         * Error on previously sent datagram
                         */
                        if (t_rcvuderr(fd, uderr) < 0) {
                                t_error("t_rcvuderr failed");
                                exit(7);
                        }
                        fprintf(stderr, "bad datagram,
                          error = %d\n", uderr->error);
                        continue;
                }
                t_error("t_rcvudata failed");
                exit(8);
        }

        /*
         * Query() processes the request and places the
         * response in ud->udata.buf, setting ud->udata.len
         */
        query(ud);

        if (t_sndudata(fd, ud, 0) < 0) {
                t_error("t_sndudata failed");
                exit(9);
        }
}
}
```

(continued on next page)

```
query()
{
        /* Merely a stub for simplicity */
}
```

Read/Write Client

The following code represents the connection-mode read/write client program described in the section "A Read/Write Interface." This client establishes a transport connection with a server, and then uses cat (1) to retrieve the data sent by the server and write it to its standard output. This client will communicate with each of the connection-mode servers presented in the guide.

```
#include <stdio.h>
#include <tiuser.h>
#include <fcntl.h>
#include <stropts.h>

#define SRV_ADDR   1        /* server's well known address */

main()
{
        int fd;
        int nbytes;
        int flags = 0;
        char buf[1024];
        struct t_call *sndcall;
        extern int t_errno;

        if ((fd = t_open("/dev/tivc", O_RDWR, NULL)) < 0) {
                t_error("t_open failed");
                exit(1);
        }

        if (t_bind(fd, NULL, NULL) < 0) {
                t_error("t_bind failed");
                exit(2);
        }

        /*
         * By assuming that the address is an integer value,
         * this program may not run over another protocol.
         */

        if ((sndcall = (struct t_call *)t_alloc(fd,
          T_CALL, T_ADDR)) == NULL) {
                t_error("t_alloc failed");
                exit(3);
        }

        sndcall->addr.len = sizeof(int);
        *(int *)sndcall->addr.buf = SRV_ADDR;

        if (t_connect(fd, sndcall, NULL) < 0) {
                t_error("t_connect failed for fd");
                exit(4);
        }
```

(continued on next page)

```
        if (ioctl(fd, I_PUSH, "tirdwr") < 0) {
                perror("I_PUSH of tirdwr failed");
                exit(5);
        }

        close(0);
        dup(fd);

        execl("/usr/bin/cat", "/usr/bin/cat", 0);

        perror("execl of /usr/bin/cat failed");
        exit(6);
}
```

Event-Driven Server

The following code represents the connection-mode server program described in the section "Advanced Topics." This server manages multiple connect indications in an event-driven manner. Either connection-mode client presented earlier will communicate with this server.

```
#include <tiuser.h>
#include <fcntl.h>
#include <stdio.h>
#include <poll.h>
#include <stropts.h>
#include <signal.h>

#define NUM_FDS         1
#define MAX_CONN_IND    4
#define SRV_ADDR        1               /* server's well known address */

int conn_fd;                            /* server connection here */
extern int t_errno;

/* holds connect indications */
struct t_call *calls[NUM_FDS][MAX_CONN_IND];

main()
{
        struct pollfd pollfds[NUM_FDS];
        struct t_bind *bind;
        int i;

        /*
         * Only opening and binding one transport endpoint,
         * but more could be supported
         */
        if ((pollfds[0].fd = t_open("/dev/tivc", O_RDWR, NULL))
          < 0) {
                t_error("t_open failed");
                exit(1);
        }

        if ((bind = (struct t_bind *)t_alloc(pollfds[0].fd,
          T_BIND, T_ALL)) == NULL) {
                t_error("t_alloc of t_bind structure failed");
                exit(2);
        }
        bind->qlen = MAX_CONN_IND;
        bind->addr.len = sizeof(int);
        *(int *)bind->addr.buf = SRV_ADDR;

        if (t_bind(pollfds[0].fd, bind, bind) < 0) {
                t_error("t_bind failed");
                exit(3);
        }
```

(continued on next page)

Programmer's Guide: Networking Interfaces

```
        /*
         * Was the correct address bound?
         */
        if (*(int *)bind->addr.buf != SRV_ADDR) {
                fprintf(stderr, "t_bind bound wrong address\n");
                exit(4);
        }

        pollfds[0].events = POLLIN;

        while (1) {
                if (poll(pollfds, NUM_FDS, -1) < 0) {
                        perror("poll failed");
                        exit(5);
                }

                for (i = 0; i < NUM_FDS; i++) {

                        switch (pollfds[i].revents) {

                        default:
                                perror("poll returned error event");
                                exit(6);

                        case 0:
                                continue;

                        case POLLIN:
                                do_event(i, pollfds[i].fd);
                                service_conn_ind(i, pollfds[i].fd);
                        }
                }
        }
}

do_event(slot, fd)
{
        struct t_discon *discon;
        int i;

        switch (t_look(fd)) {

        default:
                fprintf(stderr,"t_look: unexpected event\n");
                exit(7);
```

(continued on next page)

```
case T_ERROR:
        fprintf(stderr,"t_look returned T_ERROR event\n");
        exit(8);

case -1:
        t_error("t_look failed");
        exit(9);

case 0:
        /* since POLLIN returned, this should not happen */
        fprintf(stderr,"t_look returned no event\n");
        exit(10);

case T_LISTEN:
        /*
         * find free element in calls array
         */
        for (i = 0; i < MAX_CONN_IND; i++) {
                if (calls[slot][i] == NULL)
                        break;
        }

        if ((calls[slot][i] = (struct t_call *)t_alloc(fd,
          T_CALL, T_ALL)) == NULL)
        {
                t_error("t_alloc of t_call structure failed");
                exit(11);
        }

        if (t_listen(fd, calls[slot][i]) < 0) {
                t_error("t_listen failed");
                exit(12);
        }
        break;

case T_DISCONNECT:
        discon = (struct t_discon *)t_alloc(fd,
          T_DIS, T_ALL);

        if (t_rcvdis(fd, discon) < 0) {
                t_error("t_rcvdis failed");
                exit(13);
        }
```

(continued on next page)

```
                    /*
                     * find call ind in array and delete it
                     */
                    for (i = 0; i < MAX_CONN_IND; i++) {
                            if (discon->sequence ==
                                calls[slot][i]->sequence) {
                                        t_free(calls[slot][i], T_CALL);
                                        calls[slot][i] = NULL;
                            }
                    }
                    t_free(discon, T_DIS);
                    break;
            }
    }

service_conn_ind(slot, fd)
{
        int i;

        for (i = 0; i < MAX_CONN_IND; i++) {
                if (calls[slot][i] == NULL)
                        continue;
                if ((conn_fd = t_open("/dev/tivc",
                  O_RDWR, NULL)) < 0) {
                        t_error("open failed");
                        exit(14);
                }
                if (t_bind(conn_fd, NULL, NULL) < 0) {
                        t_error("t_bind failed");
                        exit(15);
                }

                if (t_accept(fd, conn_fd, calls[slot][i]) < 0) {
                        if (t_errno == TLOOK) {
                                    t_close(conn_fd);
                                    return;
                        }
                        t_error("t_accept failed");
                        exit(16);
                }
                t_free(calls[slot][i], T_CALL);
                calls[slot][i] = NULL;

                run_server(fd);
        }
}
```

(continued on next page)

```
connrelease()
{
        /* conn_fd is global because needed here */
        if (t_look(conn_fd) == T_DISCONNECT) {
                fprintf(stderr, "connection aborted\n");
                exit(12);
        }

        /* else orderly release indication - normal exit */
        exit(0);
}

run_server(listen_fd)
int listen_fd;
{
        int nbytes;
        FILE *logfp;                    /* file pointer to log file */
        char buf[1024];

        switch (fork()) {

        case -1:
                perror("fork failed");
                exit(20);

        default: /* parent */

                /* close conn_fd and then go up and listen again */
                if (t_close(conn_fd) < 0) {
                        t_error("t_close failed for conn_fd");
                        exit(21);
                }
                return;

        case 0:          /* child */

                /* close listen_fd and do service */
                if (t_close(listen_fd) < 0) {
                        t_error("t_close failed for listen_fd");
                        exit(22);
                }
                if ((logfp = fopen("logfile", "r")) == NULL) {
                        perror("cannot open logfile");
```

(continued on next page)

```
                    exit(23);
        }

        signal(SIGPOLL, connrelease);
        if (ioctl(conn_fd, I_SETSIG, S_INPUT) < 0) {
                perror("ioctl I_SETSIG failed");
                exit(24);
        }
        if (t_look(conn_fd) != 0) {  /* disconnect already there? */
                fprintf(stderr, "t_look: unexpected event\n");
                exit(25);
        }

        while ((nbytes = fread(buf, 1, 1024, logfp)) > 0)
                if (t_snd(conn_fd, buf, nbytes, 0) < 0) {
                        t_error("t_snd failed");
                        exit(26);
                }

        if (t_sndrel(conn_fd) < 0) {
                t_error("t_sndrel failed");
                exit(27);
        }
        pause(); /* until orderly release indication arrives */
    }
}
```

Glossary

The following terms apply to the Transport Interface:

Abortive release

An abrupt termination of a transport connection, which may result in the loss of data.

Asynchronous execution

The mode of execution in which Transport Interface routines will never block while waiting for specific asynchronous events to occur, but instead will return immediately if the event is not pending.

Client

The transport user in connection-mode that requests a transport connection.

Connection establishment

The phase in connection-mode that enables two transport users to create a transport connection between them.

Connection-mode

A circuit-oriented mode of transfer in which data are passed from one user to another over an established connection in a reliable, sequenced manner.

Connectionless-mode

A mode of transfer in which data are passed from one user to another in self-contained units with no logical relationship required among multiple units.

Connection release

The phase in connection-mode that terminates a previously established transport connection between two users.

Datagram

A unit of data transferred between two users of the connectionless-mode service.

Data transfer

The phase in connection-mode or connectionless-mode that supports the transfer of data between two transport users.

Expedited data

Data that are considered urgent. The specific semantics of expedited data are defined by the transport protocol that provides the transport service.

Expedited transport service data
> The amount of expedited user data the identity of which is preserved from one end of a transport connection to the other (that is, an expedited message).

Local management
> The phase in either connection-mode or connectionless-mode in which a transport user establishes a transport endpoint and binds a transport address to the endpoint. Functions in this phase perform local operations, and require no transport layer traffic over the network.

Orderly release
> A procedure for gracefully terminating a transport connection with no loss of data.

Peer user
> The user with whom a given user is communicating above the Transport Interface.

Server
> The transport user in connection-mode that offers services to other users (clients) and enables these clients to establish a transport connection to it.

Service indication
> The notification of a pending event generated by the provider to a user of a particular service.

Service primitive
> The unit of information passed across a service interface that contains either a service request or service indication.

Service request
> A request for some action generated by a user to the provider of a particular service.

Synchronous execution
> The mode of execution in which Transport Interface routines may block while waiting for specific asynchronous events to occur.

Transport address
> The identifier used to differentiate and locate specific transport endpoints in a network.

Transport connection
>
> The communication circuit that is established between two transport users in connection-mode.

Transport endpoint
>
> The local communication channel between a transport user and a transport provider.

Transport Interface
>
> The library routines and state transition rules that support the services of a transport protocol.

Transport provider
>
> The transport protocol that provides the services of the Transport Interface.

Transport service data unit
>
> The amount of user data whose identity is preserved from one end of a transport connection to the other (that is, a message).

Transport user   The user-level application or protocol that accesses the services of the Transport Interface.

Virtual circuit   A transport connection established in connection-mode. The following acronyms are used throughout this guide:

CLTS	Connectionless Transport Service
COTS	Connection Oriented Transport Service
ETSDU	Expedited Transport Service Data Unit
TSDU	Transport Service Data Unit

3 The Sockets Interface

Programmer's Guide: Networking Interfaces

Background

Sockets was first introduced in 1981 as part of the Berkeley 4.2 Software Distribution. A significant application base has been written using this interface. Sockets has now been added to UNIX System V Release 4 as part of the BSD/System V unification.

Different approaches are possible within the sockets framework. This chapter discusses these approaches and then illustrates them with a series of sample programs. The programs demonstrate the use of both datagram socket and stream socket communication. The chapter is divided into the following sections: The "Basics" section introduces the sockets routines and the basic model of communication. "Supporting Routines" describes some of the library functions that may be used to build distributed applications. The section on the "Client/Server Model" discusses the model used in developing applications and includes examples of the two major types of servers. "Advanced Topics" discusses issues that may be relevant for more sophisticated users.

Basics

A basic building block for communication is the socket. A socket is an endpoint of communication to which a name may be bound. Each socket in use has a type and one or more associated processes. Sockets exist within communications domains. Domains are abstractions that imply both an addressing structure (address family) and a set of protocols which implement socket types within the domain (protocol family). Communications domains are introduced to bundle common properties of processes communicating through sockets. One such property is the scheme used to name sockets. In the UNIX domain, sockets are named with UNIX pathnames; for example, a socket may be named /dev/foo. Sockets normally exchange data only with sockets in the same domain (it may be possible to cross between communications domains, but only if some translation process is performed). The UNIX system socket interface facilities support several separate communications domains: for example, the UNIX domain, for on-system communication; and the Internet domain, which is used by processes that communicate using the DARPA standard communication protocols. The underlying communication facilities provided by these domains have a significant influence on the internal system implementation as well as the interface to socket facilities available to a user. For example, a socket operating in the UNIX domain sees a subset of the error conditions that are possible when operating in the Internet domain.

Socket Types

Sockets have types that reflect the communication properties visible to a user. Processes are presumed to communicate only between sockets of the same type, although there is nothing that prevents communication between sockets of different types should the underlying communication protocols support this.

There are several types of sockets currently available:

- A stream socket provides for the bidirectional, reliable, sequenced, and unduplicated flow of data without record boundaries. A pair of connected stream sockets provides an interface nearly identical to that of pipes.

- A datagram socket supports bidirectional flow of data that is not promised to be sequenced, reliable, or unduplicated. That is, a process receiving messages on a datagram socket may find messages duplicated and possibly in an order different from the order in which they were sent. An important characteristic of a datagram socket is that record boundaries in

Programmer's Guide: Networking Interfaces

the data are preserved. Datagram sockets closely model the facilities found in many contemporary packet switched networks such as the Ethernet.

■ A raw socket provides access to the underlying communication protocols that support socket abstractions. These sockets are normally datagram oriented, although their exact characteristics are dependent on the interface provided by the protocol. Raw sockets are not intended for the general user; they have been provided mainly for users interested in developing new communication protocols, or gaining access to some of the more esoteric facilities of an existing protocol. The use of raw sockets is considered under "Advanced Topics" below.

Socket Creation

The socket () system call is used to create a socket:

        s = socket(domain, type, protocol);

This call requests that the system create a socket in the specified domain and of the specified type. If the protocol is left unspecified (a value of 0), the system will select an appropriate protocol from those that comprise the domain and that may be used to support the requested socket type. A descriptor (a small integer) that may be used in later system calls that operate on sockets is returned. The domain is specified as one of the manifest constants defined in the file <sys/socket.h>. For the UNIX domain the constant is AF_UNIX; for the Internet domain, it is AF_INET.

| NOTE | The constants named AF_*whatever* show the address format to use in interpreting names. |

The socket types are also defined in <sys/socket.h> and one of SOCK_STREAM, SOCK_DGRAM, or SOCK_RAW must be specified. To create a stream socket in the Internet domain the following call might be used:

        s = socket(AF_INET, SOCK_STREAM, 0);

This call would result in a stream socket being created with the TCP protocol providing the underlying communication support. To create a datagram socket for on-machine use the call might be:

```
s = socket (AF_UNIX, SOCK_DGRAM, 0);
```

The default protocol (used when the protocol argument to the socket () call is 0) should be correct for most situations. However, it is possible to specify a protocol other than the default; this will be covered in the "Advanced Topics" section below.

A socket call may fail for several reasons. Aside from the rare occurrence of lack of memory (ENOBUFS), a socket request may fail because the request is for an unknown protocol (EPROTONOSUPPORT), or because the request is for a type of socket for which there is no supporting protocol (EPROTOTYPE).

Binding Local Names

A socket is created without a name. Until a name is bound to a socket, processes have no way to reference it and consequently no messages may be received on it. Communicating processes are bound by an association. In the Internet domain, an association is composed of local and foreign addresses, and local and foreign ports, while in the UNIX domain, an association is composed of local and foreign pathnames.

 NOTE The phrase "foreign pathname" means a pathname created by a foreign process, not a pathname on a foreign system.

In most domains, associations must be unique. In the Internet domain there may never be duplicate tuples, such as:

```
<protocol, local address, local port, foreign address, foreign port>
```

UNIX domain sockets need not always be bound to a name, but when bound there may never be duplicate tuples of the type:

```
<protocol, local pathname, foreign pathname>
```

Currently, the pathnames may not refer to files already existing on the system, though this may change in future releases.

The bind() system call allows a process to specify half of an association, for example

        `<local address, local port> (or <local pathname>)`

while the connect() and accept() primitives are used to complete a socket's association.

The bind() system call is used as follows:

        `bind(s, name, namelen);`

The bound name is a variable length byte string that is interpreted by the supporting protocol(s). Its interpretation may vary between communication domains (this is one of the properties that comprises a domain). Whereas Internet domain names contain an Internet address and port number, UNIX domain names contain a pathname and a family. The family is always AF_UNIX. The following code would be used to bind the name /tmp/foo to a UNIX domain socket:

```
#include <sys/un.h>
...
struct sockaddr_un addr;
...
strcpy(addr.sun_path, "/tmp/foo");
addr.sun_family = AF_UNIX;
bind(s, (struct sockaddr *) &addr, strlen(addr.sun_path) +
    sizeof (addr.sun_family));
```

Note that in determining the size of a UNIX domain address, null bytes are not counted, which is why strlen() is used. The file name referred to in addr.sun_path is created as a socket in the system file space. The caller must, therefore, have write permission in the directory where addr.sun_path is to reside, and the file should be deleted by the caller when it is no longer needed.

In binding an Internet address things become more complicated. The call itself is similar,

```
#include <sys/types.h>
#include <netinet/in.h>
...
struct sockaddr_in sin;
...
bind(s, (struct sockaddr *) &sin, sizeof sin);
```

but the selection of what to place in the address sin requires some discussion.
We will come back to the problem of formulating Internet addresses in the
"Supporting Routines" section when the library routines used in name resolu-
tion are discussed.

Connection Establishment

Connection establishment is usually asymmetric, with one process a client and
the other a server . The server, when willing to offer its advertised services,
binds a socket to a well-known address associated with the service and then
passively listens on its socket. It is then possible for an unrelated process to
rendezvous with the server. The client requests services from the server by initiating a connection to the server's socket. On the client side the connect ()
call is used to initiate a connection. In the UNIX domain, this might appear as:

```
struct sockaddr_un server;
...
connect(s, (struct sockaddr *)&server,
        strlen(server.sun_path) + sizeof (server.sun_family));
```

while in the Internet domain, it might be:

```
struct sockaddr_in server;
...
connect(s, (struct sockaddr *)&server, sizeof server);
```

server would contain either the UNIX pathname, or the Internet address and port number of the server to which the client process wishes to speak. If the client process's socket is unbound at the time of the connect call, the system will automatically select and bind a name to the socket if necessary. See "Signals and Process Groups" below. This is the usual way that local addresses are bound to a socket.

An error is returned if the connection was unsuccessful (however, any name automatically bound by the system remains). Otherwise, the socket is associated with the server and data transfer may begin. Some of the more common errors returned when a connection attempt fails are:

ETIMEDOUT   After failing to establish a connection over a period of time, the system stopped attempting the connection. This may occur when the destination host is down or when problems in the network result in lost transmissions.

ECONNREFUSE

      The host refused service. This usually occurs when a server process is not present at the requested name.

ENETDOWN or EHOSTDOWN

      These operational errors are returned based on status information delivered to the client host by the underlying communication services.

ENETUNREACH or EHOSTUNREACH

      These operational errors can occur either because the network or host is unknown (no route to the network or host is present), or because of status information returned by intermediate gateways or switching nodes. The status returned is not always sufficient to distinguish between a network that is down and a host that is down.

For a server to receive a client's connection it must perform two steps after binding its socket. The first is to listen for incoming connection requests. With a socket marked as listening, the second step is to accept () a connection:

```
struct sockaddr_in from;
...
listen(s, 5);
fromlen = sizeof from;
newsock = accept(s, (struct sockaddr *)&from, &fromlen);
```

The first parameter to the listen() call is the socket on which the connection is to be established. The second parameter to the listen() call specifies the maximum number of outstanding connections that may be queued awaiting acceptance by the server process. (For the UNIX domain, from would be declared as a struct sockaddr_un but nothing different would need to be done as far as fromlen is concerned. In the examples that follow, only Internet routines will be discussed.) A new descriptor is returned on receipt of a connection (along with a new socket). If the server wishes to find out who its client is, it may supply a buffer for the client socket's name. The value-result parameter fromlen is initialized by the server to indicate how much space is associated with from. It is then modified on return to reflect the true size of the name. If the client's name is not of interest, the second parameter may be a null pointer.

accept() normally blocks. That is, accept() will not return until a connection is available or the system call is interrupted by a signal to the process. Further, there is no way for a process to indicate that it will accept connections only from a specific individual or individuals. It is up to the user process to consider who the connection is from and close down the connection if it does not wish to speak to the process. If the server process wants to accept connections on more than one socket, or wants to avoid blocking on the accept call, there are alternatives; they will be considered in the "Advanced Topics" section below.

Data Transfer

With a connection established, data may begin to flow. There are several calls
for sending and receiving data. With the peer entity at each end of a connection
anchored, a user can send or receive a message without specifying the peer.
Here, the normal `read()` and `write()` system calls are usable:

```
write(s, buf, sizeof buf);
read(s, buf, sizeof buf);
```

In addition to `read()` and `write()`, the calls `send()` and `recv()` may be
used:

```
send(s, buf, sizeof buf, flags);
recv(s, buf, sizeof buf, flags);
```

While `send()` and `recv()` are virtually identical to `read()` and `write()`,
the extra `flags` argument is important. The flags, defined in
`<sys/socket.h>`, may be specified as a non-zero value if one or more of the
following is required:

MSG_OOB	send/receive out-of-band data
MSG_PEEK	look at data without reading
MSG_DONTROUTE	send data without routing packets

Out-of-band data is specific to stream sockets. The option to have data sent
without routing applied to the outgoing packets is currently used only by the
routing table management process and is unlikely to be of interest to most
users. However, the ability to preview data is of interest. When `MSG_PEEK` is
specified with a `recv()` call, any data present is returned to the user but
treated as still unread. That is, the next `read()` or `recv()` call applied to the
socket will return the data previously previewed.

Closing Sockets

Once a socket is no longer of interest, it may be discarded by applying a
`close()` to the descriptor,

        close(s);

If data is associated with a socket that promises reliable delivery (for example, a
stream socket) when a close takes place, the system will continue to attempt to
transfer the data. However, if the data is still undelivered after a fairly long
period of time, it will be discarded. If a user has no use for pending data, a
`shutdown()` may be performed on the socket before closing it. This call is of
the form:

        shutdown(s, how);

where how is 0 if the user is no longer interested in reading data, 1 if no more
data will be sent, and 2 if no data is to be sent or received.

The following two code samples illustrate how to initiate and accept an Internet
domain stream connection.

Figure 3-1: Initiating an Internet Domain Stream Connection

```
#include <sys/types.h>
#include <sys/socket.h>
#include <netinet/in.h>
#include <netdb.h>
#include <stdio.h>

#define DATA "Half a league, half a league . . ."

/*
 * This program creates a socket and initiates a connection with the socket
 * given in the command line.  One message is sent over the connection and
 * then the socket is closed, ending the connection.  The form of the command
 * line is: streamwrite hostname portnumber
 */

main(argc, argv)
        int argc;
        char *argv[];
```

(continued on next page)

Figure 3-1: Initiating an Internet Domain Stream Connection (continued)

```
{
        int sock;
        struct sockaddr_in server;
        struct hostent *hp, *gethostbyname();
        char buf[1024];

        /* Create socket. */
        sock = socket(AF_INET, SOCK_STREAM, 0);
        if (sock < 0) {
                perror("opening stream socket");
                exit(1);
        }
        /* Connect socket using name specified by command line. */
        server.sin_family = AF_INET;
        hp = gethostbyname(argv[1]);
        if (hp == 0) {
                fprintf(stderr, "%s: unknown host\n", argv[1]);
                exit(2);
        }
        memcpy((char *)&server.sin_addr, (char *)hp->h_addr,
          hp->h_length);
        server.sin_port = htons(atoi(argv[2]));

        if (connect(sock,
          (struct sockaddr *)&server, sizeof server ) < 0) {
                perror("connecting stream socket");
                exit(1);
        }
        if (write(sock, DATA, sizeof DATA ) < 0)
                perror("writing on stream socket");
        close(sock);
        exit(0);
}
```

Figure 3-2: Accepting an Internet Domain Stream Connection

```
#include <sys/types.h>
#include <sys/socket.h>
#include <netinet/in.h>
#include <netdb.h>
#include <stdio.h>
#define TRUE 1

/*
 * This program creates a socket and then begins an infinite loop.  Each time
 * through the loop it accepts a connection and prints out messages from it.
 * When the connection breaks, or a termination message comes through, the
 * program accepts a new connection.
 */

main()
{
        int sock, length;
        struct sockaddr_in server;
        int msgsock;
        char buf[1024];
        int rval;

        /* Create socket. */
        sock = socket(AF_INET, SOCK_STREAM, 0);
        if (sock < 0) {
                perror("opening stream socket");
                exit(1);
        }
        /* Name socket using wildcards. */
        server.sin_family = AF_INET;
        server.sin_addr.s_addr = INADDR_ANY;
        server.sin_port = 0;
        if (bind(sock, (struct sockaddr *)&server, sizeof server ) < 0) {
                perror("binding stream socket");
                exit(1);
        }
        /* Find out assigned port number and print it out. */
        length = sizeof server;
        if (getsockname(sock, (struct sockaddr *)&server,
          &length) < 0) {
                perror("getting socket name");
                exit(1);
        }
        printf("Socket port #%d\n", ntohs(server.sin_port));
```

(continued on next page)

Programmer's Guide: Networking Interfaces

Figure 3-2: **Accepting an Internet Domain Stream Connection** (continued)

```
/* Start accepting connections. */
listen(sock, 5);
do {
        msgsock = accept(sock, (struct sockaddr *)0, (int *)0);
        if (msgsock == -1)
                perror("accept");
        else do {
                memset(buf, 0, sizeof buf );
                if ((rval = read(msgsock, buf, 1024)) < 0)
                        perror("reading stream message");
                if (rval == 0)
                        printf("Ending connection\n");
                else
                        printf("-->%s\n", buf);
        } while (rval != 0);
        close(msgsock);
} while (TRUE);
/*
 * Since this program has an infinite loop, the socket "sock" is
 * never explicitly closed.  However, all sockets will be closed
 * automatically when a process is killed or terminates normally.
 */
exit(0);
}
```

Connectionless Sockets

Up to this point we have been concerned primarily with connection-oriented sockets. However, connectionless interactions typical of the datagram facilities found in contemporary packet switched networks are also supported. A datagram socket provides a symmetric interface to data exchange. While processes are still likely to be client and server process, there is no requirement for connection establishment. Instead, each message includes the destination address.

The Sockets Interface

Datagram sockets are created as described above under "Socket Creation." If a particular local address is needed, the `bind()` operation must precede the first data transmission. Otherwise, the system will set the local address and/or port when data is first sent. To send data, the `sendto()` call is used:

```
sendto(s, buf, buflen, flags, (struct sockaddr *)
    &to, tolen);
```

The `s`, `buf`, `buflen`, and `flags` parameters are used the same as with connection-oriented sockets. The `to` and `tolen` values are used to indicate the address of the intended recipient of the message. When using an unreliable datagram interface, it is unlikely that any errors will be reported to the sender. When information is present locally that allows the system to recognize a message that can not be delivered (for instance when a network is unreachable), the call will return −1 and the global value `errno` will contain the error number.

To receive messages on an unconnected datagram socket, the `recvfrom()` call is used:

```
recvfrom(s, buf, buflen, flags, (struct sockaddr *)
    &from, &fromlen);
```

The `fromlen` parameter initially contains the size of the `from` buffer; it is modified on return to show the size of the address from which the datagram was received.

In addition to the two calls mentioned above, datagram sockets may also use the `connect()` call to associate a socket with a specific destination address. Here, any data sent on the socket without explicitly specifying the destination address will automatically be addressed to the connected peer, and only data received from that peer will be delivered to the user. Only one connected address is permitted for each socket at one time. A second connect will change the destination address, and a connect to a null address (domain `AF_UNSPEC`) will disconnect. Connect requests on datagram sockets return immediately; the system simply records the peer's address. By contrast, a connection request on a stream socket initiates establishment of an end-to-end connection.

`accept()` and `listen()` are not used with datagram sockets.

While a datagram socket is connected, errors from recent `send()` calls may be returned asynchronously. These errors may be reported on subsequent operations on the socket, or a special socket option used with `getsockopt`, `SO_ERROR`, may be used to interrogate the error status.

Figure 3-3: Reading Internet Domain Datagrams

```
#include <sys/types.h>
#include <sys/socket.h>
#include <netinet/in.h>
#include <stdio.h>

/*
 * The include file <netinet/in.h> defines sockaddr_in as follows:
 * struct sockaddr_in {
 *       short    sin_family;
 *       u_short  sin_port;
 *       struct in_addr sin_addr;
 *       char     sin_zero[8];
 * };
 *
 * This program creates a datagram socket, binds a name to it, then reads
 * from the socket.
 */
main()
{
        int sock, length;
        struct sockaddr_in name;
        char buf[1024];

        /* Create socket from which to read. */
        sock = socket(AF_INET, SOCK_DGRAM, 0);
        if (sock < 0) {
                perror("opening datagram socket");
                exit(1);
        }
        /* Create name with wildcards. */
        name.sin_family = AF_INET;
        name.sin_addr.s_addr = INADDR_ANY;
        name.sin_port = 0;
        if (bind(sock, (struct sockaddr *)&name,
          sizeof name ) < 0) {
                perror("binding datagram socket");
                exit(1);
        }
        /* Find assigned port value and print it out. */
        length = sizeof(name);
        if (getsockname(sock, (struct sockaddr *)&name,
          &length) < 0) {
                perror("getting socket name");
                exit(1);
```

(continued on next page)

Figure 3-3: Reading Internet Domain Datagrams (continued)

```
    }
        printf("Socket port #%d\n", ntohs(name.sin_port));
        /* Read from the socket. */
        if (read(sock, buf, 1024) < 0)
                perror("receiving datagram packet");
        printf("-->%s\n", buf);
        close(sock);
        exit(0);
    }
```

Figure 3-4: Sending an Internet Domain Datagram

```
    #include <sys/types.h>
    #include <sys/socket.h>
    #include <netinet/in.h>
    #include <netdb.h>
    #include <stdio.h>

    #define DATA "The sea is calm, the tide is full . . ."

    /*
     * Here I send a datagram to a receiver whose name I get from the command
     * line arguments.  The form of the command line is:
     * dgramsend hostname portnumber
     */

    main(argc, argv)
        int argc;
        char *argv[];
    {
        int sock;
        struct sockaddr_in name;
        struct hostent *hp, *gethostbyname();

        /* Create socket on which to send. */
        sock = socket(AF_INET, SOCK_DGRAM, 0);
```

(continued on next page)

Figure 3-4: **Sending an Internet Domain Datagram** (continued)

```
if (sock < 0) {
        perror("opening datagram socket");
        exit(1);
}
/*
 * Construct name, with no wildcards, of the socket to send to.
 * gethostbyname returns a structure including the network address
 * of the specified host.  The port number is taken from the command
 * line.
 */
hp = gethostbyname(argv[1]);
if (hp == 0) {
        fprintf(stderr, "%s: unknown host\n", argv[1]);
        exit(2);
}
memcpy( (char *)&name.sin_addr, (char *)hp->h_addr,
  hp->h_length);
name.sin_family = AF_INET;
name.sin_port = htons(atoi(argv[2]));
/* Send message. */
if (sendto(sock, DATA, sizeof DATA , 0,
  (struct sockaddr *)&name, sizeof name) < 0)
        perror("sending datagram message");
close(sock);
exit(0);
}
```

Input/Output Multiplexing

The ability to multiplex I/O requests among multiple sockets or files is a facility that is often used in developing applications. The select() call is used for this type of input/output multiplexing:

```
#include <sys/time.h>
#include <sys/types.h>
#include <sys/select.h>
    ...

fd_set readmask, writemask, exceptmask;
struct timeval timeout;
    ...
select(nfds, &readmask, &writemask, &exceptmask, &timeout);
```

`select()` takes pointers to three sets as arguments. One pointer is to the set of file descriptors on which the caller wishes to be able to read data; one is to those descriptors to which data is to be written; and one is to pending exceptional conditions. Out-of-band data is the only exceptional condition currently implemented. If the user is not interested in certain conditions (i.e., read, write, or exceptions), the corresponding argument to the `select()` should be a properly cast null pointer.

Each set is a structure containing an array of long integer bit masks. The size of the array is set by `FD_SETSIZE`. The array is long enough to hold one bit for each of `FD_SETSIZE` file descriptors.

The macros `FD_SET` (*fd*, *&mask*), and `FD_CLR` (*fd*, *&mask*) have been provided for adding and removing file descriptor `fd` in the set `mask`. The set should be zeroed before use, and the macro `FD_ZERO` (*&mask*) has been provided to clear the set `mask`.

The `nfds` argument specifies the range of file descriptors (i.e., one plus the value of the largest descriptor) to be examined in a set.

A timeout value may be specified if the selection is not to last more than a predetermined period of time. If the fields in `timeout` are set to 0, the selection takes the form of a poll, returning immediately. If the last parameter is a NULL pointer, the selection will block indefinitely.

NOTE To be more specific, if the last parameter is a NULL pointer, a return takes place only when a descriptor is selectable, or when a signal is received by the caller, interrupting the system call.

select() normally returns the number of file descriptors selected. If the select() call returns because the timeout has expired, the value 0 is returned. If the select() terminates because of an error or interrupt, a −1 is returned with the error number in errno, and with the file descriptor masks unchanged.

Assuming a successful return, the three sets will indicate which file descriptors are ready to be read from, written to, or have exceptional conditions pending.

The status of a file descriptor in a select mask may be tested with the FD_ISSET (*fd*, &*mask*) macro, which returns a non-zero value if fd is a member of the set mask, and 0 if it is not.

To determine if there are connections waiting on a socket to be used with an accept() call, select() can be used, followed by a FD_ISSET (*fd*, &*mask*) macro to check for read readiness on the appropriate socket. If FD_ISSET returns a non-zero value, indicating permission to read, then a connection is pending on the socket.

As an example, to read data from two sockets, s1 and s2, as it is available from each and with a five-second timeout, the following code might be used:

Figure 3-5: Using select() to Check for Pending Connections

```
#include <sys/types.h>
#include <sys/socket.h>
#include <sys/time.h>
#include <netinet/in.h>
#include <netdb.h>
#include <stdio.h>
#define TRUE 1

/*
 * This program uses select to check that someone is trying to connect
 * before calling accept.
 */

main()
{
        int sock, length;
        struct sockaddr_in server;
        int msgsock;
        char buf[1024];
        int rval;
        fd_set ready;
        struct timeval to;

        /* Create socket. */
        sock = socket(AF_INET, SOCK_STREAM, 0);
        if (sock < 0) {
                perror("opening stream socket");
                exit(1);
        }
        /* Name socket using wildcards. */
        server.sin_family = AF_INET;
        server.sin_addr.s_addr = INADDR_ANY;
        server.sin_port = 0;
        if (bind(sock, (struct sockaddr *)&server,
          sizeof server) < 0) {
                perror("binding stream socket");
                exit(1);
        }
        /* Find out assigned port number and print it out. */
        length = sizeof server;
        if (getsockname(sock, (struct sockaddr *)&server,
          &length) < 0) {
                perror("getting socket name");
                exit(1);
```

(continued on next page)

Figure 3-5: Using `select()` **to Check for Pending Connections** (continued)

```
        }
        printf("Socket port #%d\n", ntohs(server.sin_port));

        /* Start accepting connections. */
        listen(sock, 5);
        do {
                FD_ZERO(&ready);
                FD_SET(sock, &ready);
                to.tv_sec = 5;
                if (select(sock + 1, &ready, (fd_set *)0,
                   (fd_set *)0, &to) < 0) {
                        perror("select");
                        continue;
                }
                if (FD_ISSET(sock, &ready)) {
                        msgsock = accept(sock, (struct sockaddr *)0,
                           (int *)0);
                        if (msgsock == -1)
                                perror("accept");
                        else do {
                                memset(buf, 0, sizeof buf);
                                if ((rval = read(msgsock, buf, 1024)) < 0)
                                        perror("reading stream message");
                                else if (rval == 0)
                                        printf("Ending connection\n");
                                else
                                        printf("-->%s\n", buf);
                        } while (rval > 0);
                        close(msgsock);
                } else
                        printf("Do something else\n");
        } while (TRUE);
        exit(0);
}
```

In previous versions of `select()`, its arguments were pointers to integers instead of pointers to `fd_set`s. This type of call will still work as long as the number of file descriptors being examined is less than the number of bits in an integer; however, the methods illustrated above should be used in all current programs.

select() provides a synchronous multiplexing scheme. The SIGIO and SIGURG signals described in the "Advanced Topics" section below may be used to provide asynchronous notification of output completion, input availability, and exceptional conditions.

Supporting Routines

The discussion in the "Basics" section above mentions the possible need to locate and construct network addresses when using the communication facilities in a distributed environment. To aid in this task several routines have been added to the standard C run-time library. In this section we will consider the new routines provided to manipulate network addresses.

Locating a service on a remote host requires many levels of mapping before client and server may communicate. A service is assigned a name that is intended for human consumption; e.g., the login server on host monet. This name, and the name of the peer host, must then be translated into network addresses that are not necessarily suitable for human consumption. Finally, the address must then be used in locating a physical location and route to the service. The specifics of these three mappings are likely to vary between network architectures. For instance, it is desirable for a network not to require hosts to be named in such a way that their physical location is known by the client host. Instead, underlying services in the network may discover the location of the host at the time a client host wishes to communicate. This ability to have hosts named independent of their location may induce overhead in connection establishment, as a discovery process must take place, but allows a host to be physically mobile without requiring it to notify its clientele of its current location.

Standard routines are provided for mapping host names to network addresses, network names to network numbers, protocol names to protocol numbers, and service names to port numbers and the appropriate protocol to use in communicating with the server process. The file <netdb.h> must be included when using any of these routines.

Host Names

An Internet host name to address mapping is represented by the hostent structure:

```
struct hostent {
    char *h_name;        /* official name of host */
    char **h_aliases;    /* alias list */
    int  h_addrtype;     /* host address type (e.g., AF_INET) */
    int  h_length;       /* length of address */
    char **h_addr_list;  /* list of addresses, null terminated */
};
#define h_addr h_addr_list[0]  /* first address, network byte order */
```

The routine gethostbyname(3N) takes an Internet host name and returns a hostent structure, while the routine gethostbyaddr(3N) maps Internet host addresses into a hostent structure. The routine inet_ntoa(3N) maps an Internet host address into an ASCII string for printing by log and error messages.

The official name of the host and its public aliases are returned by these routines, along with the address type (domain) and a null terminated list of variable length addresses. This list of addresses is required because it is possible for a host to have many addresses, all having the same name. The h_addr definition is provided for backward compatibility, and is defined to be the first address in the list of addresses in the hostent structure.

Network Names

As for host names, routines for mapping network names to numbers, and back, are provided. These routines return a netent structure:

```
/*
 * Assumption here is that a network number
 * fits in 32 bits -- probably a poor one.
 */
struct netent {
    char *n_name;           /* official name of net */
    char **n_aliases;       /* alias list */
    int  n_addrtype;        /* net address type */
    int  n_net;             /* network number, host byte order */
};
```

The routines getnetbyname(3N), getnetbyaddr(3N), and getnetent(3N) are the network counterparts to the host routines described above.

Protocol Names

For protocols, the protoent structure defines the protocol-name mapping used with the routines getprotobyname(3N), getprotobynumber(3N), and getprotoent(3N):

```
struct protoent {
    char *p_name;           /* official protocol name */
    char **p_aliases;       /* alias list */
    int  p_proto;           /* protocol number */
};
```

The Sockets Interface

Service Names

Information regarding services is a bit more complicated. A service is expected to reside at a specific port and use a particular communication protocol. This view is consistent with the Internet domain, but inconsistent with other network architectures. Further, a service may reside on multiple ports. If this occurs, the higher level library routines will have to be bypassed or extended.

A service mapping is described by the servent structure:

```
struct servent {
    char *s_name;           /* official service name */
    char **s_aliases;       /* alias list */
    int s_port;             /* port number, network byte order */
    char *s_proto;          /* protocol to use */
};
```

The routine getservbyname(3N) maps service names to a servent structure by specifying a service name and, optionally, a qualifying protocol. Thus the call

```
        sp = getservbyname("telnet", (char *) 0);
```

returns the service specification for a telnet server using any protocol, while the call

```
        sp = getservbyname("telnet", "tcp");
```

returns only that telnet server that uses the TCP protocol. The routines getservbyport(3N) and getservent(3N) are also provided. The get-servbyport() routine has an interface similar to that provided by get-servbyname(); an optional protocol name may be specified to qualify lookups.

Miscellaneous

With the support routines described above, an Internet application program should rarely have to deal directly with addresses. This allows services to be developed as much as possible in a network independent fashion. It is clear, however, that purging all network dependencies is very difficult. So long as the user is required to supply network addresses when naming services and sockets there will always be some network dependency in a program. For example, the normal code included in client programs, such as the remote login program, is of the form shown in Figure 3-6. (This example will be considered in more detail in the "Client/Server Model" section below.)

Aside from the address-related database routines, there are several other routines available in the run-time library that are of interest to users. These are intended mostly to simplify manipulation of names and addresses. Table 3-1 summarizes the routines for manipulating variable length byte strings and handling byte swapping of network addresses and values.

Table 3-1: Run-Time Library Routines

Call	Synopsis
memcmp(s1, s2, n)	Compare byte-strings; 0 if same, not 0 otherwise
memcpy(s1, s2, n)	Copy n bytes from s2 to s1
memset(base, value, n)	Set n bytes to value starting at base
htonl(val)	32-bit quantity from host into network byte order
htons(val)	16-bit quantity from host into network byte order
ntohl(val)	32-bit quantity from network into host byte order
ntohs(val)	16-bit quantity from network into host byte order

The byte swapping routines are provided because the operating system expects addresses to be supplied in network order. On some architectures, such as the VAX, host byte ordering is different from network byte ordering. Consequently, programs are sometimes required to byte swap quantities. The library routines that return network addresses provide them in network order so that they may simply be copied into the structures provided to the system. Users should therefore encounter byte swapping problems only when interpreting network addresses. For example, the following code will print out an Internet port:

```
printf("port number %d\n", ntohs(sp->s_port));
```

On certain machines, where these routines are not needed, they are defined as null macros.

Figure 3-6: Remote Login Client Code

```
#include <sys/types.h>
#include <sys/socket.h>
#include <netinet/in.h>
#include <stdio.h>
#include <netdb.h>
        ...
main(argc, argv)
        int argc;
        char *argv[];
{
        struct sockaddr_in server;
        struct servent *sp;
        struct hostent *hp;
        int s;
        ...
        sp = getservbyname("login", "tcp");
        if (sp == NULL) {
                fprintf(stderr, "rlogin: tcp/login: unknown service\n");
                exit(1);
        }
        hp = gethostbyname(argv[1]);
        if (hp == NULL) {
                fprintf(stderr, "rlogin: %s: unknown host\n", argv[1]);
                exit(2);
        }
        memset((char *)&server, 0, sizeof server);
        memcpy((char *)&server.sin_addr, hp->h_addr, hp->h_length);
        server.sin_family = hp->h_addrtype;
        server.sin_port = sp->s_port;
        s = socket(AF_INET, SOCK_STREAM, 0);
        if (s < 0) {
                perror("rlogin: socket");
                exit(3);
        }
        ...
        /* Connect does the bind for us */
```

(continued on next page)

Figure 3-6: Remote Login Client Code (continued)

```
        if (connect(s, (struct sockaddr *)&server, sizeof server) < 0) {
                perror("rlogin: connect");
                exit(5);
        }
        ...
        exit(0);
}
```

Client/Server Model

The most commonly used paradigm in building distributed applications is the client/server model. In this scheme client applications request services from a server process. This implies an asymmetry in establishing communication between the client and server that has been examined in the "Basics" section above. In this section we will look more closely at the interactions between client and server, and consider some of the problems in developing client and server applications.

The client and server require a well known set of conventions before service may be rendered (and accepted). This set of conventions comprises a protocol that must be implemented at both ends of a connection. Depending on the situation, the protocol may be symmetric or asymmetric. In a symmetric protocol, either side may play the master or slave roles. In an asymmetric protocol, one side is immutably recognized as the master, with the other as the slave. An example of a symmetric protocol is the TELNET protocol used in the Internet for remote terminal emulation. An example of an asymmetric protocol is the Internet file transfer protocol, FTP. No matter whether the specific protocol used in obtaining a service is symmetric or asymmetric, when accessing a service there is a client process and a server process. We will first consider the properties of server processes, then client processes.

A server process normally listens at a well known address for service requests. That is, the server process remains dormant until a connection is requested by a client's connection to the server's address. At such a time the server process "wakes up" and services the client, performing whatever appropriate actions the client requests of it.

Alternative schemes that use a service server may be used to eliminate a flock of server processes clogging the system while remaining dormant most of the time. For Internet servers, this scheme has been implemented via inetd, the so called "internet super-server." inetd listens at a variety of ports, determined at start-up by reading a configuration file. When a connection is requested to a port on which inetd is listening, inetd executes the appropriate server program to handle the client. With this method, clients are unaware that an intermediary such as inetd has played any part in the connection. inetd will be described in more detail in the "Advanced Topics" section below.

Servers

In the UNIX system, most servers are accessed at well known Internet addresses or UNIX domain names. The form of their main loop is illustrated by the following code form the remote-login server:

Figure 3-7: Remote Login Server

```
main(argc, argv)
        int argc;
        char *argv[];
{
        int f;
        struct sockaddr_in from;
        struct sockaddr_in sin;
        struct servent *sp;

        sp = getservbyname("login", "tcp");
        if (sp == NULL) {
                fprintf(stderr,
                        "rlogind: tcp/login: unknown service\n");
                exit(1);
        }
        ...
#ifndef DEBUG
        /* Disassociate server from controlling terminal. */
        ...
#endif

        sin.sin_port = sp->s_port;   /* Restricted port */
        sin.sin_addr.s_addr = INADDR_ANY;
        ...
        f = socket(AF_INET, SOCK_STREAM, 0);
        ...
        if (bind(f, (struct sockaddr *)&sin, sizeof sin) < 0) {
                ...
        }
        ...
        listen(f, 5);
        for (;;) {
                int g, len = sizeof from;

                g = accept(f, (struct sockaddr *) &from, &len);
                if (g < 0) {
```

(continued on next page)

The Sockets Interface

Figure 3-7: Remote Login Server (continued)

```
                        if (errno != EINTR)
                                syslog(LOG_ERR, "rlogind: accept: %m");
                        continue;
                }
                if (fork() == 0) {
                        close(f);
                        doit(g, &from);
                }
                close(g);
        }
        exit(0);
}
```

The first step taken by the server is look up its service definition:

```
sp = getservbyname("login", "tcp");
if (sp == NULL) {
        fprintf(stderr,
                "rlogind: tcp/login: unknown service\n");
        exit(1);
}
```

The result of the getservbyname() call is used in later portions of the code to define the Internet port at which it listens for service requests (indicated by a connection). Some standard port numbers are given in the file /usr/include/netinet/in.h for backward compatibility purposes.

Step two is to disassociate the server from the controlling terminal of its invoker:

```
for (i = getdtablesize()-1; i >= 0; --i)
        close(i);

open("/dev/null", O_RDONLY);
dup2(0, 1);
dup2(0, 2);

i = open("/dev/tty", O_RDWR);
if (i >= 0) {
        ioctl(i, TIOCNOTTY, 0);
        close(i);
}
```

This step is important as the server will likely not want to receive signals delivered to the process group of the controlling terminal. Note, however, that once a server has disassociated itself it can no longer send reports of errors to a terminal, and must log errors via `syslog()`.

Once a server has established a pristine environment, it creates a socket and begins accepting service requests. The `bind()` call is required to insure the server listens at its expected location. Note that the remote login server listens at a restricted port number, and must therefore be run with a user-id of root. This concept of a "restricted port number" is covered in the "Advanced Topics" section below.

The main body of the loop is simple:

```
for (;;) {
        int g, len = sizeof from;

        g = accept(f, (struct sockaddr *)&from, &len);
        if (g < 0) {
                if (errno != EINTR)
                        syslog(LOG_ERR, "rlogind: accept: %m");
                continue;
        }
        if (fork() == 0) {  /* Child */
                close(f);
                doit(g, &from);
        }
        close(g);            /* Parent */
}
```

An accept() call blocks the server until a client requests service. This call could return a failure status if the call is interrupted by a signal such as SIGCHLD (to be discussed in the "Advanced Topics" section below). Therefore, the return value from accept() is checked to insure a connection has been established, and an error report is logged via syslog() if an error has occurred.

With a connection in hand, the server then forks a child process and invokes the main body of the remote login protocol processing. Note how the socket used by the parent for queuing connection requests is closed in the child, while the socket created as a result of the accept() is closed in the parent. The address of the client is also handed the doit() routine because it requires it in authenticating clients.

Clients

The client side of the remote login service was shown earlier in Figure 3-6. One can see the separate, asymmetric roles of the client and server clearly in the code. The server is a passive entity, listening for client connections, while the client process is an active entity, initiating a connection when invoked.

Let us consider more closely the steps taken by the client remote login process. As in the server process, the first step is to locate the service definition for a remote login:

```
sp = getservbyname("login", "tcp");
if (sp == NULL) {
        fprintf(stderr,
                "rlogin: tcp/login: unknown service\n");
        exit(1);
}
```

Next the destination host is looked up with a gethostbyname() call:

```
hp = gethostbyname(argv[1]);
if (hp == NULL) {
        fprintf(stderr, "rlogin: %s: unknown host\n", argv[1]);
        exit(2);
}
```

With this done, all that is required is to establish a connection to the server at the requested host and start up the remote login protocol. The address buffer is cleared, then filled in with the Internet address of the foreign host and the port number at which the login process resides on the foreign host:

```
memset((char *)&server, 0, sizeof server);
memcpy((char *) &server.sin_addr, hp->h_addr, hp->h_length);
server.sin_family = hp->h_addrtype;
server.sin_port = sp->s_port;
```

A socket is created, and a connection initiated. Note that connect() implicitly performs a bind() call, since s is unbound.

The Sockets Interface

```
s = socket(hp->h_addrtype, SOCK_STREAM, 0);
if (s < 0) {
        perror("rlogin: socket");
        exit(3);
}
...
if (connect(s, (struct sockaddr *)&server,
 sizeof server) < 0) {
        perror("rlogin: connect");
        exit(4);
}
```

The details of the remote login protocol will not be considered here.

Connectionless Servers

While connection-based services are the norm, some services are based on the use of datagram sockets. One, in particular, is the rwho service, which provides users with status information for hosts connected to a local area network. This service, while predicated on the ability to broadcast information to all hosts connected to a particular network, is of interest as an example usage of datagram sockets.

A user on any machine running the rwho server may find out the current status of a machine with the ruptime program. The output generated is illustrated in Figure 3-8.

Figure 3-8: Output of ruptime **Program**

```
arpa      up    9:45,       5 users, load   1.15,   1.39,   1.31
cad       up    2+12:04,    8 users, load   4.67,   5.13,   4.59
calder    up    10:10,      0 users, load   0.27,   0.15,   0.14
dali      up    2+06:28,    9 users, load   1.04,   1.20,   1.65
degas     up    25+09:48,   0 users, load   1.49,   1.43,   1.41
ear       up    5+00:05,    0 users, load   1.51,   1.54,   1.56
ernie     down  0:24
esvax     down  17:04
oz        down  16:09
statvax   up    2+15:57,    3 users, load   1.52,   1.81,   1.86
```

Status information for each host is periodically broadcast by rwho server processes on each machine. The same server process also receives the status information and uses it to update a database. This database is then interpreted to generate the status information for each host. Servers operate autonomously, coupled only by the local network and its broadcast capabilities.

Note that the use of broadcast for such a task is fairly inefficient, as all hosts must process each message, whether or not using an rwho server. Unless such a service is sufficiently universal and is frequently used, the expense of periodic broadcasts outweighs the simplicity.

The rwho server, in a simplified form, is pictured below. It performs two separate tasks. The first is to act as a receiver of status information broadcast by other hosts on the network. This job is carried out in the main loop of the program. Packets received at the rwho port are interrogated to insure they've been sent by another rwho server process, then are time stamped with their arrival time and used to update a file indicating the status of the host. When a host has not been heard from for an extended period of time, the database interpretation routines assume the host is down and report this information on the status reports. This algorithm is prone to error, as a server may be down while a host is up.

Figure 3-9: rwho **Server**

```
main()
{
        ...
        sp = getservbyname("who", "udp");
        net = getnetbyname("localnet");
        sin.sin_addr = inet_makeaddr(net->n_net, INADDR_ANY);
        sin.sin_port = sp->s_port;
        ...
        s = socket(AF_INET, SOCK_DGRAM, 0);
        ...
        on = 1;
        if (setsockopt(s, SOL_SOCKET, SO_BROADCAST, &on,
         sizeof on) < 0) {
                syslog(LOG_ERR, "setsockopt SO_BROADCAST: %m");
                exit(1);
        }
        bind(s, (struct sockaddr *) &sin, sizeof sin);
        ...
        signal(SIGALRM, onalrm);
        onalrm();
        for (;;) {
                struct whod wd;
                int cc, whod, len = sizeof from;

                cc = recvfrom(s, (char *)&wd, sizeof (struct whod),
                        0, (struct sockaddr *)&from, &len);
                if (cc <= 0) {
                        if (cc < 0 && errno != EINTR)
                                syslog(LOG_ERR, "rwhod: recv: %m");
                        continue;
                }
                if (from.sin_port != sp->s_port) {
                        syslog(LOG_ERR, "rwhod: %d: bad from port",
                                ntohs(from.sin_port));
                        continue;
                }
                ...
                if (!verify(wd.wd_hostname)) {
                        syslog(LOG_ERR, "rwhod: bad host name from %x",
                                ntohl(from.sin_addr.s_addr));
                        continue;
                }
                (void) sprintf(path, "%s/whod.%s", RWHODIR,
                        wd.wd_hostname);
```

(continued on next page)

Figure 3-9: rwho Server (continued)

```
                    whod = open(path, O_WRONLY|O_CREAT|O_TRUNC, 0666);
                    ...
                    (void) time(&wd.wd_recvtime);
                    (void) write(whod, (char *)&wd, cc);
                    (void) close(whod);
            }
        exit(0);
    }
```

The second task performed by the server is to supply information regarding the status of its host. This involves periodically acquiring system status information, packaging it up in a message and broadcasting it on the local network for other rwho servers to hear. The supply function is triggered by a timer and runs off a signal. Locating the system status information is somewhat involved, but uninteresting. Deciding where to transmit the resultant packet is somewhat problematic, however.

Status information must be broadcast on the local network. For networks that do not support the notion of broadcast another scheme must be used to simulate or replace broadcasting. One possibility is to list the known neighbors (based on the status messages received from other rwho servers). This, unfortunately, requires some bootstrapping information, for a server will have no idea what machines are its neighbors until it receives status messages from them. Therefore, if all machines on a net are freshly booted, no machine will have any known neighbors and thus never receive, or send, any status information. This is the identical problem faced by the routing table management process in propagating routing status information. The standard solution, unsatisfactory as it may be, is to inform one or more servers of known neighbors and request that they always communicate with these neighbors. If each server has at least one neighbor supplied to it, status information may then propagate through a neighbor to hosts that are not (possibly) directly neighbors. If the server is able to support networks that provide a broadcast capability, as well as those that do not, then networks with an arbitrary topology may share status information.

The Sockets Interface

NOTE Programmers must be concerned about loops, however. If a host is connected to multiple networks, it will receive status information from itself. This
can lead to an endless, wasteful, exchange of information.

It is important that software operating in a distributed environment not have
any site-dependent information compiled into it. This would require a separate
copy of the server at each host and make maintenance a severe headache. The
UNIX system attempts to isolate host-specific information from applications by
providing system calls that return the necessary information. (An example of
such a system call is the gethostname(3N) call that returns the host's official
name.) The ioctl() call allows you to find the collection of networks to
which a host is directly connected. Further, a local network broadcasting
mechanism has been implemented at the socket level. Combining these two
features allows a process to broadcast on any directly connected local network
that supports the notion of broadcasting in a site independent manner. This
solves the problem of deciding how to propagate status information with rwho,
or more generally in broadcasting. Such status information is broadcast to connected networks at the socket level, where the connected networks have been
obtained via the appropriate ioctl() calls. The specifics of such broadcastings
are complex, however, and will be covered in the "Advanced Topics" section
below.

Advanced Topics

Several facilities have yet to be discussed. For most programmers, the mechanisms already described will suffice in building distributed applications. However, others will find the need to use some of the features that we consider in this section.

Out Of Band Data

The stream socket abstraction includes the notion of out of band data. Out of band data is a logically independent transmission channel associated with each pair of connected stream sockets. Out of band data is delivered to the user independently of normal data. The abstraction defines that the out of band data facilities must support the reliable delivery of at least one out of band message at a time. This message may contain at least one byte of data, and at least one message may be pending delivery to the user at any one time. For communications protocols (such as TCP) that support only in-band signaling (i.e., the urgent data is delivered in sequence with the normal data), the system normally extracts the data from the normal data stream and stores it separately. This allows users to choose between receiving the urgent data in order and receiving it out of sequence without having to buffer all the intervening data. It is possible to "peek" (via MSG_PEEK) at out of band data. If the socket has a process group, a SIGURG signal is generated when the protocol is notified of its existence. A process can set the process group or process id to be informed by the SIGURG signal via the appropriate fcntl() call, as described below for SIGIO. If multiple sockets may have out of band data awaiting delivery, a select() call for exceptional conditions may be used to determine those sockets with such data pending. Neither the signal nor the select show the arrival of the out-of-band data, but only notification that it is pending.

In addition to the information passed, a logical mark is placed in the data stream to specify the point at which the out of band data was sent. The remote login and remote shell applications use this facility to propagate signals between client and server processes. When a signal flushes any pending output from the remote process(es), all data up to the mark in the data stream is discarded.

To send an out of band message the MSG_OOB flag is supplied to a send() or sendto() calls, while to receive out of band data MSG_OOB should be specified when doing a recvfrom() or recv() call (unless out of band data is taken in line, in which case the MSG_OOB flag is not needed). To find out if the read pointer is currently pointing at the mark in the data stream, the SIOCATMARK ioctl is provided:

```
ioctl(s, SIOCATMARK, &yes);
```

If yes is 1 on return, the next read will return data after the mark. Otherwise (assuming out of band data has arrived), the next read will provide data sent by the client before transmission of the out of band signal. The routine used in the remote login process to flush output on receipt of an interrupt or quit signal is shown in the following example. This code reads the normal data up to the mark (to discard it), then reads the out-of-band byte.

Figure 3-10: Flushing Terminal I/O on Receipt of Out Of Band Data

```
#include <sys/ioctl.h>
#include <sys/file.h>
    ...
oob()
{
        int out = FWRITE;
        char waste[BUFSIZ];
        int mark;

        /* flush local terminal output */
        ioctl(1, TIOCFLUSH, (char *)&out);
        for (;;) {
                if (ioctl(rem, SIOCATMARK, &mark) < 0) {
                        perror("ioctl");
                        break;
                }
                if (mark)
                        break;
                (void) read(rem, waste, sizeof waste);
        }
        if (recv(rem, &mark, 1, MSG_OOB) < 0) {
                perror("recv");
                ...
        }
        ...
}
```

A process may also read or peek at the out-of-band data without first reading up to the mark. This is more difficult when the underlying protocol delivers the urgent data in-band with the normal data, and only sends notification of its presence ahead of time (e.g., the TCP protocol used to provide socket streams in the Internet domain). With such protocols, the out-of-band byte may not yet have arrived when a recv() is done with the MSG_OOB flag. In that case, the call will return an error of EWOULDBLOCK. Worse, there may be enough in-band data in the input buffer that normal flow control prevents the peer from sending the urgent data until the buffer is cleared. The process must then read enough of the queued data before the urgent data may be delivered.

Certain programs that use multiple bytes of urgent data and must handle multiple urgent signals (e.g., telnet(1)) need to retain the position of urgent data within the socket stream. This treatment is available as a socket-level option, SO_OOBINLINE; see setsockopt(3N) for usage. With this option, the position of urgent data (the "mark") is retained, but the urgent data immediately follows the mark within the normal data stream returned without the MSG_OOB flag. Reception of multiple urgent indications causes the mark to move, but no out-of-band data are lost.

Non-Blocking Sockets

It is occasionally convenient to make use of sockets that do not block; that is, I/O requests that cannot complete immediately and would therefore cause the process to be suspended awaiting completion are not executed, and an error code is returned. Once a socket has been created via the socket() call, it may be marked as non-blocking by fcntl() as follows:

```
#include <fcntl.h>
#include <sys/file.h>
...
int     s;
...
s = socket(AF_INET, SOCK_STREAM, 0);
...
if (fcntl(s, F_SETFL, FNDELAY) < 0)
        perror("fcntl F_SETFL, FNDELAY");
        exit(1);
}
...
```

When performing non-blocking I/O on sockets, one must be careful to check for the error EWOULDBLOCK (stored in the global variable errno), which occurs when an operation would normally block, but the socket it was performed on is marked as non-blocking. In particular, accept(), connect(), send(), recv(), read(), and write() can all return EWOULDBLOCK, and processes should be prepared to deal with such return codes. If an operation such as a send() cannot be done in its entirety, but partial writes are sensible (for example, when using a stream socket), the data that can be sent immediately will be processed, and the return value will show the amount actually sent.

Interrupt Driven Socket I/O

The SIGIO signal allows a process to be notified via a signal when a socket (or more generally, a file descriptor) has data waiting to be read. Use of the SIGIO facility requires three steps: First, the process must set up a SIGIO signal handler by use of the signal() or sigvec() calls. Second, it must set the process id or process group id that is to receive notification of pending input to its own process id, or the process group id of its process group (note that the default process group of a socket is group zero). This can be done by using a fcntl() call. Third, it must enable asynchronous notification of pending I/O requests with another fcntl() call. Sample code to allow a given process to receive information on pending I/O requests as they occur for a socket s is given in Figure 3-11 With the addition of a handler for SIGURG, this code can also be used to prepare for receipt of SIGURG signals.

Figure 3-11: Use of Asynchronous Notification of I/O Requests

```
#include <fcntl.h>
#include <sys/file.h>
...
int      io_handler();
...
signal(SIGIO, io_handler);

/* Set the process receiving SIGIO/SIGURG signals to us. */

if (fcntl(s, F_SETOWN, getpid()) < 0) {
        perror("fcntl F_SETOWN");
        exit(1);
}

/* Allow receipt of asynchronous I/O signals. */

if (fcntl(s, F_SETFL, FASYNC) < 0) {
        perror("fcntl F_SETFL, FASYNC");
        exit(1);
}
```

Signals and Process Groups

Because of the existence of the SIGURG and SIGIO signals, each socket has an associated process number, just as is done for terminals. This value is initialized to zero, but may be redefined at a later time with the F_SETOWN fcntl(), such as was done in the code above for SIGIO.

To set the socket's process id for signals, positive arguments should be given to the fcntl() call. To set the socket's process group for signals, negative arguments should be passed to fcntl().

The only acceptable arguments to these system calls are the caller's process id or a negative process group having the same absolute value as the caller's process id (the process must be the process group leader of its own process group). Therefore, the only allowed recipient of SIGURG and SIGIO signals is the calling process.

Note that the process number shows either the associated process id or the associated process group; it is impossible to specify both at the same time. A similar fcntl(), F_GETOWN, is available for determining the current process number of a socket.

Note that the receipt of SIGURG and SIGIO can also be enabled by using the ioctl() call to assign the socket to the user's process group:

```
. . .
/* oobdata is the out-of-band data handling routine */
signal(SIGURG, oobdata);
. . .
int pid = -getpid();

if (ioctl(client, SIOCSPGRP, (char *)&pid) < 0) {
        perror("ioctl: SIOCSPGRP");
}
. . .
```

Another signal that is useful when building server processes is SIGCHLD. This signal is delivered to a process when any child processes have changed state. Normally servers use the signal to "reap" child processes that have exited without explicitly awaiting their termination or periodically polling for exit status. For example, the remote login server loop shown in Figure 3-7 may be augmented as follows:

Figure 3-12: Use of the SIGCHLD Signal

```
int reaper();
...
signal(SIGCHLD, reaper);
listen(f, 5);
for (;;) {
        int g, len = sizeof from;

        g = accept(f, (struct sockaddr *)&from, &len,);
        if (g < 0) {
                if (errno != EINTR)
                        syslog(LOG_ERR, "rlogind: accept: %m");
                continue;
        }
        ...
}
...
#include <wait.h>
reaper()
{
        int status;

        while (wait(&status) > 0)
                continue;
}
```

If the parent server process fails to reap its children, several zombie processes may be created.

Selecting Specific Protocols

If the third argument to the socket() call is 0, socket() will select a default protocol to use with the returned socket of the type requested. The default protocol is usually correct, and alternate choices are not usually available. However, when using "raw" sockets to communicate directly with lower-level protocols or hardware interfaces, the protocol argument may be important for setting up demultiplexing. For example, raw sockets in the Internet domain may be used to implement a new protocol above IP, and the socket will receive packets only for the protocol specified. To obtain a particular protocol one determines the protocol number as defined within the protocol domain. For the Internet domain one may use one of the library routines discussed in the "Supporting Routines" section above, such as `getprotobyname()`:

```
#include <sys/types.h>
#include <sys/socket.h>
#include <netinet/in.h>
#include <netdb.h>
...
pp = getprotobyname("newtcp");
s = socket(AF_INET, SOCK_STREAM, pp->p_proto);
```

This would result in a socket s using a stream based connection, but with protocol type of newtcp instead of the default tcp.

Address Binding

As was mentioned in the "Basics" section, binding addresses to sockets in the Internet domain can be complex. As a brief reminder, these associations are composed of local and foreign addresses, and local and foreign ports. Port numbers are allocated out of separate spaces, one for each system and one for each domain on that system. Through the bind() system call, a process may specify half of an association, the *<local address, local port>* part, while the connect() and accept() primitives are used to complete a socket's association by specifying the *<foreign address, foreign port>* part. Since the association is created in two steps the association uniqueness requirement mentioned previously could be violated unless care is taken. Further, it is unrealistic to expect user programs always to know proper values to use for the local address and local port since a host may reside on multiple networks and the set of allocated port numbers is not directly accessible to a user.

To simplify local address binding in the Internet domain the notion of a wild-card address has been provided. When an address is specified as INADDR_ANY (a manifest constant defined in <netinet/in.h>), the system interprets the address as any valid address. For example, to bind a specific port number to a socket, but leave the local address unspecified, the following code might be used:

```
#include <sys/types.h>
#include <netinet/in.h>
...
struct sockaddr_in sin;
...
s = socket(AF_INET, SOCK_STREAM, 0);
sin.sin_family = AF_INET;
sin.sin_addr.s_addr = htonl(INADDR_ANY);
sin.sin_port = htons(MYPORT);
bind(s, (struct sockaddr *) &sin, sizeof sin);
```

Sockets with wildcarded local addresses may receive messages directed to the specified port number, and sent to any of the possible addresses assigned to a host. For example, if a host has addresses 128.32.0.4 and 10.0.0.78, and a socket is bound as above, the process will be able to accept connection requests that are addressed to 128.32.0.4 or 10.0.0.78. If a server process wished to only allow hosts on a given network connect to it, it would bind the address of the host on the appropriate network.

In a similar fashion, a local port may be left unspecified (specified as zero), in which case the system will select an appropriate port number for it. For example, to bind a specific local address to a socket, but to leave the local port number unspecified:

```
hp = gethostbyname(hostname);
if (hp == NULL) {
    ...
}
memcpy((char *) sin.sin_addr, hp->h_addr, hp->h_length);
sin.sin_port = htons(0);
bind(s, (struct sockaddr *) &sin, sizeof sin);
```

The system selects the local port number based on two criteria. The first is that Internet ports below IPPORT_RESERVED (1024) are reserved for privileged users (i.e., the super user); Internet ports above IPPORT_USERRESERVED (5000) are reserved for non-privileged servers. The second is that the port number is not currently bound to some other socket. To find a free Internet port number in the privileged range the `rresvport()` library routine may be used as follows to return a stream socket in with a privileged port number:

```
int lport = IPPORT_RESERVED - 1;
int s;
        ...
s = rresvport(&lport);
if (s < 0) {
        if (errno == EAGAIN)
                fprintf(stderr, "socket: all ports in use\n");
        else
                perror("rresvport: socket");
        ...
}
```

This restriction was placed on port allocation to allow processes executing in a "secure" environment to do authentication based on the originating address and port number. For example, the `rlogin(1)` command allows users to log in across a network without being asked for a password, provided that two conditions are met: First, the name of the system the user is logging in from must be in the file `/etc/hosts.equiv` on the system being logged in to (or the system name and the user name must be in the user's `.rhosts` file in the user's home directory). Second, the user's `rlogin` process must come from a privileged port on the machine from which the user is logging in. The port number and network address of the machine from which the user is logging in can be determined either from the `accept()` call (the `from` result), or the `getpeername()` call.

In certain cases the algorithm used by the system in selecting port numbers is unsuitable for an application. This is because associations are created in a two step process. For example, the Internet file transfer protocol, FTP, specifies that data connections must always originate from the same local port. However, duplicate associations are avoided by connecting to different foreign ports. In this situation the system would disallow binding the same local address and port number to a socket if a previous data connection's socket still existed. To override the default port selection algorithm, an option call must be performed before address binding:

```
     . . .
int       on = 1;
     . . .
setsockopt(s, SOL_SOCKET, SO_REUSEADDR, &on, sizeof on);
bind(s, (struct sockaddr *) &sin, sizeof sin);
```

With the above call, local addresses may be bound that are already in use. This does not violate the uniqueness requirement as the system still checks at connect time to be sure any other sockets with the same local address and port do not have the same foreign address and port. If the association already exists, the error EADDRINUSE is returned.

Broadcasting and Determining Network Configuration

By using a datagram socket, it is possible to send broadcast packets on many networks connected to the system. The network itself must support broadcast; the system provides no simulation of broadcast in software. Broadcast messages can place a high load on a network since they force every host on the network to service them. Consequently, the ability to send broadcast packets has been limited to sockets that are explicitly marked as allowing broadcasting. Broadcast is typically used for one of two reasons: it is desired to find a resource on a local network without prior knowledge of its address, or important functions such as routing require that information be sent to all accessible neighbors.

To send a broadcast message, a datagram socket should be created:

```
     s = socket(AF_INET, SOCK_DGRAM, 0);
```

The socket is marked as allowing broadcasting,

```
     int    on = 1;
     setsockopt(s, SOL_SOCKET, SO_BROADCAST, &on, sizeof on);
```

and at least a port number should be bound to the socket:

```
sin.sin_family = AF_INET;
sin.sin_addr.s_addr = htonl(INADDR_ANY);
sin.sin_port = htons(MYPORT);
bind(s, (struct sockaddr *) &sin, sizeof sin);
```

The destination address of the message to be broadcast depends on the
network(s) on which the message is to be broadcast. The Internet domain supports a shorthand notation for broadcast on the local network, the address
INADDR_BROADCAST (defined in <netinet/in.h>. To determine the list of
addresses for all reachable neighbors requires knowledge of the networks to
which the host is connected. Since this information should be obtained in a
host-independent fashion and may be impossible to derive, the UNIX system
provides a method of retrieving this information from the system data structures. The SIOCGIFCONF ioctl call returns the interface configuration of a
host as a single ifconf structure; this structure contains a "data area" that is
made up of an array of ifreq structures, one for each address domain supported by each network interface to which the host is connected. These structures are defined in <net/if.h> as follows:

```
struct ifreq {
#define IFNAMSIZ    16
    char ifr_name[IFNAMSIZ];        /* if name, e.g., "en0" */
    union {
        struct sockaddr ifru_addr;
        struct sockaddr ifru_dstaddr;
        char ifru_oname[IFNAMSIZ]; /* other if name */
        struct sockaddr ifru_broadaddr;
        short ifru_flags;
        int ifru_metric;
        char ifru_data[1];             /* interface dependent data */
        char ifru_enaddr[6];
    } ifr_ifru;

#define ifr_addr      ifr_ifru.ifru_addr      /* address */
#define ifr_dstaddr   ifr_ifru.ifru_dstaddr   /* other end of p-to-p link */
#define ifr_oname     ifr_ifru.ifru_oname     /* other if name */
#define ifr_broadaddr ifr_ifru.ifru_broadaddr /* broadcast address */
#define ifr_flags     ifr_ifru.ifru_flags     /* flags */
#define ifr_metric    ifr_ifru.ifru_metric    /* metric */
#define ifr_data      ifr_ifru.ifru_data      /* for use by interface */
#define ifr_enaddr    ifr_ifru.ifru_enaddr    /* ethernet address */
};
```

The call that obtains the interface configuration is:

```
struct ifconf ifc;
char buf[BUFSIZ];

ifc.ifc_len = sizeof buf;
ifc.ifc_buf = buf;
if (ioctl(s, SIOCGIFCONF, (char *) &ifc) < 0) {
        ...
}
```

After this call buf will contain a list of ifreq structures, one for each network to which the host is connected. These structures will be ordered first by interface name and then by supported address families. ifc.ifc_len will have been modified to reflect the number of bytes used by the ifreq structures.

For each structure there exists a set of "interface flags" that tell whether the network corresponding to that interface is up or down, point to point or broadcast, etc. The `SIOCGIFFLAGS` `ioctl` retrieves these flags for an interface specified by an `ifreq` structure as follows:

```
struct ifreq *ifr;

ifr = ifc.ifc_req;

for (n=ifc.ifc_len/sizeof (struct ifreq);
        --n >= 0; ifr++) {
        /*
         * We must be careful that we don't use an interface
         * devoted to an address domain other than those intended
         */
        if (ifr->ifr_addr.sa_family != AF_INET)
                continue;
        if (ioctl(s, SIOCGIFFLAGS, (char *) ifr) < 0) {
                ...
        }
        /*
         * Skip boring cases
         */
        if ((ifr->ifr_flags & IFF_UP) == 0 ||
            (ifr->ifr_flags & IFF_LOOPBACK) ||
            (ifr->ifr_flags &
            (IFF_BROADCAST | IFF_POINTOPOINT)) == 0)
                continue;
}
```

Once the flags have been obtained, the broadcast address must be obtained. With broadcast networks this is done via the `SIOCGIFBRDADDR` `ioctl`, while for point-to-point networks the address of the destination host is obtained with `SIOCGIFDSTADDR`.

```
struct sockaddr dst;

if (ifr->ifr_flags & IFF_POINTOPOINT) {
        if (ioctl(s, SIOCGIFDSTADDR, (char *) ifr) < 0) {
                ...
        }
        memcpy((char *) &dst, (char *) &ifr->ifr_dstaddr,
                sizeof ifr->ifr_dstaddr);
} else if (ifr->ifr_flags & IFF_BROADCAST) {
        if (ioctl(s, SIOCGIFBRDADDR, (char *) ifr) < 0) {
                ...
        }
        memcpy((char *) &dst, (char *) &ifr->ifr_broadaddr,
                sizeof ifr->ifr_broadaddr);
}
```

After the appropriate `ioctl()`s have obtained the broadcast or destination address (now in `dst`), the `sendto()` call may be used:

```
sendto(s, buf, buflen, 0, (struct sockaddr *)&dst,
        sizeof dst);
```

In the above loop one `sendto()` occurs for every interface to which the host is connected that supports the notion of broadcast or point-to-point addressing. If a process only wished to send broadcast messages on a given network, code similar to that outlined above would be used, but the loop would need to find the correct destination address.

Received broadcast messages contain the sender's address and port, as datagram sockets are bound before a message is allowed to go out.

Socket Options

It is possible to set and get several options on sockets via the `setsockopt()` and `getsockopt()` system calls. These options include such things as marking a socket for broadcasting, not to route, to linger on close, etc. The general forms of the calls are:

```
setsockopt(s, level, optname, optval, optlen);
```

and

```
getsockopt(s, level, optname, optval, optlen);
```

The parameters to the calls are as follows: s is the socket on which the option is to be applied. `level` specifies the protocol layer on which the option is to be applied; usually this is the "socket level," indicated by the symbolic constant `SOL_SOCKET`, defined in `<sys/socket.h>`. The option is specified in `optname`, and is a symbolic constant also defined in `<sys/socket.h>`. `optval` and `optlen` point to the value of the option (usually, whether the option is to be turned on or off), and the length of the value of the option, respectively. For `getsockopt()`, `optlen` is a value-result parameter, initially set to the size of the storage area pointed to by `optval`, and modified on return to show the amount of storage used.

An example should help clarify things. It is sometimes useful to determine the type (e.g., stream, datagram, etc.) of an existing socket; programs invoked by `inetd` (described below) may need to do this task using the `SO_TYPE` socket option and the `getsockopt()` call:

```
#include <sys/types.h>
#include <sys/socket.h>

int type, size;

size = sizeof (int);

if (getsockopt(s, SOL_SOCKET, SO_TYPE, (char *) &type,
        &size) < 0) {
    ...
}
```

After the `getsockopt()` call, `type` will be set to the value of the socket type, as defined in `<sys/socket.h>`. If, for example, the socket were a datagram socket, `type` would have the value corresponding to `SOCK_DGRAM`.

inetd

One of the daemons provided with the UNIX sytem is `inetd`, the so called "Internet super-server." `inetd` is invoked at boot time by the Service Access Controller, and determines the services for which it is to listen from the file `/etc/inetd.conf`. Once this information has been read and a pristine environment created, `inetd` proceeds to create one socket for each service it is to listen for, binding the appropriate port number to each socket.

`inetd` then performs a `select()` on all these sockets for read availability, waiting for somebody wishing a connection to the service corresponding to that socket. `inetd` then performs an `accept()` on the socket in question, `fork()`s, `dup()`s the new socket to file descriptors 0 and 1 (stdin and stdout), closes other open file descriptors, and `exec()`s the appropriate server.

Servers making use of `inetd` are considerably simplified, as `inetd` takes care of most of the communication work required in establishing a connection. The server invoked by `inetd` expects the socket connected to its client to be on file descriptors 0 and 1, and may immediately do operations such as `read()`, `write()`, `send()`, or `recv()`. Indeed, servers may use buffered I/O as provided by the `stdio` conventions, as long as they remember to use `fflush()` when appropriate.

One call that may be of interest to individuals writing servers to be invoked by `inetd` is the `getpeername()` call, which returns the address of the peer (process) connected on the other end of the socket. For example, to log the Internet address in "dot notation" (e.g., "128.32.0.4") of a client connected to a server under `inetd`, the following code might be used:

```
struct sockaddr_in name;
int namelen = sizeof name;
...
if (getpeername(0,
        (struct sockaddr *)&name, &namelen) < 0) {
        syslog(LOG_ERR, "getpeername: %m");
        exit(1);
} else
        syslog(LOG_INFO, "Connection from %s",
                inet_ntoa(name.sin_addr));
...
```

While the getpeername() call is especially useful when writing programs to
run with inetd, it can be used under other circumstances.

4 Sockets Migration and Sockets-to-TLI Conversion

Sockets Migration and Sockets-to-TLI Conversion

This chapter provides an introduction to the issues involved in porting a sockets application to TLI and includes notes on the differences between BSD sockets and System V Release 4 sockets that programmers must be aware of. Although existing sockets applications can be rewritten for TLI relatively easily, such ports are not necessary for sockets applications that are to run only over TCP/IP or UDP/IP networks. However, TLI is the preferred programming interface for accessing transport services and it is recommended that programmers writing new applications for System V Release 4 use TLI.

Both TLI and sockets routines are defined in terms of communications paths identified by file descriptors. These file descriptors are known as "transport endpoints" for TLI and as "sockets" for the socket interface. In most cases, there are parallel routines for each transport function. For example, the TLI routine t_open() returns a file descriptor that identifies a transport endpoint; the routine socket() returns a file descriptor that identifies a socket. Table 4-1 at the end of this section shows the parallels among TLI and sockets interface routines.

This chapter will highlight the areas in which there is no direct correspondence between TLI and sockets routines. The examples will first show code that uses the socket interface and then show how to rewrite the program using TLI.

The last section of the chapter documents differences between System V Release 4 sockets and BSD sockets. Programmers must be aware of these differences before moving BSD sockets applications to System V Release 4.

System V socket calls are implemented as library routines. Application programs that use sockets should be compiled and linked with socket libraries:

```
cc prog.c -dy -lsocket -lnsl
```

Connection Mode

Both TLI and sockets support two distinct types of service: connection oriented and connectionless.

Establishing Socket Connections: Client Code

When creating a socket, the type of service must be specified (for example, SOCK_STREAM, SOCK_DGRAM, SOCK_RAW). The service type determines whether connection-oriented or connectionless semantics are used. For a simple example of connection establishment, consider the client side of a stream-oriented application, as in Figure 4-1. It must initiate a connection by first creating a stream socket and then using the connect () call to establish communication with a preexisting socket on a server machine.

Figure 4-1: Client Side of Stream-Oriented Application

```
#include <sys/types.h>
#include <sys/socket.h>
#include <netinet/in.h>
#include <netdb.h>
#include <stdio.h>

main(argc, argv)
        int argc;
        char *argv[];
{
        int sock;
        struct sockaddr_in server;
        struct hostent *hp, *gethostbyname();
        struct servent *sp, *getservbyname();

        /* create socket */
        sock = socket(AF_INET, SOCK_STREAM, 0);
        if (sock < 0) {
                perror("opening stream socket");
                exit(1);
        }
        /* connect socket using name specified by command line */
        server.sin_family = AF_INET;
        hp = gethostbyname(argv[1]);
```

(continued on next page)

Figure 4-1: Client Side of Stream-Oriented Application (continued)

```
if (hp == 0) {
        fprintf(stderr, "%s: unknown host\n", argv[1]);
        exit(2);
}
memcpy((char *)&server.sin_addr, (char *)hp->h_addr,
  hp->h_length);
sp = getservbyname(argv[2], "tcp");
if (sp == 0) {
  fprintf(stderr, "%s: unknown service\n", argv[2]);
  exit(3);
}
server.sin_port = sp -> s_port;

if (connect(sock, (struct sockaddr *)&server,
  sizeof server ) < 0) {
        perror("connecting stream socket");
        exit(1);
}
}
```

Notice the calls to gethostbyname() and getservbyname(). These are the socket-oriented network directory services described under "Socket-Based Datagrams." They take a host and service name, respectively, and return the host network address and the service port. The service port number can be thought of as a machine-specific service address. Certain well-known services are assumed to have specific TCP port numbers in the 1-to-1023 range. Some applications hard code these port numbers rather than using get‐servbyname().

When porting sockets applications to TLI, calls to gethostbyname() and get‐servbyname(), as well as hard-coded TCP port numbers, should be replaced by calls to the netdir_getbyname() routine.

If the target socket exists and is prepared to handle a connection, the connection will complete successfully and the program can begin to send messages. Messages will be delivered in order without message boundaries. The connection is destroyed when both sockets are closed.

NOTE Some transports hold the connection open briefly in case more data are sent. The user may also have directed the system to wait. For more information, see the discussion of the SO_LINGER option on the getsockopt(3N) manual page.

Establishing TLI Connections: Client Code

The TLI connection mode transport service is also circuit (stream) oriented, enabling data to be transferred over an established connection in a reliable, sequenced manner. Typical TLI client code is shown in Figure 4-2.

Figure 4-2: TLI Client Code

```
#include <stdio.h>
#include <netdir.h>
#include <netconfig.h>

extern int t_errno;

main()
{
        int fd;
        struct netconfig *nconf;
        void *handlep;

        /*
         * select an appropriate network
         */

        if ((handlep = setnetpath()) == NULL) {
                nc_perror("Error in initializing networks");
                exit(1);
        }

        /*
         * try all transports until finding one that matches
         * the users stated preferences
         */

        while ((nconf = getnetpath(handlep)) != NULL) {
                if (nconf->nc_semantics == NC_TPI_COTS)
                        break;
```

(continued on next page)

Figure 4-2: TLI Client Code (continued)

```
        }

        if (nconf == NULL) {
                fprintf(stderr, "no transports available\n");
                exit(1);
        }

        if ((fd = t_open(nconf->nc_device, O_RDWR, NULL)) < 0) {
                t_error("t_open failed");
                exit(2);
        }

        if (t_bind(fd, NULL, NULL) < 0) {
                t_error("t_bind failed");
                exit(3);
        }

        endnetpath(handlep);
}
```

Network selection is used by TLI applications to find the device filename associated with the requested transport protocol. The device filename that matches the protocol is passed to t_open(). t_open() then returns a file descriptor that identifies a new transport endpoint, and optionally (by way of its third argument), the default characteristics of the transport provider associated with that endpoint (and indirectly specified by the first argument). t_bind() then binds the new transport endpoint to the transport address contained in its second argument. The typical client doesn't care what its own address is because no other process will try to access it. The second and third arguments in the example are therefore NULL.

Establishing Socket Connections: Server Code

Connection establishment for a server process is slightly different. The process must bind itself to an address and wait for clients to connect to it. Figure 4-3 shows how a sockets server is bound to its known address:

Figure 4-3: Sockets Server Code

```
#include <sys/types.h>
#include <sys/socket.h>
#include <netinet/in.h>
#include <netdb.h>
#include <stdio.h>

#define  SRV_PORT  2

main(argc,argv)
int      argc;
char     *argv[];
{
        int                     sock;
        struct sockaddr_in server;
        int                     msgsock;
        char                    buf[BUFSIZ];

        /* create socket */

        sock = socket(AF_INET, SOCK_STREAM, 0);
        if (sock < 0) {
                perror("opening stream socket");
                exit(1);
        }

        /* name socket */

        server.sin_family = AF_INET
        server.sin_addr.s_addr = INADDR_ANY;
        server.sin_port = SRV_PORT;
        if (bind(sock, (struct sockaddr *)&server), sizeof server) < 0) {
                perror("binding stream socket");
                exit(2);
        }

        /* the server now does a listen and accept */

}
```

In the example, the server explicitly asks to be bound to port SRV_PORT.

Establishing TLI Connections: Server Code

The equivalent code for a TLI server process is shown in Figure 4-4.

Figure 4-4: TLI Server Code

```
#include <stdio.h>
#include <fcntl.h>
#include <netconfig.h>
#include <netdir.h>
#include <tiuser.h>

#define   SRV_ADDR  2

main(argc,argv)
int       argc;
char      *argv[];
{
          struct nd_hostserve         hostserv;
          int                         fd;
          char                        buf[BUFSIZ];
          struct netconfig   *nconf;
          struct t_bind               *bind;
          void                        *handlep;
          extern int                  t_errno;

          if ( argc != 3 ) {
                  fprintf(stderr, "USAGE: %s host service\n", argv[0]);
                  exit(1);
          }
          hostserv.h_host = argv[1];
          hostserv.h_serv = argv[2];

          if ((handlep = setnetpath()) == NULL) {
                  nc_perror("setnetpath");
                  exit(2);
          }
          /*
           * select an appropriate transport and
           * get address for remote host/service
           */
          while ((nconf = getnetpath(handlep)) != NULL) {
                  if (nconf->nc_semantics == NC_TPI_COTS)
                          break;
          }
```

(continued on next page)

Figure 4-4: TLI Server Code (continued)

```
        if (nconf -- NULL) {
                fprintf(stderr, "no connection mode transport\n");
                exit(3);
        }

        if ((fd = t_open(nconf->nc_device, O_RDWR, NULL)) < 0) {
                t_error("t_open failed");
                fprintf(stderr, "unable to open %s\n", nconf->nc_device);
                exit(4);
        }
        endnetpath(handlep);

        if ((bind = (struct t_bind *)t_alloc(fd, T_BIND, T_ALL)) -- NULL) {
                t_error("t_alloc of t_bind structure failed");
                exit(5);
        }

        /*
         * for simplicity in this example, assume the
         * address is an integer
         */

        bind->qlen = 1;
        bind->addr.len = sizeof(int);
        *(int *)bind->addr.buf = SRV_ADDR;

        /* 2nd arg NULL -> bind to any address */

        if (t_bind(fd, bind, bind) < 0) {
                t_error("t_bind failed");
                exit(6);
        }

        /* was the correct address bound? */

        if (*(int *)bind->addr.buf != SRV_ADDR) {
                t_error("t_bind bound wrong address");
                exit(7);
        }

        /* the server now does a listen and accept */


}
```

The examples show two significant differences between sockets and TLI. First, since TLI server applications work over any transport provider, they use the Network Selection and Name-to-Address Mapping features in order to be protocol independent; sockets applications use fixed addresses.

A second difference is in the behavior of the TLI and sockets bind routines when an address is invalid or unavailable. The sockets bind() routine fails. The TLI t_bind() routine may bind to another address instead. For this reason, TLI servers should check that the address returned by t_bind() as its third argument is correct.

Connectionless Mode

Connectionless-mode transport services, in contrast to connection-oriented services, are message-oriented and support transfer in self-contained units (datagrams) with no necessary logical relationship to each other. Sockets and TLI both provide connectionless-mode service.

All the information required to deliver a datagram (for example, a destination address) is presented to the transport provider, together with the data to be transmitted, in a single service access. A given service access need not relate to any other service access. Each unit of data transmitted is entirely self-contained, and can be independently routed by the transport provider.

Socket-Based Datagrams

The differences between socket library datagrams and the connectionless service provided by TLI parallel the differences between sockets and TLI connection-oriented service described above. Figure 4-5 gives the code necessary to send an Internet domain datagram to a receiver whose host and service names are given as command line arguments.

Figure 4-5: Sending Internet Domain Datagram

```
#include <sys/types.h>
#include <sys/socket.h>
#include <netinet/in.h>
#include <netdb.h>
#include <stdio.h>
#define DATA "It was the best of times.  It was the worst of times."

/*
 * The form of the command line is:
 *                 dgramsend hostname servicename
 */

main(argc, argv)
        int argc;
        char *argv[];
{
        struct servent *sp, *getservbyname();
        int sock;
        struct sockaddr_in name;
        struct hostent *hp, *gethostbyname();

        /* create socket on which to send */
        sock = socket(AF_INET, SOCK_DGRAM, 0);
        if (sock < 0) {
                perror("opening datagram socket");
                exit(1);
        }
        /*
         * Find the socket to send to.  gethostbyname() returns a structure
         * including the network address of the specified host.  The port
         * number is taken from the command line.
         */
        hp = gethostbyname(argv[1]);
        if (hp == 0) {
                fprintf(stderr, "%s: unknown host\n", argv[1]);
                exit(2);
        }
        memcpy((char *)&name.sin_addr, (char *)hp->h_addr,
          hp->h_length);
        name.sin_family = AF_INET;
        sp = getservbyname(argv[2], "tcp");
        if (sp == 0) {
          fprintf(stderr, "%s: unknown service\n", argv[2]);
          exit(3);
        }
```

(continued on next page)

Figure 4-5: Sending Internet Domain Datagram (continued)

```
        server.sin_port = sp->s_port;

        /* send message */
        if (sendto(sock, DATA, sizeof DATA , 0,
            (struct sockaddr *)&name, sizeof name) < 0)
                    perror("sending datagram message");
        close(sock);
        exit(0);
    }
```

The program looks up the host address and the service port (both given on the command line) by calling gethostbyname() and getservbyname(). The host network address and service port number are in the structures returned by these two library routines. They are copied into the structure that specifies the destination of the message.

TLI Datagrams

TLI connectionless service is functionally similar to sockets datagram service. The sockets address management routines gethostbyname() and get-servbyname() are replaced by netdir_getbyname() for both connection-oriented and connectionless service.

The TLI code in Figure 4-6 sends a datagram to a receiver whose host and service names are given on the command line:

Figure 4-6: TLI Datagram Code

```
#include <stdio.h>
#include <fcntl.h>
#include <netconfig.h>
#include <netdir.h>
#include <tiuser.h>
/*
 * the form of the command line is:
 *              dgramsend hostname servicename
 */
main(argc,argv)
int     argc;
char    *argv[];
{
        int                     fd;
        struct nd_hostserve     hostserv;
        struct nd_addrlist *addrs;
        struct netconfig   *nconf;
        struct t_unitdata *ud;
        void                    *handlep;
        extern int              t_errno;

        if ( argc != 3 ) {
                fprintf(stderr, "USAGE: %s host service\n", argv[0]);
                exit(1);
        }
        hostserv.h_host = argv[1];
        hostserv.h_serv = argv[2];

        if ((handlep = setnetconfig()) == NULL) {
                nc_perror ("setnetconfig failed");
                exit(1);
        }

        /*
         * select an appropriate transport and
         * get address for remote host/service
         */
        while ((nconf = getnetconfig(handlep)) != NULL) {
                if (nconf->nc_semantics == NC_TPI_CLTS &&
                        netdir_getbyname(nconf, &hostserv, &addrs) == 0) {
                        break;
                }
        }

        if (nconf == NULL) {
```

(continued on next page)

Figure 4-6: TLI Datagram Code (continued)

```
                fprintf(stderr,
                "no address for host %s service %s\n", argv[1], argv[2]);
                exit(2);
        }

        if ((fd = t_open(nconf->nc_device, O_RDWR, NULL)) < 0) {
                t_error("t_open failed");
                fprintf(stderr, "unable to open %s\n", nconf->nc_device);
                exit(3);
        }

        if (t_bind(fd, NULL, NULL) < 0) {
                t_error("t_bind failed");
                exit(4);
        }

        if ((ud = (struct t_unitdata *)t_alloc(fd, T_UNITDATA, T_ALL))
        == NULL ) {
                t_error("t_alloc of t_unitdata structure failed");
                exit(5);
        }
        /*
         * use first address returned by netdir_getbyname()
         * filldata() will fill in the data to be sent
         */
        ud->addr = addrs->n_addrs;
        filldata(ud->udata);

        endnetconfig(handlep);

        /* send the datagram */
        if (t_sndudata(fd, ud) <0 ) {
                t_error("t_sndudata failed");
                exit(6);
        }

        exit(0);
}
```

For more information about the functions t_open, t_bind, and t_sndudata, see the manual pages t_open(3N), t_bind(3N), and t_sndudata(3N).

Synchronous and Asynchronous Modes

Transport services are inherently asynchronous, with events occurring independently of the actions of the transport user. For example, a user may be sending data over a transport connection when an asynchronous disconnect indication arrives. The user must somehow be informed that the connection has been broken. Both the socket interface and TLI provide an asynchronous mode for managing such events. Asynchronous mode is most useful for applications that expect long delays between events and have other tasks that they can perform in the meantime.

A socket is put into asynchronous mode by calling fcntl() and specifying O_NDELAY or O_NONBLOCK. Once in asynchronous mode, all relevant primitives — send(), read(), etc. — return EWOULDBLOCK whenever they encounter situations that would have caused them to block if they had been in synchronous mode.

The TLI non-blocking mode is also specified with the O_NDELAY or O_NONBLOCK flag. The O_NDELAY and O_NONBLOCK flags can be used when the transport provider is initially opened with the t_open() function, or later with the fcntl() call. If the TLI blocking mode is used, these cause the error code EAGAIN to be returned (see the *Programmer's Reference Manual*, Section 2, Introduction).

There are different levels of asynchronous operation. Specifying O_NDELAY or O_NONBLOCK puts a socket into non-blocking mode. For true asynchronous operation, however, it is also necessary to test for asynchronous events. Socket-based applications normally use select(3N) to test for asynchronous events.

TLI–based applications should use poll(2) to test for asynchronous events. select() is supported only for compatibility with older applications.

Both TLI and sockets provide mechanisms for asynchronous event notification. Sockets uses fcntl() to request that the system issue a SIGIO signal when it becomes possible to perform I/O on a given file descriptor. TLI uses the I_SETSIG ioctl. This causes the system to send the process a SIGPOLL signal when the I/O event specified actually occurs. The TLI mechanism is the more powerful of the two, since it allows users to specify the precise kind of I/O event they want to be signaled on (see the streamio(7) manual page for the possible kinds of events).

A process that issues functions in synchronous mode must still be able to recognize certain asynchronous events immediately and act on them if necessary. Eight such asynchronous events are specified for TLI and cover both connection-oriented and connectionless modes (see the t_look(3N) manual page). TLI routines that encounter trouble return the special transport error TLOOK. The user can then use the t_look() function to identify the event that generated the error. Alternatively, the transport user can use t_look() to poll the transport endpoint periodically for asynchronous events. If a sockets function encounters trouble, the primitive will return an errno value directly.

Error Handling

TLI attempts to separate communications errors from system errors by defining two levels of errors:

- **Library level errors.** Each library function has one or more error returns and indicates failure with a −1. An external integer, t_errno, holds the specific error number when such an failure occurs. This value is set when errors occur but is not cleared by successful library calls. It should therefore be tested only after an error has been indicated. A diagnostic function, t_error(), is provided for printing out information on the current transport error.

- **System errors.** The standard external variable errno, is used to report system errors. Such errors can, of course, affect TLI functioning. When they do, t_errno is set to TSYSERR and errno is set to indicate the specific system error that occurred. The state of the transport provider may change if a transport error occurs.

The socket interface provides a similar facility with getsockopt() when called with an option of SO_ERROR.

Sockets-to-TLI Conversion

Table 4-1 shows some approximate TLI/−sockets equivalents. The comment field describes the differences. Where there is no comment, either the functions are the same or there is no equivalent function in one or the other interface.

Table 4-1: Table of TLI/Sockets Equivalents.

TLI function	Socket function	Comments
t_open()	socket()	
−	socketpair()	
t_bind()	bind()	t_bind() sets the queue depth for passive sockets, but bind() doesn't. For sockets, the queue length is specified in the call to listen().
t_optmgmt()	getsockopt() setsockopt()	t_optmgmt() manages only transport options. getsockopt() and setsockopt() can manage options at the transport layer, but also at the socket layer and at arbitrary protocol layers.
t_unbind()	−	
t_close()	close()	
t_getinfo()	getsockopt()	t_getinfo() returns information about the transport. getsockopt() can return information about the transport and the socket.
t_getstate()	−	
t_getname()	getsockname()	
t_sync()	−	
t_alloc()	−	
t_free()	−	
t_look()	−	getsockopt with the SO_ERROR option returns the same kind of error information as t_look().
t_error()	perror()	

Programmer's Guide: Networking Interfaces

Table 4-1: Table of TLI/Sockets Equivalents. (continued)

TLI function	Socket function	Comments
t_connect()	connect()	A connect() can be done without first binding the local endpoint. The endpoint must be bound before calling t_connect(). A connect() can be done on a connectionless endpoint to set the default destination address for datagrams.
t_rcvconnect()	–	
t_listen()	listen()	t_listen() waits for connection indications. listen() merely sets the queue depth.
t_accept()	accept	
t_snd()	send() sendto() sendmsg()	sendto() and sendmsg() operate in connection mode as well as datagram mode.
t_rcv()	recv() recvfrom() recvmsg()	recvfrom() and recvmsg() operate in connection mode as well as datagram mode.
t_snddis()	–	
t_rcvdis()	–	
t_sndrel()	shutdown()	
t_rcvrel()	–	
t_sndudata()	sendto() sendmsg()	
t_rcvudata()	recvfrom() recvmsg()	
t_rcvuderr()	–	
read() write()	read() write()	In TLI, you must push the tirdwr module before calling read() or write(); in sockets, it is sufficient just to call read() or write().

Moving Sockets Applications to System V Release 4

Although System V Release 4 sockets and the BSD sockets implementation are largely compatible, there are some differences an application programmer must be aware of before moving a BSD sockets-based application to System V Release 4. These differences are described in Table 4-2.

Table 4-2: Differences in Sockets Implementations

BSD	UNIX System V Release 4.0
Connection-Mode Primitives	
connect()	
If connect() is called on an unbound socket, the protocol determines whether or not the endpoint will be bound before the connection takes place.	When connect(), is called on an unbound socket, that socket is always bound to an address selected by the transport provider.
Data Transfer Primitives	
write()	
write() will fail with errno set to ENOTCONN if it is used on an unconnected socket.	A call to write() will appear to succeed, but the data will be discarded. The socket error option SO_ERROR will be set to ENOTCONN if this occurs.
write() can be used on type SOCK_DGRAM sockets (either AF_UNIX or AF_INET domains) to send zero length data.	A call to write() will return −1, with errno set to ERANGE. The functions send(), sendto(), or sendmsg() should be used to send zero length data.

Table 4-2: Differences in Sockets Implementations (continued)

BSD	UNIX System V Release 4.0
read()	
A call to read() will fail with errno set to ENOTCONN if read() is used on an unconnected socket which needs to be connected.	A call to read() will return zero bytes read if the socket is in blocking mode. If the socket is in non-blocking mode, it will return a −1 with errno set to EAGAIN.
sendmsg() and readmsg()	
If the MSG_PEEK flag has been set when sendmsg() is called, and access rights are available, the access rights will be copied, leaving them available for reading by a subsequent call to recvmsg().	If the MSG_PEEK flag is specified in a call to recvmsg(), and access rights are available, the access rights will be transferred to the user buffer associated with the receiving socket. They are then destroyed, and the transferring socket has no further access to them. They are therefore unavailable to a subsequent call to recvmsg(). Any data associated with the access rights will also be copied to the user buffer and will not be available to recvmsg().
Information Primitives	
getsockname()	
getsockname() will work when a previously existing connection has been closed.	getsockname() will return −1 and errno will be set to EPIPE if a previously existing connection has been closed.

Table 4-2: Differences in Sockets Implementations (continued)

BSD	UNIX System V Release 4.0
ioctl( ) and fcntl( )	
`SIOCSPGRP/FIOSETOWN/F_SETOWN()`	
The `SIOCSPGRP/FIOSETOWN/F_SETOWN` `ioctl()`'s and the `F_SETOWN` `fcntl()` take as argument a positive process id or negative process group indentifying the intended recipient list of subsequent `SIGURG` and `SIGIO` signals.	This is not the case in SVR4. The only acceptable arguments to these system calls is the caller's process id or a negative process group which has the same absolute value as the caller's process id. In other words, the only recipient of `SIGURG` and `SIGIO` signals is the calling process.
Local Management	
`bind()`	
`bind()` uses the credentials of the user at the time of the `bind()` call to determine whether the port requested should be allocated or not.	A call to `socket()` causes the user's credentials to be remembered and used to validate addresses used in `bind()`.
`setsockopt()`	
`setsockopt()` can be used at any time during the life of a socket.	Because of the state diagram specified by the Transport Provider Interface (TPI), a `setsockopt()` operation on a transport provider conforming to this specification will fail if issued on a socket that is not bound to a local address.

Table 4-2: Differences in Sockets Implementations (continued)

BSD	UNIX System V Release 4.0
	Specifically, if a socket is unbound and `setsockopt()` is used, then the operation will succeed in the `AF_INET` domain, but will fail in the `AF_UNIX`
`shutdown()`	
If `shutdown` is called with the value of *how* equal to zero, further attempts to receive data will return zero bytes (EOF).	Calling `shutdown` with the value of *how* equal to zero will not cause further attempts to receive data to return zero bytes if the `read(2)` system call is used and the socket is in nonblocking mode. In this case `read` will return −1 with `errno` set to `EAGAIN`. If one of the socket receive primitives is used, the correct result (EOF) will be returned.
If `shutdown()` is called with the value of *how* equal to 2, further atempts to receive data will return EOF. Attempts to send data will return −1 with `errno` set to `EPIPE` with a `SIGPIPE` issued.	The same results will occur, except that attempts to send data using the `write` system call will cause `errno` to be set to EIO. As in the above case, if a socket primitive is used, the correct `errno` will be returned.
If `shutdown()` is called with a value of two for *how*, further attempts to receive data will return EOF, and attempts to send data will return −1 with `errno` set to `EPIPE` with a `SIG-PIPE` issued.	The same results will occur, except that attempts to send data using the `write()` system call will cause `errno` to be set to `EIO`. If a socket primitive is used, the correct `errno` will be returned.

Table 4-2: Differences in Sockets Implementations (continued)

BSD	UNIX System V Release 4.0
Signals	
SIGIO	
SIGIO is delivered every time new data are appended to the socket input queue.	SIGIO is delivered only when data are appended to a socket queue that was previously empty.
SIGURG	
A SIGURG is delivered every time new data is anticipated or actually arrives.	A SUGURG is delivered only when there is no urgent data already pending.
S_ISSOCK	
The ISSOCK macro takes the mode of a file as an argument. It returns 1 if the file represents a socket and 0 otherwise.	The ISSOCK macro does not exist. In SVR4, a socket is defined as a file descriptor associated with a streams character device that has the socket module pushed onto it.
S_IFSOCK()	
This file type identifies a socket descriptor.	There is no socket file type, and this #define does not exist.
Miscellaneous	
If an invalid buffer is specified in a function, the function will normally return −1 with errno set to EFAULT.	If an invalid buffer is specified in a function, the user's program will probably coredump.
If ls −1 is executed on a directory that contains a UNIX domain socket, an s will be printed on the left side of the mode field.	If ls −1 is executed on a directory that contains a UNIX domain socket, a p will be printed on the left side of the mode field.

Table 4-2: Differences in Sockets Implementations (continued)

BSD	UNIX System V Release 4.0
Executing ls −F will cause an equals sign (=) to be printed after any filename that represents a UNIX domain socket.	Nothing will be printed after a filename that represents a UNIX domain socket.

Index

A

abortive release   2: 13, 36
accept(3N)   3: 7, 34
address
  binding   3: 48
  wildcard   3: 48
asynchronous mode   2: 28, 51, 63,
  4: 14–15
authentication   3: 50

B

bind(3N)   3: 52
binding local names   3: 4
broadcasting   3: 51
byte swapping   3: 27

C

clients   2: 11, 16, 24–26, 38–39, 4: 2
client/server model   3: 29
close(2)   2: 48–50
communication, C run-time routines
  3: 27
connect requests   2: 11–13, 17, 20–31,
  34–35, 51–65, 69
  multiple   2: 81
connection errors   3: 7
connection establishment   2: 10–12,
  23–31
  using sockets   3: 6
connection release   2: 13, 36–39
  table of routines   2: 13
connectionless sockets   3: 13
connectionless-mode   2: 7, 14, 40–47,
  4: 9–13

example of transaction server
  2: 77–79
servers   3: 36
state table   2: 67
connection-mode   2: 7–13, 16–39, 47,
  4: 2–9
  client side   4: 4–5
  example of client   2: 71–72
  example of server   2: 73–76, 81–87
  server side   4: 6–9
  state table   2: 68

D

data transfer   2: 12, 31–36, 43–45, 3: 9
  during connection   2: 24
  in byte stream mode   2: 32
  message interface   2: 32
  table of routines   2: 12
datagram
  errors   2: 45–46
  Internet domain   3: 15–16
  socket   3: 2
device names   2: 70, 4: 5
disconnect requests   2: 26–31, 33,
  35–38, 49–51, 57–60, 63, 69

E

event handling   2: 26–27
event-driven TLI software, example
  of   2: 52–60
expedited data   2: 35

BUSINESS REPLY MAIL

FIRST CLASS MAIL PERMIT NUMBER 126 PITTSFIELD, MA

POSTAGE WILL BE PAID BY ADDRESSEE

Bob Oblack
TEKTRONIX, INC.
P O BOX 1520
PITTSFIELD MA 01202-9864

☒ ☐

YES! I'd like more information about Tek's calibration offer.

YES! Tempt me with what's new in Tek's oscilloscope lineup.

offer expires xxxx June 30 xx

Help us serve you better . . .

1. Is our long-term support meeting your needs?

☒ Yes   ☐ No

2. Is it easy for you to use Tektronix customer services?

☒ Yes   ☐ No

3. Are your instrument certifications maintained by your company's calibration lab?

☒ Yes   ☐ No

4. Do you have interest in Tektronix maintaining all your Tek and non-Tek instruments?

☐ Yes   ☒ No

NAME _____

TITLE OR POSITION _____

COMPANY _____

MAIL STATION, BLDG., DEPT. _____

ADDRESS _____

CITY, STATE, ZIP _____

PHONE/EXTENSION _____

```
BOB COMSTOCK
GENERAL ELECTRIC COMPANY
BUILDING SEVEN
43 ELECTRONIC PARKWAY
SYRACUSE NY 13201          ALL
```

38W-8406-0

03W-188521-01A

Contents

9   Remote Procedure Calls: Protocol Specification

10   RPC Administration

11   The YP Service

Index: Remote Procedure Calls

Figures and Tables

5 Introduction to Remote Procedure Calls

Introduction to RPC

The Remote Procedure Calls (RPC) mechanism is a high-level communications paradigm for network applications. By use of RPC, programs on networked platforms can communicate with remote (and local) resources.

Organization of Technical Information

This chapter, "Introduction to Remote Procedure Calls", provides an overview of the RPC mechanism and the programming tools and protocols that support RPC. Terms used throughout this section are defined.

The "rpcgen Programming Guide" chapter provides instruction on the use of rpcgen, the compiler used for creating C-language programs that use RPC. The RPC programming language is described in this chapter.

The "Remote Procedure Call Programming Guide" chapter describes in detail the C-language interface to the RPC environment. The RPC interface allows programmers access to RPC at various levels, from high to low. High level RPC provides transparency and portability. Lower levels offer greater control of the communications. This chapter includes guidance on selecting an appropriate level for a given application.

External Data Representation (XDR) is the protocol used by RPC for platform-independent data communications. The "External Data Representation Standard: Protocol Specification" chapter is an XDR reference for RPC programmers.

The "Remote Procedure Calls: Protocol Specification" chapter is a complete RPC programming reference.

Definitions

Bottom Level   Lowest of the four lower RPC levels; programs written to this level can control many transport-specific details.

connection-oriented transport   Connection-oriented transports are reliable and support byte-stream deliveries of unlimited data size.

connectionless transport	Connectionless transports have less overhead than connection-orient transports but are less reliable and maximum data transmissions are limited by buffer sizes.
datagram transport	See *connectionless transport*.
deserializing	Converting data from XDR format to a machine-specific representation.
Expert Level	Second-lowest of the four lower RPC levels; programs written to this level can: control client and server characteristics; interface with rpcbind; manipulate service dispatch.
Intermediate Level	Second-highest of the four lower RPC levels; programs written to this level specify the transport they require.
network client	A process that makes remote procedure calls to services.
network service	A collection of one or more remote programs.
ping	A call to procedure 0 of an RPC program. Pinging is used to verify the existence and accessibility of a remote program. Pinging can also be used to time network communications.
remote program	Software that implements one or more remote procedures.
RPC language	A C-like programming language recognized by the rpcgen compiler.
RPC Package	The collection of software and documentation used to implement and support remote procedure calls in System V. The RPC Package implements and is a superset of the functionality of the RPC Protocol.
RPC Protocol	The message-passing protocol that is the basis of the RPC package.

RPC/XDR	See *RPC language*.
serializing	Converting data from a machine-specific representation to XDR format.
server	Software that implements network services.
Simplified Interface	The simplest level of the RPC package.
transport	Refers to the fourth layer of the Reference Model of Open Systems Interconnection (OSI).
Top Level	Highest of the four lower RPC levels; programs written to this level specify the type of transport they require.
universal address	A machine-independent representation of a network address.
virtual circuit transport	See *connection-oriented transport*.
XDR language	A protocol specification language for data representation. RPC language builds on and is a superset of XDR.

RPC Overview

RPC allows network applications to use specialized kinds of procedure calls designed to hide the details of underlying networking mechanisms. RPC is transport independent, able to take advantage of whatever kinds of networking mechanisms (such as TCP/IP or ISO) may be available. RPC implements a logical client–to–server communications system designed specifically for the support of network applications. Generic facilities, such as rpcbind, associate network services with universal network addresses.

Refer to Figure 5-1. With RPC, the client makes a procedure call that sends data packets to the server, as necessary. When these packets arrive, the server calls a dispatch routine, performs whatever service is requested, sends back the reply, and the procedure call returns to the client.

Figure 5-1: Network Communication with the Remote Procedure Call

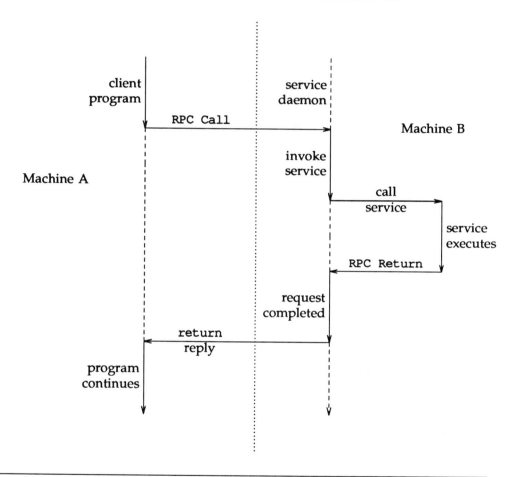

Programming with RPC produces programs that are designed to run within a client/server network model. Such programs use RPC mechanisms to avoid the details of interfacing to the network, and provide network services to their callers without requiring that the caller be aware of the existence and function of the underlying network. For example, a program can simply call rusers(), a C routine that returns the number of users on a remote machine. The caller is not

Introduction to Remote Procedure Calls

explicitly aware of using RPC — the call to rusers() is as simple as a call to malloc().

This section addresses only the C interface to RPC, but remote procedure calls can be made from any language. Note too that although this section describes the use of RPC for communication between processes on different machines, RPC works just as well for communication between different processes on the same machine.

The following paragraphs provide capsule overviews of the key components and leading characteristics of RPC. Descriptions will address:

- "RPC Versions and Numbers" — RPC uses a program number, program version, procedure number tuple to uniquely identify procedures that can be called via RPC.

- "Network Selection" — Programs can be written to operate over specific transports and transport types, or can be written to operate over system- or user-chosen transports.

- "The rpcbind Facility" — rpcbind is a facility used to associate network services with universal network addresses.

- "The Lower RPC Levels" — The lower RPC levels available to client and server programs allow for greater control of RPC communications.

- "External Data Representation (XDR)" — Data transmitted between RPC clients and servers is encoded in XDR transfer syntax.

RPC Versions and Numbers

Each RPC procedure is uniquely identified by a program number, version number, and procedure number.

The program number identifies a group of related remote procedures, each of which has a different procedure number. Each program also has a version number, so when a minor change is made to a remote service (adding a new procedure, for example), a new program number does not have to be assigned.

To call a procedure to find the number of remote users, for example, you would look up the appropriate program, version and procedure number in a reference manual (just as you would look up the name of a memory allocator if you wanted to allocate memory).

RPC programs should be assigned program numbers according to rules detailed in the "Program Number Assignment" sub-section of the "Remote Procedure Calls: Protocol Specification" chapter in this guide.

Network Selection

Network selection is a simple way by which users and applications may dynamically select transports, according to both their preferences and the available transports. It is based on two mechanisms, the /etc/netconfig database, which lists the transports available on the host and identifies them by type, and the optional environmental variable NETPATH, which allows the user to specify preferences among the transports available in /etc/netconfig that are acceptable to the application.

 NOTE To create a service for a particular transport, an application must interface to RPC at a level below the *top level*, i.e., the level composed of clnt_create() and its associated routines. Only then can it specify the types of transports that it prefers. See below for details about the various RPC levels.

The /etc/netconfig file contains several lines, each of which corresponds to an available transport. Here are some possible entries:

```
# The Network Configuration File.
#
# Each entry is of the form:
#
# network_id semantics flags protofamily protoname device nametoaddr_libs
#
ticlts tpi_clts v loopback - /dev/ticlts /usr/lib/straddr.so
ticots tpi_cots v loopback - /dev/ticots /usr/lib/straddr.so
ticotsord tpi_cots_ord v loopback - /dev/ticotsord /usr/lib/straddr.so
starlan tpi_cots v osinet - /dev/starlan /usr/lib/straddr.so
starlang tpi_clts v osinet - /dev/starlang /usr/lib/straddr.so
tcp tpi_cots_ord v inet tcp /dev/tcp /usr/lib/tcpip.so
udp tpi_clts v inet udp /dev/udp /usr/lib/tcpip.so
icmp tpi_raw - inet icmp /dev/icmp /usr/lib/tcpip.so
rawip tpi_raw - inet - /dev/rawip /usr/lib/tcpip.so
```

For the details about /etc/netconfig, and about the applications interface to
it, see the getnetconfig(3N) manual page and the "Network Services"
Chapter in the *System Administrator's Guide*. Here, we just want to mention a
few points:

- Each entry contains an identifier (the first field) which gives the network
  identifier by which the transport is commonly known.

- Each entry also contains a flag or set of flags (the third field) that
  identifies it by type — the v flag, for example, identifies any transport
  that is 'visible.'

- The last field names a run-time linkable module that contains the name-
  to-address translation routines associated with the transport. (See below).

- The loopback transports are required for registering services with
  rpcbind. They are local transports, available only to local clients and
  servers, and hence are more secure than other transports.

The format of NETPATH is simple: an ordered list of network identifiers
separated by colons (:) (for example: udp:tcp:starlan). By setting NETPATH,
the user can specify the order in which the application should try the various
networks. If NETPATH is not set, the system defaults to all visible transports
specified in /etc/netconfig, in the order they appear.

NOTE   Applications can choose to ignore a user's NETPATH.

RPC divides selectable transports into the following types:

netpath   Choose from those transports that have been specified in the NETPATH environment variable. If NETPATH is not set, the system defaults to all visible transports specified in /etc/netconfig, in the order they appear.

" "   (null) — same as selecting netpath.

visible   Choose those transports that have the visible flag ('v') set in their /etc/netconfig entries.

circuit_v   Same as visible, but restricted to connection-oriented transports.

datagram_v   Same as visible, but restricted to connectionless transports.

circuit_n   Choose from whatever is defined in NETPATH, but restrict to connection-oriented transports.

datagram_n   Choose from whatever is defined in NETPATH, but restrict to connectionless transports.

udp   (Obsolete. For backwards compatibility.) — specifies Internet User Datagram Protocol (UDP).

tcp   (Obsolete. For backwards compatibility.) — specifies Internet Transmission Control Protocol (TCP).

When a transport-dependent application begins execution, it begins by calling the setnetconfig(), getnetconfig() and endnetconfig() routines, using them to search /etc/netconfig for a transport of appropriate type. This information is then stored in local data structures of type struct netconfig and is available for later use. setnetconfig(), getnetconfig(), and endnetconfig() are described on the getnetconfig(3N) manual page; the Network Selection Administrative file /etc/netconfig is described on the netconfig(4) manual page.

Taken together, these mechanisms allow a fine degree of control over network selection: a user can specify a preferred transport, and if it is reasonable, applications will use it. In cases where the specified transport is inappropriate (as, for example, when a remote server does not support a specified transport) the application should automatically try others with the right characteristics.

Name-to-Address Translation

Each transport has an associated set of routines that convert between universal network addresses (string representations of transport addresses) and their local address representation. These universal addresses are passed around within the RPC system (for example, between `rpcbind` and a client). When any programming interface to the transport layer is made, a transport-specific name-to-address translation routine is called to convert the universal address into local form. Each transport has associated with it a run-time loadable library that contains the name-to-address translation routines associated with it. The main translation routines are:

`netdir_getbyname:`	Translates from host/service pairs and a `netconfig` structure (e.g. `server1`, `rpcbind`) to a set of `netbuf` addresses. `netbuf`'s are Transport Layer Interface (TLI) structures that are used at run-time to contain transport-specific addresses.
`netdir_getbyaddr:`	Translates from `netbuf` addresses and a `netconfig` structure into host/service pairs.
`uaddr2taddr:`	Translates from universal addresses and a `netconfig` structure to `netbuf` addresses.
`taddr2uaddr:`	Translates from `netbuf` addresses and a `netconfig` structure to universal addresses.

For more details on these routines, see the `netdir`(3N) manual page.

The rpcbind Facility

Client programs need a way to find server programs; that is, they need a way to look up the addresses of server programs. Network transport services do not themselves provide such a service; they merely provide process-to-process message transfer across a network. A message is sent to a transport-specific network address. A network address is a logical communications channel; by waiting on a network address, a process receives messages from the network.

RPC, being transport independent, makes no assumptions about the structure of a network address. It deals with universal addresses, specified only as null-terminated strings of characters. RPC translates universal addresses into local transport addresses by using routines specific to each transport provider. For more details on these routines, see the netdir(3N) manual page.

Operating systems provide (differing) mechanisms by which a process can wait on a network address, i.e, synchronize its activity with arriving messages. Thus, messages are not sent across networks to receiving processes, but rather to the transport address at which receiving processes pick them up. Transport addresses are valuable because they allow message receivers to be specified in a way that is independent of the conventions of the receiving operating system. The rpcbind protocol defines a network service that provides a standard way for clients to look up the transport address of any remote program supported by a server. Because the rpcbind protocol can be implemented for any transport, it provides a single solution to a general problem that works for all clients, all servers and all networks.

Address Registration

Because rpcbind is responsible for mapping network services to their addresses, its address must be well known. The name-to-address translation routines for any particular transport should know and reserve a particular address for rpcbind.

In the Internet domain, this problem is solved by always assigning rpcbind the port number 111. Unfortunately, this simple solution is not acceptable on all transports.

rpcbind begins each session by registering its location on each of the transports supported by the host. rpcbind is the only network service that must have such a well-known address. The address must be well-known for a given transport because rpcbind is responsible for registering the addresses of other network services and making those addresses available to network clients. Thus, services make their addresses available to clients by registering their addresses with their host's rpcbind daemon. Thereafter, the addresses of the services are available to rpcinfo(1M) and to programs using library routines specified in rpcbind(3N).

RPC-based servers typically get mapped to network addresses at run time, and then they register with rpcbind, and neither they nor their clients can make any assumptions about what those network addresses will be.

rpcbind is started by the system or RPC administrator. Both server programs and client programs call rpcbind.

NOTE Although client and server programs and client and server machines are usually distinct, they need not be. A server program can also be a client program, as when an NFS server calls an rpcbind server. Likewise, when a client program directs a "remote" procedure call to its own machine, the machine acts as both client and server.

As part of its initialization, a server program calls its host's rpcbind daemon to register itself in the host's registered-address map. Whereas server programs call rpcbind to update address maps, clients call them to query those maps. To find a remote program's address, a client sends an RPC call message to a server machine's rpcbind daemon; if the remote program is on the server, the daemon returns the relevant address in an RPC reply message. The client program can then send RPC call messages to that address.

The rpcbind protocol (for details, see the "Remote Procedure Calls: Protocol Specification" chapter) provides a procedure, RPCBPROC_CALLIT(), with which rpcbind can assist a client in making a remote procedure call. A client program passes the target procedure's program number, version number, procedure number (for a discussion of these numbers, see the "Remote Procedure Call Programming Guide" chapter) and arguments in an RPC call message. rpcbind then looks up the target procedure's address in the address map and sends an RPC call message, including the arguments received from the client, to the target procedure.

When the target procedure returns results, RPCBPROC_CALLIT() passes them on to the client program. It also returns the target procedure's address so the client can later call it directly.

The RPC library provides an interface to all rpcbind procedures. Some of the RPC library procedures also call rpcbind automatically for client and server programs.

The rpcinfo Command

rpcinfo is a shell command that reports current RPC registration information known to rpcbind (and can be used, by administrators, to delete registrations). rpcinfo can be used to find all the RPC services registered on a specified host and to report their universal addresses and the transports for which they are registered. It can also be used to call (ping) a specific version of a specific program on a specific host using a TCP or UDP transport, and to report whether a response is received. For details, see rpcinfo(1M).

The Lower RPC Levels

There are various levels at which it is possible to interface to the RPC library services. These levels are described in detail in the "Remote Procedure Call Programming Guide" chapter. Understanding the lower levels of RPC is helpful but not necessary if you plan to use rpcgen to generate your RPC applications. For usage of rpcgen, refer to the "rpcgen Programming Guide" chapter.

Figure 5-2 illustrates client-side lower level interfaces, that are available for transport-handle creation. Figure 5-3 illustrates transport-handle creation for an RPC server. Note the similarity of hierarchies on each side.

Figure 5-2: Client-Side RPC Lower Levels

```
          clnt_create(host, prog, vers, nettype)
```
"Top Level" - transport is selected by network type.
```
                              |
                              |
                    (Network Selection)
```
Application controls transport selection below this point.
```
                              |
                              |
          clnt_tp_create(host, prog, vers, netconfig)
```
"Intermediate Level" - application knows what transport it will use.
```
                              |
                              |
               (Name-to-Address Translation)
                              |
                              |
             clnt_tli_create(fd, netconfig, ...)
```
"Expert Level" - Application can now directly manipulate the transport.
```
                              |
                              |
             ----------------------------------
             |                                |
             |                                |
       clnt_dg_create()              clnt_vc_create()
```
*"Bottom Level" - Only **very** specialized applications need access to this level.*

Figure 5-3: Server-Side RPC Lower Levels

```
svc_create(dispatch, prog, vers, nettype)
```
"Top Level" - transport is selected by network type.

```
                  |
                  |
          (Network Selection)
```
Application controls transport selection below this point.

```
                  |
                  |
svc_tp_create (dispatch, prog, vers, netconfig)
```
"Intermediate Level" - application knows what transport it will use.

```
                  |
                  |
     (Name-to-Address Translation)
                  |
                  |
    svc_tli_create(fd, netconfig, ...)
```
"Expert Level" - Application can now directly manipulate the transport.

```
                  |
                  |
   ------------------------------
   |                          |
   |                          |
svc_dg_create()          svc_vc_create()
```
"Bottom Level" - Only very specialized applications need access to this level.

External Data Representation

RPC uses External Data Representation (XDR), a protocol for the machine-independent description and encoding of data. XDR is useful for transferring data between different computer architectures.

RPC can handle arbitrary data structures, regardless of different machines' byte orders or structure layout conventions, by always converting them to XDR representation sending them over the wire. The process of converting from a particular machine representation to XDR format is called *serializing*, and the reverse process is called *deserializing*. For a detailed discussion of XDR, see the ''External Data Representation Standard: Protocol Specification'' chapter.

6   rpcgen Programming Guide

Introduction

An Overview of rpcgen

rpcgen is a compiler. It accepts a remote program interface definition written in a language, called RPC Language. RPC Language is similar to C. rpcgen produces a C language output for RPC programs. This output includes:

- stub versions of the client routines

- a server skeleton

- XDR filter routines for both parameters and results

- a header file that contains common definitions

- (optionally) dispatch tables that the server can use to check authorizations and then invoke service routines.

rpcgen's output files can be compiled and linked in the usual way.

The client stubs interface with the RPC library and effectively hide the transport from their callers. The server skeleton similarly hides the transport from the server procedures that are to be invoked by remote clients.

The developer writes server procedures (in any language that observes system calling conventions) and links them with the server skeleton produced by rpcgen to get an executable server program. To use a remote program, the programmer writes an ordinary main program that makes local procedure calls to the client stubs produced by rpcgen. Linking this program with stubs produced by rpcgen creates an executable program. (At present the main program must be written in C.)

rpcgen options can be used to suppress stub generation and to specify the transport to be used by the server skeleton.

rpcgen reduces the development time that would otherwise be spent coding and debugging low-level routines, at a small cost in efficiency and flexibility. For speed-critical applications, though, rpcgen allows programmers to mix low-level code with high-level code. Hand-written routines can be linked with the rpcgen output without any difficulty. Also, one may proceed by using rpcgen output as a starting point, and then rewriting it as necessary. (For a discussion of RPC programming without rpcgen, see the "Remote Procedure Call Programming Guide" chapter.)

Organization of Technical Information

This chapter provides rpcgen tutorial and user information.

The section titled "An rpcgen Tutorial" describes through examples how a programmer can use rpcgen to do such things as:

- convert an application to run over a network
- use rpcgen to create XDR routines
- make use of rpcgen-supported preprocessing directives.

The "Common RPC Programming Techniques" section suggests some coding and rpcgen usage techniques.

Finally, the "RPC Language Reference" provides a complete description of the RPC programming language recognized by the rpcgen compiler.

An rpcgen Tutorial

The details of programming applications to use Remote Procedure Calls can be overwhelming. Perhaps most daunting is the writing of the XDR routines necessary to convert procedure arguments and results into their XDR format and vice-versa.

Fortunately, rpcgen(1) exists to help programmers write RPC applications simply and directly. rpcgen does most of the dirty work, allowing programmers to debug the main features of their application, instead of requiring them to spend most of their time on their transport interface code.

This section presents some basic rpcgen programming examples.

Converting Local Procedures into Remote Procedures

Assume an application that runs on a single machine. Suppose we want to convert it to run over the network. Here we will show such a conversion by way of a simple example program that prints a message to the console. The source file for the original program might look like:

```
/* printmsg.c: print a message on the console */
#include <stdio.h>
main(argc, argv)
        int argc;
        char *argv[];
{
        char *message;
        if (argc != 2) {
                fprintf(stderr, "usage: %s <message>\n", argv[0]);
                exit(1);
        }
        message = argv[1];
        if (!printmessage(message)) {
                fprintf(stderr, "%s: couldn't print your message\n",
                        argv[0]);
                exit(1);
        }
        printf("Message Delivered!\n");
        exit(0);
}
/* Print a message to the console. */
/* Return a boolean indicating whether the message was actually printed. */
printmessage(msg)
        char *msg;
{
        FILE *f;
        f = fopen("/dev/console", "w");
        if (f == NULL) {
                return (0);
        }
        fprintf(f, "%s\n", msg);
        fclose(f);
        return (1);
}
```

For local use on a single machine, this program could be compiled and executed as follows:

```
$ cc printmsg.c -o printmsg
$ printmsg "Hello, there."
Message delivered!
$
```

If the printmessage () function were turned into a remote procedure, it could be called from anywhere in the network. It is not difficult to make a procedure remote.

NOTE In the context of RPC programming, it has become acceptable to use the term *procedure* to refer to a C-language *function*. The terms are used interchangeably in this guide.

In general, it is necessary to figure out what the types are for all procedure inputs and outputs. Here, the procedure printmessage () takes a string as input, and returns an integer as output. Knowing this, we can write a protocol specification in RPC language that describes the remote version of printmessage (). The RPC language source code for such a specification might look like:

```
/* msg.x: Remote message printing protocol */

program MESSAGEPROG {
        version MESSAGEVERS {
                int PRINTMESSAGE(string) = 1;
        } = 1;
} = 0x20000001;
```

Remote procedures are always declared as being part of remote programs. The above is actually a declaration for an entire remote program, one that contains the single procedure PRINTMESSAGE.

NOTE In the context of RPC programming, the term *"remote* program" actually refers to a collection of (related) *procedures*.

In this example, the PRINTMESSAGE procedure is declared to be procedure 1, in version 1 of the remote program whose number is 0x20000001. [Refer to "Program Number Assignment" in the "Remote Procedure Calls: Protocol Specification" chapter for guidance on choice of program numbers.]

By convention, all RPC services provide for a procedure 0; a call to a remote program's procedure 0 should do nothing (a "no-op") except succeed. To *ping* means to call procedure 0 of a remote program. Pinging is used to verify the existence and accessibility of a remote program.

Using rpcgen, no null procedure (procedure 0) need be written because rpcgen generates it automatically.

Notice that the program and procedure names are declared with all capital letters. This is not required, but is a good convention to follow.

Notice also that the argument type is string and not char * as it would be in C. This is because a char * in C is ambiguous. Programmers usually intend it to mean a null-terminated string of characters, but it could also represent a pointer to a single character or a pointer to an array of characters. In RPC language, a null-terminated string is unambiguously called a string.

There are just two more things to write:

- the remote procedure itself
- the main client program that calls it

Here's one possible definition of a remote procedure to implement the PRINTMESSAGE procedure we declared above:

```
/*
 * msg_proc.c: implementation of the remote procedure "printmessage"
 */

#include <stdio.h>
#include <rpc/rpc.h>          /* always needed */
#include "msg.h"              /* msg.h will be generated by rpcgen */
/*
 * Remote version of "printmessage"
 */
int *
printmessage_1(msg)
        char **msg;
{
        static int result; /* must be static! */
        FILE *f;

        f = fopen("/dev/console", "w");
        if (f == NULL) {
                result = 0;
                return (&result);
        }
        fprintf(f, "%s\n", *msg);
        fclose(f);
        result = 1;
        return (&result);
}
```

Notice that the declaration of the remote procedure `printmessage_1()` differs from that of the local procedure `printmessage()` in three ways:

- It takes a pointer to a string instead of a string itself. This is true of all remote procedures: they always take pointers to their arguments rather than the arguments themselves.

- It returns a pointer to an integer instead of an integer itself. This is also characteristic of remote procedures: they return pointers to their results.

When rpcgen is used, it is essential to have result (in this example) declared as static.

In the code generated by rpcgen, the result address is converted to XDR format *after* the remote procedure returns. If the result were declared local to the remote procedure, references to its address would be invalid after the remote procedure returned. So the result *must* be declared static when rpcgen is used.

- It has _1 appended to its name. In general, all remote procedures called by rpcgen are named by the following rule: the procedure name in the program definition (here PRINTMESSAGE) is converted to all lower-case letters, an underbar (_) is appended to it, and the version number (here 1) is appended.

The last thing to do is declare the main client program that will call the remote procedure. Here is one possibility:

```
/*
 * rprintmsg.c: remote version of "printmsg.c"
 */
#include <stdio.h>
#include <rpc/rpc.h>        /* always needed    */
#include "msg.h"            /* msg.h will be generated by rpcgen */

main(argc, argv)
        int argc;
        char *argv[];
{
        CLIENT *cl;
        int *result;
        char *server;
        char *message;

        if (argc != 3) {
                fprintf(stderr,
                "usage: %s host message\n", argv[0]);
                exit(1);
        }
```

(continued on next page)

```
/*
 * Save values of command line arguments
 */
server = argv[1];
message = argv[2];

/*
 * Create client "handle" used for calling MESSAGEPROG on the
 * server designated on the command line.
 */
cl = clnt_create(server, MESSAGEPROG, MESSAGEVERS,
   "visible");
if (cl == NULL) {
        /*
         * Couldn't establish connection with server.
         * Print error message and die.
         */
        clnt_pcreateerror(server);
        exit(1);
}


/*
 * Call the remote procedure "printmessage" on the server
 */
result = printmessage_1(&message, cl);
if (result == NULL) {
        /*
         * An error occurred while calling the server.
         * Print error message and die.
         */
        clnt_perror(cl, server);
        exit(1);
}
/*
 * Okay, we successfully called the remote procedure.
 */
if (*result == 0) {
        /*
         * Server was unable to print our message.
         * Print error message and die.
         */
        fprintf(stderr, "%s: %s couldn't print your message\n",
                argv[0], server);
                exit(1);
}
```

(continued on next page)

```
        /*
         * The message got printed on the server's console
         */
        printf("Message delivered to %s!\n", server);
        exit(0);
    }
```

There are four things to note here:

- First a client *handle* is created using the RPC library routine
  `clnt_create()` . This client handle will be passed to the stub routines
  that call the remote procedure. (The client handle can be created in other
  ways as well, see the "Remote Procedure Call Programming Guide"
  chapter for details.)

- The last parameter to `clnt_create()` is ``visible'', which specifies
  that any transport noted as visible in /etc/netconfig can be used.

- The remote procedure `printmessage_1()` is called exactly the same
  way as it is declared in `msg_proc.c` except for the inserted client handle
  as the second argument. It also returns a pointer to the result instead of
  the result itself.

- The remote procedure call can fail in two ways. The RPC mechanism
  itself can fail or, alternatively, there can be an error in the execution of the
  remote procedure. In the former case, the remote procedure [in this case
  `print_message_1()`] returns with a NULL. In the later case, however,
  the details of error reporting are application dependent. Here, the error is
  being reported via `*result`.

Here's how to put all the pieces together:

```
$ rpcgen msg.x
$ cc rprintmsg.c msg_clnt.c -o rprintmsg -lnsl
$ cc msg_proc.c msg_svc.c -o msg_server -lnsl
```

Two programs are compiled here: the client program `rprintmsg` and the server program `msg_server`. Before doing this, `rpcgen` was used to fill in the missing pieces.

Here is what `rpcgen` (called without any flags) did with the input file `msg.x`:

1. It created a header file called `msg.h` that contained `#define` statements for `MESSAGEPROG`, `MESSAGEVERS` and `PRINTMESSAGE` for use in the other modules.

2. It created the client "stub" routines in the `msg_clnt.c` file. Here there is only one, the `printmessage_1()` routine, that was called from the `rprintmsg` client program. If the name of an rpcgen input file is `FOO.x`, the client stubs output file is called `FOO_clnt.c`.

3. It created the server program in `msg_svc.c` that calls `printmessage_1()` from `msg_proc.c`. The rule for naming the server output file is similar to the previous one: for an input file called `FOO.x`, the output server file is named `FOO_svc.c`.

 NOTE If invoked with the `-T` argument, `rpcgen` creates an additional output file that contains index information used for the dispatching of service routines.

Once created, the server should be copied to a remote machine and run. (If the machines are homogeneous, the server can be copied as a binary. Otherwise, the source files will need to be copied to and compiled on the remote machine.) For this example, the remote machine is called `remote` and the local machine is called `local`. The server is started from the shell on the remote system:

```
remote$ msg_server
```

NOTE Server processes, like `msg_server`, created with `rpcgen` always run in the background. It is not necessary to follow the server's invocation with an ampersand (&). Servers generated by `rpcgen` can also be invoked with port monitors like `listen` and `inetd`, instead of from the command line.

Thereafter, a user on `local` can print a message on the console of system `remote` as follows:

```
local$ rprintmsg remote "Hello, there."
```

Using `rprintmsg`, a user can print a message on any system console (including the `local` console) if the server `msg_server` is running on the target system.

Generating XDR Routines with rpcgen

The previous example illustrated the automatic generation of client and server RPC code. `rpcgen` may also be used to generate XDR routines, i.e., the routines necessary to convert local data structures into XDR format and vice-versa.

This example presents a complete RPC service: a remote directory listing service, built using `rpcgen` not only to generate stub routines, but also to generate the XDR routines.

Here is the protocol description file:

Programmer's Guide: Networking Interfaces

```
/*
 * dir.x: Remote directory listing protocol
 */
const MAXNAMELEN = 255;                  /* maximum length of a directory entry */
typedef string nametype<MAXNAMELEN>;     /* a directory entry */
typedef struct namenode *namelist;       /* a link in the listing */

/*
 * A node in the directory listing
 */
struct namenode {
        nametype name;                   /* name of directory entry */
        namelist next;                   /* next entry */
};

/*
 * The result of a READDIR operation.
 */
union readdir_res switch (int errno) {
case 0:
        namelist list;       /* no error: return directory listing */
default:
        void;                /* error occurred: nothing else to return */
};

/*
 * The directory program definition
 */
program DIRPROG {
        version DIRVERS {
                readdir_res
                READDIR(nametype) = 1;
        } = 1;
} = 0x20000076;
```

NOTE Types (like readdir_res in the example above) can be defined using the struct, union and enum keywords. These keywords should not be used in later declarations of variables of those types. For example, if you define a union foo, you should declare using only foo and not union foo.

rpcgen compiles RPC unions into C structures. It is an error to declare RPC unions using the union keyword.

Running rpcgen on dir.x creates four output files. First are the basic three described previously: those containing the header file, client stub routines and server skeleton.

The fourth contains the XDR routines necessary for converting instances of declared data types from host platform representation into XDR format, and vice-versa. These routines are output in the file dir_xdr.c.

For each data type used in the .x file, rpcgen assumes that the RPC/XDR library contains a routine whose name is the name of the datatype, prepended by xdr_ (e.g. xdr_int). If a data type is defined in the .x file, then rpcgen generates the required xdr_ routine.

If there are no such data types definitions, in an RPC source file (e.g. msg.x), then an _xdr.c file will not be generated.

An RPC programmer may write a .x source file that uses a data type not supported by the RPC/XDR library, and deliberately omit defining the type (in the .x file); if so, the programmer has to provide that xdr_ routine. This is a way for programmers to provide their own customized xdr_ routines. See the "Remote Procedure Call Programming Guide" chapter for more details on passing arbitrary data types.

Here is the server-side implementation of the READDIR procedure.

```
/*
 * dir_proc.c: remote readdir implementation
 */
#include <rpc/rpc.h>                    /* Always needed */
#include <dirent.h>
#include "dir.h"                        /* Created by rpcgen */

extern int errno;
extern char *malloc();
extern char *strdup();

readdir_res *
readdir_1(dirname)
        nametype *dirname;
{

        DIR *dirp;
        struct dirent *d;
        namelist nl;
        namelist *nlp;
        static readdir_res res; /* must be static! */

        /*
         * Open directory
         */
        dirp = opendir(*dirname);
        if (dirp == NULL) {
                res.errno = errno;
                return (&res);
        }
        /*
         * Free previous result
         */
        xdr_free(xdr_readdir_res, &res);
        /*
         * Collect directory entries.
         * Memory allocated here will be freed by xdr_free
         * next time readdir_1 is called
         */
        nlp = &res.readdir_res_u.list;
        while (d = readdir(dirp)) {
                nl = *nlp = (namenode *) malloc(sizeof(namenode));
                nl->name = strdup(d->d_name);
                nlp = &nl->next;
        }
        *nlp = NULL;
```

(continued on next page)

```
        /*
         * Return the result
         */
        res.errno = 0;
        closedir(dirp);
        return (&res);
}
```

Here is the client side program to call the server:

```
/*
 * rls.c: Remote directory listing client
 */

#include <stdio.h>
#include <rpc/rpc.h>        /* always need this */
#include "dir.h"            /* will be generated by rpcgen */

extern int errno;

main(argc, argv)
        int argc;
        char *argv[];

{
        CLIENT *cl;
        char *server;
        char *dir;
        readdir_res *result;
        namelist nl;

        if (argc != 3) {
                fprintf(stderr, "usage: %s host directory\n",
                    argv[0]);
                exit(1);
        }

        /*
         * Remember what our command line arguments refer to
         */
```

(continued on next page)

Programmer's Guide: Networking Interfaces

```
        server = argv[1];
        dir = argv[2];

        /*
         * Create client "handle" used for calling MESSAGEPROG on the
         * server designated on the command line.  We tell the RPC package
         * to use any visible transport when contacting the server.
         */

        cl = clnt_create(server, DIRPROG, DIRVERS, "visible");
        if (cl == NULL) {
                /*
                 * Couldn't establish connection with server.
                 * Print error message and die.
                 */
                clnt_pcreateerror(server);
                exit(1);
        }

        /*
         * Call the remote procedure readdir on the server
         */

        result = readdir_1(&dir, cl);
        if (result == NULL) {
                /*
                 * An error occurred while calling the server.
                 * Print error message and die.
                 */
                clnt_perror(cl, server);
                exit(1);
        }

        /*
         * Okay, we successfully called the remote procedure.
         */

        if (result->errno != 0) {
                /*
                 * A remote system error occurred.
                 * Print error message and die.
                 */
                errno = result->errno;
                perror(dir);
                exit(1);
        }
```

(continued on next page)

```
/*
 * Successfully got a directory listing.
 * Print it out.
 */

for (nl = result->readdir_res_u.list; nl != NULL;
    nl = nl->next) {
            printf("%s\n", nl->name);
}

exit(0);
}
```

Again using the hypothetical systems named local and remote, the files can be compiled and run as follows:

```
remote$  rpcgen dir.x
remote$  cc -c dir_xdr.c
remote$  cc rls.c dir_clnt.c dir_xdr.o -o rls -lnsl
remote$  cc dir_svc.c dir_proc.c dir_xdr.o -o dir_svc -lnsl

remote$  dir_svc
```

After installing an executable copy of rls on system local, a user on that system can list the contents of /usr/share/lib on system remote as follows:

```
local$  rls remote /usr/share/lib
.

..
ascii
eqnchar
greek
kbd
marg8
tabclr
tabs
tabs4
local$
```

Using Preprocessing Directives

The rpcgen compiler supports C and other preprocessing features.

C-preprocessing is performed on rpcgen input files before they are compiled.
All C-preprocessing directives are legal within a .x file. Five symbols may be
defined by rpcgen, depending on the type of output file being generated. The
symbols are:

Symbol	Usage
RPC_HDR	For header-file output
RPC_XDR	For XDR routine output
RPC_SVC	For server-skeleton output
RPC_CLNT	For client stub output
RPC_TBL	For index table output

The rpcgen compiler provides an additional preprocessing feature: any line
that begins with a percent sign (%) is passed directly into the output file,
without any interpretation of the line.

The % feature is not always useful, owing to a limitation: The rpcgen compiler may not place the lines where the programmer intended.

Here is a simple example that illustrates rpcgen preprocessing features:

```
/*
 * time.x: Remote time protocol
 */
program TIMEPROG {
        version TIMEVERS {
                        unsigned int TIMEGET(void) = 1;
                } = 1;
} = 0x20000044;

#ifdef RPC_SVC
%int *
%timeget_1()
%{
%       static int thetime;
%
%       thetime = time(0);
%       return (&thetime);
%}
#endif
```

Common RPC Programming Techniques

This section suggests some coding and rpcgen usage techniques.

network types	rpcgen can produce for specific transport types (or even specific transports)
timeout changes	client default timeout periods can be changed
authentication	clients may authenticate themselves to servers; interested servers can examine client authentication information
define statements	C-preprocessing symbols can be defined on rpcgen command lines
broadcast calls	servers need not send NULL replies to broadcast calls
port monitor support	port monitors can "listen" for RPC servers
dispatch tables	programs can access server dispatch tables
debugging	clients and servers created with rpcgen can be linked and run on a single system for debugging purposes

Network Types (transport selection)

The rpcgen compiler takes optional arguments that allow a programmer to specify a desired network type or even a specific network identifier. (For details about network selection, see the "Remote Procedure Call Programming Guide" chapter.)

 NOTE In the context of RPC programming, the term *network* is frequently used (as here) as a synonym for *transport* or *transport type*.

The −s flag creates a server that responds to requests on all transports of a specified type. For example, the invocation

```
rpcgen −s datagram_n prot.x
```

writes a server to standard output that responds to any of the connectionless

transports specified in the NETPATH environment variable (or in
/etc/netconfig, if NETPATH is not defined or does not specify any connectionless transports).

Similarly, the −n flag creates a server that responds only to requests from the
transport specified by a single network identifier.

 Be careful using servers created by rpcgen with the −n flag. Because
network identifiers are host-specific, the server produced may not run on
other hosts in the expected way.

Timeout Changes

After sending a request to the server, a client program waits for a default
amount of time (25 seconds) to receive a reply. This timeout may be changed
using the clnt_control() routine. [See rpc(3N).]

 When considering timeout periods, be sure to allow for the minimal
amount of time required for "round trip" communications over the network.

Here is a small code fragment to illustrate the use of clnt_control():

```
struct timeval tv;
CLIENT *cl;

cl = clnt_create("somehost", SOMEPROG, SOMEVERS, "visible");
if (cl == NULL) {
        exit(1);
}
tv.tv_sec = 60;    /* change timeout to 1 minute */
tv.tv_usec = 0;
clnt_control(cl, CLSET_TIMEOUT, &tv);
```

Client Authentication

The client create routines do not, by default, have any facilities for client authentication, but the client may sometimes want (or be required) to authenticate itself to the server. Doing so is trivial, and looks about like this:

 WARNING The following example illustrates one of the *least* secure authentication methods in common use. See the "Remote Procedure Call Programming Guide" for information on the more secure DES authentication technique.

```
CLIENT *cl;

cl = client_create("somehost", SOMEPROG, SOMEVERS, "visible");
if (cl != NULL) {
        /* To set AUTH_SYS style authentication */
        cl->cl_auth = authsys_createdefault();
}
```

Servers that want to know more about an RPC call can check authentication information. For example, getting authentication information is important to servers that want to achieve some level of security. This extra information is actually supplied to the server as a second argument. (For details, see the structure of svc_req, in the "Authentication" section of the "Remote Procedure Call Programming Guide" chapter.

Here is an example of a remote procedure whose server checks client authentication information. This is a rewrite of the printmessage_1() that is developed in the "An rpcgen Tutorial" section. The rewritten procedure will only allow root users to print a message to the console:

```
int *
printmessage_1(msg, rq)
        char **msg;
        struct svc_req      *rq;
{
        static int result; /* Must be static */
        FILE *f;
        struct authsys_parms *aup;

        aup = (struct authsys_parms *)rq->rq_clntcred;
        if (aup->aup_uid != 0) {
                result = 0;
                return (&result);
        }

        /*
         * Same code as before.
         */
}
```

rpcgen Command-line Define Statements

The rpcgen compiler provides a means for defining C-preprocessing symbols
and assigning values to them from the command line. Command-line define
statements can, for example, be used to compile conditional debugging code
that is compiled only when the DEBUG symbol is defined. For example:

```
$ rpcgen -DDEBUG proto.x
```

Server Response to Broadcast Calls

When a procedure is known to have been called via broadcast RPC, and the called procedure determines that it cannot provide the client with a useful response, it is usually best for the server to send no reply back to the client. This reduces network traffic.

To prevent the server from replying, a remote procedure can return NULL as its result. The server code generated by rpcgen will detect this and not send out a reply.

Here is an example of a procedure that replies only if it thinks it is an NFS server:

```
void *
reply_if_nfsserver_1()
{
        char notnull;       /* just here so we can use its address */

        if (access("/etc/exports", F_OK) < 0) {
                return (NULL);      /* prevent RPC from replying */
        }
        /*
         * assign notnull a non-null value so RPC will send out a reply
         */
        return ((void *)&notnull);
}
```

> **NOTE** If a procedure returns type void *, it *must* return a non-NULL pointer if it wants RPC to send a reply.

Port Monitor Support

Port monitors such as `inetd` and `listen` can monitor network addresses for specified RPC services. Whenever a request comes in for a particular service, the port monitor spawns a server process to provide for it. After the call has been serviced, the server can exit. This has the advantage of conserving system resources: fewer blocked processes waiting for work.

It may be useful for services to wait for a specified interval after satisfying a service request, on the chance that another request will follow. If there is no call within the specified time, the server will exit and some port monitors, like `inetd`, will continue to monitor for the server. If a later request for the service occurs, the port monitor will give the request to a waiting server process (if any), rather than spawning a new process.

 When monitoring for a server, some port monitors, like `listen`, *always* spawn a new process in response to a service request. If it is known that a server will be used with such a monitor, the server should exit immediately on completion.

By default, services created using `rpcgen` wait for 120 seconds after servicing a request before exiting. The programmer can, however, change that interval with the −K flag.

```
$ rpcgen -K 20 proto.x
```

Here the server will wait only for 20 seconds before exiting. To create a server that exits immediately, −K 0 can be used. To create a server that never exits (a normal server), the appropriate argument is −K −1.

All servers generated by `rpcgen` assume the following support from port monitors:

- the name of the transport provider is passed through the environment variable NLS_PROVIDER

- the connection is passed on an open TLI file descriptor 0

See the "Using Port Monitors" section of the "Remote Procedure Call Programming Guide" chapter for a further discussion of port monitors.

Dispatch Tables

It is sometimes useful for programs to have access to dispatch tables used by the RPC package. For example, the server dispatch routine may need to check authorization and then invoke the service routine; or a client library may want to deal with the details of storage management and XDR data conversion.

When invoked with the −T option, rpcgen generates RPC dispatch tables for each program defined in the protocol description file, *proto*.x, in the file *proto*_tbl.i. For sample protocol description file, dir.x, given in the "Generating XDR Routines with rpcgen" section, above, a dispatch table file created by rpcgen would be called dir_tbl.i. The suffix .i stands for "index."

Each entry in the dispatch table is a struct rpcgen_table, defined in the header file proto.h as follows:

```
struct rpcgen_table {
        char        *(*proc) ();
        xdrproc_t   xdr_arg;
        unsigned    len_arg;
        xdrproc_t   xdr_res;
        unsigned    len_res;
};
```

where

proc   is a pointer to the service routine,

xdr_arg   is a pointer to the input (argument) xdr_ routine,

len_arg   is the length in bytes of the input argument,

xdr_res   is a pointer to the output (result) xdr_ routine, and

len_res   is the length in bytes of the output result.

The table, named `dirprog_1_table` for the example, is indexed by procedure number. The variable `dirprog_1_nproc` contains the number of entries in the table.

An example of how to locate a procedure in the dispatch tables is shown by the routine `find_proc ()` :

```
struct rpcgen_table *
find_proc(proc)
        long      proc;
{
        if (proc >= dirprog_1_nproc)
                /* error */
        else
                return (&dirprog_1_table[proc]);
}
```

Each entry in the dispatch table contains a pointer to the corresponding service routine. However, that service routine is usually not defined in the client code. To avoid generating unresolved external references, and to require only one source file for the dispatch table, the `rpcgen` service routine initializer is `RPCGEN_ACTION (proc_ver)`.

This way, the same dispatch table can be included in both the client and the server. Use the following define when compiling the client:

```
#define RPCGEN_ACTION(routine)        0
```

and use this define when compiling the server:

```
#define RPCGEN_ACTION(routine)        routine
```

Debugging with rpcgen

When programming with rpcgen, the client program and the server procedure can be tested together as a single program by linking them with each other rather than with the client and server stubs. To do this, calls to RPC library routines [e.g. clnt_create()], have to be commented out, and client-side routines have to call server routines directly. The procedure calls will be executed as ordinary local procedure calls and the program can be debugged with a local debugger. After the program is working, the client program can be linked to the rpcgen-created client stubs and the server procedures can be linked to the rpcgen-created server skeleton.

RPC Language Reference

RPC language is an extension of the XDR language. The sole extension is the addition of the `program` and `version` types.

For a complete description of the XDR language syntax, see the "External Data Representation: Protocol Specification" chapter. For a description of the RPC extensions to the XDR language, see the "Remote Procedure Calls: Protocol Specification" chapter.

RPC language is similar to C language. We describe here the syntax of the RPC language, showing a few examples along the way. We also show how the various RPC and XDR type definitions get compiled into C type definitions in the output header file.

Definitions

An RPC language file consists of a series of definitions.

> *definition-list:*
> > *definition ;*
> > *definition ; definition-list*

It recognizes six types of definitions.

> *definition:*
> > *enum-definition*
> > *const-definition*
> > *typedef-definition*
> > *struct-definition*
> > *union-definition*
> > *program-definition*

Enumerations

RPC/XDR enumerations have the same syntax as C enumerations.

> *enum-definition:*
> > enum *enum-ident* {
> > > *enum-value-list*
> >
> > }
>
> *enum-value-list:*
> > *enum-value*
> > *enum-value* , *enum-value-list*
>
> *enum-value:*
> > *enum-value-ident*
> > *enum-value-ident* = *value*

Here is a short example of an RCP/XDR enum, and the C enum to which it gets compiled.

```
enum colortype {              enum colortype {
    RED = 0,                      RED = 0,
    GREEN = 1,     -->            GREEN = 1,
    BLUE = 2                      BLUE = 2,
};                            };
                              typedef enum colortype colortype;
```

Constants

RPC/XDR symbolic constants may be used wherever an integer constant is used, for example, in array size specifications.

> *const-definition:*
> > const *const-ident* = *integer*

For example, the following defines a constant, DOZEN, equal to 12.

```
const DOZEN = 12;   -->   #define DOZEN 12
```

Typedefs

RPC/XDR typedefs have the same syntax as C typedefs.

> *typedef-definition:*
> > `typedef` *declaration*

Here is an example that defines an `fname_type` used for declaring file name strings that have a maximum length of 255 characters.

> `typedef string fname_type<255>;` `-->` `typedef char *fname_type;`

Declarations

In RPC/XDR, there are four kinds of declarations.

> *declaration:*
> > *simple-declaration*
> > *fixed-array-declaration*
> > *variable-array-declaration*
> > *pointer-declaration*

Simple Declarations: Simple declarations are just like simple C declarations.

> *simple-declaration:*
> > *type-ident variable-ident*

Example:

> `colortype color;` `--> colortype color;`

Fixed-length Array Declarations: Fixed-length array declarations are just like C array declarations:

> *fixed-array-declaration:*
> > *type-ident variable-ident [value]*

Example:

> `colortype palette[8];` `--> colortype palette[8];`

Variable-Length Array Declarations: Variable-length array declarations have no explicit syntax in C. The RPC/XDR does have a syntax; it uses angle-brackets.

> *variable-array-declaration:*
> > *type-ident variable-ident < value >*
> > *type-ident variable-ident < >*

The maximum size is specified between the angle brackets. The size may be omitted, indicating that the array may be of any size.

```
int heights<12>;    /* at most 12 items */
int widths<>;       /* any number of items */
```

Because variable-length arrays have no explicit syntax in C, these declarations are compiled into `struct` declarations. For example, the `heights` declaration gets compiled into the following `struct`:

```
struct {
        u_int heights_len;      /* # of items in array */
        int *heights_val;       /* pointer to array */
} heights;
```

Note that the number of items in the array is stored in the `_len` component and the pointer to the array is stored in the `_val` component. The first part of each of these component's names is the same as the name of the declared RPC/XDR variable.

Pointer Declarations: Pointer declarations are made in RPC/XDR exactly as they are in C. Address pointers cannot really be sent over the network, but RPC/XDR pointers are useful for sending recursive data types such as lists and trees. The type is actually called "optional-data," not "pointer," in XDR language.

> *pointer-declaration:*
> > *type-ident *variable-ident*

Example:

```
listitem *next;   -->   listitem *next;
```

Structures

An RPC/XDR `struct` is declared almost exactly like its C counterpart. It looks like the following:

> *struct-definition:*
>   `struct` *struct-ident* {
>   *declaration-list*
>
>   }
>
> *declaration-list:*
>   *declaration ;*
>   *declaration ; declaration-list*

As an example, here is an RPC/XDR structure for a two-dimensional coordinate, and the C structure that it gets compiled into in the output header file.

```
struct coord {              struct coord {
     int x;        -->           int x;
     int y;                      int y;
};                          };
                            typedef struct coord coord;
```

The output is identical to the input, except for the added `typedef` at the end of the output. This allows one to use `coord` instead of `struct coord` when declaring items.

Unions

RPC/XDR unions are discriminated unions, and look different from C unions. They are more analogous to Pascal variant records than they are to C unions.

> *union-definition:*
>   `union` *union-ident* `switch` (*simple declaration*) {
>   *case-list*
>
>   }
>
> *case-list:*
>   `case` *value* : *declaration ;*
>   `case` *value* : *declaration ; case-list*
>   `default` : *declaration ;*

Here is an example of a type that might be returned as the result of a "read data" operation: if there is no error, return a block of data; otherwise, don't return anything.

```
union read_result switch (int errno) {
case 0:
        opaque data[1024];
default:
        void;
};
```

It gets compiled into the following:

```
struct read_result {
        int errno;
        union {
                char data[1024];
        } read_result_u;
};
typedef struct read_result read_result;
```

Notice that the union component of the output struct has the name as the type name, except for the trailing _u.

Programs

RPC/XDR programs are declared using the following syntax:

program-definition:
>   program *program-ident* {
>   *version-list*
>   } = *value*

version-list:
>   version ;
>   version ; version-list

version:
>   version *version-ident* {
>   *procedure-list*
>   } = *value*

procedure-list:
>   procedure ;
>   procedure ; procedure-list

procedure:
>   type-ident procedure-ident (type-ident) = value

For example:

```
/*
 * time.x: Get or set the time.  Time is represented as seconds
 * since 0:00, January 1, 1970.
 */
program TIMEPROG {
        version TIMEVERS {
                unsigned int TIMEGET(void) = 1;
                void TIMESET(unsigned) = 2;
        } = 1;
} = 0x20000044;
```

This file compiles into these #defines in the output header file:

```
#define TIMEPROG 0x20000044
#define TIMEVERS 1
#define TIMEGET 1
#define TIMESET 2
```

Special Cases

There are a few exceptions to the rules described above.

Booleans: C has no built-in boolean type. However, the RPC library uses a boolean type called `bool_t` that is either `TRUE` or `FALSE`. Things declared as type `bool` in RPC/XDR language are compiled into `bool_t` in the output header file.

Example:

```
bool married;  --> bool_t married;
```

Strings: C has no built-in string type, but instead uses the null-terminated `char *` convention. In RPC/XDR language, strings are declared using the `string` keyword, and compiled into type `char *` in the output header file. The maximum size contained in the angle brackets specifies the maximum number of characters allowed in the strings (not counting the `NULL` character). The maximum size may be left off, indicating a string of arbitrary length.

Examples:

```
string name<32>;  --> char *name;
string longname<>;  --> char *longname;
```

Opaque Data: Opaque data is used in RPC/XDR to describe untyped data, that is, just sequences of arbitrary bytes. It may be declared either as a fixed or variable length array. Examples:

```
opaque diskblock[512]; --> char diskblock[512];

opaque filedata<1024>; --> struct {
                                 u_int filedata_len;
                                 char *filedata_val;
                             } filedata;
```

Voids: In a void declaration, the variable is not named. The declaration is just `void` and nothing else. Void declarations can only occur in two places: union definitions and program definitions (as the argument or result of a remote procedure).

7 Remote Procedure Call Programming Guide

Introduction

The RPC package provides a multi-level application programming interface for development of network applications using remote procedure calls.

At the *simplified interface* (the highest level), the package provides great *transparency*, but offers only limited control over the underlying communications mechanisms. Program development at the simplified interface can be rapid, and is directly supported by the rpcgen compiler — a C-language code generator that supports remote procedure call program development.

 NOTE The "Generating XDR Routines with rpcgen" section of the "rpcgen Programming Guide" contains the complete source for a working RPC service: a remote directory listing service that uses rpcgen to generate XDR routines as well as client and server stubs. For most applications, rpcgen and its facilities are fully adequate and the detailed information in this chapter is not required.

Interfaces to *lower levels* of the RPC package provide increasing *control* over remote procedure call communications. Programs that exercise this control pay for the power in terms of greater *complexity* of code. Effective programming at the lower levels requires knowledge of computer network fundamentals.

In order of increasing control and complexity, these levels are called the *Top Level*, *Intermediate Level*, *Expert Level* and *Bottom Level*.

This chapter is intended for programmers who wish to write network applications using remote procedure calls, and who want to use or understand the RPC mechanisms usually hidden by the rpcgen(1) protocol compiler.

An Overview of the RPC Package

The RPC interface can be seen as being divided into several distinct levels. The highest level is general, and provides for no fine control of any kind. The lower levels (four can be usefully distinguished) are available for use as necessary, and provide increasingly detailed levels of control.

NOTE For a complete specification of the routines in the RPC library, see the rpc(3N) and related manual pages.

The Simplified Interface: Here, the programmer doesn't need to consider the characteristics of the underlying transport, operating system, or other low-level implementation mechanisms. Programmers simply make remote procedure calls to routines on other machines, and need specify only the *type* of transport that they wish to use. The selling point here is simplicity. It is this level that allows RPC to pass the "hello world" test — that simple things should be simple. The routines at this level are used for most applications.

Included in the simplified interface are only three basic RPC routines:

rpc_reg()
: rpc_reg() registers a routine as an RPC routine and obtains a unique, system-wide procedure-identification number for it.

rpc_call()
: Given such a unique, system-wide procedure-identification number, rpc_call() uses it to make a remote call to that routine on a specified host.

rpc_broadcast()
: Like rpc_call(), except that it broadcasts its call message across all transports of the specified type.

The Top Level: At the top level, the interface is still simple, but the programmer does have to create client and server handles before making a call. Like the routines in the simplified interface, the routines here require a nettype argument that specifies a general class (type) of transports.

The top level essentially consists of two routines:

clnt_create()
: The generic client creation. The programmer tells clnt_create() where the server is located and the type of transport to use to get to it.

svc_create()
: Creates server handles for all the transports of the specified nettype. The programmer tells svc_create() which dispatch function should be used.

The simplified interface and the top level of RPC, while simple, are also inefficient. They do not allow the choice of a specific transport (but see the discussion of NTEPATH, below). At these levels, all routines just take a nettype argument, which serves to define the class of transport to be used. On the client side, programs do network selection, and hence may be slightly inefficient depending on the nettype. On the server side, programs may have to listen on many transports, and hence may waste system resources.

In both of these cases, however, efficiency can be improved by judicious assignment to the NETPATH environment variable. If the programmer wishes the application to run on all transports, this is the interface that should be used.

The Intermediate Level: The intermediate interface of RPC, and the two interfaces below it, allow many details to be controlled by the programmer, and for that reason their use is necessary for special applications. Programmers should only go down to the level necessary for the control needed. Programs written at these lower levels are more complicated, but also more efficient.

The intermediate differs from the two levels above it in that it allows the programmer to specify directly the transport to be used. It consists of two routines:

clnt_tp_create()   Creates a client handle for a specified transport.

svc_tp_create()   Likewise, svc_tp_create() creates a server handle for a specified transport.

The Expert Level: The expert level consists of a larger set of routines with which the programmer can specify more parameters, but those parameters are still all directly transport related. It includes the following routines:

clnt_tli_create()   Creates a client handle for a specified transport, allowing fine control of the client characteristics.

svc_tli_create()   Creates a server handle for a specified transport, allowing fine control of the server characteristics.

rpcb_set(),   Provides a programmatic interface to rpcbind, one that establishes a mapping between an RPC service and a network address.

rpcb_unset()   Destroys a mapping of the type established by rpcb_set.

rpcb_getaddr()	Provides a programmatic interface to rpcbind, one that returns the transport address of specified RPC service.
svc_reg()	Associates a given program and version number pair with a given dispatch routine.
svc_unreg()	Destroys an association of the type established by svc_reg.

The Bottom Level: The bottom level consists of routines called when the programmer requires full control, even down to the smallest details of transport options. It consists of the following routines:

clnt_dg_create()	Creates an RPC client for the specified remote program, using a connectionless transport.
svc_dg_create()	Creates an RPC server handle, using a connectionless transport.
clnt_vc_create()	Creates an RPC client for the specified remote program, using a connection-oriented transport.
svc_vc_create()	Creates an RPC server handle, using a connection-oriented transport.

Organization of Technical Information

"The Simplified Interface to RPC" section describes programming with RPC library-based services, and calling RPC functions using the simplest RPC interfaces. Programming with arbitrary data types is also addressed.

The next three sections serve as a general reference to the lower levels of the RPC package.

"The Lower Levels of RPC" section illustrates the client- and server-side programming interfaces of each of the four lower levels of the RPC package.

The "Low-level Data Structures" section provides reference information on RPC handles and the authentication structure used for secure RPC communications.

The "Low-level Program Testing Using Raw RPC" section describes *pseudo*-RPC interfaces that are provided by the package for testing purposes.

The remaining sections focus on particular aspects of low-level RPC programming.

The "Advanced RPC Programming Techniques," comments on developing RPC applications programs that take advantage of the lower level interfaces.

The "Advanced Examples" section illustrates how some important programming tasks are done using the RPC low-level interfaces.

The Simplified Interface to RPC

The easiest interface to RPC does not require the programmer to use the interface at all. "RPC Library-based Network Services" describes using functions that hide all details of the RPC package.

Some RPC services are not available as C functions, but are available as RPC programs. "Remote Procedure Call and Registration" shows how easy it is to use these services, and how easy it is to create new services that are equally simple to use.

Data types passed to and received from remote procedures can be any of a set of predefined types, or can be programmer-defined types. "Passing Arbitrary Data Types" explains how such types are declared and used.

RPC Library-based Network Services

Imagine writing a program that needs to know how many users are logged into a remote machine. This can be done by calling an RPC library routine, rusers(), as illustrated below:

```
#include <stdio.h>

/*
 * a program that calls rusers()
 */

main(argc, argv)
        int argc;
        char **argv;
{
        int num;

        if (argc != 2) {
                fprintf(stderr, "usage: %s hostname\n", argv[0]);
                exit(1);
        }
        if ((num = rusers(argv[1])) < 0) {
                fprintf(stderr, "error: rusers\n");
                exit(1);
        }
        printf("%d users on %s\n", num, argv[1]);
        exit(0);
}
```

NOTE For rusers() to work, the rusers daemon must be running on the remote host.

RPC library routines such as rusers() are in the RPC services library librpcsvc.a. Thus, the program above should be compiled with

```
$ cc program.c -lrpcsvc -lnsl
```

Here are some of the RPC service library routines available to the C programmer:

Routine	Description
rusers()	Return information about users on remote machine
rwall()	Write to specified remote machines
spray()	Spray packets to a specific machine

Remote Procedure Call and Registration

The simplest interface to the RPC functions is based on the routines
rpc_call(), rpc_reg(), and rpc_broadcast(). These functions provide
direct access to the RPC facilities, and are appropriate for programs that do not
require fine levels of control.

Using the simplified interface, the number of remote users can be gotten as follows:

```
#include <stdio.h>
#include <rpc/rpc.h>
#include <rpcsvc/rusers.h>

/*
 * a program that calls the RUSERSPROG RPC program
 */

main(argc, argv)
        int argc;
        char **argv;
{
        unsigned long nusers;
        int clnt_stat;

        if (argc != 2) {
                fprintf(stderr, "usage: rusers hostname\n");
                exit();
        }
        if (clnt_stat = rpc_call(argv[1],
          RUSERSPROG, RUSERSVERS, RUSERSPROC_NUM,
          xdr_void, 0, xdr_u_long, &nusers, "visible") != 0) {
                clnt_perrno(clnt_stat);
                exit(1);
        }
        printf("%d users on %s\n", nusers, argv[1]);
        exit(0);
}
```

The rpc_call() Routine

The simplest way of making remote procedure calls is with the RPC library routine rpc_call(). It has nine parameters.

■ The first is the name of the remote server machine.

■ The next three parameters are the program, version, and procedure numbers. Together, they identify the remote procedure to be called.

■ The fifth and sixth parameters are an XDR filter for encoding and an argument that has to be passed to the remote procedure.

- The next two parameters are an XDR filter for decoding the results returned by the remote procedure and a pointer to the place where the procedure's results are to be stored.

- Finally, there is the nettype specifier.

Multiple arguments and results are handled by embedding them in structures. If rpc_call() completes successfully, it returns zero; otherwise, it returns a nonzero value. The return codes (of type enum clnt_stat, cast to an int in the previous example) are found in <rpc/clnt.h>.

Because data types may be represented differently on different machines, rpc_call() needs both the type of, and a pointer to, the RPC argument (similarly for the result). For RUSERSPROC_NUM, the return value is an unsigned long, so rpc_call() has xdr_u_long() as its first return parameter, which says that the result is of type unsigned long; and &nusers as its second return parameter, which is a pointer to where the long result will be placed. Because RUSERSPROC_NUM takes no argument, the argument parameter of rpc_call() is xdr_void().

If rpc_call() gets no answer within a certain time period, it returns with an error code. In the example, it tries all the transports listed in /etc/netconfig that are flagged as visible. Adjusting the number of retries requires use of the lower levels of the RPC library, discussed later in this chapter. The remote server procedure corresponding to the above might look like this:

```
char *
rusers()
{
        static unsigned long nusers;

        /*
        * Code here to compute the number of users
        * and place result in variable nusers.
        */
        return((char *)&nusers);
}
```

It takes one argument, which is a pointer to the input of the remote procedure call (ignored in our example), and it returns a pointer to the result. In many versions of C, character pointers are the generic pointers, so both the input argument and the return value are cast to char *.

The rpc_reg() Routine

Normally, a server registers all the RPC calls it plans to handle, and then goes into an infinite loop waiting to service requests. If rpcgen is used to provide this functionality, it will generate much code, including a server dispatch function and support for port monitors. But programmers can also write servers themselves using rpc_reg(), and it is appropriate that they do so if they have simple applications, like the one shown as an example here. In this example, there is only a single procedure to register, so the main body of the server would look like this:

```
#include <stdio.h>
#include <rpc/rpc.h>
#include <rpcsvc/rusers.h>

char *rusers();

main ()
{
        if (rpc_reg(RUSERSPROG, RUSERSVERS, RUSERSPROC_NUM,
            rusers, xdr_void, xdr_u_long, "visible") == -1) {
                fprintf(stderr, "Couldn't Register\n");
                exit(1);
        }
        svc_run();                      /* Never returns */
        fprintf(stderr, "Error: svc_run returned!\n");
        exit(1);
}
```

The rpc_reg() routine registers a C procedure as corresponding to a given RPC procedure number. The registration is done for each of the transports of the specified type, or if the type parameter is NULL, for all the transports named in NETPATH. The first three parameters, RUSERPROG, RUSERSVERS, and RUSERSPROC_NUM are the program, version, and procedure numbers of the remote procedure to be registered; rusers is the name of the local procedure that implements the remote procedure; and xdr_void and xdr_u_long name the XDR filters for the remote procedure's arguments and results, respectively. (Multiple arguments or multiple results are passed as structures.) The last parameter specifies the desired nettype. Note that, when using rpc_reg(), programmers are not required to write their own dispatch routines.

 The svc_run() routine is used at *all* levels of RPC programming. Strictly speaking, it does not "belong" to this or to any other level.

After registering the local procedure, the server program's main procedure calls svc_run(), the RPC library's remote procedure dispatcher. It is this function that calls the remote procedures in response to RPC call messages. Note that the dispatcher in rpc_reg() takes care of decoding remote procedure arguments and encoding results, using the XDR filters specified when the remote procedure was registered.

Passing Arbitrary Data Types

In the previous example, the RPC call returned a single unsigned long. RPC can handle arbitrary data structures, regardless of different machines' byte orders or structure layout conventions, by always converting them to a standard transfer syntax called External Data Representation (XDR) before sending them over the transport. The process of converting from a particular machine representation to XDR format is called *serializing*, and the reverse process is called *deserializing*.

The type field parameters of rpc_call() and rpc_reg() can name an XDR primitive procedure, like xdr_u_long() in the previous example, or a programmer supplied procedure (that may take a maximum of two parameters). XDR has these "built-in" primitive type routines:

xdr_int()	xdr_u_int()	xdr_enum()
xdr_long()	xdr_u_long()	xdr_bool()
xdr_short()	xdr_u_short()	xdr_wrapstring()
xdr_char()	xdr_u_char()	

NOTE The routine `xdr_string()` exists, but takes more than two parameters. It cannot, therefore, be used with `rpc_call()` and `rpc_reg()`, which only pass two parameters to their XDR routines. `xdr_wrapstring()` has only two parameters, and is thus OK. It, in turn, calls `xdr_string()`.

As an example of a user-defined type routine, if a programmer wanted to send the structure:

```
struct simple {
        int a;
        short b;
} simple;
```

then `rpc_call()` would be called as:

```
rpc_call(hostname, PROGNUM, VERSNUM, PROCNUM,
        xdr_simple, &simple ...);
```

where `xdr_simple()` is written as:

```
#include <rpc/rpc.h>
#include "simple.h"

bool_t
xdr_simple(xdrsp, simplep)
        XDR *xdrsp;
        struct simple *simplep;
{
        if (!xdr_int(xdrsp, &simplep->a))
                return (FALSE);
        if (!xdr_short(xdrsp, &simplep->b))
                return (FALSE);
        return (TRUE);
}
```

An XDR routine returns nonzero (true in the C sense) if it completes success-fully, and zero otherwise. A complete description of XDR is provided in the "External Data Representation Standard: Protocol Specification" chapter. Note that the above routine could have been generated automatically by using the rpcgen compiler.

In addition to the built-in primitives, there are also some prefabricated building blocks:

```
xdr_array()     xdr_bytes()     xdr_reference()
xdr_vector()    xdr_union()     xdr_pointer()
xdr_string()    xdr_opaque()
```

To send a variable array of integers, the array might be packaged as a structure like this:

```
struct varintarr {
        int *data;
        int arrlnth;
} arr;
```

and sent by an RPC call such as:

```
rpc_call(hostname, PROGNUM, VERSNUM, PROCNUM,
        xdr_varintarr, &arr...);
```

with xdr_varintarr() defined as:

```
bool_t
xdr_varintarr(xdrsp, arrp)
        XDR *xdrsp;
        struct varintarr *arrp;
{
        return (xdr_array(xdrsp, &arrp->data, &arrp->arrlnth,
                MAXLEN, sizeof(int), xdr_int));
}
```

The xdr_array() routine takes as parameters the XDR handle, a pointer to the array, a pointer to the size of the array, the maximum allowable array size, the size of each array element, and an XDR routine for handling each array element.

If the size of the array is known in advance, one can use xdr_vector(), which serializes fixed-length arrays.

```
int intarr[SIZE];

bool_t
xdr_intarr(xdrsp, intarr)
        XDR *xdrsp;
        int intarr[];
{
        return (xdr_vector(xdrsp, intarr, SIZE, sizeof(int),
                xdr_int));
}
```

XDR always converts quantities to 4-byte multiples when serializing. Thus, if either of the examples above involved characters instead of integers, each character would occupy 32 bits. That is the reason for the XDR routine xdr_bytes(), which is like xdr_array() except that it packs characters; xdr_bytes() has four parameters, similar to the first four parameters of xdr_array().

For null-terminated strings, there is the xdr_string() routine, which is the same as xdr_bytes() without the length parameter. On serializing it gets the string length from strlen(), and on deserializing it creates a null-terminated string.

Here is a final example that calls the previously written `xdr_simple()` as well as the built-in functions `xdr_string()` and `xdr_reference()`, which chases pointers:

```
struct finalexample {
        char *string;
        struct simple *simplep;
} finalexample;

bool_t
xdr_finalexample(xdrsp, finalp)
        XDR *xdrsp;
        struct finalexample *finalp;
{
        if (!xdr_string(xdrsp, &finalp->string, MAXSTRLEN))
                return (FALSE);
        if (!xdr_reference(xdrsp, &finalp->simplep,
          sizeof(struct simple), xdr_simple))
                return (FALSE);
        return (TRUE);
}
```

Note that we could as easily call `xdr_simple()` here instead of `xdr_reference()`.

The Lower Levels of RPC

In the examples given for programming at the simplied interface, RPC takes care of almost as many details as would the rpcgen compiler. RPC does so by choosing defaults for almost everything, including the transport protocol.

This section shows how to control these details by using lower levels of the RPC library. The reader is assumed to be familiar with the Transport Level Interface (TLI).

There are several reasons for using lower levels of RPC:

- A program may need to directly control the selection of the transport protocol, which at the simplified interface level, can be done only by use of the NETPATH variable.

- A program may need to allocate and free memory while serializing or deserializing with XDR routines. There are no facilities for doing so available at the higher level. (For details, see "Memory Allocation with XDR" in the "Advanced Examples" section of this chapter.)

The following sections illustrate programming at the lower levels of RPC.

"The Top Level" describes RPC interfaces that allow for control of transport selection by type.

"The Intermediate Level" section describes those interfaces that allow a programmer to choose a specific transport.

"The Expert Level" section describes routines that:

- allow program control of client and server characteristics

- provide an interface to rpcbind

Finally, the section on "The Bottom Level" describes routines that control most details of transport options.

For detailed descriptions of RPC routines, see rpc(3N).

The Top Level

At the top level, the application can specify the *type* of transport that it wants to use, but not an individual transport. This level differs from the simplified interface to RPC in that the application is responsible for creating its own transport handles, on both the client and server sides.

Top Level: The Client Side

Assume we have the following header file:

```
/*
 * time_prot.h
 */

#include <rpc/types.h>

struct timev {
        int second;
        int minute;
        int hour;
};
typedef struct timev timev;

bool_t xdr_timev(xdrsp, resp)
        XDR *xdrsp;
        struct timev *resp;
{
        if (!xdr_int(xdrsp, &resp->second))
                return (FALSE);
        if (!xdr_int(xdrsp, &resp->minute))
                return (FALSE);
        if (!xdr_int(xdrsp, &resp->hour))
                return (FALSE);
        return (TRUE);
}

#define TIME_PROG ((u_long)76)
#define TIME_VERS ((u_long)1)
#define TIME_GET ((u_long)1)
```

The following code implements the client side of a trivial date service, written at the top level:

```
#include <stdio.h>
#include <rpc/rpc.h>
#include "time_prot.h"

#define TOTAL (30)

/*
 * Caller of trivial date service
 * usage: calltime hostname
 */
main(argc,argv)
        int argc;
        char *argv[];
{
        struct timeval timeout;
        CLIENT *client;
        enum clnt_stat stat;
        struct timev timev;
        char *nettype;

        if (argc != 2 && argc != 3) {
                fprintf(stderr,"usage: %s host [nettype]\n",argv[0]);
        }

        if (argc == 2)
                nettype = "netpath";           /* Default */
        else
                nettype = argv[2];
        client = clnt_create(argv[1], TIME_PROG, TIME_VERS,
          nettype);
        if (client == NULL) {
                clnt_pcreateerror("Couldn't create client");
                exit(1);
        }
        timeout.tv_sec = TOTAL;
        timeout.tv_usec = 0;
        stat = clnt_call(client, TIME_GET, xdr_void, NULL,
          xdr_timev, &timev, timeout);
        if (stat != RPC_SUCCESS) {
                clnt_perror(client, "Call failed");
                exit(1);
        }
        printf("%s: %02d:%02d:%02d GMT\n", nettype, timev.hour,
          timev.minute, timev.second);
        exit(0);
}
```

Note that, when this program is run, if `nettype` is not given on the command line, the code assigns it to point to the string `"netpath"`. Whenever the routines in the RPC libraries encounter this string, they consult the NETPATH environment variable for the user's list of acceptable network identifiers.

If the client handle cannot be created, the reason for the failure can be printed using `clnt_pcreateerror()`, or the error status can be obtained via the global variable `rpc_createerr`.

After the client handle is created, `clnt_call()` is used to make the remote call. It takes as arguments the remote procedure number, an XDR filter for the input argument and the argument pointer, an XDR filter for the result and the result pointer, and the time-out period of the call. Normally, this last should not be 0. In this particular example there are no arguments, and thus `xdr_void()` has been specified.

Top Level: The Server Side

Here's the code for the time server:

```
#include <stdio.h>
#include <rpc/rpc.h>
#include "time_prot.h"

static void time_prog();

main(argc,argv)
        int argc;
        char *argv[];
{
        int transpnum;
        char *nettype;

        if (argc == 2)
                nettype = argv[1];
        else
                nettype = "netpath";        /* Default */
        transpnum = svc_create(time_prog, TIME_PROG, TIME_VERS,
          nettype);
        if (transpnum == 0) {
                fprintf(stderr,"%s: cannot create %s service.\n",
                  argv[0], nettype);
```

(continued on next page)

```
                exit (1);
        }
        svc_run ();
}

/*
 * The server dispatch function
 */
static void
time_prog (rqstp, transp)
        struct svc_req *rqstp;
        SVCXPRT *transp;
{
        struct timev rslt;
        long thetime;

        switch (rqstp->rq_proc) {
        case NULLPROC:
                svc_sendreply (transp, xdr_void, NULL);
                return;

        case TIME_GET:
                break;

        default:
                svcerr_noproc (transp);
                return;
        }

        thetime = time (0);
        rslt.second = thetime % 60;
        thetime /= 60;
        rslt.minute = thetime % 60;
        thetime /= 60;
        rslt.hour = thetime % 24;
        if (! svc_sendreply (transp, xdr_timev, &rslt)) {
                svcerr_systemerr (transp);
        }
}
```

svc_create() returns the number of transports on which it could create
server handles. time_prog() is the dispatch function called by svc_run()
whenever there's a request for its given program and version number.

Here the remote procedure takes no arguments. Had arguments been required,

```
svc_getargs(transport, XDR_filter, argument_pointer)
```

could have been used to deserialize (XDR decode) the arguments. In such cases, `svc_freeargs()` should be used to free up the arguments after the actual call has been made. The server reply results are sent back to the client using `svc_sendreply()`.

It is recommended that rpcgen be used to generate the dispatch function which can later be customized.

When rpcgen is used to generate the dispatch function, `svc_sendreply()` is called only after the actual procedure has returned, and hence it is essential to have rslt (in this example) declared as static within that actual procedure.

In this example, rslt is not declared as static because `svc_sendreply()` is called from within the dispatch function.

The Intermediate Level

At the intermediate level, the application directly chooses the transport it wishes to use, factoring the value of NETPATH and the contents of /etc/netconfig into the choice as it sees fit.

Intermediate Level: The Client Side

The following code implements the client side of the same time service shown above, but written to the intermediate level of the RPC package.

Here, the programmer requires the user to name, on the command line, the transport over which the call will be made:

Programmer's Guide: Networking Interfaces

```
#include <stdio.h>
#include <rpc/rpc.h>
#include <netconfig.h>                    /* For netconfig structure */
#include "time_prot.h"

#define TOTAL (30)

/*
 *  Caller of trivial date service
 *  usage: calltime hostname netid
 */
main(argc,argv)
        int argc;
        char *argv[];
{
        struct netconfig *nconf;

        /* Declarations from previous example */

        if (argc != 3) {
                fprintf(stderr,"usage: %s host netid\n",argv[0]);
        }
        nettype = argv[2];
        if ((nconf = getnetconfigent(nettype)) == NULL) {
                fprintf(stderr, "Bad netid type: %s\n", nettype);
                exit(1);
        }
        client = clnt_tp_create(argv[1], TIME_PROG, TIME_VERS,
          nconf);
        if (client == NULL) {
                clnt_pcreateerror("Could not create client");
                exit(1);
        }

        /* Same as previous example after this point */

}
```

The netconfig structure can be obtained by a call to
getnetconfigent(nettype). (See getnetconfig(3N) for more details.)

At this level, the program must explicitly make all decisions about network-selection.

Intermediate Level: The Server Side

Here's the corresponding server. The administrator who starts the service is required to name, on the command line, the transport over which the service is provided:

```
#include <stdio.h>
#include <rpc/rpc.h>
#include <netconfig.h>                /* For netconfig structure */
#include "time_prot.h"

static void time_prog();

/* Service to supply Greenwich mean time */
/* usage: server netid */

main(argc,argv)
        int argc;
        char *argv[];
{
        SVCXPRT *transp;
        struct netconfig *nconf;

        if (argc == 1) {
                fprintf(stderr, "usage: server netid \n");
                exit(1);
        }

        if ((nconf = getnetconfigent(argv[1])) == NULL) {
                fprintf(stderr, "Could not find info on %s\n",
                  argv[1]);
                exit(1);
        }

        transp = svc_tp_create(time_prog, TIME_PROG, TIME_VERS,
          nconf);

        if (transp == NULL) {
                fprintf(stderr,"%s: cannot create %s service.\n",
                  argv[0], argv[1]);
                exit(1)
                }

        svc_run();
}
static void
time_prog(rqstp, transp)
        struct svc_req *rqstp;
        SVCXPRT *transp;
```

(continued on next page)

```
(
          /* Code identical to Top Level version */
)
```

The Expert Level

At the expert level, network selection is done exactly as at the intermediate level. The only difference here is in the level of control that the application has over the details of the transport's configuration. Control at this level is much greater. These examples illustrate that control, which is exercised using the `clnt_tli_create()` and `svc_tli_create()` routines.

Expert Level: The Client Side

Here is the client side of some code that implements a version of `clntudp_create()` (the client-side creation routine for the UDP transport) in terms of `clnt_tli_create()`. The example shows how to do network selection based on the family of the transport one wishes to use.

`clnt_tli_create()` is normally used to create a client handle when:

- the application wants to pass an open file descriptor, which may or may not be bound

- the programmer wants to feed the server's address to the client

- the programmer wants to specify the send and receive buffer size (here, 8800 bytes)

```
#include <stdio.h>
#include <rpc/rpc.h>
#include <netconfig.h>
#include <netinet/in.h>
/*
 * In an earlier implementation of RPC, the only transports supported
 * were TCP/IP and UDP/IP. Here they are shown based on the Berkeley
 * socket, but implemented on the top of TLI/Streams.
 */
CLIENT *
clntudp_create(raddr, prog, vers, wait, sockp)
        struct sockaddr_in *raddr;   /* Remote address */
        u_long prog;                 /* Program number */
        u_long vers;                 /* Version number */
        struct timeval wait;         /* Time to wait */
        int *sockp;                  /* fd pointer */
{
        CLIENT *cl;                  /* Client handle */
        int madefd = FALSE;          /* Is fd opened here */
        int fd = *sockp;             /* fd */
        struct t_bind *tbind;        /* bind address */
        struct netconfig *nconf;     /* netconfig structure */
        void *handlep;

        if ((handlep = setnetconfig()) == 0) { /* No transports available */
                rpc_createerr.cf_stat = RPC_UNKNOWNPROTO;
                return ((CLIENT *)NULL);
        }
        /*
         * Try all the transports till it gets one which is
         * connectionless, family is INET and name is UDP
         */
        while (nconf = getnetconfig(handlep)) {
                if ((nconf->nc_semantics == NC_TPI_CLTS) &&
                    (strcmp(nconf->nc_protofmly, NC_INET) == 0) &&
                    (strcmp(nconf->nc_proto, NC_UDP) == 0))
                        break;
        }
        if (nconf == NULL) {
                rpc_createerr.cf_stat = RPC_UNKNOWNPROTO;
                goto err;
        }
        if (fd == RPC_ANYSOCK) {
                fd = t_open(nconf->nc_device, O_RDWR, NULL);
                if (fd == -1) {
                        rpc_createerr.cf_stat = RPC_SYSTEMERROR;
```

(continued on next page)

```
                        goto err;
                }
                madefd = TRUE;      /* The fd was opened here */
        }
        if (raddr->sin_port == 0) { /* remote addr unknown */
                u_short sport;

                /*
                 * rpcb_getport() is a user provided routine
                 * which will call rpcb_getaddr and translate
                 * the netbuf address to port number.
                 */
                sport = rpcb_getport(raddr, prog, vers, nconf);
                if (sport == 0) {
                        rpc_createerr.cf_stat = RPC_PROGUNAVAIL;
                        goto err;
                }
                raddr->sin_port = sport;
        }


        /* Transform sockaddr_in to netbuf */
        tbind = (struct t_bind *)t_alloc(fd, T_BIND, T_ADDR);
        if (tbind == NULL) {
                rpc_createerr.cf_stat = RPC_SYSTEMERROR;
                goto err;
        }
        (void) memcpy(tbind->addr.buf, (char *)raddr,
          (int)tbind->addr.maxlen);
        tbind->addr.len = tbind->addr.maxlen;

        /* Bind endpoint to a reserved address */
        (void) bind_resv(fd);
        cl = clnt_tli_create(fd, nconf, &(tbind->addr), prog,
          vers, 8800, 8800);
        (void) endnetconfig(handlep);       /* Close the netconfig file */
        (void) t_free((char *)tbind, T_BIND);
        if (cl) {
                *sockp = fd;
                if (madefd == TRUE) {
                        /* fd should be closed while destroying the handle */
                        (void) CLNT_CONTROL(cl, CLSET_FD_CLOSE, NULL);
                }
                /* Set the retry time */
                (void) CLNT_CONTROL(cl, CLSET_RETRY_TIMEOUT, &wait);
                return (cl);
        }
```

(continued on next page)

```
err:
        if (madefd == TRUE)
                (void) t_close(fd);
        (void) endnetconfig(handlep);
        return ((CLIENT *)NULL);
}
```

The network selection is done using the library functions setnetconfig(), getnetconfig(), and endnetconfig(). (Note that endnetconfig() is not called until after the call to clnt_tli_create(), near the end of the example.)

clntudp_create() can be passed an open fd, but if not (fd == RPC_ANYSOCK), it will open its own using the netconfig structure for UDP.

If the remote address is not known, (raddr->sin_port == 0), then it is obtained from the remote rpcbind. Note the call to bind_clnt_resv(), which serves to bind a transport endpoint to a reserved address. This call is necessary because there is no notion of a reserved address in RPC under TLI, as there is in both TCP and UDP. The implementation of this routine is of no interest here, because it is entirely transport specific. What is of interest is the scaffolding necessary to call it.

After the client handle has been created, the programmer can suitably customize it using calls to clnt_control(). Here, the RPC library closes the file descriptor while destroying the handle (as it usually does with a call to clnt_destroy() when it opens the fd itself) and sets the retry timeout period.

Expert Level: The Server Side

Below is the corresponding server code. It implements svcudp_create() in terms of svc_tli_create(), and calls the user provided bind_resv() to bind the transport endpoint to a reserved address.

`svc_tli_create()` is normally used when the application needs a fine degree of control, and especially if it is necessary to:

- pass an open file descriptor to the application
- pass the user's bind address
- set the send and receive buffer sizes (here being set to 8800 bytes)

The `fd` argument may be unbound when passed in. If it is, then it is bound to a given address, and the address is stored in a handle. If the bind address is set to `NULL`, and if the `fd` is initially unbound, it will be bound to any suitable address.

NOTE It is the responsibility of the programmer to use `rpcb_set()` to register the service with `rpcbind`.

```
#include <stdio.h>
#include <rpc/rpc.h>
#include <netconfig.h>
#include <netinet/in.h>

/*
 * On the server side
 */
SVCXPRT *
svcudp_create(fd)
        register int fd;
{
        struct netconfig *nconf;
        SVCXPRT *svc;
        int madefd = FALSE;
        int port;
        void *handlep;

        if ((handlep = setnetconfig()) == 0) { /* No transports available */
                nc_perror("server");
                return ((SVCXPRT *)NULL);
        }
        /*
         * Try all the transports till it gets one which is
```

(continued on next page)

```
        * a connection less, family is INET and name is UDP
        */
        while (nconf = getnetconfig(handlep)) {
                if ((nconf->nc_semantics == NC_TPI_CLTS) &&
                    (strcmp(nconf->nc_protofmly, NC_INET) == 0) &&
                    (strcmp(nconf->nc_proto, NC_UDP) == 0))
                        break;
        }
        if (nconf == NULL) {
                endnetconfig(handlep);
                fprintf(stderr, "UDP transport not available\n");
                return ((SVCXPRT *)NULL);
        }
        if (fd == RPC_ANYFD) {
                fd = t_open(nconf->nc_device, O_RDWR, NULL);
                if (fd == -1) {
                        (void) endnetconfig();
                        (void) fprintf(stderr,
                        "svcudp_create: could not open connection\n");
                        return ((SVCXPRT *)NULL);
                }
                madefd = TRUE;
        }

        /*
        * Bind Endpoint to a reserved address
        */
        port = bind_resv(fd);
        svc = svc_tli_create(fd, nconf, (struct t_bind *)NULL,
          8800, 8800);
        (void) endnetconfig(handlep);
        if (svc == (SVCXPRT *)NULL) {
                if (madefd)
                        (void) t_close(fd);
                return ((SVCXPRT *)NULL);
        }
        if (port == -1)
                /* Specifically set xp_port now */
                svc->xp_port =
                    ((struct sockaddr_in *)svc->xp_ltaddr.buf)->sin_port;
        else
                svc->xp_port = port;
        return (svc);
}
```

The network selection here is done in a similar way as in `clntudp_create()`.

`svcudp_create()` is set up to receive an open `fd`, but if it does not, it will open one itself using the selected `netconfig` structure.

`bind_resv()` is a user-provided function that binds the `fd` to a reserved port if the caller is a superuser.

The Bottom Level

At the bottom-level interface to RPC, the application can control all options, transport-related and otherwise. `clnt_tli_create()`, and the other expert-level RPC interface routines are implemented on top of these bottom-level routines.

The programmer should not normally be using these low-level routines.

These routines are responsible for creating their own data structures, their own buffer management, the creation of their own RPC headers, etc.

Callers of these routines [like the expert level routine `clnt_tli_create()`] are responsible for initializing the `cl_netid` and `cl_tp` fields within the client handle. The bottom level routines `clnt_dg_create()` and `clnt_vc_create()` are themselves responsible for populating the `clnt_ops` and `cl_private` fields.

For a created handle, `cl_netid` is the network identifier (e.g. udp) of the transport and `cl_tp` is the device name of that transport (e.g. /dev/udp).

Bottom Level: The Client Side

The example here shows the use of local variables to control the exact details of the calls to `clnt_vc_create()` and `clnt_dg_create()`. Thus, these routines allow control of the transport to the lowest level:

```
switch (tinfo.servtype) {
        case T_COTS:
        case T_COTS_ORD:
                cl = clnt_vc_create(fd, svcaddr, prog, vers,
                    sendsz, recvsz);
                break;
        case T_CLTS:
                cl = clnt_dg_create(fd, svcaddr, prog, vers,
                    sendsz, recvsz);
                break;
        default:
                goto err;
}
```

Bottom Level: The Server Side

And, again, on the server side:

```
/* call transport specific function. */

switch(tinfo.servtype) {
        case T_COTS_ORD:
        case T_COTS:
                xprt = svc_vc_create(fd, sendsz, recvsz);
                break;

        case T_CLTS:
                xprt = svc_dg_create(fd, sendsz, recvsz);
                break;
        default:
                goto err;
}
```

Low-level Data Structures

For reference, here are the client- and server-side RPC handles, as well as an authentication structure.

```
/*
 * Client rpc handle.
 * Created by individual implementations
 * Client is responsible for initializing auth
 */
typedef struct {
    AUTH    *cl_auth;                       /* authenticator */
    struct clnt_ops {
        enum clnt_stat  (*cl_call)();  /* call remote procedure */
        void            (*cl_abort)();    /* abort a call */
        void            (*cl_geterr)();   /* get specific error code */
        bool_t          (*cl_freeres)();  /* frees results */
        void            (*cl_destroy)();  /* destroy this structure */
        bool_t          (*cl_control)();  /* the ioctl() of rpc */
    } *cl_ops;
    caddr_t         cl_private;       /* private stuff */
    char            *cl_netid;        /* network token */
    char            *cl_tp;           /* device name */
} CLIENT;
```

The client-side handle contains an authentication structure. For a client program authenticate itself, it must initialize the cl_auth field to an appropriate authentication structure:

```
/*
 * Auth handle, interface to client side authenticators.
 */
typedef struct {
        struct  opaque_auth     ah_cred;  /* credentials */
        struct  opaque_auth     ah_verf;  /* verifier */
        union   des_block       ah_key;   /* DES key */
        struct auth_ops {
            void    (*ah_nextverf)();
            int     (*ah_marshal)();       /* nextverf & serialize */
            int     (*ah_validate)();      /* validate verifier */
            int     (*ah_refresh)();       /* refresh credentials */
            void    (*ah_destroy)();       /* destroy this structure */
        } *ah_ops;
        caddr_t ah_private;                             /* Private data */
} AUTH;
```

Within the AUTH structure, ah_cred contains the caller's credentials, and
ah_verf contains the information necessary to verify those credentials. (See
"Authentication" in the "Advanced RPC Programming Techniques" section for
more details.)

Here is the server-side transport handle:

```
/*
 * Server side transport handle
 */
typedef struct {
    int          xp_fd;           /* associated file descriptor */
    u_short      xp_port;         /* associated port number (obsolete) */
    struct xp_ops {
        bool_t          (*xp_recv)();    /* receive incoming requests */
        enum xprt_stat  (*xp_stat)();    /* get transport status */
        bool_t          (*xp_getargs)(); /* get arguments */
        bool_t          (*xp_reply)();   /* send reply */
        bool_t          (*xp_freeargs)();/* free mem allocated for args */
        void            (*xp_destroy)(); /* destroy this struct */
    } *xp_ops;
    int          xp_addrlen;      /* length of remote addr. Obsolete */
    char         *xp_tp;          /* transport provider device name */
    char         *xp_netid;       /* network token */
    struct netbuf    xp_ltaddr;   /* local transport address */
    struct netbuf    xp_rtaddr;   /* remote transport address */
    char         xp_raddr[16];    /* remote address. Obsolete */
    struct opaque_auth xp_verf;   /* raw response verifier */
    caddr_t      xp_p1;           /* private: for use by svc ops */
    caddr_t      xp_p2;           /* private: for use by svc ops */
    caddr_t      xp_p3;           /* private: for use by svc lib */
} SVCXPRT;
```

xp_fd is the file descriptor associated with the handle. Two or more server handles can share the same file descriptor.

xp_netid is the network identifier (e.g. udp) of the transport on which this handle was created and xp_tp is the device name associated with that transport.

xp_ltaddr is the server's own bind address, while xp_rtaddr is the address of the remote caller and hence may change from call to call.

xp_netid, xp_tp and xp_ltaddr are initialized by svc_tli_create() and other expert-level routines.

The rest of the fields are initialized by the bottom-level server routines svc_dg_create() and svc_vc_create().

Low-level Program Testing Using Raw RPC

There are two *pseudo*-RPC interface routines provided to support program testing. These routines, `clnt_raw_create()` and `svc_raw_create()`, do not involve the use of any real transport. They exist to help the developer debug and test the non-communications-oriented aspects of an application before running it over a real network.

Here's an example of their use:

```
/*
 * A simple program to increment a number by 1
 */
#include <stdio.h>
#include <rpc/rpc.h>
#include <rpc/raw.h>

struct timeval TIMEOUT = {0, 0};
static void server();

main (argc, argv)
        int argc;
        char **argv;
{
        CLIENT *cl;
        SVCXPRT *svc;
        int num = 0, ans;

        if (argc == 2)
                num = atoi(argv[1]);
        svc = svc_raw_create();
        if (svc == NULL) {
                fprintf(stderr, "Could not create server handle\n");
                exit(1);
        }
        svc_reg(svc, 200000, 1, server, 0);
        cl = clnt_raw_create(200000, 1);
        if (cl == NULL) {
                clnt_pcreateerror("raw");
                exit(1);
        }
        if (clnt_call(cl, 1, xdr_int, &num, xdr_int, &ans,
            TIMEOUT) != RPC_SUCCESS) {
                clnt_perror(cl, "raw");
                exit(1);
        }
        printf("Client: number returned %d\n", ans);
```

(continued on next page)

Programmer's Guide: Networking Interfaces

```
        exit(0) ;
}

static void
server(rqstp, transp)
        struct svc_req *rqstp;
        SVCXPRT *transp;
{
        int num;

        switch(rqstp->rq_proc) {
        case 0:
                if (svc_sendreply(transp, xdr_void, 0) == NULL) {
                        fprintf(stderr, "error in null proc\n");
                        exit (1);
                }
                return;
        case 1:
                break;
        default:
                svcerr_noproc(transp);
                return;
        }
        if (!svc_getargs(transp, xdr_int, &num)) {
                svcerr_decode(transp);
                return;
        }
        num++;
        if (svc_sendreply(transp, xdr_int, &num) == NULL) {
                fprintf(stderr, "error in sending answer\n");
                exit (1);
        }
        return;
}
```

Note the following points:

- The server is not registered with rpcbind, and svc_run() is not called. The last parameter to svc_reg() is 0, which means that it will not register with rpcbind.

- All the RPC calls occur within the same thread of control.

- It is necessary that the server be created before the client.

- `svc_raw_create()` takes no parameters.

- The server dispatch routine is the same as it is for normal RPC servers.

Advanced RPC Programming Techniques

This section addresses areas of occasional interest to programmers using the lower level interfaces of the RPC package. The topics discussed are:

`select()` on the server side	if calling `svc_run()` is not feasible, a server can call the dispatcher directly
broadcast RPC	details of the broadcast mechanism are described
batching	efficiency is gained if a series of calls can be batched
authentication	two methods in common use are described
port	details are provided for interfacing with the `inetd` and `listener` port monitors
versions	how programs with multiple versions are serviced

select() on the Server Side

Suppose a process is processing RPC requests while performing some other activity. If the other activity involves periodically updating a data structure, the process can set an alarm signal before calling `svc_run()`.

If the other activity involves waiting on a file descriptor, however, the `svc_run()` call will not work.

Below is the code for `svc_run()`. Note that `svc_fdset` is a bit mask of all the file descriptors that RPC is using for services. The mask can change every time *any* RPC library routine is called, because descriptors are constantly being opened and closed:

```
void
svc_run ()
{
        fd_set readfds;
        extern int errno;

        for (;;) {
                readfds = svc_fdset;
                switch (select(_rpc_dtbsize(), &readfds,
                (fd_set *)0, (fd_set *)0, (struct timeval *)0)) {

                case -1:
                        if (errno == EINTR) {
                                continue;
                        }
                        /*
                         * log an error: svc_run: select failed
                         */
                        return;
                case 0:
                        continue;
                default:
                        svc_getreqset(&readfds);
                }
        }
}
```

A process can bypass svc_run() and call svc_getreqset() (the dispatcher) directly. Given the file descriptors of the transport endpoints associated with the programs being waited on, the process can have its own select() that waits on both the RPC file descriptors, and its own descriptors.

Broadcast RPC

rpcbind is a daemon that converts RPC program numbers into network addresses comprehensible to any transport provider. rpcbind supports broadcast RPC. Here are the main differences between broadcast RPC and normal RPC calls:

■ Normal RPC expects one answer, whereas broadcast RPC expects many answers (one or more answer from each responding machine).

■ Broadcast RPC can only be performed on connectionless protocols that support broadcasting, such as UDP.

■ The implementation of broadcast RPC treats all unsuccessful responses as garbage by filtering them out. Thus, if there is a version mismatch between the broadcaster and a remote service, the user of broadcast RPC never knows.

■ All broadcast messages are sent to rpcbind's network address. Thus, only services that register themselves with rpcbind are accessible via the broadcast RPC mechanism.

■ The size of broadcast requests is limited to the MTU (Maximum Transfer Unit) of the local network. For Ethernet, the MTU is 1500 bytes.

The following illustrates how rpc_broadcast () is used and describes its arguments:

```
#include <rpc/clnt.h>
#include <rpc/rpcb_clnt.h>
    . . .
enum clnt_stat      clnt_stat;
    . . .
clnt_stat = rpc_broadcast(prognum, versnum, procnum,
    inproc, in, outproc, out, eachresult, nettype)
            u_long      prognum;        /* program number */
            u_long      versnum;        /* version number */
            u_long      procnum;        /* procedure number */
            xdrproc_t   inproc;         /* xdr routine for args */
            caddr_t     in;             /* pointer to args */
            xdrproc_t   outproc;        /* xdr routine for results */
            caddr_t     out;            /* pointer to results */
            resultproc_t    eachresult;/* call with each result gotten */
            char        *nettype;       /* transport type */
```

The procedure eachresult () is called each time a valid result is obtained. It returns a boolean that specifies whether the user wants more responses.

```
bool_t done;
    . . .
done = eachresult(resultsp, raddr, nconf)
        caddr_t resultsp;
        struct netbuf *addr;      /* Addr of responding machine */
        struct netconfig *nconf; /* Transport which responded */
```

If done is TRUE, then broadcasting stops and rpc_broadcast() returns successfully. Otherwise, the routine waits for another response. The request is
rebroadcast after a few seconds of waiting. If no responses come back, the routine returns with RPC_TIMEDOUT.

Batching

The RPC architecture is designed so that clients send a call message, and wait
for servers to reply that the call succeeded. This implies that clients do not
compute while servers are processing a call. This is inefficient if the client does
not want or need an acknowledgement for every message sent. It is possible for
clients to continue computing while waiting for a response, using RPC batch
facilities.

RPC messages can be placed in a "pipeline" of calls to a desired server; this is
called batching. Batching assumes that:

- each RPC call in the pipeline requires no response from the server, and
  the server does not send a response message

- the pipeline of calls is transported on a reliable byte stream transport such
  as TCP/IP

Because the server does not respond to every call, the client can generate new
calls in parallel with the server executing previous calls. Furthermore, the
TCP/IP implementation can buffer up many call messages, and send them to
the server in one write() system call. This overlapped execution greatly
decreases the interprocess communication overhead of the client and server
processes, and the total elapsed time of a series of calls.

Because the batched calls are buffered, the client should eventually do a non-batched call to flush the pipeline.

An example of batching follows. Assume a string rendering service (like a window system) has two similar calls: one renders a string and returns void results, while the other renders a string and remains silent. The service (using the TCP/IP transport) may look like:

```
#include <stdio.h>
#include <rpc/rpc.h>
#include "windows.h"

void windowdispatch();

main ()
{
        int num;

        num = svc_create(windowdispatch, WINDOWPROG,
            WINDOWVERS, "tcp");
        if (num == 0){
                fprintf(stderr, "can't create an RPC server\n");
                exit(1);
        }
        svc_run();  /* Never returns */
        fprintf(stderr, "should never reach this point\n");
}

void
windowdispatch(rqstp, transp)
        struct svc_req *rqstp;
        SVCXPRT *transp;
{
        char *s = NULL;

        switch (rqstp->rq_proc) {
        case NULLPROC:
                if (!svc_sendreply(transp, xdr_void, 0))
                        fprintf(stderr, "can't reply to RPC call\n");
                return;
        case RENDERSTRING:
                if (!svc_getargs(transp, xdr_wrapstring, &s)) {
                        fprintf(stderr, "can't decode arguments\n");
                        /*
                        * Tell caller an error occurred
```

(continued on next page)

```
                         */
                         svcerr_decode(transp);
                         break;
            }
            /*
             * Code here to render the string s
             */
            if (!svc_sendreply(transp, xdr_void, NULL))
                         fprintf(stderr, "can't reply to RPC call\n");
            break;
        case RENDERSTRING_BATCHED:
            if (!svc_getargs(transp, xdr_wrapstring, &s)) {
                         fprintf(stderr, "can't decode arguments\n");
                         /*
                          * We are silent in the face of protocol errors
                          */
                         break;
            }
            /*
             * Code here to render string s, but send no reply!
             */
            break;
        default:
            svcerr_noproc(transp);
            return;
        }
        /*
         * Now free string allocated while decoding arguments
         */
        svc_freeargs(transp, xdr_wrapstring, &s);
}
```

Of course, the service could have one procedure that takes the string and a
boolean that specifies whether the procedure should respond.

To take advantage of batching (using the code above), the client must make RPC
calls on a TCP-based transport. The calls must have the following attributes:

- the XDR routine for the result must be zero (NULL)
- the RPC call's timeout must be zero

Here is an example of a client that uses batching to render a bunch of strings; the batching is flushed when the client gets a null string (EOF):

```
#include <stdio.h>
#include <rpc/rpc.h>
#include "windows.h"

main(argc, argv)
        int argc;
        char **argv;
{
        struct timeval total_timeout;
        register CLIENT *client;
        enum clnt_stat clnt_stat;
        char buf[1000], *s = buf;

        if ((client = clnt_create(argv[1], WINDOWPROG,
            WINDOWVERS, "tcp")) == NULL) {
                clnt_pcreateerror("clnt_create");
                exit(1);
        }
        total_timeout.tv_sec = 0;
        total_timeout.tv_usec = 0;
        while (scanf("%s", s) != EOF) {
                clnt_call(client, RENDERSTRING_BATCHED,
                        xdr_wrapstring, &s, xdr_void, NULL, total_timeout);
        }

        /* Now flush the pipeline */

        total_timeout.tv_sec = 20;
        clnt_stat = clnt_call(client, NULLPROC, xdr_void, NULL,
                xdr_void, NULL, total_timeout);
        if (clnt_stat != RPC_SUCCESS) {
                clnt_perror(client, "rpc");
                exit(1);
        }
        clnt_destroy(client);
        exit(0);
}
```

Because the server sends no message, the clients cannot be notified of any of the failures that may occur.

Batching Performance

The following illustrates the benefits that may be gained from batching.

The above example was completed to render all the lines in a 2000 line file. The rendering service did nothing but throw the lines away.

The example was run in four configurations, with the following results:

Configuration	Time
machine to itself, regular RPC	50 seconds
machine to itself, batched RPC	16 seconds
machine to another, regular RPC	52 seconds
machine to another, batched RPC	10 seconds

Running `fscanf()` on the same file only requires six seconds. These timings show the advantage of protocols that allow for overlapped execution.

Authentication

In the examples presented so far, the caller never identified itself to the server, and the server never required an ID from the caller. Some network services, such as a network filesystem, require stronger security than what has been presented so far.

Every RPC call is subjected to a *style* of authentication by the RPC package on the server. Similarly, the RPC client package generates and sends authentication parameters suitable for the style of authentication in effect. The default authentication style is AUTH_NONE (none).

Just as different transports can be used when creating RPC clients and servers, different forms of authentication can be associated with RPC clients.

The authentication subsystem of the RPC package is open ended. That is, numerous styles of authentication are easy to support; programmers can design their own authentication style and easily configure the RPC package to support it.

In addition to AUTH_NONE, the RPC package already supports the following authentication styles:

AUTH_SYS   An authentication style based on traditional System V operating system process permissions authentication.

AUTH_SHORT   An alternate form of AUTH_SYS used by some servers for efficiency. Client programs using AUTH_SYS authentication should be prepared to receive AUTH_SHORT response verifiers from some servers. See "Authentication Protocols" in the "Remote Procedure Calls: Protocol Specification" chapter for details.

AUTH_DES   An authentication style based on DES encryption techniques.

AUTH_NONE: The Client Side

When a caller creates a new RPC client handle as in:

```
clnt = clnt_create(host, prognum, versnum, nettype)
```

the appropriate transport instance defaults the associated authentication handle to be

```
clnt->cl_auth = authnone_create();
```

> **NOTE** If the programmer creates a new style of authentication, the programmer is responsible for destroying it with auth_destroy(clnt->cl_auth). This should always be done, to conserve memory.

AUTH_NONE: The Server Side

Service implementors have a harder time dealing with authentication issues because the RPC package passes the service dispatch routine a request that has an arbitrary authentication style associated with it. Consider the fields of a request handle passed to a service dispatch routine:

```
/*
 * An RPC Service request
 */
struct svc_req {
        u_long    rq_prog;              /* service program number */
        u_long    rq_vers;              /* service protocol vers num */
        u_long    rq_proc;              /* desired procedure number */
        struct opaque_auth rq_cred;    /* raw credentials from wire */
        caddr_t   rq_clntcred;         /* credentials (read only) */
        SVCXPRT   *rq_xprt;            /* associated transport */
};
```

The `rq_cred` is mostly opaque, except for one field of interest: the style or flavor of authentication credentials:

```
/*
 * Authentication info. Mostly opaque to the programmer.
 */
struct opaque_auth {
        enum_t    oa_flavor;           /* style of credentials */
        caddr_t   oa_base;             /* address of more auth stuff */
        u_int     oa_length;           /* not to exceed MAX_AUTH_BYTES */
};
```

The RPC package guarantees the following to the service dispatch routine:

- The request's `rq_cred` is well formed. Thus the service implementor may inspect the request's `rq_cred.oa_flavor` to determine the style of authentication the caller used. The service implementor may also wish to inspect the other fields of `rq_cred` if the style is not one supported by the RPC package.

■ The request's `rq_clntcred` field is either `NULL` or points to a well
formed structure that corresponds to a supported style of authentication
credentials. Remember that only `AUTH_NONE`, `AUTH_SYS`, `AUTH_SHORT`
and `AUTH_DES` styles are currently supported, so (currently)
`rq_clntcred` could be cast only as a pointer to an `authsys_parms`,
`short_hand_verf`, or `authdes_cred` structure. If `rq_clntcred` is
`NULL`, the service implementor may wish to inspect the other (opaque)
fields of `rq_cred` if the service knows about a new type of authentication
that the RPC package does not know about.

AUTH_SYS Authentication

The RPC client can choose to use `AUTH_SYS` style authentication by setting
`clnt->cl_auth` after creating the RPC client handle:

```
clnt->cl_auth = authsys_create_default();
```

This causes each RPC call associated with `clnt` to carry with it the following
authentication credentials structure:

```
/*
 * AUTH_SYS style credentials.
 */
struct authsys_parms {
        u_long  aup_time;        /* credentials creation time */
        char    *aup_machname;   /* host name where client is */
        uid_t   aup_uid;         /* client's effective uid */
        gid_t   aup_gid;         /* client's current group id */
        u_int   aup_len;         /* element length of aup_gids */
        gid_t   *aup_gids;       /* array of groups user is in */
};
```

These fields are set by `authsys_create_default()` by invoking the
appropriate system calls.

The following shows the server for a remote procedure, RUSERPROC_n, that computes the number of users on the network. As a trivial demonstration of authentication usage, this server checks AUTH_SYS credentials and does not service requests from callers whose uid is 16:

```
nuser(rqstp, transp)
        struct svc_req *rqstp;
        SVCXPRT *transp;
{

        struct authsys_parms *SYS_cred;
        uid_t uid;
        unsigned long nusers;

        /*
         * we don't care about authentication for null proc
         */
        if (rqstp->rq_proc == NULLPROC) {
                if (!svc_sendreply(transp, xdr_void, 0)) {
                        fprintf(stderr, "can't reply to RPC call\n");
                        return (1);
                }
                return;
        }
        /*
         * now get the uid
         */
        switch (rqstp->rq_cred.oa_flavor) {
        case AUTH_SYS:
                SYS_cred =
                        (struct authsys_parms *)rqstp->rq_clntcred;
                uid = SYS_cred->aup_uid;
                break;
        case AUTH_NONE:
        default:
                svcerr_weakauth(transp);
                return;
        }
        switch (rqstp->rq_proc) {
        case RUSERSPROC_n:
                /*
                 * make sure caller is allowed to call this proc
                 */
                if (uid == 16) {
                        svcerr_systemerr(transp);
                        return;
```

(continued on next page)

```
          }
          /*
           * Code here to compute the number of users
           * and assign it to the variable nusers
           */
          if (!svc_sendreply(transp, xdr_u_long, &nusers)) {
                  fprintf(stderr, "can't reply to RPC call\n");
                  return (1);
          }
          return;
  default:
          svcerr_noproc(transp);
          return;
  }
}
```

A few things should be noted here:

- It is customary not to check the authentication parameters associated with the NULLPROC (procedure number zero).

- The server should call svcerr_weakauth() if the authentication parameter's type is not suitable for the service.

- The service protocol itself should return status for access denied; in this example, the protocol does not have such a status, so the service primitive svcerr_systemerr() is called instead.

The last point underscores the relation between the RPC authentication package and the services: RPC deals only with *authentication* and not with individual services' *access control*. The services themselves must establish access control policies and reflect these policies as return statuses in their protocols.

AUTH_DES Authentication

AUTH_DES authentication is recommended for programs that require more security than that offered by the AUTH_SYS style of authentication.

AUTH_SYS authentication is easy to defeat. For example, instead of using authsys_create_default(), a program could call authsys_create(), and then change the RPC authentication handle to give itself any desired user ID and hostname.

The details of the AUTH_DES authentication protocol are complicated and are not explained here. See the "Remote Procedure Calls: Protocol Specification" chapter for the details.

For AUTH_DES authentication to work, the keyserv(1M) daemon must be running on both the server and client machines. The users on these machines need public/secret key pairs assigned by the network administrator in the pub-lickey(4) database. And, they need to have decrypted their secret keys using the keylogin(1) command.

AUTH_DES: The Client Side

If a client wishes to use AUTH_DES authentication, it must set its authentication handle appropriately. Here is an example:

```
cl->cl_auth = authdes_seccreate(servername, 60, server, NULL);
```

The first argument is the network name or "netname" of the owner of the server process. Typically, server processes are root processes and their netname can be derived using the following call:

```
char servername[MAXNETNAMELEN];

host2netname(servername, rhostname, NULL);
```

Here, rhostname is the hostname of the machine the server process is running on. host2netname() populates servername to contain this root process's netname. If the server process was run by a regular user, one could use the call user2netname() instead. Here is an example for a server process with the same user ID as the client:

```
char servername[MAXNETNAMELEN];

user2netname(servername, getuid(), NULL);
```

The last argument to both of these calls, user2netname() and
host2netname(), is the name of the naming domain where the server is
located. The NULL used here means "use the local domain name."

The second argument to authdes_seccreate() is a lifetime for the credential. Here it is set to sixty seconds. What that means is that the credential will
expire 60 seconds from now. If some mischievous program tries to reuse the
credential, the server RPC subsystem will recognize that it has expired and will
not grant any requests. If the same mischievous program tries to reuse the
credential within the sixty second lifetime, it will still be rejected, because the
server RPC subsystem remembers credentials it has seen in the near past, and
will not grant requests to duplicates.

The third argument to authdes_seccreate() is the name of the host to synchronize with. For AUTH_DES authentication to work, the server and client
must agree on the time. Here we pass the hostname of the server itself, so the
client and server will both be using the same time: the server's time. The argument can be NULL, which means "don't bother synchronizing." A program
should pass NULL only if sure the client and server are already synchronized.

The final argument to authdes_seccreate() is the address of a DES encryption key to use for encrypting timestamps and data. If this argument is NULL,
as it is in this example, a random key will be chosen. The client may find out
the encryption key being used by consulting the ah_key field of the authentication handle.

AUTH_DES: The Server Side

The server side is simpler than the client side. Here is the previous example
rewritten to use the AUTH_DES style instead of AUTH_SYS:

```
#include <rpc/rpc.h>
    . . .
    . . .
nuser(rqstp, transp)
        struct svc_req *rqstp;
        SVCXPRT *transp;
{
        struct authdes_cred *DES_cred;
        uid_t uid;
        gid_t gid;
        int gidlen;
        gid_t gidlist[10];
        /*
         * we don't care about authentication for null proc
         */

        if (rqstp->rq_proc == NULLPROC) {
                /* same as before */
        }

        /*
         * now get the uid
         */
        switch (rqstp->rq_cred.oa_flavor) {
        case AUTH_DES:
                DES_cred =
                   (struct authdes_cred *) rqstp->rq_clntcred;
                if (! netname2user(DES_cred->adc_fullname.name,
                    &uid, &gid, &gidlen, gidlist)) {
                        fprintf(stderr, "unknown user: %s\n",
                          DES_cred->adc_fullname.name);
                        svcerr_systemerr(transp);
                        return;
                }
                break;
        case AUTH_NONE:
        default:
                svcerr_weakauth(transp);
                return;
        }

        /*
         * The rest is the same as before
         */
```

Note the use of the routine `netname2user()`, the inverse of `user2netname()`: it takes a network ID and converts to a local system ID. `netname2user()` also supplies the group IDs, not used in this example, but which may be useful to other programs.

Using Port Monitors

An RPC server can be started from port monitors such as `inetd` and `listener`. These port monitors listen for requests for the services, and spawn servers in response to those requests. The forked server process is passed the file descriptor 0 on which the request has been accepted. For `inetd`, after the server has serviced the request, it may exit immediately or wait a given interval of time for another service request to come in.

 NOTE For the `listener`, servers should exit immediately because the `listener` will always spawn a new process rather than give a request to a waiting server process.

The following routine can be used to create a service:

```
transp = svc_tli_create(0, nconf, NULL, 0, 0)
```

nconf is the `netconfig` structure of the transport on which the request came in.

Because the port monitors have already registered the service with `rpcbind`, there is no need for the service to register itself. Nevertheless, it must call `svc_reg()`:

```
svc_reg(transp, PROGNUM, VERSNUM, dispatch, NULL)
```

The `netconfig` structure here is NULL.

NOTE Programmers should study `rpcgen`-generated server stubs to better see the sequence in which these routines are called.

For connection-oriented transports, the following routine provides a lower level interface:

```
transp = svc_fd_create(0, recvsize, sendsize);
```

The file descriptor passed here is 0. The user may set the value of *recvsize* or *sendsize* to any appropriate buffer size. If they use a 0 in either case, a system default size will be chosen. This routine should be used by application servers that do not do any listening of their own, i.e., servers that simply do their job and return.

Using inetd

The format of entries in `/etc/inetd.conf` for RPC services is as follows:

rpc_prog/vers socket_type `rpc/`*proto flags uid pathname args*

where *rpc_prog* is the symbolic name of the program as it appears in `rpc(4)`, *vers* is the version number, *socket_type* is one of `dgram` or `stream` for connectionless or virtual circuit transport, respectively, *proto* is transport protocol, such as `tcp` or `udp` and must make sense with respect to the specified *socket_type*; *flags* is one of `wait` or `nowait`, *uid* must exist in `/etc/passwd`, *pathname* is the full path name of the server daemon and *args* are arguments to be passed to the daemon when it is invoked. For example:

```
mountd dgram rpc/udp wait root /usr/sbin/rpc.mountd rpc.mount
```

For more information, see `inetd.conf(4)`.

Using the listener

We will assume here that the reader already knows the details of setting up the
listener process and of using pmadm. The following shows how to use pmadm
to add RPC services:

pmadm −a −p *pm_tag* −s *svctag* −i *id* −v *ver* \
        −m `nlsadmin −c *command* −D −R *prog:vers*`

Here −a means to add a service, −p *pm_tag* specifies a tag associated with the
port monitor providing access to the service, −s *svctag* is the server's identifying
code, −i *id* is the /etc/passwd user ID assigned to service *svctag*, −v *ver* is
the version number for the port monitor's database file and −m specifies the
nlsadmin command for invoking the service. nlsadmin may have additional
arguments. For example, to add version 1 of a remote program server named
rusersd the pmadm command might be:

```
# pmadm -a -p tcp -s rusers -i root -v 4 \
>          -m 'nlsadmin -c /usr/sbin/rpc.ruserd -D -R 100002:1'
```

Here, the command is given root permissions, installed in version 4 of the
listener database file, and is made available over TCP transports.

 NOTE
Because of the complexity of the arguments and options that can follow the
pmadm −a invocation, it may be convenient to use a command script or the
menu system to add RPC services. If you use the menu system, enter
sysadm ports, then choose the port_services option.

After adding a service, the listener must be reinitialized before the service
will be available. This is accomplished by stopping, then retarting the listener,
as follows (note that rpcbind must be running):

```
# sacadm -k -p pmtag          # stop the listener
# sacadm -s -p pmtag          # start the listener
```

For more information, see the listen(1M), pmadm(1M), sacadm(1M) and sysadm(1M) manual pages and the *System Administrator's Guide.*

Advanced Examples

This section contains examples.

"Versions" shows how to register multiple versions of a remote procedure.

"Connection-oriented Transports" shows a remote copy program.

"Callback Procedures" shows how a server can be made to place a "client call" back to a client that calls it.

"Memory Allocation With XDR" illustrates how this is done.

Versions

By convention, the first version number of program PROG is PROGVERS_ORIG and the most recent version is PROGVERS.

Suppose there is a new version of the ruser program that returns an unsigned short rather than a long. If we name this version RUSERSVERS_SHORT, then a server that wants to support both versions would do a double register. The same server handle would be used for both of these registrations.

```
if (!svc_reg(transp, RUSERSPROG, RUSERSVERS_ORIG,
    nuser, nconf)) {
        fprintf(stderr, "can't register RUSER service\n");
        exit(1);
}
if (!svc_reg(transp, RUSERSPROG, RUSERSVERS_SHORT,
    nuser, nconf)) {
        fprintf(stderr, "can't register RUSER service\n");
        exit(1);
}
```

Both versions can be handled by the same C procedure:

```
nuser(rqstp, transp)
    struct svc_req *rqstp;
    SVCXPRT *transp;
{
    unsigned long nusers;
    unsigned short nusers2;

    switch (rqstp->rq_proc) {
    case NULLPROC:
        if (!svc_sendreply(transp, xdr_void, 0)) {
            fprintf(stderr, "can't reply to RPC call\n");
            return (1);
        }
        return (0);
    case RUSERSPROC_NUM:
            /*
             * Code here to compute the number of users
             * and assign it to the variable nusers
             */
        nusers2 = nusers;
        switch (rqstp->rq_vers) {
        case RUSERSVERS_ORIG:
            if (!svc_sendreply(transp, xdr_u_long,
              &nusers)) {
                fprintf(stderr,"can't reply to RPC call\n");
            }
            break;
        case RUSERSVERS_SHORT:
            if (!svc_sendreply(transp, xdr_u_short,
              &nusers2)) {
                fprintf(stderr,"can't reply to RPC call\n");
            }
            break;
        }
    default:
        svcerr_noproc(transp);
        return;
    }
    return (0);
}
```

Connection-Oriented Transports

Here is an example that copies a file from one system to another. The initiator of the RPC send call takes its standard input and sends it to the server receive, which prints it on standard output. This also illustrates an XDR procedure that behaves differently on serialization than on deserialization.

```c
/*
 * The xdr routine:     on decode, read from wire, write onto fp
 *                      on encode, read from fp, write onto wire
 */
#include <stdio.h>
#include <rpc/rpc.h>

xdr_rcp(xdrs, fp)
        XDR *xdrs;
        FILE *fp;
{
        unsigned long size;
        char buf[BUFSIZ], *p;

        if (xdrs->x_op == XDR_FREE)/* nothing to free */
                return 1;
        while (1) {
                if (xdrs->x_op == XDR_ENCODE) {
                        if ((size = fread(buf, sizeof(char), BUFSIZ,
                            fp)) == 0 && ferror(fp)) {
                                fprintf(stderr, "can't fread\n");
                                return (1);
                        }
                }
                p = buf;
                if (!xdr_bytes(xdrs, &p, &size, BUFSIZ))
                        return 0;
                if (size == 0)
                        return 1;
                if (xdrs->x_op == XDR_DECODE) {
                        if (fwrite(buf, sizeof(char), size,
                            fp) != size) {
                                fprintf(stderr, "can't fwrite\n");
                                return (1);
                        }
                }
        }
}
```

Note that in the following two screens, the serializing and deserializing is done only by `xdr_bytes()`.

```
/* The sender routines */

#include <stdio.h>
#include <netdb.h>
#include <rpc/rpc.h>
#include <sys/socket.h>
#include <sys/time.h>

main(argc, argv)
        int argc;
        char **argv;
{
        int xdr_rcp();

        if (argc < 2) {
                fprintf(stderr, "usage: %s servername\n", argv[0]);
                exit(1);
        }
        if (callcots(argv[1], RCPPROG, RCPPROC, RCPVERS,
          xdr_rcp, stdin, xdr_void, 0) != 0) {
                exit(1);
        }
        exit(0);
}

callcots(host, prognum, procnum, versnum, inproc, in, outproc, out)
        char *host, *in, *out;
        xdrproc_t inproc, outproc;
{
        enum clnt_stat clnt_stat;
        register CLIENT *client;
        struct timeval total_timeout;

        if ((client = clnt_create(host, prognum, versnum,
          "circuit_v")) == NULL) {
                perror("clnt_create");
                return (-1);
        }
        total_timeout.tv_sec = 20;
        total_timeout.tv_usec = 0;
        clnt_stat = clnt_call(client, procnum,
                inproc, in, outproc, out, total_timeout);
        clnt_destroy(client);
```

(continued on next page)

```
            if (clnt_stat != RPC_SUCCESS) {
                    clnt_perror("callcots");
            }
            return ((int)clnt_stat);
    }
```

```
/*
 * The receiving routines
 */
#include <stdio.h>
#include <rpc/rpc.h>
main ()
{
        int rcp_service(), xdr_rcp();

        if (svc_create(rpc_service, RCPPROG, RCPVERS,
          "circuit_v") == 0) {
                fprintf("svc_create: error\n");
                exit(1);
        }
        svc_run();   /* never returns */
        fprintf(stderr, "svc_run should never return\n");
}

rcp_service(rqstp, transp)
        register struct svc_req *rqstp;
        register SVCXPRT *transp;
{
        switch (rqstp->rq_proc) {
        case NULLPROC:
                if (svc_sendreply(transp, xdr_void, 0) == 0) {
                        fprintf(stderr, "err: rcp_service");
                        return (1);
                }
                return;
        case RCPPROC:
                if (!svc_getargs(transp, xdr_rcp, stdout)) {
                        svcerr_decode(transp);
                        return (1);
                }
                if (!svc_sendreply(transp, xdr_void, 0)) {
```

(continued on next page)

```
                              fprintf(stderr, "can't reply\n");
                              return (1);
                    }
                    return (0);
         default:
                    svcerr_noproc(transp);
                    return (1);
          }
    }
```

Note that on the server side no explicit action was taken after receiving the arguments. This is because xdr_rcp() did all the necessary dirty work automatically.

Callback Procedures

Occasionally, it is useful to have a server become a client, and make an RPC call back to the client process. An example is remote debugging, where the client is a window system program, and the server is a debugger running on the remote machine. Most of the time, the user clicks a mouse button at the debugging window, which converts this to a debugger command, and then makes an RPC call to the server (where the debugger is actually running), telling it to execute that command. However, when the debugger hits a breakpoint, the roles are reversed, and the debugger wants to make an rpc call to the window program, so that it can inform the user that a breakpoint has been reached.

To do an RPC callback, a program number is needed to make the RPC call. Because this will be a dynamically generated program number, it should be in the transient range, 0x40000000 - 0x5fffffff. In the following example, the routine gettransient() returns a valid program number in the transient range, and registers it with rpcbind. The call to rpcb_set() is a test and set operation, in that it indivisibly tests whether a program number has already been registered, and if it has not, then reserves it.

```
#include <stdio.h>
#include <rpc/rpc.h>
#include <netconfig.h>

gettransient(vers, nconf, address)
        int vers;
        struct netconfig *nconf;
        struct netbuf *address;
{
        static int prog = 0x40000000;

        while (! rpcb_set(prog++, vers, nconf, address))
                continue;
        return (prog - 1);
}
```

The following program illustrates how to use the gettransient() routine.
The client makes an RPC call to the server, passing it a transient program
number. Then the client waits around to receive a callback from the server at
that program number. The server registers the program EXAMPLEPROG, so that
it can receive the RPC call informing it of the callback program number. Then
at some random time (on receiving an ALRM signal in this example), it sends a
callback RPC call, using the program number it received earlier.

```
/*
 * client
 */
#include <stdio.h>
#include <rpc/rpc.h>
#include <netconfig.h>
#include "example.h"

main(argc, argv)
        int argc;
        char **argv;
{
        SVCXPRT *xprt;
        struct netconfig *nconf;
        int prognum;
        enum clnt_stat stat;

        if (argc != 3) {
                fprintf(stderr, "usage: clnt host transport\n");
                exit (1);
        }
        nconf = getnetconfigent(argv[2]);
        if (nconf == NULL) {
                fprintf(stderr, "unknown transport\n");
                exit (1);
        }
        xprt = svc_tli_create(RPC_ANYFD, nconf,
          (struct t_bind *)NULL, 0, 0);
        if (xprt == (SVCXPRT *)NULL) {
                fprintf(stderr, "could not create server handle\n");
                exit (1);
        }
        prognum = gettransient(1, nconf, &xprt->xp_ltaddr);
        fprintf(stderr, "client gets prognum %d\n", prognum);
        if (svc_reg(xprt, prognum, 1, callback, NULL)
          == FALSE) {
                fprintf(stderr, "could not register service\n");
                exit(1);
        }
        stat = rpc_call(argv[1], EXAMPLEPROG, EXAMPLEVERS,
          EXAMPLEPROC_CALLBACK, xdr_int, &prognum, xdr_void,
          NULL, NULL);
        if (stat != RPC_SUCCESS) {
                clnt_perrno(stat);
                exit(1);
        }
        svc_run();
```

(continued on next page)

```
            exit(1);
     }

callback(rqstp, transp)
        register struct svc_req *rqstp;
        register SVCXPRT *transp;
{
        switch (rqstp->rq_proc) {
                case 0:
                        if (!svc_sendreply(transp, xdr_void, 0)) {
                                fprintf(stderr, "err: exampleprog\n");
                                return (1);
                        }
                        return (0);
                case 1:
                        if (!svc_getargs(transp, xdr_void, 0)) {
                                svcerr_decode(transp);
                                return (1);
                        }
                        fprintf(stderr, "client got callback\n");
                        if (!svc_sendreply(transp, xdr_void, 0)) {
                                fprintf(stderr, "err: exampleprog");
                                return (1);
                        }
                        return (0);
        }
        return (2);
}
```

This example shows how `svc_tli_create()` can be used when it is necessary to explicitly chose the program number by calling `rpcb_set()` until it succeeds. (Here it was not required that a service be registered on a given transport, and the example could simply have used a "generic" network type.) After creating the handle, `svc_reg()` is called (with the last parameter given as NULL) to register the dispatch function with the dispatcher. Once the server side is ready, it then notifies the actual server of its dynamic program number with `rpc_call()`. On success it then waits for requests from the remote server.

In the following example, the server makes an RPC call to the client on an ALARM signal, but only if the client has passed the program number to the server. This server example illustrates the simplicity of the code when one is using `rpc_reg()`.

```
/*
 * server
 */
#include <stdio.h>
#include <rpc/rpc.h>
#include <sys/signal.h>
#include "example.h"

char *getnewprog();
char *hostname;
int docallback();
int pnum;          /* program number for callback routine */

main ()
{
        if (argc != 2) {
                fprint(stderr, "usage: server hostname\n");
                exit (1);
        }
        hostname = argv[1];
        rpc_reg(EXAMPLEPROG, EXAMPLEVERS, EXAMPLEPROC_CALLBACK,
          getnewprog, xdr_int, xdr_void, NULL);
        signal(SIGALRM, docallback);
        alarm(10);
        svc_run();
        fprintf(stderr, "Error: svc_run shouldn't return\n");
}

char *
getnewprog(pnump)
        char *pnump;
{
        pnum = *(int *)pnump;
        return NULL;
}

docallback ()
{
        int ans;

        if (pnum == 0) {
                alarm (10);
                return;
        }
        ans = rpc_call(hostname, pnum, 1, 1, xdr_void, 0,
          xdr_void, 0, NULL);
```

(continued on next page)

```
      if (ans != RPC_SUCCESS) {
              fprintf(stderr, "server: ");
              clnt_perrno(ans);
      }
}
```

Memory Allocation with XDR

XDR routines not only do input and output, they also do memory allocation.

The second parameter of xdr_array() is a pointer to an array, rather than the array itself.

 NOTE This is true for most XDR routines. The indirection is necessary because these routines often allocate memory.

If it is NULL, then xdr_array() allocates space for the array and returns a pointer to it, putting the size of the array in the third argument. As an example, consider the following XDR routine xdr_chararr1(), which deals with a fixed array of bytes with length SIZE:

```
xdr_chararr1(xdrsp, chararr)
        XDR *xdrsp;
        char chararr[];
{
        char *p;
        int len;

        p = chararr;
        len = SIZE;
        return (xdr_bytes(xdrsp, &p, &len, SIZE));
}
```

If space has already been allocated in `chararr`, it can be called from a server like this:

```
char chararr[SIZE];

svc_getargs(transp, xdr_chararr1, chararr);
```

To have XDR to do the allocation, this routine must be rewritten in the following way:

```
xdr_chararr2(xdrsp, chararrp)
        XDR *xdrsp;
        char **chararrp;
{
        int len;

        len = SIZE;
        return (xdr_bytes(xdrsp, chararrp, &len, SIZE));
}
```

Then the RPC call might look like this:

```
char *arrptr;

arrptr = NULL;
svc_getargs(transp, xdr_chararr2, &arrptr);
/*
 * Use the result here
 */
svc_freeargs(transp, xdr_chararr2, &arrptr);
```

Note that, after being used, the character array should normally be freed with `svc_freeargs()`. `svc_freeargs()` will not attempt to free any memory if the variable indicating it is NULL. For example, in the routine `xdr_finalexample()`, given earlier, if `finalp->string` were NULL, then it would not be freed. The same is true for `finalp->simplep`.

To summarize:

- Each XDR routine is responsible for serializing, deserializing, and freeing memory.

- When an XDR routine is called from `rpc_call()`, the serializing part is used.

- When called from `svc_getargs()`, the deserializer is used.

- When called from `svc_freeargs()`, the memory deallocator is used.

When building simple programs like those given as examples in this section, a programmer does not have to worry about the three modes.

8 External Data Representation Standard: Protocol Specification

Introduction to XDR

XDR is a standard for the description and encoding of data. The XDR protocol is useful for transferring data between different computer architectures and has been used to communicate data between such diverse machines as the 3B2, Sun Workstation, VAX, IBM-PC, and Cray. XDR fits into the ISO presentation layer and is roughly analogous in purpose to X.409, ISO Abstract Syntax Notation. The major difference between the two is that XDR uses implicit typing, while X.409 uses explicit typing.

XDR uses a language to describe data formats and can only be used to describe data; it is not a programming language. This language makes it possible to describe intricate data formats in a concise manner. The XDR language is similar to the C language. Protocols such as RPC (Remote Procedure Call) and the NFS (Network File System) use XDR to describe the format of their data.

The XDR standard makes the following assumption: that bytes (or octets) are portable, where a byte is defined to be 8 bits of data.

Basic Block Size

The representation of all items requires a multiple of four bytes (or 32 bits) of data. The bytes are numbered 0 through n−1. The bytes are read or written to some byte stream such that byte m always precedes byte m+1. The n bytes are followed by enough (0 to 3) residual zero bytes, r, to make the total byte count a multiple of four.

Choosing the XDR block size requires a tradeoff. Choosing a small size such as two makes the encoded data small, but causes alignment problems for machines that are not aligned on these boundaries. A large size such as eight means the data will be aligned on virtually every machine, but causes the encoded data to grow too large. Four was chosen as a compromise. Four is big enough to support most architectures efficiently, except for rare machines such as the eight-byte aligned Cray. Four is also small enough to keep the encoded data restricted to a reasonable size.

The same data should encode into the same thing on all machines, so that encoded data can be significantly compared or checksummed. Forcing the padded bytes to be zero ensures this.

This chapter uses graphic box notation for illustration and comparison. In most illustrations, each box (delimited by a plus sign at the 4 corners and vertical bars and dashes) depicts a byte. Ellipses (. . .) between boxes show zero or more additional bytes where required:

A Block

```
+--------+--------+...+--------+--------+...+--------+
| byte 0 | byte 1 |...|byte n-1|   0    |...|   0    |
+--------+--------+...+--------+--------+...+--------+
|<----------n bytes---------->|<------r bytes------>|
|<----------n+r (where (n+r) mod 4 = 0)>----------->|
```

Organization of Technical Information

The "XDR Data Type Declarations" section describes each atomic data type that can be represented using XDR.

"Other XDR Declarations" describe constants, type definitions, and optional data (an alternate way to express certain kinds of unions).

"The XDR Language Specification" section provides a formal definition of the XDR language.

"An Example of an XDR Data Description" shows how XDR might be used to describe a file.

XDR Data Type Declarations

Each of the sections that follow:

- describe a data type defined in the XDR standard
- show how that data type is declared in the language
- include a graphic illustration of the encoding

For each data type in the language we show a general paradigm declaration. Note that angle brackets (< and >) denote variable length sequences of data and square brackets ([and]) denote fixed-length sequences of data. n, m and r denote integers. For the full language specification and more formal definitions of terms such as *identifier* and *declaration*, refer to "The XDR Language Specification", below.

For some data types, more specific examples are included. A more extensive example of a data description is in the section "An Example of XDR Data Representation".

Integer

Description

An XDR signed integer is a 32-bit datum that encodes an integer in the range [-2147483648,2147483647]. The integer is represented in two's complement notation; the most and least significant bytes are 0 and 3, respectively.

Declaration

Integers are declared as follows:

        int *identifier*;

Encoding

Integer

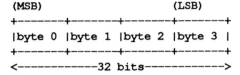

```
(MSB)                       (LSB)
+-------+-------+-------+-------+
|byte 0 |byte 1 |byte 2 |byte 3 |
+-------+-------+-------+-------+
<------------32 bits------------>
```

Unsigned Integer

Description

An XDR unsigned integer is a 32-bit datum that encodes a nonnegative integer in the range [0,4294967295]. The integer is represented by an unsigned binary number whose most and least significant bytes are 0 and 3, respectively.

Declaration

An unsigned integer is declared as follows:

    unsigned int *identifier*;

Encoding

Unsigned Integer

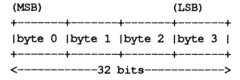

```
(MSB)                       (LSB)
+-------+-------+-------+-------+
|byte 0 |byte 1 |byte 2 |byte 3 |
+-------+-------+-------+-------+
<------------32 bits------------>
```

Enumeration

Description

Enumerations have the same representation as signed integers and are handy for describing subsets of the integers.

Declaration

Enumerated data is declared as follows:

> enum { *name-identifier* = *constant*, ... } *identifier*;

For example, an enumerated type could represent the three colors red, yellow, and blue as follows:

> enum { RED = 2, YELLOW = 3, BLUE = 5 } colors;

It is an error to assign to an enum an integer that has not been assigned in the enum declaration.

Encoding

See "Integer," above.

Boolean

Description

Booleans are important enough and occur frequently enough to warrant their own explicit type in the standard. Booleans are integers of value 0 or 1.

Declaration

Booleans are declared as follows:

> bool *identifier*;

This is equivalent to:

> enum { FALSE = 0, TRUE = 1 } *identifier*;

Encoding

See "Integer," above.

Hyper Integer and Unsigned Hyper Integer

Description

The standard also defines 64-bit (8-byte) numbers called hyper int and unsigned hyper int whose representations are the obvious extensions of integer and unsigned integer, defined above. They are represented in two's complement notation; the most and least significant bytes are 0 and 7, respectively.

Declaration

Hyper integers are declared as follows:

       hyper int *identifier*;

       unsigned hyper int *identifier*;

Encoding

Hyper Integer

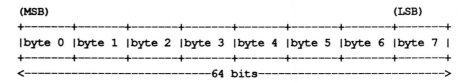

```
(MSB)                                                            (LSB)
+-------+-------+-------+-------+-------+-------+-------+-------+
|byte 0 |byte 1 |byte 2 |byte 3 |byte 4 |byte 5 |byte 6 |byte 7 |
+-------+-------+-------+-------+-------+-------+-------+-------+
<-----------------------------64 bits-------------------------->
```

Floating-point

Description

The standard defines the floating-point data type `float` (32 bits or 4 bytes). The encoding used is the IEEE standard for normalized single-precision floating-point numbers [1]. The following three fields describe the single-precision floating-point number:

S: The sign of the number. Values 0 and 1 represent positive and negative, respectively. One bit.

E: The exponent of the number, base 2. Eight bits are devoted to this field. The exponent is biased by 127.

F: The fractional part of the number's mantissa, base 2. 23 bits are devoted to this field.

Therefore, the floating-point number is described by:

```
(-1)**S * 2**(E-Bias) * 1.F
```

Declaration

Single-precision floating-point data is declared as follows:

```
float identifier;
```

Encoding

Single-Precision Floating Point

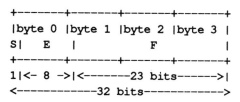

```
+--------+--------+--------+--------+
|byte 0  |byte 1  |byte 2  |byte 3  |
S|   E    |        F        |
+--------+--------+--------+--------+
1|<- 8 ->|<-------23 bits------>|
<------------32 bits------------>
```

Just as the most and least significant bytes of an integer are 0 and 3, the most and least significant bits of a single-precision floating-point number are 0 and

31. The beginning bit (and most significant bit) offsets of S, E, and F are 0, 1, and 9, respectively.

 NOTE These offsets refer to the logical positions of the bits, *not* to their physical locations (which vary from medium to medium).

The IEEE specifications should be consulted about the encoding for signed zero, signed infinity (overflow), and denormalized numbers (underflow) [1]. According to IEEE specifications, the NaN (not a number) is system dependent and should not be used externally.

Double-Precision Floating-point

Description

The standard defines the encoding for the double-precision floating-point data type double (64 bits or 8 bytes). The encoding used is the IEEE standard for normalized double-precision floating-point numbers [1]. The standard encodes the following three fields, which describe the double-precision floating-point number:

S: The sign of the number. Values 0 and 1 represent positive and negative, respectively. One bit.

E: The exponent of the number, base 2. 11 bits are devoted to this field. The exponent is biased by 1023.

F: The fractional part of the number's mantissa, base 2. 52 bits are devoted to this field.

Therefore, the floating-point number is described by:

```
(-1)**S * 2**(E-Bias) * 1.F
```

Declaration

double *identifier;*

Encoding

Double-Precision Floating Point

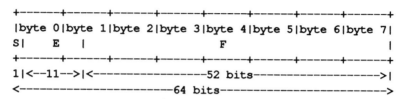

```
+------+------+------+------+------+------+------+------+
|byte 0|byte 1|byte 2|byte 3|byte 4|byte 5|byte 6|byte 7|
S|   E  |                   F                          |
+------+------+------+------+------+------+------+------+
1|<--11-->|<------------------52 bits------------------>|
 <-----------------------64 bits----------------------->
```

Just as the most and least significant bytes of an integer are 0 and 3, the most and least significant bits of a double-precision floating- point number are 0 and 63. The beginning bit (and most significant bit) offsets of S, E , and F are 0, 1, and 12, respectively.

> **NOTE** These offsets refer to the logical positions of the bits, *not* to their physical locations (which vary from medium to medium).

The IEEE specifications should be consulted about the encoding for signed zero, signed infinity (overflow), and denormalized numbers (underflow) [1]. According to IEEE specifications, the NaN (not a number) is system dependent and should not be used externally.

Fixed-length Opaque Data

Description

At times, fixed-length uninterpreted data needs to be passed among machines. This data is called opaque.

Declaration

Opaque data is declared as follows:

    opaque identifier[n];

where the constant n is the (static) number of bytes necessary to contain the
opaque data.

Encoding

The n bytes are followed by enough (0 to 3) residual zero bytes, r, to make the
total byte count of the opaque object a multiple of four.

Fixed-Length Opaque

```
0         1      ...
+--------+--------+...+--------+--------+...+--------+
| byte 0 | byte 1 |...|byte n-1|    0   |...|    0   |
+--------+--------+...+--------+--------+...+--------+
|<-----------n bytes---------->|<------r bytes------>|
|<-----------n+r (where (n+r) mod 4 = 0)------------>|
```

Variable-length Opaque Data

Description

The standard also provides for variable-length (counted) opaque data, defined
as a sequence of n (numbered 0 through n−1) arbitrary bytes to be the number
n encoded as an unsigned integer (as described below), and followed by the n
bytes of the sequence.

Byte b of the sequence always precedes byte b+1 of the sequence, and byte 0 of
the sequence always follows the sequence's length (count). The n bytes are followed by enough (0 to 3) residual zero bytes, r, to make the total byte count a
multiple of four.

Declaration

Variable-length opaque data is declared in the following way:

> opaque *identifier<m>;*

or

> opaque *identifier<>;*

The constant m denotes an upper bound of the number of bytes that the sequence may contain. If m is not specified, as in the second declaration, it is assumed to be $(2^{**}32) - 1$, the maximum length. For example, a filing protocol may state that the maximum data transfer size is 8192 bytes, as follows:

> opaque filedata<8192>;

Encoding

Variable-Length Opaque

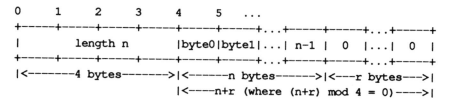

It is an error to encode a length greater than the maximum described in the specification.

String

Description

The standard defines a string of n (numbered 0 through n−1) ASCII bytes to be the number n encoded as an unsigned integer (as described above), and followed by the n bytes of the string. Byte b of the string always precedes byte b+1 of the string, and byte 0 of the string always follows the string's length. The n bytes are followed by enough (0 to 3) residual zero bytes, r, to make the total byte count a multiple of four.

Declaration

Counted byte strings are declared as follows:

    string object<m>;

or

    string object<>;

The constant m denotes an upper bound of the number of bytes that a string may contain. If m is not specified, as in the second declaration, it is assumed to be $(2**32) - 1$, the maximum length. The constant m would normally be found in a protocol specification. For example, a filing protocol may state that a file name can be no longer than 255 bytes, as follows:

    string filename<255>;

Encoding

String

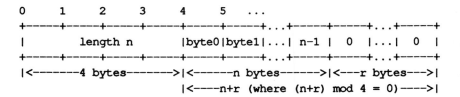

It is an error to encode a length greater than the maximum described in the specification.

Fixed-length Array

Description

Fixed-length arrays of elements numbered 0 through n−1 are encoded by individually encoding the elements of the array in their natural order, 0 through n−1. Each element's size is a multiple of four bytes. Though all elements are of the same type, the elements may have different sizes. For example, in a fixed-length array of strings, all elements are of type string, yet each element will vary in its length.

Declaration

Declarations for fixed-length arrays of homogeneous elements are in the following form:

type-name identifier [*n*] ;

Fixed-Length Array

```
+---+---+---+---+---+---+---+---+...+---+---+---+---+
|   element 0   |   element 1   |...|  element n-1  |
+---+---+---+---+---+---+---+---+...+---+---+---+---+
|<--------------------n elements------------------->|
```

Variable-length Array

Description

Counted arrays provide the ability to encode variable-length arrays of homogeneous elements. The array is encoded as the element count n (an unsigned integer) followed by the encoding of each of the array's elements, starting with element 0 and progressing through element n–1.

Declaration

The declaration for variable-length arrays follows this form:

type-name identifier<m>;

or

type-name identifier<>;

The constant *m* specifies the maximum acceptable element count of an array. Note that if *m* is not specified, as is the case in the second declaration format above, it is assumed to be (2**32) − 1.

Encoding

Counted Array

```
 0   1   2   3
+--+--+--+--+--+--+--+--+--+--+--+--+...+--+--+--+--+
|     n     | element 0 | element 1 |...|element n-1|
+--+--+--+--+--+--+--+--+--+--+--+--+...+--+--+--+--+
|<-4 bytes->|<--------------n elements------------->|
```

It is an error to encode a value of n that is greater than the maximum described in the specification.

Structure

Description

The components of the structure are encoded in the order of their declaration in the structure. Each component's size is a multiple of four bytes, though the components may be different sizes.

Declaration

Structures are declared as follows:

```
struct {
        component-declaration-A;
        component-declaration-B;

        . . .
} identifier;
```

Encoding

Structure

```
+-------------+-------------+...
| component A | component B |...
+-------------+-------------+...
```

Discriminated Union

Description

A discriminated union is a type composed of a discriminant followed by a type selected from a set of prearranged types according to the value of the discriminant. The type of discriminant is either int, unsigned int, or an enumerated type, such as bool. The component types are called *arms* of the union, and are preceded by the value of the discriminant which implies their encoding.

Declaration

Discriminated unions are declared as follows:

```
union switch (discriminant-declaration) {
        case discriminant-value-A:
                arm-declaration-A;
        case discriminant-value-B:
                arm-declaration-B;
        ...
        default:
                default-declaration;
} identifier;
```

Each case keyword is followed by a legal value of the discriminant. The default arm is optional. If it is not specified, then a valid encoding of the union cannot take on unspecified discriminant values. The size of the implied arm is always a multiple of four bytes.

Encoding

The discriminated union is encoded as its discriminant followed by the encoding of the implied arm.

Discriminated Union

```
 0   1   2   3
+---+---+---+---+---+---+---+---+
|  discriminant |  implied arm  |
+---+---+---+---+---+---+---+---+
|<---4 bytes--->|
```

Void

Description

An XDR void is a 0-byte quantity. Voids are useful for describing operations that take no data as input or no data as output. They are also useful in unions, where some arms may contain data and others do not.

Declaration

The declaration is simply as follows:

```
void;
```

Encoding

Voids are illustrated as follows:

```
++
||
++
-><- 0 bytes
```

Other XDR Declarations

Constant

The declaration for a constant follows this form:

    const name-identifier = n;

const is used to define a symbolic name for a constant; it does not declare any data. The symbolic constant may be used anywhere a regular constant may be used.

The following example defines a symbolic constant DOZEN, equal to 12.

    const DOZEN = 12;

typedef

typedef does not declare any data either, but serves to define new identifiers for declaring data. The syntax is:

    typedef declaration;

The new type name is actually the variable name in the declaration part of the typedef.

The following example defines a new type called eggbox using an existing type called egg and the symbolic constant DOZEN:

    typedef egg eggbox[DOZEN];

Variables declared using the new type name have the same type as the new type name would have in the typedef, if it was considered a variable. For example, the following two declarations are equivalent in declaring the variable fresheggs:

    eggbox   fresheggs;
    egg   fresheggs[DOZEN];

When a typedef involves a struct, enum, or union definition, there is another (preferred) syntax that may be used to define the same type. In general, a typedef of the following form:

    typedef <<struct, union, or enum definition>> identifier;

may be converted to the alternative form by removing the `typedef` part and placing the identifier after the `struct`, `enum`, or `union` keyword, instead of at the end. For example, here are the two ways to define the type `bool`:

```
typedef enum {      /* using typedef */
       FALSE = 0,
       TRUE = 1
} bool;

enum bool {         /* preferred alternative */
       FALSE = 0,
       TRUE = 1
};
```

This syntax is preferred because one does not have to go to the end of a declaration to learn the name of the new type.

Optional-data

Optional-data is a form of union. Because it occurs frequently, it has been given its own declaration syntax. It is declared as follows:

> *type-name* *identifier;

This is equivalent to the following union:

```
union switch (bool opted) {
       case TRUE:
               type-name element;
       case FALSE:
               void;
} identifier;
```

It is also equivalent to the following variable-length array declaration, because the boolean `opted` can be interpreted as the length of the array:

> *type-name identifier<1>;*

Optional-data is useful for describing recursive data-structures such as linked-lists and trees. For example, the following defines a type `stringlist` that encodes lists of arbitrary length strings:

```
struct *stringlist {
        string item<>;
        stringlist next;
};
```

It could have been equivalently declared as the following union:

```
union stringlist switch (bool opted) {
        case TRUE:
                struct {
                        string item<>;
                        stringlist next;
                } element;
        case FALSE:
                void;
};
```

or as a variable-length array:

```
struct stringlist<1> {
        string item<>;
        stringlist next;
};
```

Both of these declarations obscure the intention of the `stringlist` type, so the optional-data declaration is preferred over both of them. The optional-data type also has a close correlation to how recursive data structures are represented in high-level languages such as Pascal or C by use of pointers. The syntax is the same as that of the C language for pointers.

The XDR Language Specification

Notational Conventions

This specification uses a modified Backus-Naur Form notation for describing the XDR language. Here is a brief description of the notation:

1. The characters |, (,), [,], and * are special.

2. Terminal symbols are strings of any characters in a font.

3. Non-terminal symbols are strings of non-special *italic* characters.

4. Alternative items are separated by a vertical bar (|).

5. Optional items are enclosed in brackets.

6. Items are grouped together by enclosing them in parentheses.

7. A * following an item means 0 or more occurrences of the item.

For example, consider the following pattern:

        a very (, very)* [cold and] rainy (day | night)

An infinite number of strings match this pattern. A few of them are:

        a very rainy day
        a very, very rainy day
        a very cold and rainy day
        a very, very, very cold and rainy night

Lexical Notes

1. Comments begin with /* and end with */.

2. White space serves to separate items and is otherwise ignored.

3. An identifier is a letter followed by an optional sequence of letters, digits or underbars (_). The case of identifiers is not ignored.

4. A constant is a sequence of one or more decimal digits, optionally preceded by a minus-sign (−).

Syntax Information

declaration:

        type-specifier identifier
        | *type-specifier identifier* [*value*]
        | *type-specifier identifier* < [*value*] >
        | opaque *identifier* [*value*]
        | opaque *identifier* < [*value*] >
        | string *identifier* < [*value*] >
        | *type-specifier* * *identifier*
        | void

value:

        constant
        | *identifier*

type-specifier:

        [unsigned] int
        | [unsigned] hyper
        | float
        | double
        | bool
        | *enum-type-spec*
        | *struct-type-spec*
        | *union-type-spec*
        | *identifier*

enum-type-spec:

        enum *enum-body*

enum-body:

        {
        (*identifier* = *value*)
        (, *identifier* = *value*)*
        }

struct-type-spec:

        struct *struct-body*

struct-body:
      {
      (*declaration* ;)
      (*declaration* ;)*
      }

union-type-spec:
      union *union-body*

union-body:
      switch (*declaration*) {
      (case *value* : *declaration* ;)
      (case *value* : *declaration* ;)*
      [default : *declaration* ;]
      }

constant-def:
      const *identifier* = *constant* ;

type-def:
      typedef *declaration* ;
      | enum *identifier enum-body* ;
      | struct *identifier struct-body* ;
      | union *identifier union-body* ;

definition:
      type-def
      | *constant-def*

specification:
      definition *

Syntax Notes

1. The following are keywords and cannot be used as identifiers:

bool	const	enum	int	struct	union
case	default	float	opaque	switch	unsigned
char	double	hyper	string	typedef	void

2. Only unsigned constants may be used as size specifications for arrays. If an identifier is used, it must have been declared previously as an unsigned constant in a const definition.

3. Constant and type identifiers within the scope of a specification are in the same name space and must be declared uniquely within this scope.

4. Similarly, variable names must be unique within the scope of struct and union declarations. Nested struct and union declarations create new scopes.

5. The discriminant of a union must be of a type that evaluates to an integer. That is, int, unsigned int, bool, an enum type or any typedefed type that evaluates to one of these. Also, the case values must be legal discriminant values. Finally, a case value may not be specified more than once within the scope of a union declaration.

An Example of an XDR Data Description

Here is a short XDR data description of a thing called a file, which might be used to transfer files from one machine to another:

```
const MAXUSERNAME = 32;     /* max length of a user name */
const MAXFILELEN = 65535;   /* max length of a file */
const MAXNAMELEN = 255;     /* max length of a file name */

/* Types of files: */

enum filekind {
        TEXT = 0,       /* ascii data */
        DATA = 1,       /* raw data   */
        EXEC = 2        /* executable */
};

/* File information, per kind of file: */

union filetype switch (filekind kind) {
        case TEXT:
                void;                           /* no extra information */
        case DATA:
                string creator<MAXNAMELEN>;     /* data creator */
        case EXEC:
                string interpretor<MAXNAMELEN>; /* program interpretor */
};

/* A complete file: */

struct file {
        string filename<MAXNAMELEN>; /* name of file */
        filetype type;              /* info about file */
        string owner<MAXUSERNAME>;  /* owner of file */
        opaque data<MAXFILELEN>;    /* file data */
};
```

Suppose now that there is a user named john who wants to store his lisp program sillyprog that contains just the data (quit). His file would be encoded as follows:

Offset	Hex Bytes	ASCII	Description
0	00 00 00 09	. . . .	Length of filename = 9
4	73 69 6c 6c	sill	Filename characters
8	79 70 72 6f	ypro	... and more characters ...
12	67 00 00 00	g...	... and 3 zero-bytes of fill
16	00 00 00 02	. . . .	Filekind is EXEC = 2
20	00 00 00 04	. . . .	Length of interpretor = 4
24	6c 69 73 70	lisp	Interpretor characters
28	00 00 00 04	. . . .	Length of owner = 4
32	6a 6f 68 6e	john	Owner characters
36	00 00 00 06	. . . .	Length of file data = 6
40	28 71 75 69	(qui	File data bytes ...
44	74 29 00 00	t)..	... and 2 zero-bytes of fill

References

[1]   "IEEE Standard for Binary Floating-Point Arithmetic," ANSI/IEEE Standard 754-1985, Institute of Electrical and Electronics Engineers, August 1985.

9 Remote Procedure Calls: Protocol Specification

Introduction

This chapter specifies a message protocol used in implementing the Remote Procedure Call (RPC) package. (The message protocol is specified with the External Data Representation (XDR) language. This chapter assumes the reader is familiar with XDR. See the "External Data Representation Standard: Protocol Specification" chapter for details.)

Terminology

This chapter discusses servers, services, programs, procedures, clients, and versions.

A *server* is a process that provides remote services to clients.

A *network service* is a collection of one or more remote programs.

A *remote program* implements one or more remote procedures; the procedures, their parameters, and results are documented in the specific program's protocol specification (see the "rpcbind Protocol" below, for an example).

Network *clients* are processes that make remote procedure calls to servers. A server may support more than one version of a remote program to be forward compatible with changing protocols.

As an example of how these terms are used, consider a network file service composed of two programs. One program may deal with high-level applications such as file system access control and locking. The other may deal with low-level file IO and have procedures like "read" and "write." A client machine of the network file service would call the procedures associated with the two programs of the service on behalf of some user on the client machine.

General Attributes of the Protocol

The RPC Model

The remote procedure call model is similar to the local procedure call model. In the local case, the caller places arguments to a procedure in some well-specified location. It then transfers control to the procedure, and eventually gains back control. At that point, the results of the procedure are extracted from a well-specified location, and the caller continues execution.

The remote procedure call is similar, in that one thread of control logically winds through two processes. One is the caller's process, the other is a server's process. Conceptually, the caller process sends a call message to the server process and waits (blocks) for a reply message. The call message contains the procedure's parameters, among other things. The reply message contains the procedure's results, among other things. Once the reply message is received, the results of the procedure are extracted, and the caller's execution is resumed.

On the server side, a process is dormant awaiting the arrival of a call message. When one arrives, the server process extracts the procedure's parameters, computes the results, sends a reply message, and then awaits the next call message.

Note that in this description, only one of the two processes is active at any given time. However, this need not be the case. The RPC protocol makes no restrictions on the concurrency model implemented. For example, an implementation may choose to have RPC calls be asynchronous, so that the client may do useful work while waiting for the reply from the server. Another possibility is to have the server create a task to process an incoming request, so that the server can be free to receive other requests.

Transports and Semantics

The RPC protocol is independent of transport protocols. That is, RPC does not care how a message is passed from one process to another. The protocol deals only with specification and interpretation of messages.

It is important to point out that RPC does not attempt to ensure transport reliability. In this regard, the application must be aware of the type of transport protocol underneath RPC. If the RPC service knows it is running on top of a reliable transport such as TCP/IP, then most of the work is already done for it. On the other hand, if RPC is running on top of an unreliable transport such as UDP/IP, the service must devise its own retransmission and time-out policy. RPC does not provide this service.

Because of transport independence, the RPC protocol does not attach specific semantics to the remote procedures or their execution. Semantics can be inferred from (but should be explicitly specified by) the underlying transport protocol. For example, consider RPC running on top of an unreliable transport such as UDP/IP. If an application retransmits RPC messages after short time-outs, the only thing it can infer if it receives no reply is that the procedure was executed zero or more times. If it does receive a reply, then it can infer that the procedure was executed at least once.

A server may wish to remember previously granted requests from a client and not regrant them to insure some degree of execute-at-most-once semantics. A server can do this by taking advantage of the transaction ID that is packaged with every RPC request. The main use of this transaction ID is by the RPC client for matching replies to requests. However, a client application may choose to reuse its previous transaction ID when retransmitting a request. The server application, knowing this fact, may choose to remember this ID after granting a request and not regrant requests with the same ID. The server is not allowed to examine this ID in any other way except as a test for equality.

On the other hand, if using a reliable transport such as TCP/IP, the application can infer from a reply message that the procedure was executed exactly once, but if it receives no reply message, it cannot assume the remote procedure was not executed. Note that even if a connection-oriented protocol like TCP is used, an application still needs time-outs and reconnection to handle server crashes.

Binding and Rendezvous Independence

The act of binding a client to a service is *not* part of the remote procedure call specification. This important and necessary function is left up to some higher-level software. (The software may use RPC itself; see the "rpcbind Protocol" section, below.)

Implementors should think of the RPC protocol as the jump-subroutine instruction ("JSR") of a network; the loader (binder) makes JSR useful, and the loader itself uses JSR to accomplish its task. Likewise, the network makes RPC useful, using RPC to accomplish this task.

Authentication

The RPC protocol provides the fields necessary for a client to identify itself to a service and vice-versa. Security and access control mechanisms can be built on top of the message authentication. Several different authentication protocols can be supported. A field in the RPC header specifies the protocol being used. More information on authentication protocols can be found in the "Authentication Protocols" section, below.

Organization of Technical Information

The "RPC Protocol Requirements" section outlines the inherent features of the RPC protocol and additional features provided by the RPC package.

The "RPC Message Protocol" section defines the RPC message protocol in terms of the XDR language.

The "Authentication Protocols" section describes authentication features supported by the RPC package.

The "Record Marking Standard" section describes how RPC messages are delimited from each other when operating over a byte stream protocol transport like TPC/IP.

"The RPC Language" section provides an example of an RPC service followed by a formal definition of the RPC language.

The "rpcbind Protocol" section describes the interface to the rpcbind service.

RPC Protocol Requirements

The RPC protocol provides for the following:

- Unique specification of a procedure to be called.
- Provisions for matching response messages to request messages.
- Provisions for authenticating the caller to service and vice-versa.

In addition, the RPC package provides features that detect the following:

- RPC protocol mismatches.
- Remote program protocol version mismatches.
- Protocol errors (such as misspecification of a procedure's parameters).
- Reasons why remote authentication failed.

Programs and Procedures

The RPC call message has three unsigned fields:

- remote program number
- remote program version number
- remote procedure number

The three fields uniquely identify the procedure to be called.

Program numbers are administered by a central authority (see below).

The first implementation of a program will most likely have version number 1. Because most new protocols evolve into better, stable, and mature protocols, a version field of the call message identifies the version of the protocol the caller is using. Version numbers make speaking old and new protocols through the same server process possible.

The procedure number identifies the procedure to be called. These numbers are documented in the specific program's protocol specification. For example, a file service's protocol specification may state that its procedure number 5 is "read" and procedure number 12 is "write."

Just as remote program protocols may change over several versions, the RPC message protocol itself may change. Therefore, the call message also has in it the RPC version number, which is always equal to 2 for the version of RPC described here.

The reply message to a request message has enough information to distinguish the following error conditions:

- The remote implementation of RPC does not speak protocol version 2. The lowest and highest supported RPC version numbers are returned.

- The remote program is not available on the remote system.

- The remote program does not support the requested version number. The lowest and highest supported remote program version numbers are returned.

- The requested procedure number does not exist. (This is usually a caller side protocol or programming error.)

- The parameters to the remote procedure appear to be garbage from the server's point of view. (Again, this is usually caused by a disagreement about the protocol between client and service.)

Authentication

Provisions for authentication of caller to service and vice-versa are provided as a part of the RPC protocol. The call message has two authentication fields, the credentials and verifier. The reply message has one authentication field, the response verifier. The RPC protocol specification defines all three fields to be the following opaque type:

```
enum auth_flavor {
        AUTH_NONE    = 0,
        AUTH_SYS     = 1,
        AUTH_SHORT   = 2,
        AUTH_DES     = 3
        /* and more to be defined */
};

struct opaque_auth {
        enum_t    oa_flavor;        /* style of credentials */
        caddr_t   oa_base;          /* address of more auth stuff */
        u_int     oa_length;        /* not to exceed MAX_AUTH_BYTES */
};
```

In simple English, any opaque_auth structure is an auth_flavor enumeration followed by bytes that are opaque to the RPC protocol implementation.

The interpretation and semantics of the data contained within the authentication fields is specified by individual, independent authentication protocol specifications. (See "Authentication Protocols," below, for definitions of the various authentication protocols.)

If authentication parameters are rejected, the response message contains information stating why they are rejected.

Program Number Assignment

Program numbers are given out in groups of 0x20000000 according to the following chart:

Program Numbers	Description
0 — 1fffffff	*Defined by Sun*
20000000 — 3fffffff	*Defined by user*
40000000 — 5fffffff	*Transient*
60000000 — 7fffffff	*Reserved*
80000000 — 9fffffff	*Reserved*
a0000000 — bfffffff	*Reserved*
c0000000 — dfffffff	*Reserved*
e0000000 — ffffffff	*Reserved*

Sun Microsystems administers the first group of numbers, which should be identical for all UNIX® System V customers. If a customer develops an application that might be of general interest, that application should be given an assigned number in the first range.

The second group of numbers is reserved for specific customer applications. This range is intended primarily for debugging new programs.

The third group is reserved for applications that generate program numbers dynamically.

The final groups are reserved for future use, and should not be used.

To register a protocol specification, send a request by email to rpc@sun.com, or write to:

> RPC Administrator
> Sun Microsystems
> 2550 Garcia Ave.
> Mountain View, CA 94043

Please include a compilable rpcgen .x file describing your protocol. You will be given a unique program number in return.

The RPC program numbers and protocol specifications of standard RPC services can be found in the include files in /usr/include/rpcsvc. These services, however, constitute only a small subset of those that have been registered.

Other Uses of the RPC Protocol

The intended use of this protocol is for calling remote procedures. That is, each call message is matched with a response message. However, the protocol itself is a message-passing protocol with which other (non-RPC) protocols can be implemented. Some of the non-RPC protocols supported by the RPC package are:

Batching

Batching allows a client to send an arbitrarily large sequence of call messages to a server; batching typically uses reliable byte stream protocols (like TCP/IP) for its transport. In batching, the client never waits for a reply from the server, and the server does not send replies to batch requests. A sequence of batch calls is usually finished by a non-batch RPC call to flush the pipeline (with positive acknowledgement).

Broadcast RPC

In broadcast RPC-based protocols, the client sends a broadcast packet to the network and waits for numerous replies. Broadcast RPC uses unreliable, packet-based protocols (like UDP/IP) as its transports. Servers that support broadcast protocols only respond when the request is successfully processed, and are silent in the face of errors. Broadcast RPC uses the rpcbind service to achieve its semantics. See the "rpcbind Protocol" below, for more information.

The RPC Message Protocol

This section defines the RPC message protocol in the XDR data description
language. The message is defined in a top-down style.

```
enum msg_type {
        CALL  = 0,
        REPLY = 1
};
/*
 * A reply to a call message can take on two forms:
 * The message was either accepted or rejected.
 */
enum reply_stat {
        MSG_ACCEPTED = 0,
        MSG_DENIED   = 1
};

/*
 * Given that a call message was accepted, the following is the
 * status of an attempt to call a remote procedure.
 */
enum accept_stat {
        SUCCESS       = 0, /* RPC executed successfully       */
        PROG_UNAVAIL  = 1, /* remote hasn't exported program  */
        PROG_MISMATCH = 2, /* remote can't support version #  */
        PROC_UNAVAIL  = 3, /* program can't support procedure */
        GARBAGE_ARGS  = 4  /* procedure can't decode params   */
};


/*
 * Reasons why a call message was rejected:
 */
enum reject_stat {
        RPC_MISMATCH = 0, /* RPC version number != 2          */
        AUTH_ERROR   = 1   /* remote can't authenticate caller */
};


/*
 * Why authentication failed:
 */
enum auth_stat {
        AUTH_BADCRED      = 1,  /* bad credentials */
        AUTH_REJECTEDCRED = 2,  /* client must begin new session */
        AUTH_BADVERF      = 3,  /* bad verifier */
        AUTH_REJECTEDVERF = 4,  /* verifier expired or replayed */
        AUTH_TOOWEAK      = 5   /* rejected for security reasons */
};
```

(continued on next page)

```
/*
 * The RPC message:
 * All messages start with a transaction identifier, xid,
 * followed by a two-armed discriminated union.  The union's
 * discriminant is a msg_type which switches to one of the two
 * types of the message.  The xid of a REPLY message always
 * matches that of the initiating CALL message.  NB: The xid
 * field is only used for clients matching reply messages with
 * call messages or for servers detecting retransmissions; the
 * service side cannot treat this id as any type of sequence
 * number.
 */
struct rpc_msg {
        unsigned int xid;
        union switch (msg_type mtype) {
                case CALL:
                        call_body cbody;
                case REPLY:
                        reply_body rbody;
        } body;
};


/*
 * Body of an RPC request call:
 * In version 2 of the RPC protocol specification, rpcvers must
 * be equal to 2.  The fields prog, vers, and proc specify the
 * remote program, its version number, and the procedure within
 * the remote program to be called.  After these fields are two
 * authentication parameters: cred (authentication credentials)
 * and verf (authentication verifier).  The two authentication
 * parameters are followed by the parameters to the remote
 * procedure, which are specified by the specific program
 * protocol.
 */
struct call_body {
        unsigned int rpcvers;  /* must be equal to two (2) */
        unsigned int prog;
        unsigned int vers;
        unsigned int proc;
        opaque_auth cred;
        opaque_auth verf;
        /* procedure specific parameters start here */
};
```

(continued on next page)

```
/*
 * Body of a reply to an RPC request:
 * The call message was either accepted or rejected.
 */
union reply_body switch (reply_stat stat) {
        case MSG_ACCEPTED:
                accepted_reply areply;
        case MSG_DENIED:
                rejected_reply rreply;
} reply;

/*
 * Reply to an RPC request that was accepted by the server:
 * there could be an error even though the request was accepted.
 * The first field is an authentication verifier that the server
 * generates in order to validate itself to the caller.  It is
 * followed by a union whose discriminant is an enum
 * accept_stat.  The SUCCESS arm of the union is protocol
 * specific.  The PROG_UNAVAIL, PROC_UNAVAIL, and GARBAGE_ARGP
 * arms of the union are void.  The PROG_MISMATCH arm specifies
 * the lowest and highest version numbers of the remote program
 * supported by the server.
 */
struct accepted_reply {
        opaque_auth verf;
        union switch (accept_stat stat) {
                case SUCCESS:
                        opaque results[0];
                        /* procedure-specific results start here */
                case PROG_MISMATCH:
                        struct {
                                unsigned int low;
                                unsigned int high;
                        } mismatch_info;
                default:
                        /*
                         * Void.  Cases include PROG_UNAVAIL, PROC_UNAVAIL,
                         * and GARBAGE_ARGS.
                         */
                        void;
        } reply_data;
};
```

(continued on next page)

```
/*
 * Reply to an RPC request that was rejected by the server:
 * The request can be rejected for two reasons: either the
 * server is not running a compatible version of the RPC
 * protocol (RPC_MISMATCH), or the server refuses to
 * authenticate the caller (AUTH_ERROR).  In case of an RPC
 * version mismatch, the server returns the lowest and highest
 * supported RPC version numbers.  In case of refused
 * authentication, failure status is returned.
 */
union rejected_reply switch (reject_stat stat) {
        case RPC_MISMATCH:
                struct {
                        unsigned int low;
                        unsigned int high;
                } mismatch_info;
        case AUTH_ERROR:
                auth_stat stat;
};
```

Authentication Protocols

As previously stated, authentication parameters are opaque, but open-ended to the rest of the RPC protocol. This section defines some *flavors* of authentication that have already been implemented. Other sites are free to invent new authentication types, with the same rules of flavor number assignment as there is for program number assignment.

AUTH_NONE Authentication

Calls are often made where the caller does not authenticate itself and the server does not care who the caller is. In these cases, the flavor value (the "discriminant" of the opaque_auth "union") of the RPC message's credentials, verifier, and response verifier is AUTH_NONE. The bytes of the body field in the opaque_auth structure are undefined. It is recommended that the body length be zero when AUTH_NONE authentication is used.

AUTH_SYS Authentication

The caller of a remote procedure may wish to identify itself using traditional System V process permissions authentication. The flavor of the opaque_auth of such an RPC call message is AUTH_SYS. The bytes of the body encode the following structure:

```
struct auth_sysparms {
        unsigned int stamp;
        string machinename<255>;
        uid_t uid;
        gid_t int gid;
        gid_t int gids<10>;
};
```

stamp   is an arbitrary ID that the caller machine may generate.

machinename   is the name of the caller's machine (like "krypton").

uid   is the caller's effective user ID.

gid   is the caller's effective group ID.

gids   is a counted array of groups in which the caller is a
                          member.

The flavor of the verifier accompanying the credentials should be
AUTH_NONE. (defined above).

The AUTH_SHORT Verifier

When using AUTH_SYS authentication, the flavor of the response verifier
received in the reply message from the server may be AUTH_NONE or
AUTH_SHORT.

If AUTH_SHORT, the bytes of the response verifier's string encode a
short_hand_verf structure. This opaque structure may now be passed to the
server instead of the original AUTH_SYS credentials.

The server keeps a cache that maps shorthand opaque structures (passed back
by way of an AUTH_SHORT style response verifier) to the original credentials of
the caller. The caller can save network bandwidth and server cpu cycles by
using the new credentials.

The server may flush the shorthand opaque structure at any time. If this happens, the remote procedure call message will be rejected owing to an authentication error. The reason for the failure will be AUTH_REJECTEDCRED. At this
point, the caller may wish to try the original AUTH_SYS style of credentials.

AUTH_DES Authentication

AUTH_SYS authentication suffers from the following problems:

- Caller identification can not be guaranteed to be unique if machines with
  differing operating systems are on the same network.

- There is no verifier, so credentials can easily be faked.

AUTH_DES authentication attempts to fix these two problems.

Naming

The first problem is handled by addressing the caller by a simple string of characters instead of by an operating system specific integer. This string of characters is known as the *netname* or network name of the caller. The server should not interpret the caller's name in any way other than as the identify of the caller. Thus, netnames should be unique for every caller in the naming domain.

It is up to each operating system's implementation of AUTH_DES authentication to generate netnames for its users that insure this uniqueness when they call remote servers. Operating systems already know how to distinguish users local to their systems. It is usually a simple matter to extend this mechanism to the network. For example, a user with a user ID of 515 might be assigned the following netname: "UNIX.515@sun.com". This netname contains three items that serve to insure it is unique. Going backwards, there is only one naming domain called sun.com in the internet. Within this domain, there is only one UNIX user with user ID 515. However, there may be another user on another operating system, for example VMS, within the same naming domain that, by coincidence, happens to have the same user ID. To insure that these two users can be distinguished we add the operating system name. So one user is "UNIX.515@sun.com" and the other is "VMS.515@sun.com".

NOTE   The first field is actually a naming method rather than an operating system name. It just happens that today there is almost a one-to-one correspondence between naming methods and operating systems. If the world could agree on a naming standard, the first field could be a name from that standard, instead of an operating system name.

AUTH_DES Authentication Verifiers

Unlike AUTH_SYS authentication, AUTH_DES authentication does have a verifier so the server can validate the client's credential (and vice-versa). The contents of this verifier is primarily an encrypted timestamp. The server can decrypt this timestamp, and if it is close to what the real time is, then the client must have encrypted it correctly. The only way the client could encrypt it correctly is to know the *conversation key* of the RPC session. If the client knows the conversation key, then it must be the real client.

The conversation key is a DES [5] key that the client generates and notifies the server of in its first RPC call. The conversation key is encrypted using a public key scheme in this first transaction. The particular public key scheme used in

AUTH_DES authentication is Diffie-Hellman [3] with 192-bit keys. The details of this encryption method are described later.

The client and the server need the same notion of the current time for this to work. If network time synchronization cannot be guaranteed, then client can synchronize with the server before beginning the conversation, perhaps by consulting the Internet Time Server [4].

A server can determine if a client timestamp is valid. For any transaction after the first, the server checks for two things:

■ the timestamp is greater than the one previously seen from the same client

■ the timestamp has not expired

A timestamp is expired if the server's time is later than the sum of the client's timestamp plus what is known as the client's *window*. The window is a number the client passes (encrypted) to the server in its first transaction. The window can be thought of as a lifetime for the credential.

For the first transaction, the server checks that the timestamp has not expired. As an added check, the client sends an encrypted item in the first transaction known as the *window verifier* which must be equal to the window minus 1, or the server will reject the credential.

The client must check the verifier returned from the server to be sure it is legitimate. The server sends back to the client the encrypted timestamp it received from the client, minus one second. If the client gets anything other than this, it will reject it.

Nicknames and Clock Synchronization

After the first transaction, the server's AUTH_DES authentication subsystem returns in its verifier to the client an integer *nickname* that the client may use in its further transactions instead of passing its netname, encrypted DES key and window every time. The nickname is most likely an index into a table on the server that stores for each client its netname, decrypted DES key and window.

Though originally synchronized, client and server clocks can get out of sync. If this happens, the client RPC subsystem most likely will get back RPC_AUTHERROR at which point it should resynchronize.

A client may still get the RPC_AUTHERROR error even though it is synchronized with the server. The reason is that the server's nickname table is a limited size, and it may flush entries whenever it wants. The client should resend its original credential and the server will give it a new nickname. If a server crashes, the entire nickname table may get flushed, and all clients will have to resend their original credentials.

DES Authentication Protocol (in XDR language)

```
/*
 * There are two kinds of credentials: one in which the client uses
 * its full network name, and one in which it uses its "nickname"
 * (just an unsigned integer) given to it by the server. The
 * client must use its fullname in its first transaction with the
 * server, in which the server will return to the client its
 * nickname. The client may use its nickname in all further
 * transactions with the server. There is no requirement to use the
 * nickname, but it is wise to use it for performance reasons.
 */
enum authdes_namekind {
        ADN_FULLNAME = 0,
        ADN_NICKNAME = 1
};

/*
 * A 64-bit block of encrypted DES data
 */
typedef opaque des_block[8];

/*
 * Maximum length of a network user's name
 */
const MAXNETNAMELEN = 255;

/*
 * A fullname contains the network name of the client, an encrypted
 * conversation key and the window. The window is actually a
 * lifetime for the credential. If the time indicated in the
 * verifier timestamp plus the window has passed, then the server
 * should expire the request and not grant it. To insure that
 * requests are not replayed, the server should insist that
 * timestamps be greater than the previous one seen, unless it is
 * the first transaction. In the first transaction, the server
 * checks instead that the window verifier is one less than the
 * window.
```

(continued on next page)

```
*/
struct authdes_fullname {
        string name<MAXNETNAMELEN>;  /* name of client */
        des_block key;                /* PK encrypted conversation key */
        unsigned int window;          /* encrypted window */
};                   /* NOTE:  PK means "public key" */
/*
 * A credential is either a fullname or a nickname
 */
union authdes_cred switch (authdes_namekind adc_namekind) {
        case ADN_FULLNAME:
                authdes_fullname adc_fullname;
        case ADN_NICKNAME:
                unsigned int adc_nickname;
};
/*
 * A timestamp encodes the time since midnight, January 1, 1970.
 */
struct timestamp {
        unsigned int seconds;    /* seconds */
        unsigned int useconds;   /* and microseconds */
};
/*
 * Verifier: client variety
 */
struct authdes_verf_clnt {
        timestamp adv_timestamp;    /* encrypted timestamp     */
        unsigned int adv_winverf;   /* encrypted window verifier */
};
/*
 * Verifier: server variety
 * The server returns (encrypted) the same timestamp the client
 * gave it minus one second.  It also tells the client its nickname
 * to be used in future transactions (unencrypted).
 */
struct authdes_verf_svr {
        timestamp adv_timeverf;    /* encrypted verifier      */
        unsigned int adv_nickname; /* new nickname for client */
};
```

Diffie-Hellman Encryption

In this scheme, there are two constants, `PROOT` and `HEXMODULUS`. The particular values chosen for these for the DES authentication protocol are:

```
const PROOT = 3;
const HEXMODULUS = "d4a0ba0250b6fd2ec626e7efd637df76c716e22d0944b88b"; /* hex */
```

The way this scheme works is best explained by an example. Suppose there are two people "A" and "B" who want to send encrypted messages to each other. So, A and B each generate a random *secret key* that they do not disclose to anyone. Let these keys be represented as `SK(A)` and `SK(B)`. They also publish in a public directory their *public keys*. These keys are computed as follows:

```
PK(A) = ( PROOT ** SK(A) ) mod HEXMODULUS
PK(B) = ( PROOT ** SK(B) ) mod HEXMODULUS
```

The `**` notation is used here to represent exponentiation.

Now, both A and B can arrive at the *common key* between them, represented here as `CK(A,B)`, without disclosing their secret keys.

A computes:

```
CK(A, B) = ( PK(B) ** SK(A)) mod HEXMODULUS
```

while B computes:

```
CK(A, B) = ( PK(A) ** SK(B)) mod HEXMODULUS
```

These two can be shown to be equivalent:

`(PK(B)**SK(A)) mod HEXMODULUS = (PK(A)**SK(B)) mod HEXMODULUS`

We drop the mod `HEXMODULUS` parts and assume modulo arithmetic to simplify things:

```
PK(B) ** SK(A) = PK(A) ** SK(B)
```

Then, replace `PK(B)` by what B computed earlier and likewise for `PK(A)`.

$$((PROOT ** SK(B)) ** SK(A) = (PROOT ** SK(A)) ** SK(B)$$

which leads to:

$$PROOT ** (SK(A) * SK(B)) = PROOT ** (SK(A) * SK(B))$$

This common key CK(A, B) is not used to encrypt the timestamps used in the protocol. It is used only to encrypt a conversation key that is then used to encrypt the timestamps. The reason for doing this is to use the common key as little as possible, for fear that it could be broken. Breaking the conversation key is a far less serious offense, because conversations are comparatively short-lived.

The conversation key is encrypted using 56-bit DES keys, yet the common key is 192 bits. To reduce the number of bits, 56 bits are selected from the common key as follows. The middle-most 8-bytes are selected from the common key, and then parity is added to the lower order bit of each byte, producing a 56-bit key with 8 bits of parity.

Record Marking Standard

When RPC messages are passed on top of a byte stream protocol (like TCP/IP), it is necessary, or at least desirable, to delimit one message from another to detect and possibly recover from user protocol errors. This is called record marking (RM). One RPC message fits into one RM record.

A record is composed of one or more record fragments. A record fragment is a four-byte header followed by 0 to (2**31) − 1 bytes of fragment data. The bytes encode an unsigned binary number; as with XDR integers, the byte order is from highest to lowest.

The header encodes two values

- a boolean that specifies whether the fragment is the last fragment of the record (bit value 1 implies the fragment is the last fragment)

- a 31-bit unsigned binary value that is the length in bytes of the fragment's data.

The boolean value is the highest-order bit of the header; the length is the 31 low-order bits.

 This record specification is *not* in XDR standard form.

NOTE

The RPC Language

Just as there was a need to describe the XDR data-types in a formal language, there is also need to describe the procedures that operate on these XDR data-types in a formal language as well. We use the RPC Language for this purpose. It is an extension to the XDR language. The following example is used to describe the essence of the language.

An Example Service Described in the RPC Language

Here is an example of the specification of a simple ping program.

```
/*
 * Simple ping program
 */
program PING_PROG {
        /* Latest and greatest version */
        version PING_VERS_PINGBACK {
                void
                PINGPROC_NULL(void) = 0;

                /*
                 * Ping the caller, return the round-trip time
                 * (in microseconds).  Returns -1 if the operation
                 * timed out.
                 */
                int
                PINGPROC_PINGBACK(void) = 1;
        } = 2;

/*
 * Original version
 */
        version PING_VERS_ORIG {
                void
                PINGPROC_NULL(void) = 0;
                } = 1;
        } = 1;
} = 200000;

const PING_VERS = 2;       /* latest version */
```

The first version described is PING_VERS_PINGBACK with two procedures, PINGPROC_NULL and PINGPROC_PINGBACK.

PINGPROC_NULL takes no arguments and returns no results, but it is useful for such things as computing round-trip times from the client to the server and back again. By convention, procedure 0 of any RPC protocol should have the same semantics, and never require authentication.

The second procedure is used for the client to have the server do a reverse ping operation back to the client, and it returns the amount of time (in microseconds) that the operation used.

The next version, PING_VERS_ORIG, is the original version of the protocol and it does not contain PINGPROC_PINGBACK procedure. It is useful for compatibility with old client programs, and as this program matures it may be dropped from the protocol entirely.

The RPC Language Specification

The RPC language is identical to the XDR language, except for the added definitions described below.

program-definition:
>   `program` *program-ident* {
>   *version-list*
>   } = *value*

version-list:
>   *version* ;
>   *version* ; *version-list*

version:
>   `version` *version-ident* {
>   *procedure-list*
>   } = *value*

procedure-list:
>   *procedure* ;
>   *procedure* ; *procedure-list*

procedure:
>   *type-ident procedure-ident* (*type-ident*) = *value*

Syntax Notes

1. The following keywords are added and cannot be used as identifiers:

   > `program    version`

2. A version name cannot occur more than once within the scope of a program definition. Nor can a version number occur more than once within the scope of a program definition.

3. A procedure name cannot occur more than once within the scope of a version definition. Nor can a procedure number occur more than once within the scope of version definition.

4. Program identifiers are in the same name space as constant and type identifiers.

5. Only unsigned constants can be assigned to programs, versions and procedures.

rpcbind Protocol

rpcbind maps RPC program and version numbers to universal addresses, thus making dynamic binding of remote programs possible.

rpcbind is run at a well-known universal address, and other programs register their dynamically allocated transport addresses with it. It then makes those addresses publically available. Universal addresses are defined by the addressing authority of the given transport. They are string representations of the transport address.

rpcbind also aids in broadcast RPC. There is no fixed relationship between the addresses that a given RPC program will have on different machines, so there is no way to broadcast directly to all these programs. rpcbind, however, has a universal address. So, to broadcast to a given program, the client actually sends its message to the rpcbind process on the machine it wishes to reach. rpcbind picks up the broadcast and calls the local service specified by the client. When rpcbind gets a reply from the local service, it passes it on to the client.

rpcbind Protocol Specification (in RPC Language)

```
/*
 * rpcb_prot.x
 * RPCBIND protocol in rpc language
 */

/*
 * A mapping of (program, version, network ID) to universal address
 */
struct rpcb {
        u_long r_prog;                  /* program number */
        u_long r_vers;                  /* version number */
        string r_netid<>;               /* network id */
        string r_addr<>;                /* universal address */
};

/*
 * A list of mappings
 */
struct rpcblist {
```

(continued on next page)

```
        rpcb rpcb_map;
        struct rpcblist *rpcb_next;
};

/*
 * Arguments of remote calls
 */
struct rpcb_rmtcallargs {
        u_long prog;                    /* program number */
        u_long vers;                    /* version number */
        u_long proc;                    /* procedure number */
        opaque args_ptr<>;              /* argument */
};

/*
 * Results of the remote call
 */
struct rpcb_rmtcallres {
        string addr_ptr<>;              /* remote universal address */
        opaque results_ptr<>;           /* result */
};

/*
 * rpcbind procedures
 */
program RPCBPROG {
        version RPCBVERS {
                void
                RPCBPROC_NULL(void) = 0;

                bool
                RPCBPROC_SET(rpcb) = 1;

                bool
                RPCBPROC_UNSET(rpcb) = 2;

                string
                RPCBPROC_GETADDR(rpcb) = 3;

                rpcblist
                RPCBPROC_DUMP(void) = 4;

                rpcb_rmtcallres
                RPCBPROC_CALLIT(rpcb_rmtcallargs) = 5;

                unsigned int
```

(continued on next page)

Remote Procedure Calls: Protocol Specification

```
                    RPCBPROC_GETTIME(void) = 6;

                    struct netbuf
                    RPCBPROC_UADDR2TADDR(string) = 7;

                    string
                    RPCBPROC_TADDR2UADDR(struct netbuf) = 8;
            } = 3;
    } = 100000;
```

rpcbind Operation

rpcbind is contacted by way of an assigned address specific to the transport being used. For IP, for example, it is port number 111. Each transport has such an assigned well known address. The following is a description of each of the procedures supported by rpcbind.

The RPCBPROC_NULL Procedure

This procedure does no work. By convention, procedure zero of any protocol takes no parameters and returns no results.

The RPCBPROC_SET Procedure

When a program first becomes available on a machine, it registers itself with the rpcbind program running on the same machine. The program passes its program number *prog*, version number *vers*, network identifier *netid*, and the universal address *uaddr* on which it awaits service requests.

The procedure returns a boolean response whose value is TRUE if the procedure successfully established the mapping and FALSE otherwise. The procedure refuses to establish a mapping if one already exists for the tuple *(prog, vers, netid)*.

Note that neither *netid* nor *uaddr* can be NULL, and that *netid* should be a valid network identifier on the machine making the call.

The RPCBPROC_UNSET Procedure

When a program becomes unavailable, it should unregister itself with the rpcbind program on the same machine.

The parameters and results have meanings identical to those of RPCBPROC_SET. The mapping of the *(prog, vers, netid)* tuple with *uaddr* is deleted.

If *netid* is NULL, all mappings specified by the tuple *(prog, vers, *)* and the corresponding universal addresses are deleted.

The RPCBPROC_GETADDR Procedure

Given a program number *prog*, version number *vers*, and network identifier *netid*, this procedure returns the universal address on which the program is awaiting call requests.

The *netid* field of the argument is ignored and the *netid* is inferred from the *netid* of the transport on which the request came in.

The RPCBPROC_DUMP Procedure

This procedure lists all entries in rpcbind's database.

The procedure takes no parameters and returns a list of program, version, netid, and universal addresses.

The RPCBPROC_CALLIT Procedure

This procedure allows a caller to call another remote procedure on the same machine without knowing the remote procedure's universal address. It is intended for supporting broadcasts to arbitrary remote programs via rpcbind's universal address.

The parameters *prog*, *vers*, *proc*, and the *args_ptr* are the program number, version number, procedure number, and parameters of the remote procedure.

NOTE This procedure only sends a response if the procedure was successfully executed and is silent (no response) otherwise.

The procedure returns the remote program's universal address, and the results of the remote procedure.

The RPCBPROC_GETTIME Procedure

This procedure returns the local time on its own machine.

The RPCBPROC_UADDR2TADDR Procedure

This procedure converts universal addresses to transport (netbuf) addresses. RPCBPROC_UADDR2TADDR is equivalent to uaddr2taddr() [see netdir(3N)].

NOTE Only processes that can not link to the name-to-address library modules should use RPCBPROC_UADDR2TADDR.

The RPCBPROC_TADDR2UADDR Procedure

This procedure converts transport (netbuf) addresses to universal addresses. RPCBPROC_TADDR2UADDR is equivalent to taddr2uaddr() [see netdir(3N)].

NOTE Only processes that can not link to the name-to-address library modules should use RPCBPROC_TADDR2UADDR.

References

[1] Birrell, Andrew D. & Nelson, Bruce Jay; "Implementing Remote Procedure Calls," XEROX CSL-83-7, October 1983.

[2] Cheriton, D.; "VMTP: Versatile Message Transaction Protocol," Preliminary Version 0.3; Stanford University, January 1987.

[3] Diffie & Hellman; "New Directions in Cryptography," IEEE Transactions on Information Theory IT-22, November 1976.

[4] Harrenstien, K.; "Time Server," RFC 738; Information Sciences Institute, October 1977.

[5] National Bureau of Standards; "Data Encryption Standard," Federal Information Processing Standards Publication 46, January 1977.

[6] Postel, J.; "Transmission Control Protocol - DARPA Internet Program Protocol Specification," RFC 793; Information Sciences Institute, September 1981.

[7] Postel, J.; "User Datagram Protocol," RFC 768; Information Sciences Institute, August 1980.

10 RPC Administration

Introduction to RPC Administration

RPC administration consists of configuring administration files that:

- Establish name-to-address mapping relationships
- Start server daemons at boot time
- Prompt users for a network password at login (secure RPC)
- Edit a master machine /etc/publickey file that determines who can access secure RPC services (secure RPC)
- Start ypdaemons

Servers are started at boot time by editable system RC scripts. The file /etc/profile is edited to call keylogin to query for a network password at login time.

YP is currently the recommended default mechanism for administering secure RPC (see Chapter 11, ''The YP Service'').

RPC Administration Files

Name-to-Address Mapping

Name-to-address mapping must be in effect for RPC (secure or otherwise) to work. Refer to the "Network Services" chapter of the *System Administrator's Guide* for name-to-address mapping administrative procedures.

System RC File /etc/rc2.d/s75rpc

RPC servers can be started at system boot time. When the system comes up in init state 2, all of the scripts in /etc/rc2.d are executed. One of these scripts, /etc/rc2.d/s75rpc, starts the RPC servers.

The system administrator can edit the script to start additional servers. For reference, the default script, shipped with new systems, is shown here:

```
#ident    "@(#)initpkg:init.d/rpc    1.1.2.5"

if [ ! -d /usr/bin ]
then                         # /usr not mounted
        exit
fi
case "$1" in
        set `who -r`
        if [ $9 = "S" -o $9 = "1" -o $9 = "?" ]
        then
                if [ -x /usr/sbin/rpcbind ]
                then
                        /sbin/sh /etc/init.d/rpc rpcstart&
                else
                        exit # nothing else can do anything
                fi
        fi
        ;;
                /usr/sbin/rpcbind > /dev/console 2>&1

                if [ -x /usr/lib/netsvc/rwall/rpc.rwalld ]
                then
                        /usr/lib/netsvc/rwall/rpc.rwalld > /dev/console 2>&1
                fi
                if [ -x /usr/lib/netsvc/rusers/rpc.rusersd ]
                then
```

(continued on next page)

```
                         /usr/lib/netsvc/rusers/rpc.rusersd > /dev/console 2>&1
                fi
                if [ -x /usr/lib/netsvc/spray/rpc.sprayd ]
                then
                         /usr/lib/netsvc/spray/rpc.sprayd > /dev/console 2>&1
                fi

#               uncomment for secure RPC

#               if [ -x /usr/sbin/keyserv ]
#               then
#                        /usr/sbin/keyserv > /dev/console 2>&1
#               fi
#               if [ -x /usr/lib/netsvc/yp/ypbind ]
#               then
#                        /usr/lib/netsvc/yp/ypbind > /dev/console 2>&1
#               fi
#               if [ -x /usr/lib/netsvc/yp/ypupdated ]
#               then
#                        /usr/lib/netsvc/yp/ypupdated > /dev/console 2>&1
#               fi
#               if [ -x /usr/lib/netsvc/yp/ypserv ]
#               then
#                        /usr/lib/netsvc/yp/ypserv > /dev/console 2>&1
#               fi

                ;;
#stop all the daemons
pid=`/usr/bin/ps -e | /usr/bin/grep rpc.spra | \
        /usr/bin/sed -e 's/^  *//' -e 's/ .*//'`
if [ "${pid}" != "" ]
then
        /usr/bin/kill ${pid}
fi
pid=`/usr/bin/ps -e | /usr/bin/grep rpc.ruse | \
        /usr/bin/sed -e 's/^  *//' -e 's/ .*//'`
if [ "${pid}" != "" ]
then
        /usr/bin/kill ${pid}
fi
pid=`/usr/bin/ps -e | /usr/bin/grep rpc.rwal | \
        /usr/bin/sed -e 's/^  *//' -e 's/ .*//'`
if [ "${pid}" != "" ]
then
        /usr/bin/kill ${pid}
fi
```

(continued on next page)

```
        pid='/usr/bin/ps -e | /usr/bin/grep rpcbind | \
              /usr/bin/sed -e 's/^ *//' -e 's/ .*//''
        if [ "${pid}" != "" ]
        then
                /usr/bin/kill ${pid}
        fi

#               uncomment for secure RPC

#       pid='/usr/bin/ps -e | /usr/bin/grep keyserv | \
#             /usr/bin/sed -e 's/^ *//' -e 's/ .*//''
#       if [ "${pid}" != "" ]
#       then
#               /usr/bin/kill ${pid}
#       fi
#       pid='/usr/bin/ps -e | /usr/bin/grep ypbind | \
#             /usr/bin/sed -e 's/^ *//' -e 's/ .*//''
#       if [ "${pid}" != "" ]
#       then
#               /usr/bin/kill ${pid}
#       fi
#       pid='/usr/bin/ps -e | /usr/bin/grep ypupdated | \
#             /usr/bin/sed -e 's/^ *//' -e 's/ .*//''
#       if [ "${pid}" != "" ]
#       then
#               /usr/bin/kill ${pid}
#       fi
#       pid='/usr/bin/ps -e | /usr/bin/grep ypserv | \
#             /usr/bin/sed -e 's/^ *//' -e 's/ .*//''
#       if [ "${pid}" != "" ]
#       then
#               /usr/bin/kill ${pid}
#       fi
        ;;
*)
        echo "Usage: /etc/init.d/rpc { start | stop }"
        ;;
esac
```

NOTE The server keyserv must also be running for secure RPC to work properly. Administrators may wish to edit the RPC RC script to start keyserv at boot time. If not, keyserv will have to be started manually or by other means.

The /etc/publickey File

Secure RPC information is kept in this file, which is controlled by a domain master server. For each secure RPC user known to a master, this file contains:

- operating system name
- user ID
- RPC domain name
- public key
- secret key

The triple (*operating system, user ID, domain*) forms a unique key into this database of public/secret key pairs that are required by the RPC built-in security protocol.

NOTE The user ID field in /etc/publickey may also be a host name. This allows more than one root user per domain.

The /etc/master.d/kernel File

All machines supporting secure RPC must have what is known as a secure RPC domain name. By default, a machine's secure RPC domain name is null and (because it is null), secure RPC will not work on the machine.

A domain name can be set using the domainname(1M) command, but it will not be remembered across reboots. For preservation of the name across reboots, administrators need to edit their /etc/master.d/kernel file to set the SRPC_DOMAIN tunable to their desired secure RPC domain name. For example, to change a machine's domain name from null to finance, the system administrator would find the line:

        SRPC_DOMAIN=""

in /etc/master.d/kernel and change it to

        SRPC_DOMAIN="finance"

Secure RPC Overview

There is a security protocol, based on DES encryption, built into the RPC package. Remote programs that use secure RPC expect client users to have a public/secret key entry in a shared master /etc/publickey file. Access to secure RPC programs is controlled by the keyserv daemon which accesses the /etc/publickey file when users invoke keylogin. One /etc/publickey database exists for each secure RPC domain. In large domains (many machines), multiple physical copies of the database may exist for performance reasons. If multiple copies exist, updates will be made to the copy on the domain's master server, and copies of the master /etc/publickey will be propagated to slave servers.

Secure RPC users must be given entries in this file on the master /etc/publickey server machine by the system administrator before they can use secure RPC programs (in that domain). These users must also be given logins on the master server machine.

In addition, the administrator of every client machine should edit /etc/profile to remove the comment character that has commented out the keylogin command; in this way, keylogin will be invoked for each user at login time. Thereafter secure RPC commands and programs can be used in the same way ordinary commands and programs are used.

NOTE Every machine that allows use of secure RPC is a client machine, even if it is also a master or slave server.

One of the secure RPC commands, chkey, allows users who are logged onto only the master server machine to change their secure RPC passwords.

The .profile files of secure RPC users should be set up to call keylogout automatically at the end of a terminal session. For example:

```
# .profile code fragment

trap "keylogout" 0
```

A secure RPC user should *always* execute keylogout before logging off the system. Failure to do so is a serious security infraction.

[See sh(1) for details on use of trap for executing commands at the end of a terminal session.]

 The presence of secure RPC has no effect on remote programs that do not use the secure protocol. Such programs work normally, whether or not the user is also a secure RPC user.

RPC Domains

All machines using secure RPC must have a secure RPC domain name. One machine per domain acts as master server for the domain. The domainname(1M) command is used to set a machine's domain name. The machine's SRPC_DOMAIN tunable should also be set to the secure RPC domain name. Otherwise, the name is forgotten across reboots.

Secure RPC identifies users using a triple (*operating system, uid, domain*). Thus, users may have multiple registrations with RPC, provided all such triples are unique. For example, a user may belong to more than one *domain*, with *operating system* and *uid* identical for each.

By default, master servers know about users in their own domain. However, master servers may export their /domainkeys directories to other master servers to acquire information about users in other domains. If those other master servers have an /etc/masters file listing the local master server, they will periodically mount the local master's /domainkeys directory and copy their domain key data to a file named /domainkeys/*master_X* (path as seen by the local master) where *master_X* is the secure RPC domain name of the other master server.

Given this information, the local master server can periodically update its own /etc/publickey file to include key information records from files in /domainkeys.

Secure RPC Administration

In general, administering secure RPC is accomplished as follows:

1. A domain name is chosen (for multiple domains, more than one domain name is chosen). Secure RPC domain names are set on participating machines, using the domainname(1M) command, and the SRPC_DOMAIN tunable is set to the secure RPC domain name.

2. For each user or host to be allowed access to secure RPC services, domain master machine administrators add entries to their master /etc/publickey file.

3. keyserv and YP daemons are started.

4. Administrators start keyserv, either manually or by means of a boot-time script.

5. Administrators of client machines mount the master (or a slave) /etc/publickey file and link it as their local /etc/publickey file. They remove the comment character that has commented out the keylogin command from their machine's /etc/profile and they direct their secure RPC users to add a trap to their $HOME/.profile so that keylogout will be called when their sessions end.

The following sections detail this procedure.

 When slave servers are in use, master servers may have clients as well as slaves.

Establishing Secure RPC Domains

For many networked systems, a single secure RPC domain will suffice. Administrators are notified of the domain name, and they use the domainname(1M) command to establish that name as the secure RPC domain name for their machine. For example, to set the a machine's domain name to research:

```
# domainname research <cr>
```

For networked systems having multiple domains, the process is the same, except that two or more different domains will be in use in the network.

Administrators should also set their machine's SRPC_DOMAIN tunable to their secure RPC domain name, as described in "The /etc/master.d/kernel File" section, above. If this is not done, the domain name will be forgotten across reboots.

A machine can be part of only one domain at any given time. The decision to use single or multiple domains depends on need. In general, the advantages of multiple domains include:

- Duplicate operating system/user ID pairs can be using secure RPC (provided they are in different domains).

- Access to secure RPC programs can be made selective, if some programs are not available to all domains.

The primary advantage of using a single domain is simplified administration.

Master /etc/publickey File

The /etc/publickey file is a database of public/secret key pairs. The file contains pairs for users and hosts authorized to use secure RPC. Remote procedures that use the DES authentication protocol (built into the RPC package) expect to find public/secret key pairs (for the processes that call them) in /etc/publickey. A system administrator must therefore add an entry to /etc/publickey for each user/host to be granted access to secure RPC resources. A single /etc/publickey file (on a master server or on a collection of master and slave servers) is used and shared over the network by machines having access to the file.

NOTE Secure RPC programs are not required to be hosted by the same machine that hosts the master /etc/publickey file. The master /etc/publickey machine is not necessarily the server for *any* of the secure RPC application programs or commands.

Adding RPC Users with the newkey Command

On the domain master server machine (only), the system administrator grants a user or host access to secure RPC in that domain by adding an entry to the /etc/publickey file. This is accomplished using the newkey(1M) command.

 NOTE The newkey command must be executed on the master server machine by a user with root privileges. Furthermore, prior to using newkey, the machine's secure RPC domain name must have been set.

For example, to add an entry for the user alice the system administrator would enter the following on the master server:

```
master# newkey -u alice
password: <password> <cr>
Re-enter new passwd: <password> <cr>
```

The −u option signifies that alice is a user ID. The domain field for this entry is the domain of the master server on which this command is executed. This is the only way that user alice can get access to this particular secure RPC domain.

The newkey command can also be used with the −h option to give access to hosts, i.e., to root users on hosts on the network:

```
master# newkey -h client
password: <password> <cr>
Re-enter new passwd: <password> <cr>
```

Within the domain of secure RPC users having entries in a master
/etc/publickey file, all user names and IDs must be unique. The −h option
is provided to allow more than one root user to have access to secure RPC.
Because root users on different machines have the same name and ID, it would
be impossible for more than one of them to be a secure RPC user. The −h
option solves this problem, allowing root users to use their unique machine
name and address as a user name and ID for RPC purposes.

Network Passwords and the chkey Command

If using the YP service, client users should be notified of their passwords when
they are given access to secure RPC. Their .profile files should be modified
to execute keylogout when they log off.

Users are prompted for their secure RPC passwords when keylogin is executed by /etc/profile. After gaining access, secure RPC users logged onto
the master server machine may invoke the chkey command to assign themselves a different secret password.

For example, a user can set up a password as follows:

```
master$ chkey
New password: <password> <cr>
Re-enter new passwd: <password> <cr>
```

 NOTE Users logged onto client machines and on slave server machines cannot
change their passwords in this way. Users should login to their master
server to change their network password.

Troubleshooting Note

If all administration procedures have been performed correctly and trouble occurs, suspect that an RPC server daemon process (in particular, rpcbind) may not have been started, may have died, or may have been killed.

11 The YP Service

Introduction to YP Service

This chapter explains how to administer the YP distributed network lookup service. Information in the chapter includes:

- The YP environment
- Setting up YP servers
- Setting up a YP client
- Creating and updating maps
- YP-related commands
- Fixing YP problems

What Is YP?

YP is a distributed name service designed to meet the administrative needs of large, diverse, and evolving computing communities. It is a mechanism for identifying and locating objects and resources accessible to the community. It provides a uniform, network-wide storage and retrieval method that is both protocol– and media–independent.

By running the YP service, the system administrator can distribute administrative databases (maps) among a variety of machines and can update those databases from a centralized location in an automatic and reliable fashion, ensuring that all clients share in the same databases in a consistent manner throughout the network. Furthermore, the use of the YP "publickey" map permits running secure RPC and secure NFS across the network of machines.

The YP Elements

The YP service is composed of the following elements:

- domains
- maps
- daemons:

□ ypserv — server process

□ ypbind — binding process

□ ypupdated — server for changing map entries

■ utilities:

□ ypcat — lists data in a map

□ ypwhich — lists name of YP server

□ ypmatch — finds a key in a map

□ ypinit — builds and installs a YP database, or initializes a client

□ yppoll — gets protocol version from server

□ yppush — propagates data from master to slave YP server

□ ypset — sets binding to a particular server

□ ypxfr — transfers data from master to slave YP server

□ makedbm — creates dbm file for a YP map

The YP Environment

YP service is based on information contained in YP maps. Maps are non-ASCII administrative files, which usually derive from ASCII files traditionally found in the /etc directory. Each YP map has a mapname used by programs to access it. On a network running YP, at least one YP server per domain maintains a set of YP maps for other hosts in the domain to query.

The service is mediated by the daemons ypserv and ypbind, and updates are facilitated by the daemon ypupdated.

The YP Domain

A YP domain is an arbitrary name that designates which machines will make use of a common set of maps. Maps for each domain are located in separate directories, /var/yp/*domainname*, on the YP server (see "YP Servers"). For example, the maps for machines that belong to the domain accounting will be located in the directory /var/yp/accounting on their corresponding YP server.

No restrictions are placed on whether a machine can belong to a given domain. Assignment to a domain is done at the local level of each machine by the system administrator logged in as superuser; it can be done in any of the following three ways: modify /etc/rc2.d/s75ppc; modify /etc/master.d/kernel; or by entering the command

```
# domainname   name
```

where *name* is the name of the domain to which you want the machine to belong.

YP Machine Types

There are three types of YP machines:

■ master server

■ slave server

■ client

Any machine can be a YP client, but only machines with disks should be YP servers, either master or slave. Servers are generally also clients.

YP Servers

By definition, a YP server is a machine with a disk storing a set of YP maps that it makes available to network hosts. The YP server does not have to be the same machine as the file server, unless, of course, it is the only machine on the network with a disk.

YP servers come in two varieties, master and slave. The machine designated as YP master server contains the master set of maps that are updated as necessary. If you have only one YP server on your network, designate it as the master server. Otherwise, designate the machine you think will be best able to propagate YP updates with the least performance degradation.

You can designate additional YP servers on your network as slave servers. A slave server has a complete copy of the master's set of YP maps: Whenever the master server's maps are updated, it propagates the updates among the slave servers. The existence of slave servers allows the system administrator to distribute evenly the load implied in answering YP requests. The following diagram is a stylized representation of the relationship between master, slaves and clients:

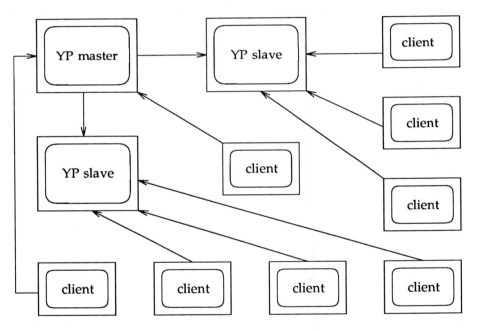

A server may be a master in regard to one map, and a slave in regard to another. However, randomly assigning maps to YP servers can cause a great deal of administrative confusion. You are strongly urged to make a single server the master for all the maps you create within a single domain. The examples in this chapter assume that one server is the master for all maps in the domain.

YP Clients

YP clients run processes that request data from maps on the servers. Clients do not care which server is the master in a given domain, since all YP servers have the same information. The distinction between master and slave server only applies to where you make the updates.

YP Binding

YP clients get information from the YP server through the binding process. Here is what happens during YP binding:

1. A program running on the client (that is, a client process) and needing information that is normally provided by a YP map, asks ypbind for the name of a server.

2. ypbind looks in the file /var/yp/binding/*domainname*/ypservers to get a list of the servers for the domain (see "Establishing the Domain" later in this chapter).

3. ypbind initiates binding to the first server on the list. If the server does not respond, it tries the next, and so on until it finds a server or exhausts the list.

4. ypbind tells the client process which server to talk to. The client then forwards the request directly to the server.

5. The ypserv daemon on the YP server handles the request by consulting the appropriate map.

6. ypserv then sends the requested information back to the client.

The binding between a client and a server can change with the network's load as the service tries to compensate for current activity; that is, a client may get information from one server at one time and from another server at a different time.

To find out which YP server is currently providing service to a client, use the ypwhich command

```
$ ypwhich hostname
```

where hostname is the name of the client. If no hostname is mentioned, ypwhich defaults to the local host (the machine on which the command is entered).

YP Maps

YP maps are one type of implementation of System V Release 4.0 administrative databases. (The other implementation is the ASCII files generally found in the /etc directory.) Information in YP maps is organized in a format similar to System V Release 4.0 dbm files. The manual pages for ypfiles(5) and dbm(3) completely explain the dbm file format. Input to makedbm must be in the form of *key/value* pairs, where *key* is the first word of each line and *value* is whatever follows in that line. The input can be from a file or from standard input (as when modified through a script; see below, "Making the Maps"). After passing through makedbm the data is collected in non-ASCII form in two files, mapname.dir and mapname.pag, both in the /var/yp/*domainname* directory.

The pairs of keys and values are preserved in the YP maps, so programs can use the keys to look up the values.

The System V Release 4.0 package includes a default YP map, publickey.byname, and a default makefile for that map.

Programmer's Guide: Networking Interfaces

Implementing the YP Service

Implementation of the YP service consists of the following steps:

1. Establishing the domain(s) for your machines
2. Writing or preparing the maps in ASCII form
3. Running the ASCII files through `makedbm`
4. Setting the master server
5. Starting daemons in the master server
6. Setting the slave server(s)
7. Starting daemons in the slave server(s)
8. Initializing the clients

The following sections will describe each of these steps.

Establishing the Domain

Before you configure machines as YP servers or clients, you must prepare the YP domain by:

- Giving it a name.

  A domain name can be up to 256 characters long. However, because your `/var/yp` directory may reside in an s5 file system, and the domain name you select may be longer than the 14-character limit that s5 imposes on filenames, the program `ypinit` makes a shortened domain name and stores it in the `/var/yp/aliases` file. The name of the database directory `/var/yp/`*domainname* will correspond to the shortened alias for the domain name.

- Designating which machines will serve or be served by the YP domain.

  Once you have chosen a domain name, make a list of network hosts that will give or receive YP service within that domain.

- Determining which machine should be master server (you can always change this at a later date).

- Listing which hosts on the network, if any, are to be slave servers.

- Finally, listing all the hosts that are to be YP clients.

You will probably want all hosts in your network's administrative domain to receive YP services, although this is not strictly necessary. If this is the case, give the YP domain the same name as the network administrative domain.

Log in as superuser to all servers, whether master or slave(s), and all clients of the YP domain. Enter the command

```
# domainname name
```

where *name* is the name of the domain.

The above is a temporary measure; edit the file in /etc/rc2.d/s75rpc that initiates YP service or edit /etc/master.d/kernel.

```
domainname name
```

where *name* is the name of the domain.

Preparing the Maps

System V Release 4.0 enables a site to use public key encryption as one of the methods for providing secure networking. If you are planning on running secure RPC or secure NFS, you may use YP to administer the /etc/publickey file.

The publickey Map

This file consists of three fields in the following format:

```
user name    user public key : user secret key
```

where *user name* may be the name of a user or of a machine, *user public key* is that key in hexadecimal notation, and *user secret key* is that key also in hexadecimal notation.

Since nobody expects you to be conversant in hexadecimal notation, the program newkey is provided to make things easier. Simply become superuser at the master server and invoke newkey for a given user by typing

```
# newkey -u username
```

or for the superuser on a given host machine by typing the following:

```
# newkey -h hostname
```

At the prompt enter the appropriate secure RPC or network password. The program will then create a new public/secret key pair in /etc/publickey, encrypted with the secure RPC or network password of the given user.

Users can later modify their own entries, or can even create them, by using the program chkey. The user simply types:

```
$ chkey
```

and then responds to prompts from the command. A typical chkey session would look like this:

```
willow$ chkey
Generating new key for username
Password: user enters password
Sending key change request to server...
Done.
willow$
```

Note that in order for newkey and chkey to run properly, the daemon ypup-dated must be running in the master server. If it is not running at this point, enter the following:

```
# /usr/lib/netsvc/yp/ypupdated
```

You must also make sure that the appropriate file in /etc/rc?.d contains the lines

```
if [ -f /usr/lib/netsvc/yp/ypupdated -a -d /var/yp/'domainname' ]
then
        /usr/lib/netsvc/yp/ypupdated
        (echo \c ' ypupdated') >/dev/console
fi
```

The ypupdated daemon consults the file /var/yp/updaters for information about which maps should be updated and how to go about it. In the case of the publickey map, changes to /etc/publickey affected through newkey or chkey are mediated by /usr/sbin/udpublickey.

Other Maps

Other maps do not need the assistance of special programs for their creation or modification. For instance, if you are planning on having distributed auto-mounter files, all you have to do is write the automounter files as they would reside in a machine's /etc directory. (For more information on the auto-mounter, see the chapter on the automounter in the "Network File System Administrator's Guide" in the *Network User's and Administrator's Guide*.)

A typical auto.master file would contain

```
#Mount-point    Map                Mount-options
/net            -hosts
/home           /etc/auto.home     -rw,intr,secure
/-              /etc/auto.direct   -ro,intr
```

A typical auto.home map would contain the following:

```
#key       mount-options    location
willow                      willow:/home/willow
cypress                     cypress:/home/cypress
poplar                      poplar:/home/poplar
pine                        pine:/export/pine
apple                       apple:/export/home
ivy                         ivy:/home/ivy
peach      -rw,nosuid       peach:/export/home
```

The following would be a typical /etc/auto.direct map:

```
/usr/local \
              /bin      -ro, soft   ivy:/export/local/sun3 \
              /share    -ro, soft   ivy:/export/local/share \
              /src      -ro, soft   ivy:/export/local/src
/usr/man                -ro, soft   oak:/usr/man \
                                    rose:/usr/man \
                                    willow:/usr/man
/usr/games              -ro, soft   peach:/usr/games
/usr/spool/news         -ro, soft   pine:/usr/spool/news
/usr/frame              -ro, soft   redwood:/usr/frame1.3 \
                                    balsa:/export/frame
```

A full explanation of what these files mean can be found in the chapter on the automounter in the *Network User's and Administrator's Guide.*

Note that these files are all in the directory /etc. These are not the maps, these are the files that you will use in order to make the maps.

The automounter recognizes the notation + at the beginning of a line as an indication to consult the corresponding YP map; this notation is permissible in a client's file in the /etc directory.

Making the Maps

Your next step, after creating the maps, is to convert these ASCII files into the non-ASCII files in dbm format that the YP service expects. The prescribed method is to use the make(1) program through a permanent Makefile.

The Default Makefile

A makefile is provided in the directory /var/yp. It contains the commands needed to transform /etc/publickey into the desired dbm format and is similar to the following:

Programmer's Guide: Networking Interfaces

```
#ident    "@(#)ypcmd:net_files/Makefile        1.1"
#+++++++++++++++++++++++++++++++++++++++++++++++++++++++++++
#         PROPRIETARY NOTICE (Combined)
#
# This source code is unpublished proprietary information
# constituting, or derived under license from AT&T's UNIX(r) System V.
# In addition, portions of such source code were derived from Berkeley
# 4.3 BSD under license from the Regents of the University of
# California.
#
#
#
#         Copyright Notice
#
# Notice of copyright on this source code product does not indicate
#  publication.
#
#         (c) 1986,1987,1988.1989  Sun Microsystems, Inc
#         (c) 1983,1984,1985,1986,1987,1988,1989  AT&T.
#          All rights reserved.
#
# Set the following variable to "-b" to have yp servers use the domain name
# resolver for hosts not in the current domain.
#B=-b
B=
DIR =/etc
DOM = `domainname`
NOPUSH = ""
YPDIR=/usr/sbin
YPDBDIR=/var/yp
YPPUSH=$(YPDIR)/yppush
MAKEDBM=$(YPDIR)/makedbm
MKNETID=$(YPDIR)/mknetid

all:      $(YPDBDIR)/$(DOM)/publickey.byname;

$(YPDBDIR)/$(DOM)/publickey.byname:  $(DIR)/publickey
        sed "/^#/d" < $(DIR)/publickey | \
              $(MAKEDBM) - $(YPDBDIR)/$(DOM)/publickey.byname;
        echo "updated publickey";
        if [ ! $(NOPUSH) ]; then \
              $(YPPUSH) publickey.byname; \
              echo "pushed publickey"; \
        else \
              : ; \
        fi
```

This makefile first creates an entry in /var/yp/aliases which translates the mapname into a shorter name to be used for the dbm file name (this is done to accomodate the 14-character limitation that s5 file systems impose on file names.) Then it eliminates all lines in /etc/publickey that start with a # (that is, comment lines) and passes the rest to makedbm. makedbm creates the files publickey.pag and publickey.dir. Both of these files are in the directory /var/yp/*domain.name*. The makefile then touches a file called publickey.time (to keep track of updates) and calls the yppush program, if applicable, to propagate the changes to all slave servers.

It is inappropriate to call make until you have set the slave servers.

Modifying the Makefile

In order for the makefile to work on the automounter files (or any other files) that you wish to propagate through YP, the following modifications must be made:

1. Modify the line that says

```
all: publickey
```

to say the following:

```
all: publickey auto.direct auto.home auto.master
```

The order is not relevant.

2. Add the following lines at the end of the makefile:

```
auto.direct: auto.direct.time
auto.home: auto.home.time
auto.master: auto.master.time
```

Programmer's Guide: Networking Interfaces

3. Add the following entry for the auto.direct map in the middle of the file, after the entry for publickey.time and before the line that reads publickey: publickey.time:

```
auto.direct.time: $(DIR)/publickey
    -if [ -f $(DIR)/auto.direct ]; then \
        echo auto.direct.byname '$(ALIAS) publickey.byname' >> $(ALIASFILE); \
        sort $(ALIASFILE) | uniq > .ypaliases; mv .ypaliases $(ALIASFILE); \
        for i in $(DOM); do \
            sed -e "/^#/d" \
                -e s/#.*$$// \
                -e "/^ *$$/d" \
                -e "/^+/d" $(DIR)/auto.direct | \
            $(MAKEDBM) - $(YPDBDIR)/'$(ALIAS) \
                -d $$i'/'$(ALIAS) auto.direct.byname'; \
        done; \
        touch auto.direct.time; \
        echo "updated auto.direct"; \
        if [ ! $(NOPUSH) ]; then \
            $(YPPUSH) auto.direct.byname; \
            echo "pushed auto.direct"; \
        else \
            : ; \
        fi \
    else \
        echo "couldn't find $(DIR)/auto.direct"; \
    fi
```

Create similar entries for auto.home and auto.master.

Setting the Master Server

The program that helps you establish the master and slave servers, and permits the initial mapping of ASCII files and their propagation, is /usr/lib/netsvc/yp/ypinit.

You use the shell script ypinit to build a fresh set of YP maps on the master server in the following way:

1. Bring the machine that is going to be your master server to single-user mode, or to a mode that is not defined as running the YP service, and log in as superuser.

2. Type

```
# cd /var/yp
# /usr/lib/netsvc/yp/ypinit -m
```

3. `ypinit` prompts for a list of other hosts that are to become YP servers. Enter the name of the server you are working on and the names of all other YP servers.

4. `ypinit` asks whether you want the procedure to die at the first non-fatal error or to continue despite non-fatal errors.

    If you choose the first option, `ypinit` will exit at the first problem; you can then fix the problem and restart `ypinit`. This is recommended if you are running `ypinit` for the first time. If you prefer to continue, you can try to fix by hand all problems that may occur, then restart `ypinit`.

    Once `ypinit` has constructed the list of servers, it calls up make(1). This program uses the instructions contained in the makefile (either the default one or the one you modified) located in /var/yp. It cleans all comment lines from the files you designated and runs makedbm on them, creating the appropriate pairs of maps and establishing the name of the master server for each map.

NOTE	For security reasons, you may want to restrict access to the master YP server.

Starting Daemons in the Master Server

The success of the remaining procedures depends on the presence of the ypserv daemon in the master server.

If your master server is still in single-user mode or at an inappropriate run-level, bring it to the run-level that is defined as allowing YP services to run. This entails having the following or similar lines in the appropriate file in the /etc/rc?.d directory:

```
if [ -f /usr/lib/netsvc/yp/ypserv -a -d /var/yp/'domainname' ]
then
        /usr/lib/netsvc/yp/ypserv
        (echo \c ' ypserv') >/dev/console
fi
if [ -d /var/yp ]; then
        /usr/lib/netsvc/yp/ypbind
        (echo \c ' ypbind') >/dev/console
fi
```

Once you have made sure that these lines are in the file, and that there is an executable file called /usr/lib/netsvc/yp/ypserv and a directory under /var/yp named after the domain name, log in as root and enter the command

```
# init #
```

where # is at least run-level 2.

Setting Slave Servers

Your network can have one or more YP slave servers. Before actually running ypinit to create the slave servers, you should take several precautions.

The domain name for each YP slave must be the same as the domain name of the YP master server. Use the domainname command on each YP slave to make sure it is consistent with the master server. Make any necessary changes to the domain name, as described in the previous section, "Setting Up the YP Domain." Do not forget to set each slave server's host name.

Make sure that the network is working properly before you set up a slave YP server. In particular, check that you can use rcp to send files from the master YP server to YP slaves. If you cannot, follow the procedures outlined in the *Network User's and Administrator's Guide* to permit the use of rcp.

Now you are ready to create a new slave server.

1. Log in to each slave server as superuser and bring the slave server to a run-level, preferably single user, that does not imply running the YP service. ypserv must not be running.

2. Change directory to /var/yp.

3. Type the following:

```
# /usr/lib/netsvc/yp/ypinit -c
```

Enter the names of the YP servers in order of preference; that is, enter first the names of the servers that are physically closest to the machine in the network. If the client is also a server, enter its name first. This initializes the client and establishes its servers for binding.

4. Type the following:

```
# /usr/lib/netsvc/yp/ypbind
```

5. Type

```
# /usr/lib/netsvc/yp/ypinit -s master
```

where master is the host name of the existing YP master server. Ideally, the named host is the master server, but it can be any host with a stable set of YP maps, such as another slave server.

6. ypinit will not prompt you for a list of other servers, as it does when you create the master server, nor will it run make again. However, it will stop executing if you have not used ypinit -c to initialize the list of servers, and it lets you choose whether or not to halt at the first non-fatal error. ypinit then calls the program ypxfr, which transfers a copy of the master's YP map set to the slave server's /var/yp/*domainname* directory.

7. When ypinit terminates in each slave, make sure that the ASCII files in the /etc directory direct whichever program reads them to the YP maps, thus ensuring homogeneity across the network. For instance, if you have added the maps auto.master, auto.home, and auto.direct to the YP maps, make a copy of each of these files in each slave by typing

```
# cp /etc/auto.home /etc/auto.home-
```

or the following:

```
# cp /etc/auto.home /etc/auto.home.old
```

Note that in the particular case of the automounter, if the invocation does not contain the −m option, then it will automatically look for a YP auto.master map. You can therefore move the auto.master file into another file:

```
# mv /etc/auto.master /etc/auto.master.orig
```

8. Edit the original files (not those with the − or .old extension) and make them refer to the YP maps. For instance, the file /etc/auto.direct should contain, as its last line, something similar to the following:

```
+auto.direct
```

Thus, whenever the automounter reads this file, it will consult the YP auto.direct map upon reaching this line.

9. The preceding procedures ensure that processes on the slave server actually use the YP services, rather than files in the local /etc. In this way, you ensure that the YP slave server is also a YP client.

10. Back up copies of the edited files. For instance, you might type the following:

```
# cp /etc/auto.direct /etc/auto.direct+
```

Repeat the procedures above for each machine you want configured as a YP slave server.

Starting Slave Server Daemons

The procedure for starting the YP daemons in a slave server is exactly the same as that used for starting the YP daemons in the master server, as explained in "Starting Daemons in the Master Server."

Setting Up a YP Client

To establish a machine as a YP client, do the following:

1. Edit the client's local files, as you did for the local files in the slave servers, so that processes consulting those files are sent to the YP maps.

2. Run

```
# /usr/lib/netsvc/yp/ypinit -c
```

to initialize the client.

3. Bring the client to the run-level defined as permitting the running of YP services, after making sure that the appropriate file in the /etc/rc2.d/s75rpc directory contains lines similar to the following:

```
if [ -d /var/yp ]; then
        /usr/lib/netsvc/yp/ypbind
        (echo \c ' ypbind')      >/dev/console
fi
```

4. Type

```
# ps -ef | grep ypbind
```

to confirm that `/usr/lib/netsvc/yp/ypbind` is running.

With the relevant files in `/etc` abbreviated and `ypbind` running, the processes on the machine will be clients of the YP servers.

At this point, you must have configured a YP server on the network and have given that server's name to `ypinit`. Otherwise, processes on the client hang if no YP server is available while `ypbind` is running.

Administering YP Maps

This section describes how to maintain the maps of an existing YP domain. Subjects discussed include:

- Updating YP maps
- Propagating a YP map
- Adding maps to an additional YP server
- Moving the master map set to a new server

Updating Existing Maps

After you have installed YP, you will discover that some maps require frequent updating while others never need to change. For example, the `publickey` map may change frequently on a large company's network. On the other hand, the `auto.master` map probably will change little, if at all.

When you need to update a map, you can use one of two updating procedures, depending on whether the map is standard or non-standard. A standard map is a map in the default set created by `ypinit` from the network databases. Non-standard maps may be any of the following:

- A map included with an application purchased from a vendor
- A map created specifically for your site
- A map existing in a form other than ASCII

The following text explains how to use various updating tools. In practice, you probably will use them only if you add non-standard maps or change the set of YP servers after the system is up and running.

Modifying Standard Maps

Use the following procedure for updating all standard maps:

1. Become superuser on the master server. (Always modify YP maps on the master server.)

2. Edit the file in /etc that has the same name as the map you want to change.

3. Type the following:

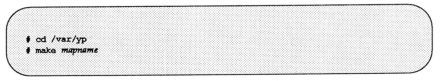

```
# cd /var/yp
# make mapname
```

The make command will then update your map according to the changes you made in its corresponding file. It will also propagate it among the servers (see the section "Propagating a YP Map" for more information).

NOTE: Do not use this procedure with the publickey map. Instead, use the new-key and chkey commands, as described in "Preparing the Maps."

Creating and Modifying Non-Standard Maps

To update a non-standard map, you edit its corresponding ASCII file. Then you rebuild the updated map using the /usr/sbin/makedbm command. [The makedbm(1M) manual page fully describes this command.] If the map has an entry in the /var/yp/Makefile, simply run make. If the map does not have an entry, try to create one following the instructions in "Making the Maps," above. Using make is the preferred method; otherwise, you will have to use makedbm by hand.

There are two different methods for using makedbm:

- Redirect the command's output to a temporary file, modify the file, then use the modified file as input to makedbm.

- Have the output of makedbm operated on within a pipeline that feeds into makedbm again directly. This is appropriate if you can update the disassembled map with either awk, sed, or a cat append.

You can use either of two possible procedures for creating new maps. The first uses an existing ASCII file as input; the second uses standard input.

In all cases, if /var/yp resides in an s5 file system, you have to create an alias for the map to deal with the 14-character limitation for file names (which, in the case of map names, is actually an 8-character limitation because of the suffixes that makedbm creates). To do this, change directory to /var/yp and enter the command:

```
echo mapname '/usr/lib/netsvc/yp/ypalias mapname' >> aliases
```

Updating Maps Built from Existing ASCII Files

Assume that an ASCII file /var/yp/mymap.asc was created with an editor or a shell script on the YP master. You want to create a YP map from this file, and locate it in the home_domain subdirectory. To do this, you type the following on the master server:

```
# cd /var/yp
# /usr/sbin/makedbm mymap.asc home_domain/mymap
```

The mymap map now exists in the directory home_domain.

Adding entries to mymap is simple. First, you must modify the ASCII file mymap.asc. (If you modify the actual dbm files without modifying the corresponding ASCII file, the modifications are lost.) Type the following:

```
# cd /var/yp
# <edit mymap.asc>
# /usr/sbin/makedbm mymap.asc home_domain/mymap
```

When you finish updating the map, propagate it to the slave servers, as described in the section "Propagating a YP Map."

Updating Maps Built from Standard Input

When no original ASCII file exists, create the YP map from the keyboard by typing input to makedbm, as shown below:

```
ypmaster# cd /var/yp
ypmaster# /usr/sbin/makedbm - home_domain/mymap
key1 value1
key2 value2
key3 value3
<ctl D>
ypmaster#
```

If later you need to modify a map that is not based on an existing file, you can use makedbm -u to disassemble the map and create a temporary ASCII intermediate file. You type the following:

```
$ cd /var/yp
$ /usr/sbin/makedbm -u home_domain/mymap > mymap.temp
```

The resulting temporary file mymap.temp has one entry per line. You can edit it as needed, using your preferred editing tools.

To update the map, you give the name of the modified temporary file to makedbm as follows:

```
$ /usr/sbin/makedbm mymap.temp home_domain/mymap
$ rm mymap.temp
```

When makedbm finishes, propagate the map to the slave servers, as described in the section "Propagating a YP Map."

The preceding paragraphs explained how to use some tools. In reality, almost everything you have to do can be done by ypinit and /var/yp/Makefile, unless you add non-standard maps to the database or change the set of YP servers after the system is already up and running.

Whether you use the makefile in /var/yp or some other procedure, a new pair of well-formed dbm files must end up in the domain directory on the master YP server.

Propagating a YP Map

When you propagate a YP map, you move it from place to place—most often from the master to all YP slave servers. Initially ypinit propagates the maps from master to slaves, as described previously. From then on, you must transfer updated maps from master to slaves by running the ypxfr command. You can run ypxfr three different ways: periodically through the root crontab file; by the ypserv daemon; and interactively on the command line.

ypxfr handles map transference in tandem with the yppush program. yppush should always be run from the master server. The makefile in the /var/yp directory automatically runs yppush after you change the master set of maps.

yppush's function is to copy, or "push," a new version of a YP map from the YP master to the slave(s). After making a list of YP servers from the ypservers map built by ypinit, yppush contacts each slave server in the list and sends it a "transfer map" request. When the request is acknowledged by the slave, the ypxfr program transfers the new map to the slave.

Using crontab with ypxfr

Maps have differing rates of change. For instance, auto.master may not change for months at a time, but publickey may change several times a day in a large organization. When you schedule map transference through the crontab command, you can designate the intervals at which individual maps are to be propagated.

To run ypxfr periodically at a rate appropriate for your map set, edit root's crontab file on each slave server and put the appropriate ypxfr entries in it [see the manual page for crontab(1)]. ypxfr contacts the master server and transfers the map only if the master's copy is more recent than the local copy.

Using Shell Scripts with ypxfr

As an alternative to creating separate `crontab` entries for each map, you may prefer to have root's `crontab` periodically run shell scripts that update the maps. You can easily modify these shell scripts to fit your site's requirements or replace them. Here is an example shell script:

```
#! /bin/sh
#
# ypxfr_1perday.sh - Do daily yp map check/updates
#
# set -xv
ypxfr publickey.byname
ypxfr auto.direct
ypxfr ypservers
```

This shell script will update once per day the maps mentioned in it, as long as root's `crontab` executes it once a day (preferably at times of low network load). You can also have scripts update maps once a week, once a month, once every hour, and so on, but be aware of the performance degradation implied in propagating the maps.

Run the same shell scripts through root's `crontab` on each slave server configured for the YP domain. Alter the exact time of execution from one server to another to avoid bogging down the master.

If you want to transfer the map from a particular slave server, use the −h *host* option of `ypxfr` within the shell script. The syntax of the commands you put in the script is

```
/usr/lib/netsvc/yp/ypxfr -h host mapname
```

where *host* is the name of the server with the maps you want to transfer, and *mapname* is the name of the requested map. If you use the −h option without specifying *host*, `ypxfr` will try to get the map from the master server.

You can use the −s *domain* option to transfer maps from another domain to your local domain. These maps should be essentially the same across domains.

Directly Invoking ypxfr

The third method of invoking ypxfr is to run it as a command. Typically, you do this only in exceptional situations − for example, when setting up a temporary YP server to create a test environment, or when trying to make a YP server that has been out of service consistent with the other servers.

Logging ypxfr's Activities

ypxfr's transfer attempts and the results can be captured in a log file. If a file called /var/yp/ypxfr.log exists, results are appended to it. No attempt to limit the size of the log file is made. To prevent it from growing indefinitely, empty it from time to time by entering

```
# cp /var/yp/ypxfr.log /var/yp/ypxfr.log.old
# cat /dev/null > /var/yp/ypxfr.log
```

You can have crontab execute these commands once a week.

To turn off logging, remove the log file.

Adding New YP Maps to the Makefile

Adding a new YP map entails getting copies of the map's dbm files into the /var/yp/domain_name directory on each of the YP servers in the domain. The actual mechanism is described above in ''Propagating a YP Map.'' This section only describes how to update the makefile so that propagation works correctly.

After deciding which YP server is the master of the map, modify /var/yp/Makefile on the master server so that you can conveniently rebuild the map. As indicated previously, different servers can be masters of different maps. This can, however, lead to administrative confusion, and it is strongly recommended that you set only one server as the master of all maps. Actual case-by-case modification is too varied to describe here, but typically a human-readable ASCII file is filtered through awk, sed, and/or grep to make it suitable for input to makedbm. Refer to the existing /var/yp/Makefile for examples and to the previous section, "Modifying the Makefile."

Use the mechanisms already in place in /var/yp/Makefile when deciding how to create dependencies that make will recognize; specifically, the use of .time files allows you to see when the makefile was last run for the map.

To get an initial copy of the map, you can have make run yppush on the YP master server. The map must be available globally before clients begin to access it.

 NOTE If the map is available from some YP servers, but not all, you will encounter unpredictable behavior from client programs.

Adding a New YP Server to the Original Set

After YP is running, you may need to create a YP slave server that you did not include in the initial set given to `ypinit`. The following procedure explains how to do this:

1. Log in to the master server as superuser.

2. Go to the YP domain directory by typing:

   ```
   # cd /var/yp/domain_name
   ```

3. Disassemble `ypservers`, as follows:

   ```
   # /usr/sbin/makedbm -u ypservers > /tmp/temp_file
   ```

   `makedbm` converts `ypservers` from dbm format to the temporary ASCII file `/tmp/temp_file`.

4. Edit `/tmp/temp_file` using your preferred text editor. Add the new slave server's name to the list of servers. Then save and close the file.

5. Run the makedbm command with `temp_file` as the input file and `ypservers` as the output file.

   ```
   # /usr/sbin/makedbm /tmp/temp_file ypservers
   ```

   Here makedbm converts `ypservers` back into dbm format.

6. Verify that the `ypservers` map is correct (since there is no ASCII file for `ypservers`) by typing the following:

```
ypslave# /usr/sbin/makedbm -u ypservers
```

NOTE If a host name is not in *ypservers*, it will not be warned of updates to the YP map files.

Here makedbm will display each entry in ypservers on your screen.

7. Set up the new slave server's YP domain directory by copying the YP map set from the master server. To do this, log in to the new YP slave as superuser and run the ypinit command:

```
ypslave# cd /var/yp
ypslave# ypinit -c
< enter the list of servers >
ypslave# /usr/lib/netsvc/yp/ypbind
ypslave# /usr/lib/netsvc/yp/ypinit -s ypmaster
```

When you are finished, complete Steps 5 and 6 in the "Setting Slave Servers" section.

Changing a Map's Master Server

To change a map's master, you first have to build it on the new YP master. The old master's name occurs as a key-value pair in the existing map (this pair is inserted automatically by makedbm). Therefore, using the existing copy at the new master or transferring a copy to the new master with ypxfr is insufficient. You have to reassociate the key with the new master's name. If the map has an ASCII source file, you should copy it in its current version to the new master.

Here are instructions for remaking a sample YP map called
`jokes.bypunchline`.

1. Log in to the new master as superuser and type the following:

```
newmaster# cd /var/yp
```

2. `/var/yp/Makefile` must have an entry for the new map before you specify the map to make. If this isn't the case, edit the makefile now (see "Making the Maps").

3. Type the following:

```
newmaster# make jokes.bypunchline
```

4. If the old master will remain a YP server, `rlogin` in to it and edit `/var/yp/Makefile`. Comment out the section of `/var/yp/Makefile` that made `jokes.bypunchline` so that it is no longer made there.

5. If `jokes.bypunchline` only exists as a dbm file, remake it on the new master by disassembling a copy from any YP server, then running the disassembled version through `makedbm`:

```
newmaster# cd /var/yp
newmaster# ypcat -k jokes.bypunchline |\
/usr/sbin/makedbm - domain/jokes.bypunchline
```

Don't forget that `jokes.bypunchline` should be in the `alias` file too.

After making the map on the new master, you must send a copy of it to the other slave servers. However, do not use `yppush`, as the other slaves will try to get new copies from the old master, rather than the new one. A typical method for circumventing this is to transfer a copy of the map from the new master back to the old master. Become superuser on the old master server and type:

```
oldmaster# /usr/lib/netsvc/yp/ypxfr -h newmaster jokes.bypunchline
```

Now it is safe to run yppush. The remaining slave servers still believe that the old master is the current master. They will attempt to get the current version of the map from the old master. When they do so, they will get the new map, which names the new master as the current master.

If this method fails, you can try this cumbersome but sure-fire option. Log in as superuser on each YP server and execute the ypxfr command shown above.

Summary of YP-Related Commands

In addition to maps, YP service also includes specialized daemons, system programs, and commands, which are summarized below.

ypserv   Looks up requested information in a map. ypserv is a daemon that runs on YP servers with a complete set of maps. At least one ypserv daemon must be present on the network for YP service to function.

ypbind   Initiates binding. ypbind is the YP binder daemon. It must be present on both clients and servers. It initiates binding by finding a ypserv process that serves maps within the domain of the requesting client. ypserv must run on each YP server. ypbind must run on all servers and clients.

ypinit   Automatically creates maps for a YP server from files located in /etc. ypinit also constructs the initial maps that are not built from files in /etc, such as ypservers. Use ypinit to set up the master YP server and the slave YP servers for the first time, as well as to initialize all clients.

make   Updates YP maps by reading the Makefile in /var/yp. You can use make to update all maps based on the files in /etc or to update individual maps. The manual page ypmake(1M) describes make functionality for YP.

makedbm   Takes an input file and converts it into dbm .dir and .pag files—valid dbm files that YP can use as maps. You can also use makedbm −u to "disassemble" a map, so that you can see the key-value pairs that comprise it.

ypxfr   Moves a YP map from one server to another, using YP itself as the transport medium. You can run ypxfr interactively, or periodically from a crontab file. It is also called by ypserv to initiate a transfer.

yppush   Copies a new version of a YP map from the YP master server to its slaves. You run it on the master YP server.

ypset   Tells a ypbind process to bind to a named YP server. ypset is not for casual use.

`yppoll`	Tells which version of a YP map is running on a server that you specify. It also lists the master server for the map.
`ypcat`	Displays the contents of a YP map.
`ypmatch`	Prints the value for one or more specified keys in a YP map. You cannot specify which YP server's version of the map you are seeing.
`ypwhich`	Shows which YP server a client is using at the moment for YP services, or, if invoked with the –m *mapname* option, which YP server is master of each of the maps.
`ypupdated`	Facilitates the updating of YP information.

Fixing YP Problems

This section explains how to clear problems encountered on networks running YP. It has two parts, one covering problems seen on a YP client and another covering problems seen on a YP server.

Debugging a YP Client

Before trying to debug a YP client, review the first part of the chapter, which explains the YP environment. Then look for the subheading in this section that best describes your problem.

Hanging Commands on the Client

The most common problem of YP clients is for a command to hang and generate console messages such as:

```
yp: server not responding for domain <domainname>. Still trying
```

Sometimes many commands begin to hang, even though the system as a whole seems normal and you can run new commands.

The message above indicates that `ypbind` on the local machine is unable to communicate with `ypserv` in the domain *domainname*. This happens when a machine running `ypserv` has crashed or is down or unavailable for any reason. It may also occur if the network or YP server is so overloaded that `ypserv` cannot get a response back to the client's `ypbind` within the timeout period.

Under these circumstances, every client on the network will experience the same or similar problems. The condition is temporary in most cases. The messages will usually go away when the YP server reboots and restarts `ypserv`, or when the load on the YP server or network itself decreases.

However, commands may hang and require direct action to clear them. The following list describes the causes of such problems and gives suggestions for fixing them:

■ The YP client has not set, or has incorrectly set, the machine's domain name. Clients must use a domain name that the YP servers know.

■ On the client, type domainname to see which domain name is set. Compare that with the actual domain name in /var/yp on the YP master server. If a machine's domain name is not the same as the server's, the machine's domain name entry in its installation scripts is incorrect. Log in as superuser, edit the client's installation scripts, and correct the domain-name entry. This assures the domain name is correct every time the machine boots. Then set domainname manually by typing the following:

```
# domainname good_domain_name
```

■ If commands still hang, make sure the server is up and running. Check other machines on your local network. If several clients also have problems, suspect a server problem. Try to find a client machine behaving normally, and type the ypwhich command on it. If ypwhich does not respond, kill it and go to a terminal on the YP server. Type the following:

```
ypserver# ps -ef | grep yp
```

Look for ypserv and ypbind processes. If a ypserv process is running, type

```
ypserver# ypwhich
```

on the YP server. If ypwhich does not respond, ypserv has probably hung, and you should restart it. Type the following while logged in as superuser:

```
ypserver# kill -9 [ypserv's pid # from ps]
ypserver# /usr/lib/netsvc/yp/ypserv
```

If ps shows no ypserv process running, start one up.

■ If the server's ypbind daemon is not running, start it up by typing the following:

```
ypserver# /usr/lib/netsvc/yp/ypbind
```

Notice that if you run ypbind and you type ypwhich immediately, ypwhich will return the error message not found in all cases. Run ypwhich again; it should now return the name of a server.

■ If commands still hang, you may try the following:

1. Kill the existing ypbind:

```
# ps -ef | grep ypbind
```

2. Restart ypbind with the ypset option that permits root to change the server:

```
# ypbind -ypsetme
```

3. Reset the server to one you know is reliable:

```
$ ypset servername
```

YP Service Is Unavailable

When most machines on the network appear to be behaving normally, but one client cannot receive YP service, that client may experience many different symptoms. For example, some commands appear to operate correctly while others terminate with an error message about the unavailability of YP. Other commands limp along in a backup-strategy mode particular to the program involved. Still other commands or daemons crash with obscure messages or no message at all. Here are messages a client in this situation may receive:

```
$ ypcat myfile
ypcat: can't bind to YP server for domain <domainname>.
        Reason: can't communicate with ypbind.
```

```
$ /usr/lib/netsvc/yp/yp/yppoll myfile
yppoll: Sorry, I can't communicate with ypbind.  I give up.
```

These symptoms usually indicate that the client's ypbind process is not running. Run ps -ef and check for ypbind. If it you do not find it, log in as superuser and start by typing the following:

```
# /usr/lib/netsvc/yp/ypbind
```

YP problems should disappear.

ypbind Crashes

If ypbind crashes almost immediately each time it is started, look for a problem in some other part of the system. Check for the presence of the rpcbind daemon by typing the following:

```
$ ps ax | grep rpcbind
```

If it is not running, reboot.

If rpcbind itself will not stay up or behaves strangely, look for more fundamental problems. Check the network software in the ways suggested in the TCP/IP section in the *Network User's and Administrator's Guide.*

You may be able to communicate with rpcbind on the problematic client from a machine operating normally. From the functioning machine, type:

```
$ rpcinfo client | grep ypbind
```

If rpcbind on the problematic machine is running normally, rpcinfo should produce an output similar to the following:

```
100007    3    tcp  0.0.0.0.12.169  ypbind  superuser
100007    3    udp  0.0.0.0.4.9  ypbind  superuser
100007    3  ticlts  Q 00 00 00  ypbind  superuser
100007    3  ticots   07 00 00 00  ypbind  superuser
100007    3  ticotsord   07 00 00 00  ypbind  superuser
100007    3  starlandg    00 15sfsc.3071900 20I 00 00 00 00 00 00 00 10 \
               00j 10 32v376 02  ypbind  superuser
100007    3  starlan   00 15sfsc.;3719900 20I 00 00 00 00 00 00 00 10 \
               00j 10 32v376 01  ypbind  superuser
```

There should be one entry per transport; in the preceding example, the entry for
udp is missing. Because ypbind was not registered for it in this case, ypbind
cannot run on udp. As long as there are other transports to run on, ypbind
should run but the omission may indicate some kind of a problem. Reboot the
machine and run rpcinfo again. If the ypbind processes are there and they
change each time you try to restart /usr/lib/netsvc/yp/ypbind, reboot the
system, even if the rpcbind daemon is running.

ypwhich Displays Are Inconsistent

When you use ypwhich several times on the same client, the resulting display
may vary because the YP server changes. This is normal. The binding of YP
client to YP server changes over time when the network or the YP servers are
busy. Whenever possible, the network stabilizes at a point where all clients get
acceptable response time from the YP servers. As long as your client machine
gets YP service, it does not matter where the service comes from. For example,
one YP server machine can get its own YP services from another YP server on
the network.

Debugging a YP Server

Before trying to debug your YP server, read about the YP environment at the
beginning of this chapter. Then look in this subsection for the heading that
most closely describes the server's problem.

Servers Have Different Versions of a YP Map

Because YP propagates maps among servers, occasionally you find different versions of the same map at YP servers on the network. This version discrepancy is normal if transient, but abnormal otherwise.

Most commonly, normal map propagation is prevented if it occurs when a YP server or router between YP servers is down. When all YP servers and the routers between them are running, ypxfr should succeed.

If a particular slave server has problems updating maps, log in to that server and run ypxfr interactively. If ypxfr fails, it will tell you why it failed, and you can fix the problem. If ypxfr succeeds, but you suspect it has occasionally failed, create a log file to enable logging of messages. As superuser type the following:

```
ypslave# cd /var/yp
ypslave# touch ypxfr.log
```

This saves all output from ypxfr. The output resembles the output ypxfr displays when run interactively, but each line in the log file is time-stamped. You may see unusual orderings in the timestamps. This is normal − the time-stamp tells you when ypxfr started to run. If copies of ypxfr ran simultaneously but their work took different amounts of time, they may actually write their summary status line to the log files in an order different from that in which they were invoked. Any pattern of intermittent failure shows up in the log. When you have fixed the problem, turn off logging by removing the log file. If you forget to remove it, it will grow without limit.

While still logged in to the problem YP slave server, inspect the root's crontab file and the ypxfr* shell scripts it invokes. Typos in these files cause propagation problems, as do failures to refer to a shell script within /var/spool/cron/crontabs/root, or failures to refer to a map within any shell script.

Also, make sure that the YP slave server is in the map ypservers within the domain. If it is not, it still operates perfectly as a server, but yppush will not tell it when a new copy of a map exists.

If the YP slave server's problem is not obvious, you can work around it while you debug it using rcp or tftp to copy a recent version of the inconsistent map from any healthy YP server. You must not do this remote copy as root, but you can probably do it while logged in as daemon. For instance, here is how you might transfer the map busted:

```
ypslave# chmod go+w /var/yp/mydomain
ypslave# su daemon
$ rcp ypmaster:/var/yp/mydomain/busted.\* /var/yp/mydomain
$ exit
ypslave# chown root /var/yp/mydomain/busted.*
ypslave# chmod go-w /var/yp/mydomain
```

Here the * character has been escaped in the command line so that it will be expanded on ypmaster, instead of locally on ypslave. Notice that the map files should be owned by root, so you must their change ownership after the transfer.

ypserv Crashes

When the ypserv process crashes almost immediately and does not stay up even with repeated activations, the debug process is virtually identical to that previously described in the subsection "ypbind Crashes." Check for the existence of the rpcbind daemon as follows:

```
ypserver$ ps -ef | grep rpcbind
```

Reboot the server if you do not find the daemon. If it is there, type

```
$ rpcinfo yp_server | grep ypserv
```

and look for output similar to the following:

```
100004    2      tcp  0.0.0.0.12.168  ypserv  superuser
100004    2      udp  0.0.0.0.4.8  ypserv  superuser
100004    2  ticlts  B 00 00 00  ypserv  superuser
100004    2  ticots   06 00 00 00  ypserv  superuser
100004    2  ticotsord   06 00 00 00  ypserv  superuser
100004    2  starlandg    00 15sfsc.2>219?00 20I 00 00 00 00 00 00 00 10 \
                 00j 10 32v376 02  ypserv  superuser
100004    2  starlan    00 15sfsc.31319?00 20I 00 00 00 00 00 00 00 10 \
                 00j 10 32v376 01  ypserv  superuser
```

Your machine will have different port numbers. As in the case of ypbind, there should be one entry per transport. If a transport is missing, ypserv has been unable to register its services with it. Reboot the machine. If the ypserv processes are there, and they change each time you try to restart /usr/lib/netsvc/yp/ypserv, reboot the machine.

Turning Off YP Services

If `ypserv` on the master is disabled, you can no longer update any of the YP maps. On the other hand, if there is no `ypserv` daemon running but clients have `ypbind` running, machines may hang indefinitely until they find a `ypserv`.

To turn off YP services safely, make sure all the clients stop running `ypbind` before `ypserv` in the master and slave servers is turned off.

Index

A

authentication 7: 46, 9: 3, 6, 14
 AUTH_DES 7: 51–53, 9: 15–18, 20
 AUTH_NONE 7: 47–48, 9: 14
 AUTH_SHORT 9: 15
 AUTH_SYS 7: 49, 9: 14
 clock synchronization 9: 17
 nicknames 9: 17

B

batch RPC 7: 42, 9: 9
binding, YP 11: 5–6
broadcast RPC 6: 25, 7: 40, 9: 9
 synopsis 7: 41

C

circuit_n transport type 5: 9
circuit_v transport type 5: 9
clients 5: 2
 handle used by rpcgen(1) 6: 10
 RPC 5: 12
clnt_create function 7: 2
clnt_dg_create function 7: 4
clnt_stat type (in RPC programming) 7: 10
clnt_tli_create function 7: 3
clnt_tp_create function 7: 3
clnt_vc_create function 7: 4
connection-oriented transports 7: 61

D

datagram_n transport type 5: 9

datagram_v transport type 5: 9
debugging with raw RPC 7: 36
debugging with rpcgen(1) 6: 29
#define, with rpcgen(1) 6: 24
deserialize 5: 2, 16
discriminated union (XDR) 8: 15
domain, YP 11: 3, 7–8
domain names, YP 11: 3

E

External Data Representation (see
  XDR)

I

inetd(1M) 6: 12, 7: 55–56

L

listen(1M) 6: 12, 7: 55, 57
loopback transport 5: 8

M

makedbm(1M) 11: 24–27
maps (YP) 11: 2, 6, 8–16, 23–30
 adding to makefile 11: 29–30
 changing server 11: 32–34
 creating 11: 24–25
 makefiles 11: 12–15
 propagating 11: 27–29
 updating 11: 23–27
master server (YP) 11: 3–6
 map changing 11: 32–34

Contents

Figures and Tables

12 Network Selection and Name-to-Address Mapping

Table of Contents   i

Network Selection

In order for network applications to be portable to different environments, the application process must have a standard interface into the number and types of networks available in any current environment. Network Selection provides a simple and consistent interface that allows user applications to select networks (at the transport level) that exist in an environment, thus enabling applications to be protocol- and media-independent. System V Networking Services applications that allow the user to influence the choice of networks will use the standard interface outlined here.

Network Selection routines may be employed by the client portion of an application when the application initiates communication with its peer application on another machine; they may also be used by the server portion of an application when it offers its service. On a machine connected to a single network, Network Selection makes it possible for the application to make use of that network without requiring application-specific action by the administrator or user. On a machine connected to multiple networks, Network Selection makes it easy for the application to try each alternative network in turn, until it succeeds in establishing communication, and to try them either in the order specified as the local "default" sequence established by the system administrator or in the order preferred by the user. It also allows server-side applications to accept requests over multiple networks.

Choosing among the available networks is the responsibility of the application. The Network Selection mechanism is intended to make that selection uniform and simple.

How Network Selection Works

The Network Selection component is built around

- a network configuration database (the /etc/netconfig file) that contains an entry for each network on the system, and

- an optional NETPATH environment variable, set by a user and containing an ordered list of network identifiers. These network identifiers match the netconfig *network ID* field and are used as links to the records in the netconfig file. The netconfig file is described in the next section.

The Network Selection application programming interface consists of a set of network configuration database access routines. One set of library routines accesses only the netconfig entries identified by the NETPATH environment

variable. These routines are described below under "Routines That Access
netconfig via NETPATH," and on the getnetpath(3N) manual page.

```
setnetpath()
getnetpath()
endnetpath()
```

Applications should use these routines that access NETPATH. They allow users
to influence the selection of transports used by the application. If an application
does not want the user to influence its decision, then the routines that access the
netconfig database directly should be used.

There is also another group of routines that accesses netconfig directly. These
routines are described below under "Routines That Access netconfig Directly,"
and on the getnetconfig(3N) manual page.

```
setnetconfig()
getnetconfig()
endnetconfig()

getnetconfigent()
freenetconfigent()
```

In addition to this chapter, the System V Network Selection component is
described in the *System Administrator's Guide*.

The netconfig File

The netconfig file is the database that describes all networks on a given
machine. Entries in the netconfig file contain the following fields:

network ID	semantics	flag	protocol family	protocol name	network device	directory lookup libraries

network ID   A locally meaningful representation of a network
name (for example, tcp or starlan). Applications
that require the name of a transport provider will
obtain the name from this field.

semantics	The semantics of the particular network. Valid semantics are:

`tpi_clts`	connectionless
`tpi_cots`	connection-oriented
`tpi_cots_ord`	connection-oriented with orderly release

Applications that require certain semantics, such as virtual circuit establishment, can use this field to determine if the transport provider has the required semantics.

flag	A string of flags associated with the transport. The only flag currently defined is a "visible" flag, which is described under 'The NETPATH Environment Variable." *flag* may take one of two values, v or a hyphen (–).
protocol family	The protocol family name of the transport provider, for example, inet or osinet. See the netconfig(4) manual page.
protocol name	The protocol name of the transport provider. If *protocol family* is inet, then *protocol name* is tcp, udp, or icmp. Otherwise the value of *protocol name* is a hyphen (–). See the netconfig(4) manual page.
network device	The full pathname of the device file to open when accessing the transport provider.
directory lookup libraries	Names of the shared libraries. This field contains the comma-separated full pathnames of the directory lookup libraries that contain Name-to-Address Mapping routines. The libraries must be shared objects.

The fields correspond to elements of the struct netconfig structure. Pointers returned by Network Selection library routines are pointers to netconfig entries in struct netconfig format. The netconfig structure is shown in Figure 12-1.

Figure 12-1: The `netconfig` **Structure**

```
struct          netconfig {
                char           *nc_netid;       /* network identifier      */
                unsigned long  nc_semantics;    /* semantics of protocol   */
                unsigned long  nc_flag;         /* flags for the protocol  */
                unsigned long  nc_protofmly;    /* family name             */
                unsigned long  nc_proto;        /* proto specific if fmly inet */
                char           *nc_device;      /* device name for network id */
                unsigned long  nc_nlookups;     /* # of entries in nc_lookups */
                char           **nc_lookups;    /* list of lookup directories */
                unsigned long  nc_unused[8];
};
```

Valid network IDs are defined by the system administrator, who is responsible
for ensuring that network IDs are locally unique. If they are not, some Network
Selection routines cannot operate in a well-defined manner. For example, it is
not possible to know which network `getnetconfigent("starlan")` will use
if there are two `netconfig` entries with the network ID `starlan`.

The system administrator also determines the order of the entries in the
`netconfig` database. The routines that retrieve entries from
`/etc/netconfig` return entries in order, beginning at the top of the file. The
order of networks in the `netconfig` file therefore becomes the default network
search path for applications using the routines described in the next section.

The `netconfig` file and the `struct netconfig` structure are described in
greater detail on the `netconfig`(4) manual page.

The NETPATH Environment Variable

In most cases the user isn't interested in which network is used for a network
operation. Typically an application uses the default network search path established by the system administrator to locate an available network. However,
when a user wants to influence the choices made by an application, the application can modify the interface by using the shell variable NETPATH and the routines described in the next section. These routines access only the networks
specified in the NETPATH variable.

NETPATH is similar to the PATH variable. It consists of a colon-separated list of network IDs. Each network ID in the NETPATH variable corresponds to the *network ID* field of a record in the netconfig file. A literal colon can be embedded as "\:" and a literal backslash as "\\". NETPATH is described on the environ(5) manual page in the *User's Reference Manual*.

Figure 12-2: Sample values for a NETPATH environment variable.

```
NETPATH=starlan:tcp
```

The set of default networks is different for the routines that access netconfig via the NETPATH environment variable (described in the next section) and the routines that access netconfig directly (described later in this chapter). The set of default networks for routines that access netconfig via NETPATH consists of the "visible" networks in the netconfig file. For routines that access netconfig directly, the set of default networks is the entire netconfig file. A network is "visible" if the system administrator has included a v flag in the flag field of that network's netconfig entry.

Routines That Access netconfig via NETPATH

The three routines described in this section access the network configuration database indirectly through the NETPATH environment variable. The user is thus able to specify the network or networks the application is to use and, if more than one network is specified, in what order they are to be tried. These routines have the following syntax:

```
#include <netconfig.h>

void *
setnetpath()

struct netconfig *
getnetpath(handlep)
void * handlep;

int
endnetpath(handlep)
void * handlep;
```

A call to setnetpath() has the effect of initializing NETPATH. It returns a
pointer to a database that contains the entries specified in a NETPATH variable.
The pointer, called a "handle," is used when traversing this database with get-
netpath(). Each call to setnetpath() returns a different database pointer.
setnetpath() must be called before the first call to getnetpath() and may
be called at any other time. setnetpath() returns NULL if the netconfig
database is not present. setnetpath() takes no arguments.

When first called, getnetpath() returns a pointer to to the netconfig database entry that corresponds to the first component of the NETPATH variable (the
instance described by the handle). NETPATH components are read from left to
right. The netconfig entry is formatted as a struct netconfig. On each
subsequent call, getnetpath() returns a pointer to the netconfig entry that
corresponds to the next component of the NETPATH variable. getnetpath()
returns NULL on end of file. A call to getnetpath() without an initial call to
setnetpath() will produce an error. getnetpath() takes a handle as an
argument.

getnetpath() silently ignores invalid NETPATH components. A NETPATH
component is invalid if there is no corresponding entry in the netconfig database.

If the NETPATH variable is unset, getnetpath() behaves as if NETPATH were
set to the sequence of "default" or "visible" networks in the netconfig database, in the order in which they are listed.

endnetpath() is called to "free" the database pointer to elements in the NET-PATH variable when processing is complete. It returns 0 on success and −1 on failure. endnetpath() will fail if setnetpath() was not called previously. endnetpath() takes the instance *handlep* as an argument.

Figure 12-3: **Sample code using** setnetpath(), getnetpath(), **and** endnetpath().

```
void *handlep;

if ((handlep = setnetpath()) == NULL) {
        nc_perror(argv[0]);
        exit(1);
}

while ((netconfigp = getnetpath(handlep)) != NULL) {
        /*
         *   netconfigp now describes a transport provider
         */
}
endnetpath(handlep);
```

Routines That Access netconfig Directly

Five functions access the network configuration database file, /etc/netconfig. They have the following syntax:

```
#include <netconfig.h>

void *
setnetconfig()

struct netconfig *
getnetconfig(handlep)
void * handlep;

int
endnetconfig(handlep)
void * handlep;
```

A call to setnetconfig() initializes the database routines. It returns a database pointer to be used when traversing the database with getnetconfig(). This database pointer is also called a handle. Each call to setnetconfig() returns a different database pointer. Each call to getnetconfig() returns the next entry in netconfig associated with the "handle" returned by set-netconfig().

When first called, getnetconfig() returns a pointer to the first entry in the netconfig database, formatted as a struct netconfig. On each subsequent call, getnetconfig() returns a pointer to the next entry in the database; it can thus be used to search the entire netconfig file. getnetconfig() returns NULL to the calling routine at end of file.

endnetconfig() may be called to "free" the database pointer when processing is complete. endnetconfig() may not be called before setnetconfig(). endnetconfig() returns 0 on success and −1 on failure (for example, if setnetconfig() was not called previously).

Figure 12-4: **Sample code using** `setnetconfig()`, `getnetconfig()`, **and** `endnetconfig()`.

```
void * handlep;
struct netconfig * netcfp;
if ((handlep = setnetconfig()) == NULL){
        nc_perror(argv[0]);
        exit(1);
}

/*
 *   transport provider information is described in netcfp.
 *   process_transport is a user-supplied routine that tries to
 *   connect to a server over transport netcfp.
 */

while ((netcfp = getnetconfig(handlep)) != NULL){
        if (process_transport(netcfp) == SUCCESS){
                break;
        }
}

endnetconfig(handlep);
```

Figure 12-5: **Sample Code Using** `getnetconfigent()` **and** `freenetconfigent()`

```
#include <netconfig.h>

struct netconfig *
getnetconfigent(netid)
        char * netid;

int
freenetconfigent(netconfigp)
struct netconfig * netconfigp;
```

getnetconfigent() returns a pointer to the struct netconfig structure corresponding to *netid*. It returns NULL if *netid* is invalid (that is, does not name an entry in the netconfig database).

freenetconfigent() frees the structure returned by getnetconfigent().

 NOTE   setnetconfig() need not be called before getnetconfigent().

Figure 12-6: Sample code using getnetconfigent() **and** freenetconfigent().

```
/*
 *   assume starlan is a netid on this machine
 */

struct netconfig * netcfp;
if ((netcfp = getnetconfigent("starlan")) == NULL) {
        nc_error("no information about starlan");
        exit(1);
}

process_transport(netcfp);

freenetconfigent(netcfp);
```

Code Examples

The following code examples are taken from the larger program at the end of this section. They show several of the ways in which the Network Selection facility may be used.

Programmer's Guide: Networking Interfaces

Looping through All "Visible" netconfig Entries

In the examples, the setnetpath() call initializes the Network Selection routines and returns a database pointer.

The getnetpath() call returns each visible entry in the /etc/netconfig file (that is, each entry that contains a v flag). Entries are returned in the order in which they appear in the file.

```
if (setnetpath() <= 0) {
        fprintf(stderr, "%s: ERROR: network selection not set\n", argv[0]);
        exit(1);
}

while ((netconfigp = getnetpath()) != NULL) {
        /*
         *    the netconfig structure contains information about the
         *    transport provider.
         */
}
```

Looping through User-defined netconfig Entries

Users can also manipulate the loop by setting the NETPATH environment variable to a colon-separated list of transport provider names (transport provider names are given in the first field of the /etc/netconfig file). If the value of NETPATH is set as follows:

```
NETPATH=tcp:starlan
```

then the loop will first return the entry corresponding to tcp, and then the entry corresponding to starlan. If NETPATH is not set in the environment, the above loop will return all visible entries in the netconfig file in the order in which they appear there.

The NETPATH environment variable allows users to define the order in which client-side applications attempt to make connections to a service. It also allows the administrator of the server machine to restrict which transport providers a service will loop through and bind to.

Looping through All netconfig Entries

An application can ignore the NETPATH variable and loop through all entries in the netconfig file — even those without a v flag:

```
if (setnetconfig() <= 0) {
        fprintf(stderr, "%s: ERROR: network selection not set\n", argv[0]);
        exit(1);
}

while ((netconfigp = getnetconfig()) != NULL) {
        /*
         *   the netconfig structure contains information about the
         *   transport provider, and NETPATH is ignored.
         */
}
```

Specifying a Single Transport Provider

The following call will obtain information about a single, named transport provider:

```
netconfigp = getnetconfigent(name);
```

Name-to-Address Mapping

The Name-to-Address Mapping feature allows an application to obtain the address of a service on a specified machine in a transport–independent manner. The Name-to-Address Mapping feature consists of the following routines:

```
netdir_getbyname
netdir_getbyaddr
netdir_free
netdir_mergeaddr
taddr2uaddr
uaddr2taddr
netdir_options
```

Each routine takes a pointer to a `struct netconfig`, which describes a transport provider. Using the directory lookup library element of the `netconfig` structure, the routine can obtain a list of shared libraries that contains transport-specific versions of itself. It will call each of these in turn until the call succeeds. For example, in UNIX System V Release 4.0, the full libraries are provided to support the Internet protocols, the ISO STARLAN protocols, and the loopback protocols.

The libraries are:

`tcpip.so`   Contains the Name-to-Address Mapping routines for the Internet protocol suite.

`straddr.so`   Contains the Name-to-Address Mapping routines for any protocol that accepts strings as addresses. ISO and the loopback protocols are examples.

The routines are described below under "The Name-to-Address Mapping Routines," and on the `netdir`(3N) manual page. The `struct netconfig` structure is described on the `netconfig`(4) manual page.

The Name-to-Address Mapping Libraries

Files for each of the libraries must be created and maintained by the system administrator.

`tcpip.so`

The routines in this dynamic library create addresses from the `/etc/hosts` and `/etc/services` files available with the TCP/IP package. The `/etc/hosts` file contains two fields, the machine's IP address and the machine name. For example:

```
192.11.108.01        bilbo
192.11.108.16        elvis
```

The `/etc/services` file contains two fields, a service name and a port number with one of two protocol specifications, either tcp or udp. For example:

```
rpcbind      111/udp
rpcbind      111/tcp
login        513/tcp
listen       1025/tcp
```

When an application uses this library to request the address of a service on a particular host, the host name must appear in the `/etc/hosts` file and the service name must appear in the `/etc/services` file. If one or the other does not appear, an error will be returned by the Name-to-Address Mapping routines.

`straddr.so`

The routines in this dynamic library create addresses from files that have the same format as the `tcpip.so` files described above. The `straddr.so` files are `/etc/net/`*transport*`/hosts` and `/etc/net/`*transport*`/services`. *transport* is the local name of the transport provider that accepts string addresses (specified in the *network ID* field of the `/etc/netconfig` file). For example, the host file for `starlan` would be `/etc/net/starlan/hosts`, and the service file for

starlan would be /etc/net/starlan/services. For starlandg, the files
would be /etc/net/starlandg/hosts and
/etc/net/starlandg/services.

Even though most string addresses do not distinguish between "host" and "service," separating the string into a host part and a service part provides consistency with other transport providers. The /etc/net/*transport*/hosts file will therefore contain a string that is considered to be the machine address, followed by the machine name. For example:

```
bilboaddr     bilbo
elvisaddr     elvis
frodoaddr     frodo
```

The /etc/net/*transport*/services file contains service names followed by strings identifying the service ports. For example:

```
rpcbind    rpc
listen     serve
```

The routines create the full string address by combining the "host address" and the "service port," separating the two with a dot ("."). For example, the address of the "listen" service on bilbo would be bilboaddr.serve, and the address of the "rpcbind" service on bilbo would be bilboaddr.rpc.

When an application requests the address of a service on a particular host on a transport provider that uses this library, the host name must appear in /etc/net/*transport*/hosts and the service name must appear in /etc/net/*transport*/services. If one or the other does not appear, the Name-to-Address Mapping routines will return an error.

Using the Name-to-Address Mapping Routines

```
int
netdir_getbyname(netconfig, nd_hostserv, nd_addrlist)
struct netconfig        *netconfig;
struct nd_hostserv      *nd_hostserv;
struct nd_addrlist      **nd_addrlist;

int
netdir_getbyaddr(netconfig, nd_hostservlist, netbuf)
struct netconfig        *netconfig;
struct nd_hostservlist  **nd_hostservlist;
struct netbuf           *netbuf;

void
netdir_free(ptr, type)
char    *ptr;
int     type;

char *
taddr2uaddr(netconfig, addr)
struct netconfig        *netconfig;
struct netbuf           *addr;

struct netbuf *
uaddr2taddr(netconfig, addr)
struct netconfig        *netconfig;
char                    *addr;

int
netdir_options(netconfig, option, fd, pointer_to_args)
struct netconfig        *netconfig;
int                     option;
int                     fd;
char                    *pointer_to_args;

void
netdir_perror(s)
char    *s;

char *
netdir_sperror()
```

netdir_getbyname

The netdir_getbyname() routine maps the machine and service name specified in the nd_hostserv structure to a collection of addresses of the type understood by the transport identified in the netconfig structure. The nd_addrlist parameter returns a pointer to the addresses. To find all addresses of a machine and service (on all available transports), repeatedly call the netdir_getbyname() routine with each netconfig structure returned by the getnetpath(3N) call.

netdir_getbyaddr

The netdir_getbyaddr() routine maps addresses into machine and service names. Given an address in the netbuf parameter, this routine returns a list of machine name and service name pairs that would yield that address (a pointer to the list of machine and service name pairs is returned in the nd_hostservlist parameter.)

netdir_free

The netdir_free() routine frees the structures allocated by the name-to-address translation routines. The parameters can take the following values:

Type	Pointer
ND_HOSTSERVLIST	pointer to nd_hostservlist structure allocated by netdir_getbyaddr()
ND_ADDRLIST	pointer to nd_addrlist structure allocated by netdir_getbyname()

taddr2uaddr

The taddr2uaddr() routine translates the address given in the netbuf structure (which is an address for the transport provider given in the netconfig structure) and returns a "universal address" representation of the address. A "universal address" is a machine architecture-independent character representation of the address.

uaddr2taddr

The `uaddr2taddr` routine takes a "universal address" and translates it back into a `netbuf` structure. The `netconfig` parameter specifies which transport provider the address is valid for.

netdir_options

The `netdir_options()` routine provides an interface to transport specific capabilities (for example, applications can take advantage of the "broadcast address" and "reserved port" facilities provided by the User Datagram Protocol (UDP)).

The `netconfig` structure specifies a transport provider. The *option* argument specifies the transport-specific action to take. The third argument is a file descriptor (which may or may not be used depending upon *option*). The fourth argument is a a pointer to operation-specific data.

The following values may be used for *option*:

`ND_SET_BROADCAST`	This option sets the transport provider up to allow for broadcast (if the transport provider supports broadcast). *fd* is a file descriptor into the transport provider (for example, the result of a `t_open()` of `/dev/udp`). *pointer_to_args* is not used. If successful, broadcast operations may be done on *fd*.
`ND_SET_RESERVEDPORT`	Allows the application to bind to a reserved port, if allowed by the transport provider specified. *fd* is a file descriptor into the transport (it must not be bound to an address). If *pointer_to_args* is `NULL`, *fd* will be bound to a reserved port. If *pointer_to_args* is a pointer to a `netbuf` structure, an attempt will be made to bind to a reserved port on the specified address.
`ND_CHECK_RESERVEDPORT`	If the concept of a reserved port exists for a transport provider, `ND_CHECK_RESERVEDPORT` is used to verify that an address corresponds to a reserved port. *fd* is not used. *pointer_to_args* is a pointer to a `netbuf` structure that contains an address. This option returns 0 only if the

address specified in *pointer_to_args* is reserved.

ND_MERGEADDR   Used to transform a locally meaningful address into an address that client machines can connect to. For example, the Transmission Control Protocol (TCP) has the concept of 0.0.0.0 as a locally meaningful address. ND_MERGEADDR can be used to translate the 0.0.0.0 address into a "real" address that is understood by client machines. *fd* is not used with this option. *pointer_to_args* is a pointer to a nd_mergearg structure, which has the following form:

```
struct nd_mergearg {
        char *s_uaddr;   /* server's universal address */
        char *c_uaddr;   /* client's universal address */
        char *m_uaddr;   /* the result */
}
```

netdir_perror

The netdir_perror() routine prints onto standard output the error message stating why one of the name-to-address mapping routines failed. The error message is preceded by the string given as an argument.

netdir_sperror

The netdir_sperror() routine returns a string containing the error message stating why one of the name-to-address mapping routines failed.

Figure 12-7: Code example: Using Network Selection and Name-to-Address Mapping.

```
#include <netconfig.h>
#include <netdir.h>
#include <tiuser.h>

/*** The following is a segment of a procedure. ***/

struct nd_hostserv   nd_hostserv;    /* contains host and service information */
struct netconfig     *netconfigp;    /* contains information about each network */
struct nd_addrlist   *nd_addrlistp;  /* list of addresses for the service */
struct netbuf        *netbufp;       /* the address of the service */
int                  i;              /* counts the number of addresses */
void                 *handlep;       /* a handle into network selection */

/*
 * Set the host structure to reference the "date" service on machine "gandalf"
 */

nd_hostserv.h_host = "gandalf";
nd_hostserv.h_serv = "date";

/*
 * Initialize the network selection mechanism.
 */

if ((handlep = setnetpath()) == NULL) {
        nc_perror(argv[0]);
        exit(1);
}
/*
 * Loop through the transport providers.
 */

while ((netconfigp = getnetpath(handlep)) != NULL) {
        /*
         * Print out the information associated with the transport
         * provider described in the "netconfig" structure.
         */

        printf("Transport provider name: %s\n",   netconfigp->nc_netid);
        printf("Transport protocol family: %s\n", netconfigp->nc_protofmly);
        printf("The transport device file: %s\n", netconfigp->nc_device);
        printf("Transport provider semantics: ");
```

(continued on next page)

Figure 12-7: Code example: Using Network Selection and Name-to-Address Mapping. (continued)

```
            switch (netconfigp->nc_semantics) {
              case NC_TPI_COTS:
                    printf("virtual circuit\n");
                    break;
              case NC_TPI_COTS_ORD:
                    printf("virtual circuit with orderly release\n");
                    break;
              case NC_TPI_CLTS:
                    printf("datagram\n");
            }

            /*
             *   Get the addresses for service "date" on machine "gandalf"
             *   over the transport provider specified in the netconfig structure.
             */
            if (netdir_getbyname(netconfigp, &nd_hostserv, &nd_addrlistp) != 0) {
                    printf("Cannot determine the address for the service\n");
                    netdir_perror(argv[0]);
                    continue;
            }

            printf("There are <%d> addresses for the date service on gandalf:\n",
                    nd_addrlistp->n_cnt);

            /*
             *   Print out all addresses for service "date" on machine "gandalf"
             *   on the current transport provider.
             */
            netbufp = nd_addrlistp->n_addrs;
            for (i = 0; i < nd_addrlistp->n_cnt; i++) {
                    printf("%s\n", taddr2uaddr(netconfigp, netbufp));
                    netbufp++;
            }
      }
   endnetconfig(handlep);
```

Index

I

Internet, support for protocols   12: 13

N

name-to-address mapping   12: 13–21
  routines   12: 16–21
netconfig(4)   12: 2–10, 12
netdir_free function   12: 17
netdir_getbyaddr function   12: 17
netdir_getbyname function   12: 17
netdir_options function   12: 18
netdir_perror function   12: 19
netdir_sperror function   12: 19
NETPATH environment variable   12: 2,
    4–7, 12
network, configuration file   12: 2–10,
    12
network addressing   12: 13–21
  string address providers   12: 14
  TCP/IP   12: 14
network selection   12: 1–15
  code examples   12: 10–12

S

services(4)   12: 14
STARLAN, support for protocols
    12: 13
straddr.so file   12: 14–15

T

taddr2uaddr function   12: 17
TCP (Transmission Control Protocol)
    12: 14, 19

TCP/IP, network addressing   12: 14
tcpip.so file   12: 14

U

uaddr2taddr function   12: 18

Contents

Index: Writing a Port Monitor for the Service Access Facility

Figures and Tables

13 Writing a Port Monitor for the Service Access Facility

Introduction

The Service Access Facility (SAF) generalizes the procedures for service access so that login access on the local system and network access to local services are managed in similar ways. Under the SAF, systems may access services using a variety of port monitors, including ttymon, the listener, and port monitors written expressly for a user's application. The Service Access Facility is fully documented in the "Service Access" chapter of the *System Administrator's Guide*. It is assumed that programmers who are writing port monitors to be used on a System V Release 4 system are familiar with that chapter.

Beginning with System V Release 4, ttymon replaces getty and uugetty for local access to login service and is available for other types of access to the local system. The "Service Access" chapter of the *System Administrator's Guide* describes managing ttymon port monitors ("The Port Monitor ttymon") and defining terminal line settings for TTY ports ("Terminal Line Settings").

The listener provides network access over any network that conforms to the Transport Interface (TLI) protocol. The listener is also documented in the Service Access chapter of the *System Administrator's Guide*. TLI is documented in Chapter 2 of this volume, "Transport Interface Programming."

Service Access Facility manual pages are included in the *System Administrator's Reference Manual* and in Appendix A of this volume.

Programmers of networking applications should also see Chapter 12 of this volume, "Network Selection and Name-to-Address Mapping."

This chapter gives a brief description of the functions a port monitor must perform to run under the Service Access Facility; the message format required for port monitor interface with the SAF; the way in which the SAF administers port monitors; and the requirements for port monitors registered with the SAF. The chapter also contains a section on configuration files, the language in which configuration scripts are written, and the doconfig() function, which interprets these scripts. Finally, it includes code for a simple port monitor that may be used as a model.

Overview of the Service Access Facility

The manner in which a port monitor monitors and manages access ports is specific to the port monitor and not to any component of the Service Access Facility. Users may therefore extend their systems by developing and installing their own port monitors. It is one of the important features of the Service Access Facility that it can be extended in this way by users.

From the point of view of the Service Access Facility, a service is a process that is started. There are no restrictions on the functions a service may provide.

The Service Access Facility consists of a controlling process, the Service Access Controller (SAC), and two administrative levels corresponding to two levels in the supporting directory structure. The top administrative level is concerned with port monitor administration, the lower level with service administration.

From an administrative point of view, the Service Access Facility consists of the following components:

- The Service Access Controller
- A per-system configuration script
- The SAC administrative file
- The SAC administrative command sacadm
- Port monitors
- Optional per-port monitor configuration scripts
- An administrative file for each port monitor, named _pmtab
- The administrative command pmadm
- Optional per-service configuration scripts

The Service Access Controller

The Service Access Controller is the Service Access Facility's controlling process. The SAC is started by init(1M) by means of an entry in /etc/inittab. Its function is to maintain the port monitors on the system in the state specified by the system administrator.

The administrative command sacadm is used to tell the SAC to change the state of a port monitor. sacadm can also be used to add or remove a port monitor from SAC supervision and to list information about port monitors known to the SAC.

The SAC's administrative file contains a unique tag for each port monitor known to the SAC and the pathname of the command used to start each port monitor.

The SAC performs three main functions. Briefly:

- it customizes its own environment
- it starts the appropriate port monitors
- it polls its port monitors and initiates recovery procedures when necessary

Basic Port Monitor Functions

A port monitor is a process that is responsible for monitoring a set of homogeneous, incoming ports on a machine. A port monitor's major purpose is to detect incoming service requests and to dispatch them appropriately.

A port is an externally-seen access point on a system. A port may be an address on a network (TSAP or PSAP), a hardwired terminal line, an incoming phone line, etc. The definition of what constitutes a port is strictly a function of the port monitor itself.

A port monitor performs certain basic functions. Some of these are required to conform to the Service Access Facility (SAF); others may be specified by the requirements and design of the port monitor itself.

Port monitors have two main functions:

- managing ports and
- monitoring ports for indications of activity

Port Management

The first function of a port monitor is to manage a port. The actual details of how a port is managed are defined by the person who defines the port monitor. A port monitor is not restricted to handling a single port; it may handle multiple ports simultaneously.

 NOTE Some examples of port management are setting the line speed on incoming phone connections, binding an appropriate network address, reinitializing the port when the service terminates, outputting a prompt, etc.

Activity Monitoring

The second function of a port monitor is to monitor the port or ports for which it is responsible for indications of activity. Two types of activity may be detected.

- The first is an indication to the port monitor to take some port monitor-specific action. Pressing the <break> key to indicate that the line speed should be cycled is an example of a port monitor-specific activity. Not all port monitors need to recognize and respond to the same indications. The indication used to attract the attention of the port monitor is defined by the person who defines the port monitor.

- The second is an incoming service request. When a service request is received, a port monitor must be able to determine which service is being requested from the port on which the request is received. Note that the same service may be available on more than one port.

Other Port Monitor Functions

Restricting Access to the System: Enabling and Disabling Port Monitors and Ports

A port monitor must be able to restrict access to the system without disturbing services that are still running. In order to do this, a port monitor must maintain two internal states: *enabled* and *disabled*. The port monitor starts in the state indicated by the ISTATE environment variable provided by the sac. (See "The Service Access Controller/Port Monitor Interface," below.)

Enabling and Disabling a Port Monitor

Enabling or disabling a port monitor affects all ports for which the port monitor is responsible. If a port monitor is responsible for a single port, only that port will be affected. If a port monitor is responsible for multiple ports, the entire collection of ports will be affected.

Enabling or disabling a port monitor is a dynamic operation: it causes the port monitor to change its internal state. The effect does not persist across new invocations of the port monitor.

Enabling and Disabling a Port

Enabling or disabling an individual port, however, is a static operation: it causes a change to an administrative file. The effect of this change will persist across new invocations of the port monitor.

Creating utmp Entries

Port monitors are responsible for creating utmp entries with the type field set to USER_PROCESS for services they start, if this action has been specified (that is, if –fu was specified in the pmadm line that added the service). These utmp entries may in turn be modified by the service. When the service terminates, the utmp entry must be set to DEAD_PROCESS.

Port Monitor Process IDs and Lock Files

When a port monitor starts, it writes its process id into a file named _pid in the current directory and places an advisory lock on the file.

Changing the Service Environment: Running doconfig()

Before invoking the service designated in the port monitor administrative file, _pmtab, a port monitor must arrange for the per-service configuration script to be run (if one exists) by calling the library function doconfig(3N). Because the per-service configuration script may specify the execution of restricted commands, as well as for other security reasons, port monitors are invoked with root permissions. The details of how services are invoked are specified by the person who defines the port monitor.

Files: The Port Monitor Administrative File

A port monitor's current directory contains an administrative file named _pmtab. _pmtab is maintained by the pmadm command in conjunction with a port monitor-specific administrative command. Port monitor-specific commands are discussed below.

 NOTE The port monitor-specific administrative command for a listen port monitor is nlsadmin(1M); the port monitor-specific administrative command for ttymon is ttyadm. Any port monitor written by a user must be provided with an administrative command specific to that port monitor to perform similar functions.

Programmer's Guide: Networking Interfaces

Files: Per-service Configuration Files

A port monitor's current directory also contains the per-service configuration scripts, if they exist. The names of the per-service configuration scripts correspond to the service tags in the _pmtab file.

Private Port Monitor Files

A port monitor may create private files in the directory /var/saf/*tag*, where *tag* is the name of the port monitor. Examples of private files are log files or temporary files.

Terminating a Port Monitor

A port monitor must terminate itself gracefully on receipt of the signal SIGTERM. The termination sequence is the following:

■ The port monitor enters the *stopping* state; no further service requests are accepted.

■ Any attempt to re-enable the port monitor will be ignored.

■ The port monitor yields control of all ports for which it is responsible. It must be possible for a new instantiation of the port monitor to start correctly while a previous instantiation is stopping.

■ The advisory lock on the process id file is released. Once this lock is released, the contents of the process id file are undefined and a new invocation of the port monitor may be started.

The Service Access Controller/Port Monitor Interface

The sac creates two environment variables for each port monitor it starts:

- PMTAG and
- ISTATE

PMTAG is set to a unique port monitor tag by the sac. The port monitor uses this tag to identify itself in response to sac messages. ISTATE is used to indicate to the port monitor what its initial internal state should be. ISTATE is set to "enabled" or "disabled" to indicate that the port monitor is to start in the *enabled* or *disabled* state, respectively. The sac performs a periodic sanity poll of the port monitors.

The sac communicates with port monitors through FIFOs. A port monitor should open _pmpipe, in the current directory, to receive messages from the sac and ../_sacpipe to send return messages to the sac.

Message Formats

This section describes the messages that may be sent from the sac to a port monitor (sac messages), and from a port monitor to the sac (port monitor messages). These messages are sent through FIFOs and are in the form of C structures (see the section "The Header File sac.h").

sac Messages

The format of messages from the sac is defined by the structure sacmsg:

```
struct  sacmsg {
        int     sc_size;      /* size of optional data portion */
        char    sc_type;      /* type of message */
};
```

The sac may send four types of messages to port monitors. The type of message is indicated by setting the sc_type field of the sacmsg structure to one of the following:

SC_STATUS	status request
SC_ENABLE	enable message
SC_DISABLE	disable message
SC_READDB	message indicating that the port monitor's _pmtab file should be read

sc_size indicates the size of the optional data part of the message. It is discussed under "Message Classes," below. For System V Release 4, sc_size should always be set to 0.

A port monitor must respond to every message sent by the sac.

Port Monitor Messages

The format of messages from a port monitor to the sac is defined by the structure pmmsg:

```
struct  pmmsg {
      char    pm_type;        /* type of message */
      unchar  pm_state;       /* current state of port monitor */
      char    pm_maxclass;    /* maximum message class this
                                 port monitor understands */
      char    pm_tag[PMTAGSIZE + 1];
                              /* port monitor's tag */
      int     pm_size;        /* size of optional data portion */
};
```

Port monitors may send two types of messages to the sac. The type of message is indicated by setting the pm_type field of the pmmsg structure to one of the following:

PM_STATUS	state information
PM_UNKNOWN	negative acknowledgement

For both types of messages, the pm_tag field is set to the port monitor's tag and the pm_state field is set to the port monitor's current state. Valid states are:

PM_STARTING	starting
PM_ENABLED	enabled
PM_DISABLED	disabled
PM_STOPPING	stopping

The current state reflects any changes caused by the last message from the sac.

The status message is the normal return message. The negative acknowledgment should be sent only when the message received is not understood.

pm_size indicates the size of the optional data part of the message. pm_maxclass is used to specify a message class. Both are discussed under "Message Classes" below. For System V Release 4, pm_maxclass should always be set to 1 and sc_size should always be set to 0.

Port monitors may never initiate messages; they may only respond to messages that they receive.

Message Classes

The concept of "message class" has been included to accommodate possible SAF extensions. The messages described above are all "class 1" messages. None of these messages contains a variable data portion; all pertinent information is contained in the message header.

If new messages are added to the protocol, they will be defined as new message classes (for example, class 2). The first message the sac sends to a port monitor will always be a class 1 message. Since all port monitors, by definition, understand class 1 messages, the first message the sac sends is guaranteed to be understood. In its response to the sac, the port monitor sets the pm_maxclass field to the maximum message class number for that port monitor. The sac will not send messages to a port monitor from a class with a larger number than the value of pm_maxclass. Requests that require messages of a higher class than the port monitor can understand will fail. For System V Release 4, pm_maxclass should always be set to 1.

NOTE For any given port monitor, messages of class pm_maxclass and messages of all classes with values lower than pm_maxclass are valid. Thus, if the pm_maxclass field is set to 3, the port monitor understands messages of classes 1, 2, and 3.

Port monitors may not generate messages; they may only respond to messages. A port monitor's response must be of the same class as the originating message.

Since only the sac can generate messages, this protocol will function even if the port monitor is capable of dealing with messages of a higher class than the sac can generate.

pm_size (an element of the pmmsg structure) and sc_size (an element of the sacmsg structure) indicate the size of the optional data part of the message. The format of this part of the message is undefined. Its definition is inherent in the type of message. For System V Release 4, both sc_size and pm_size should always be set to 0.

The Port Monitor Administrative Interface

The SAC Administrative File _sactab

The SAC's administrative file contains information about all the port monitors for which the SAC is responsible. This file exists on the delivered system. Initially, it is empty except for a single comment line which contains the version number of the Service Access Controller. Port monitors are added to the system by making entries in the SAC's administrative file. These entries should be made using the administrative command sacadm with a –a option. sacadm is also used to remove entries from the SAC's administrative file.

Each entry in the SAC's administrative file contains the following information:

PMTAG   A unique tag that identifies a particular port monitor. The system administrator is responsible for naming a port monitor. This tag is then used by the Service Access Controller (SAC) to identify the port monitor for all administrative purposes.

PMTAG may consist of up to 14 alphanumeric characters.

PMTYPE   The type of the port monitor. In addition to its unique tag, each port monitor has a type designator. The type designator identifies a group of port monitors that are different invocations of the same entity. ttymon and listen are examples of valid port monitor types. The type designator is used to facilitate the administration of groups of related port monitors. Without a type designator, the system administrator has no way of knowing which port monitor tags correspond to port monitors of the same type.

PMTYPE may consist of up to 14 alphanumeric characters.

FLGS   The flags that are currently defined are:

               d   When started, do not enable the port monitor.

               x   Do not start the port monitor.

If no flag is specified, the default action is taken. By default a port monitor is started and enabled.

RCNT   The number of times a port monitor may fail before being placed in a failed state. Once a port monitor enters the failed state, the SAC will not try to restart it. If a count is not specified when the entry is created, this field is set to 0. A restart count of 0 indicates that the port monitor is not to be restarted when it fails.

COMMAND   A string representing the command that will start the port monitor. The first component of the string, the command itself, must be a full pathname.

The Port Monitor Administrative File _pmtab

Each port monitor will have two directories for its exclusive use. The current directory will contain files defined by the SAF (_pmtab, _pid) and the per-service configuration scripts, if they exist. The directory /var/saf/*pmtag*, where *pmtag* is the tag of the port monitor, is available for the port monitor's private files.

Each port monitor has its own administrative file. The pmadm command should be used to add, remove, or modify service entries in this file. Each time a change is made using pmadm, the corresponding port monitor rereads its administrative file. Each entry in a port monitor's administrative file defines how the port monitor treats a specific port and what service is to be invoked on that port.

Some fields must be present for all types of port monitors. Each entry must include a service tag to identify the service uniquely and an identity to be assigned to the service when it is started (for example, root).

NOTE   The combination of a service tag and a port monitor tag uniquely define an instance of a service. The same service tag may be used to identify a service under a different port monitor.

The record must also contain port monitor specific data (for example, for a ttymon port monitor, this will include the prompt string which is meaningful to ttymon). Each type of port monitor must provide a command that takes the necessary port monitor-specific data as arguments and outputs these data in a form suitable for storage in the file. The ttyadm(1M) command does this for ttymon and nlsadmin(1M) does it for listen. For a user-defined port monitor, a similar administrative command must also be supplied.

Each service entry in the port monitor administrative file must have the following format and contain the information listed below:

svctag:*flgs*:*id*: reserved: reserved: reserved:*pmspecific*# *comment*

SVCTAG
A unique tag that identifies a service. This tag is unique only for the port monitor through which the service is available. Other port monitors may offer the same or other services with the same tag. A service requires both a port monitor tag and a service tag to identify it uniquely.

SVCTAG may consist of up to 14 alphanumeric characters.

FLGS
Flags with the following meanings may currently be included in this field:

    x   Do not enable this port.
           By default the port is enabled.

    u   Create a utmp entry for this service.
           By default no utmp entry is created for the service.

Note that port monitors may ignore the u flag if creating a utmp entry for the service is not appropriate to the manner in which the service is to be invoked. Some services may not start properly unless utmp entries have been created for them (for example, login).

ID
The identity under which the service is to be started. The identity has the form of a login name as it appears in /etc/passwd.

PMSPECIFIC
Examples of port monitor-specific information are addresses, the name of a process to execute, or the name of a STREAMS pipe to pass a connection through. This information will vary to meet the needs of each different type of port monitor.

COMMENT
A comment associated with the service entry.

Each port monitor administrative file must contain one special comment of
the form:

VERSION=*value*

where *value* is an integer that represents the port monitor's version number.
The version number defines the format of the port monitor administrative file.
This comment line is created automatically when a port monitor is added to
the system. It appears on a line by itself, before the service entries.

The SAC Administrative Command sacadm

sacadm is the administrative command for the upper level of the Service Access
Facility hierarchy, that is, for port monitor administration (see the sacadm(1M)
manual page and the "Service Access" chapter of the *System Administrator's
Guide*). Under the Service Access Facility, port monitors are administered by
using the sacadm command to make changes in the SAC's administrative file.
sacadm performs the functions listed below.

- print requested port monitor information from the SAC administrative file

- add or remove a port monitor

- enable or disable a port monitor

- start or stop a port monitor

- install or replace a per-system configuration script

- install or replace a per-port monitor configuration script

- ask the SAC to reread its administrative file

The Port Monitor Administrative Command pmadm

pmadm is the administrative command for the lower level of the Service Access Facility hierarchy, that is, for service administration (see the manual page pmadm(1M) and the "Service Access" chapter of the *System Administrator's Guide*). A port may have only one service associated with it although the same service may be available through more than one port. pmadm performs the following functions:

- print service status information from the port monitor's administrative file

- add or remove a service

- enable or disable a service

- install or replace a per-service configuration script

Note that in order to identify an instance of a service uniquely, the pmadm command must identify both the service (−s) and the port monitor or port monitors through which the service is available (−p or −t).

A Port Monitor's "Port Monitor-Specific" Administrative Command

In the previous section, two pieces of information included in the _pmtab file were described: the port monitor's version number and the port monitor-specific part of the service entries in the port monitor's _pmtab file. When a new port monitor is added, the version number must be known so that the _pmtab file can be correctly initialized. When a new service is added, the port monitor-specific part of the _pmtab entry must be formatted correctly.

Each port monitor must have an administrative command to perform these two tasks. The person who defines the port monitor must also define such an administrative command and its input options. When the command is invoked with these options, the information required for the port monitor-specific part of the service entry must be correctly formatted for inclusion in the port monitor's _pmtab file and must be written to the standard output. To request the version number the command must be invoked with a −V option; when it is invoked in this way, the port monitor's current version number must be written to the standard output.

Programmer's Guide: Networking Interfaces

If the command fails for any reason during the execution of either of these tasks, nothing should be written to standard output.

The Port Monitor/Service Interface

The interface between a port monitor and a service is determined solely by the service. Two mechanisms for invoking a service will be presented here as examples.

New Service Invocations

The first interface is for services that are started anew with each request. This interface requires the port monitor to first fork(2) a child process. The child will eventually become the designated service by performing an exec(2). Before the exec(2) happens, the port monitor may take some port monitor-specific action; however, one action that must occur is the interpretation of the per-service configuration script, if one is present. This is done by calling the library routine doconfig(3N).

Standing Service Invocations

The second interface is for invocations of services that are actively running. To use this interface, a service must have one end of a stream pipe open and be prepared to receive connections through it.

Port Monitor Requirements

To implement a port monitor, several generic requirements must be met. This section summarizes these requirements. In addition to the port monitor itself, an administrative command must be supplied.

Initial Environment

When a port monitor is started, it expects an initial execution environment in which:

- it will have no file descriptors open
- it will not be a process group leader
- it will have an entry in /etc/utmp of type LOGIN_PROCESS
- an environment variable, ISTATE, will be set to "enabled" or "disabled" to indicate the port monitor's correct initial state
- an environment variable, PMTAG, will be set to the port monitor's assigned tag
- the directory that contains the port monitor's administrative files will be its current directory
- the port monitor will be able to create private files in the directory /var/saf/*tag*, where *tag* is the port monitor's tag
- the port monitor will be running with user id 0 (root)

Important Files

Relative to its current directory, the following key files exist for a port monitor:

_config   The port monitor's configuration script. The port monitor configuration script is run by the Service Access Controller. The Service Access Controller is started by init(1M) as a result of an entry in /etc/inittab that calls sac(1M).

_pid   The file into which the port monitor writes its process id.

_pmtab	The port monitor's administrative file. This file contains information about the ports and services for which the port monitor is responsible.
_pmpipe	The FIFO through which the port monitor will receive messages from the sac.
svctag	The per-service configuration script for the service with the tag *svctag*.
../_sacpipe	The FIFO through which the port monitor will send messages to the sac.

Responsibilities

A port monitor is responsible for performing the tasks described below in addition to its port monitor-specific function.

Miscellaneous Tasks

A port monitor must perform the following miscellaneous tasks during its normal operation:

- Write its process id into the file _pid and place an advisory lock on the file.

- Terminate gracefully on receipt of the signal SIGTERM.

- Follow the protocol for message exchange with the sac.

Service Related Tasks

A port monitor must perform the following tasks during service invocation:

- Create a utmp entry if the requested service has the "u" flag set in _pmtab.

NOTE Port monitors may ignore this flag if creating a utmp entry for the service does not make sense because of the manner in which the service is to be invoked. On the other hand, some services may not start properly unless utmp entries have been created for them.

- Interpret the per-service configuration script for the requested service, if it exists, by calling the doconfig(3N) library routine.

Configuration Files and the Configuration Language

Configuration Files

The Per-System Configuration File

The per-system configuration file, /etc/saf/_sysconfig, is delivered empty. It may be used to customize the environment for all services on the system by writing a command script in the interpreted language described in this chapter and on the doconfig(3N) manual page. When the SAC is started, it calls the doconfig() function to interpret the per-system configuration script. The SAC is started when the system enters multi-user mode.

Per-Port Monitor Configuration Files

Per-port monitor configuration scripts (/etc/saf/*pmtag*/_config) are optional. They allow the user to customize the environment for any given port monitor and for the services that are available through the ports for which that port monitor is responsible. Per-port monitor configuration scripts are written in the same language used for per-system configuration scripts.

The per-port monitor configuration script is interpreted when the port monitor is started. The port monitor is started by the Service Access Controller after the SAC has itself been started and after it has run its own configuration script, /etc/saf/_sysconfig.

The per-port monitor configuration script may override defaults provided by the per-system configuration script.

Per-Service Configuration Files

Per-service configuration files allow the user to customize the environment for a specific service. For example, a service may require special privileges that are not available to the general user. Using the language described in the doconfig(3N) manual page, the programmer can write a script that will grant or limit such special privileges to a particular service offered through a particular port monitor.

The per-service configuration may override defaults provided by higher-level configuration scripts. For example, the per-service configuration script may specify a set of STREAMS modules other than the default set.

The Configuration Language

The language in which configuration scripts are written consists of a sequence of commands, each of which is interpreted separately. The following reserved keywords are defined: assign, push, pop, runwait, and run. The comment character is #. Blank lines are not significant. No line in a command script may exceed 1024 characters.

assign *variable=value*

> Used to define environment variables. *variable* is the name of the environment variable and *value* is the value to be assigned to it. The value assigned must be a string constant; no form of parameter substitution is available. *value* may be quoted. The quoting rules are those used by the shell for defining environment variables. assign will fail if space cannot be allocated for the new variable or if any part of the specification is invalid.

push *module1*[, *module2, module3, . . .*]

> Used to push STREAMS modules onto the stream designated by *fd* (see doconfig(3N)). *module1* is the name of the first module to be pushed, *module2* is the name of the second module to be pushed, etc. The command will fail if any of the named modules cannot be pushed. If a module cannot be pushed, the subsequent modules on the same command line will be ignored and modules that have already been pushed will be popped.

pop [*module*]

> Used to pop STREAMS modules off the designated stream. If pop is invoked with no arguments, the top module on the stream is popped. If an argument is given, modules will be popped one at a time until the named module is at the top of the stream. If the named module is not on the designated stream, the stream is left as it was and the command fails. If *module* is the special keyword ALL, then all modules on the stream will be popped. Note that only modules above the topmost driver are affected.

runwait *command*

> The runwait command runs a command and waits for it to complete. *command* is the pathname of the command to be run. The command is run with /bin/sh −c prepended to it; shell scripts may thus be executed from configuration scripts. The runwait command will fail if

Programmer's Guide: Networking Interfaces

command cannot be found or cannot be executed, or if *command* exits with a non-zero status.

run *command*

The run command is identical to runwait except that it does not wait for *command* to complete. *command* is the pathname of the command to be run. run will not fail unless it is unable to create a child process to execute the command.

Although they are syntactically indistinguishable, some of the commands available to run and runwait are interpreter built-in commands. Interpreter built-ins are used when it is necessary to alter the state of a process within the context of that process. The doconfig interpreter built-in commands are similar to the shell special commands and, like these, they do not spawn another process for execution. See sh(1). The initial set of built-in commands is:

        cd
        ulimit
        umask

Printing, Installing, and Replacing Configuration Scripts

This section describes the form of the SAC and port monitor administrative commands used to install the three types of configuration scripts. Per-system and per-port monitor configuration scripts are administered using the sacadm command. Per-service configuration scripts are administered using the pmadm command.

Per-System Configuration Scripts

        sacadm −G [−z *script*]

The −G option is used to print or replace the per-system configuration script. The −G option by itself prints the per-system configuration script. The −G option in combination with a −z option replaces /etc/saf/_sysconfig with the contents of the file *script*. Other combinations of options with a −G option are invalid.

Per-Port Monitor Configuration Scripts

sacadm −g −p *pmtag* [−z *script*]

The −g option is used to print, install, or replace the per-port monitor configuration script. A −g option requires a −p option. The −g option with only a −p option prints the per-port monitor configuration script for port monitor *pmtag*. The −g option with a −p option and a −z option installs the file *script* as the per-port monitor configuration script for port monitor *pmtag*, or, if /etc/saf/*pmtag*/_config exists, it replaces _config with the contents of *script*. Other combinations of options with −g are invalid.

Per-Service Configuration Scripts

pmadm −g −p *pmtag* −s *svctag* [−z *script*]
pmadm −g −s *svctag* −t *type* −z *script*

Per-service configuration scripts are interpreted by the port monitor before the service is invoked.

NOTE   The SAC interprets both its own configuration file, _sysconfig, and the port monitor configuration files. Only the per-service configuration files are interpreted by the port monitors.

The −g option is used to print, install, or replace a per-service configuration script. The −g option with a −p option and a −s option prints the per-service configuration script for service *svctag* available through port monitor *pmtag*. The −g option with a −p option, a −s option, and a −z option installs the per-service configuration script contained in the file *script* as the per-service configuration script for service *svctag* available through port monitor *pmtag*. The −g option with a −s option, a −t option, and a −z option installs the file *script* as the per-service configuration script for service *svctag* available through any port monitor of type *type*. Other combinations of options with −g are invalid.

Interpreting Configuration Scripts: doconfig()

The library routine doconfig(), defined in libnsl.so, interprets the configuration scripts contained in the files /etc/saf/*pmtag*/_sysconfig (the per-system configuration file), and /etc/saf/_config (per-port monitor configuration files); and in /etc/saf/*pmtag*/*svctag* (per-service configuration files). Its syntax is:

```
# include <sac.h>

int doconfig (int fd, char *script, long rflag);
```

script is the name of the configuration script; *fd* is a file descriptor that designates the stream to which stream manipulation operations are to be applied; *rflag* is a bitmask that indicates the mode in which *script* is to be interpreted. *rflag* may take two values, NORUN and NOASSIGN, which may be or'd. If *rflag* is zero, all commands in the configuration script are eligible to be interpreted. If *rflag* has the NOASSIGN bit set, the assign command is considered illegal and will generate an error return. If *rflag* has the NORUN bit set, the run and runwait commands are considered illegal and will generate error returns.

If a command in the script fails, the interpretation of the script ceases at that point and a positive integer is returned; this number indicates which line in the script failed. If a system error occurs, a value of −1 is returned.

If a script fails, the process whose environment was being established should *not* be started.

In the example, doconfig() is used to interpret a per-service configuration script.

```
                    . . .

if ((i = doconfig (fd, svctag, 0)) != 0){
        error ("doconfig failed on line %d of script %s", i, svctag);
}
```

Sample Configuration Scripts

Sample Per-System Configuration Script

The _sysconfig file in the example sets the time zone variable, TZ.

```
assign TZ=EST5EDT        # set TZ
runwait echo SAC is starting > /dev/console
```

Sample Per-Port Monitor Configuration Script

In the hypothetical _config file in the figure, the command
/usr/bin/daemon is assumed to start a daemon process that builds and holds
together a STREAMS multiplexor. By installing this configuration script, the
command can be executed just before starting the port monitor that requires it.

```
# build a STREAMS multiplexor
run /usr/bin/daemon
runwait echo $PMTAG is starting > /dev/console
```

Sample Per-Service Configuration Script

The following per-service configuration script does two things: It specifies the
maximum file size for files created by a process by setting the process's ulimit
to 4096. It also specifies the protection mask to be applied to files created by
the process by setting umask to 077.

```
runwait ulimit 4096
runwait umask 077
```

Sample Port Monitor Code

The following is an example of a "null" port monitor which does nothing except respond to messages from the Service Access Controller (sac).

```
# include <stdio.h>
# include <unistd.h>
# include <fcntl.h>
# include <signal.h>
# include <sac.h>

char    *getenv();

char    Scratch[BUFSIZ];        /* scratch buffer             */
char    Tag[PMTAGSIZE];         /* port monitor's tag         */
FILE    *Fp;                    /* file pointer for log file  */
FILE    *Tfp;                   /* file pointer for pid file  */
char    State;                  /* port monitor's current state */


main(argc, argv)
int argc;
char *argv[];
{
        char *istate;

        strcpy(Tag, getenv("PMTAG"));

/*
 * open up a log file in port monitor's private directory
 */

        sprintf(Scratch, "/var/saf/%s/log", Tag);
        Fp = fopen(Scratch, "a+");
        if (Fp == NULL)
                exit(1);
        log(Fp, "starting");

/*
 * retrieve initial state (either "enabled" or "disabled") and set
 * State accordingly
 */

        istate = getenv("ISTATE");
        sprintf(Scratch, "ISTATE is %s", istate);
        log(Fp, Scratch);
        if (!strcmp(istate, "enabled"))
                State = PM_ENABLED;
```

(continued on next page)

```
        else if (!strcmp(istate, "disabled"))
                State = PM_DISABLED;
        else {
                log(Fp, "invalid initial state");
                exit(1);
        }
        sprintf(Scratch, "PMTAG is %s", Tag);
        log(Fp, Scratch);

/*
 * set up pid file and lock it to indicate that we are active
 */

        Tfp = fopen("_pid", "w");
        if (Tfp == NULL) {
                log(Fp, "couldn't open pid file");
                exit(1);
        }
        if (lockf(fileno(Tfp), F_TEST, 0) < 0) {
                log(Fp, "pid file already locked");
                exit(1);
        }
        fprintf(Tfp, "%d", getpid());
        rewind(Tfp);
        log(Fp, "locking file");
        if (lockf(fileno(Tfp), F_LOCK, 0) < 0) {
                log(Fp, "lock failed");
                exit(1);
        }

/*
 * handle poll messages from the sac...this function never returns
 */

        handlepoll();
        pause();
        fclose(Tfp);
        fclose(Fp);
}


handlepoll()
{
        int pfd;                /* file descriptor for incoming pipe   */
        int sfd;                /* file descriptor for outgoing pipe   */
        struct sacmsg sacmsg;   /* incoming message                    */
```

(continued on next page)

```
        struct pmmsg pmmsg;       /* outgoing message                    */
/*
 * open pipe for incoming messages from the sac
 */

        pfd = open("_pmpipe", O_RDWR);
        if (pfd < 0) {
                log(Fp, "_pmpipe open failed");
                exit(1);
        }

/*
 * open pipe for outgoing messages to the sac
 */

        sfd = open("../_sacpipe", O_RDWR);
        if (sfd < 0) {
                log(Fp, "_sacpipe open failed");
                exit(1);
        }

/*
 * start to build a return message; we only support class 1 messages
 */

                strcpy(pmmsg.pm_tag, Tag);
                pmmsg.pm_size = 0;
                pmmsg.pm_maxclass = 1;

/*
 * keep responding to messages from the sac
 */

        for (;;) {
                if (read(pfd, &sacmsg, sizeof(sacmsg)) != sizeof(sacmsg)) {
                        log(Fp, "_pmpipe read failed");
                        exit(1);
                }

/*
 * determine the message type and respond appropriately
 */

                switch (sacmsg.sc_type) {
                case SC_STATUS:
```

(continued on next page)

Writing a Port Monitor for the Service Access Facility

```
                log(Fp, "Got SC_STATUS message");
                pmmsg.pm_type = PM_STATUS;
                pmmsg.pm_state = State;
                break;
        case SC_ENABLE:
                /* note internal state change below */
                log(Fp, "Got SC_ENABLE message");
                pmmsg.pm_type = PM_STATUS;
                State = PM_ENABLED;
                pmmsg.pm_state = State;
                break;
        case SC_DISABLE:
                /* note internal state change below */
                log(Fp, "Got SC_DISABLE message");
                pmmsg.pm_type = PM_STATUS;
                State = PM_DISABLED;
                pmmsg.pm_state = State;
                break;
        case SC_READDB:
                /* if this were a fully functional port monitor */
                /* it would read _pmtab here and take           */
                /* appropriate action                           */
                log(Fp, "Got SC_READDB message");
                pmmsg.pm_type = PM_STATUS;
                pmmsg.pm_state = State;
                break;
        default:
                sprintf(Scratch, "Got unknown message <%d>", sacmsg.sc_type);
                log(Fp, Scratch);
                pmmsg.pm_type = PM_UNKNOWN;
                pmmsg.pm_state = State;
                break;
        }

/*
 * send back a response to the poll indicating current state
 */

        if (write(sfd, &pmmsg, sizeof(pmmsg)) != sizeof(pmmsg)) {
                log(Fp, "sanity response failed");
        }
    }
}
```

(continued on next page)

```
/*
 * general logging function
 */

log(fp, msg)
FILE *fp;
char *msg;
{
        fprintf(fp, "%d; %s\n", getpid(), msg);
        fflush(fp);
}
```

The Header File sac.h

```
# define IDLEN           4        /* length in bytes of a utmp id */
# define SC_WILDC        Oxff     /* wild character for utmp ids */
# define PMTAGSIZE       14       /* maximum length in bytes for a port monitor tag */


/*
 * values for rflag in doconfig()
 */

# define NOASSIGN        Ox1      /* don't allow assign operations */
# define NORUN           Ox2      /* don't allow run or runwait operations */



/*
 * message to SAC (header only).  This header is forever fixed.  The
 * size field (pm_size) defines the size of the data portion of the
 * message, which follows the header.  The form of this optional
 * data portion is defined strictly by the message type (pm_type).
 */

struct   pmmsg {
         char        pm_type;               /* type of message */
         unchar      pm_state;              /* current state of port monitor */
         char        pm_maxclass;           /* max message class this
                                               port monitor understands */
         char        pm_tag[PMTAGSIZE + 1]; /* port monitor's tag */
         int         pm_size;               /* size of optional data portion */
};



/*
 * pm_type values
 */

# define PM_STATUS       1                  /* status response */
# define PM_UNKNOWN      2                  /* an unknown message was received */

/*
 * pm_state values
 */

/*
 * Class 1 responses
 */

# define PM_STARTING     1                  /* port monitor in starting state */
```

(continued on next page)

```
# define PM_ENABLED       2              /* port monitor in enabled state */
# define PM_DISABLED      3              /* port monitor in disabled state */
# define PM_STOPPING      4              /* port monitor in stopping state */

/*
 * message to port monitor
 */

struct  sacmsg {
        int     sc_size;                /* size of optional data portion */
        char    sc_type;                /* type of message */
};


/*
 * sc_type values
 * These represent commands that the SAC sends to a port monitor.  These
 * commands are divided into "classes" for extensibility.  Each subsequent
 * "class" is a superset of the previous "classes" plus the new commands
 * defined within that "class".  The header for all commands is identical;
 * however, a command may be defined such that an optional data portion may
 * be sent in addition to the header.  The format of this optional data piece
 * is self-defining based on the command.  Important note:  the first message
 * sent by the SAC will always be a class 1 message.  The port monitor
 * response will indicate the maximum class that it is able to understand.
 * Another note is that port monitors should only respond to a message with
 * an equivalent class response (i.e. a class 1 command causes a class 1
 * response).
 */

/*
 * Class 1 commands (currently, there are only class 1 commands)
 */

# define SC_STATUS        1              /* status request */
# define SC_ENABLE        2              /* enable request */
# define SC_DISABLE       3              /* disable request */
# define SC_READDB        4              /* read pmtab request */

/*
 * 'errno' values for Saferrno, note that Saferrno is used by
 * both pmadm and sacadm and these values are shared between
 * them
 */
```

(continued on next page)

Writing a Port Monitor for the Service Access Facility

```
# define E_BADARGS       1        /* bad args or ill-formed command line */
# define E_NOPRIV        2        /* user not privileged for operation */
# define E_SAFERR        3        /* generic SAF error */
# define E_SYSERR        4        /* system error */
# define E_NOEXIST       5        /* invalid specification */
# define E_DUP           6        /* entry already exists */
# define E_PMRUN         7        /* port monitor is running */
# define E_PMNOTRUN      8        /* port monitor is not running */
# define E_RECOVER       9        /* in recovery */
```

Service Access Facility Logic Diagram and Directory Structure

The first figure below is a logical diagram of the Service Access Facility. The second figure is the corresponding directory structure diagram; the list following it describes each of the files and directories.

Figure 13-1: Service Access Facility logical framework.

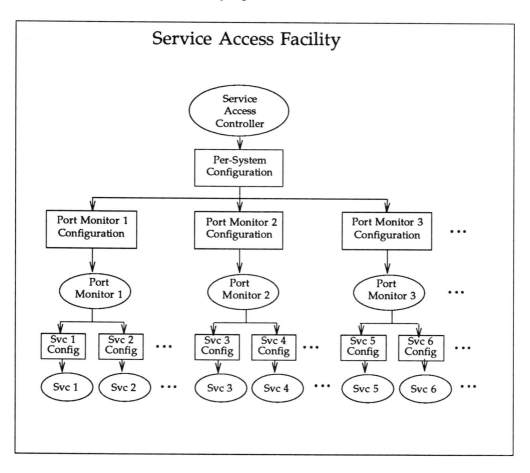

Figure 13-2: Service Access Facility directory structure.

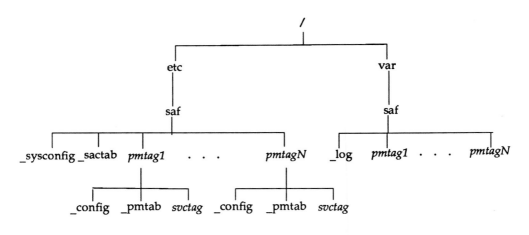

/etc/saf/_sysconfig	The per-system configuration script.
/etc/saf/_sactab	The SAC's administrative file. Contains information about the port monitors for which the SAC is responsible.
/etc/saf/*pmtag*	The home directory for port monitor *pmtag*.
/etc/saf/*pmtag*/_config	The per-port monitor configuration script for port monitor *pmtag*.
/etc/saf/*pmtag*/_pmtab	Port monitor *pmtag*'s administrative file. Contains information about the services for which *pmtag* is responsible.
/etc/saf/*pmtag*/*svctag*	The file in which the per-service configuration script for service *svctag* (available through port monitor *pmtag*) is placed.
/var/saf/_log	The SAC's log file.

Programmer's Guide: Networking Interfaces

/var/saf/*pmtag*   The directory for files created by port monitor *pmtag*, for example its log file.

Index

T

Manual Pages

Appendix A contains all Section 3N (Network Programming) manual pages for UNIX System V Release 4.0. Most of the manual pages correspond to the documents in this volume: TLI and Sockets, RPC (including XDR, secure RPC, and RPC services), and Network Selection and Name-to-Address Mapping. Other manual pages related to network programming but not specific to the contents of the volume are also included, however. The documentation that corresponds to these manual pages appears in other parts of the document set, for example, in the *Network User's and Administrator's Guide* (TCP) or the *System Administrator's Guide* (listen).

Table of Contents

1. Commands

3. Functions

4. File Formats

5. Miscellaneous Facilities

7. Special Files

Permuted Index

Programmer's Guide: Networking Interfaces

Programmer's Guide: Networking Interfaces

Programmer's Guide: Networking Interfaces

NAME
chkey – change user encryption key

SYNOPSIS
chkey

DESCRIPTION
The chkey command prompts for a password and uses it to encrypt a new user encryption key. The encrypted key is stored in the publickey(4) database.

This command should be executed only on the master server for the publickey(4) database.

SEE ALSO
keylogin(1), keylogout(1), publickey(4), keyserv(1M), newkey(1).

NAME

keylogin – decrypt and store secret key

SYNOPSIS

keylogin

DESCRIPTION

The keylogin command prompts for a password, and uses it to decrypt the user's secret key stored in the publickey(4) database. Once decrypted, the user's key is stored by the local key server process, **keyserv**(1M), to be used by any secure network service, such as NFS.

SEE ALSO

chkey(1), keylogout (1), publickey(4), keyserv(1M), newkey(1).

NAME

rpcgen – an RPC protocol compiler

SYNOPSIS

rpcgen *infile*

rpcgen [–D*name*[=*value*]] [–T] [–K *secs*] *infile*

rpcgen –c|–h|–l|–m|–t [–o *outfile*] *infile*

rpcgen –s *nettype* [–o *outfile*] *infile*

rpcgen –n *netid* [–o *outfile*] *infile*

DESCRIPTION

rpcgen is a tool that generates C code to implement an RPC protocol. The input to rpcgen is a language similar to C known as RPC Language (Remote Procedure Call Language).

rpcgen is normally used as in the first synopsis where it takes an input file and generates up to four output files. If the *infile* is named proto.x, then rpcgen will generate a header file in proto.h, XDR routines in proto_xdr.c, server-side stubs in proto_svc.c, and client-side stubs in proto_clnt.c. With the –T option, it will also generate the RPC dispatch table in proto_tbl.i.

The server created can be started both by the port monitors (for example, inetd or listen) or by itself. When it is started by a port monitor, it creates servers only for the transport for which the file descriptor 0 was passed. The name of the transport must be specified by setting up the environmental variable PM_TRANSPORT. When the server generated by rpcgen is executed, it creates server handles for all the transports specified in NETPATH environment variable, or if it is unset, it creates server handles for all the visible transports from /etc/netconfig file. Note: the transports are chosen at run time and not at compile time. When the server is self-started, it backgrounds itself by default. A special define symbol RPC_SVC_FG can be used to run the server process in foreground.

The second synopsis provides special features which allow for the creation of more sophisticated RPC servers. These features include support for user provided #defines and RPC dispatch tables. The entries in the RPC dispatch table contain:

* pointers to the service routine corresponding to that procedure,
* a pointer to the input and output arguments
* the size of these routines

A server can use the dispatch table to check authorization and then to execute the service routine; a client library may use it to deal with the details of storage management and XDR data conversion.

The other three synopses shown above are used when one does not want to generate all the output files, but only a particular one. Some examples of their usage is described in the EXAMPLE section below. When rpcgen is executed with the –s option, it creates servers for that particular class of transports. When executed with the –n option, it creates a server for the transport specified by *netid*. If *infile* is not specified, rpcgen accepts the standard input.

The C preprocessor, cc −E [see cc(1)], is run on the input file before it is actually interpreted by rpcgen. For each type of output file, rpcgen defines a special preprocessor symbol for use by the rpcgen programmer:

RPC_HDR   defined when compiling into header files
RPC_XDR   defined when compiling into XDR routines
RPC_SVC   defined when compiling into server-side stubs
RPC_CLNT   defined when compiling into client-side stubs
RPC_TBL   defined when compiling into RPC dispatch tables

Any line beginning with '%' is passed directly into the output file, uninterpreted by rpcgen.

For every data type referred to in *infile*, rpcgen assumes that there exists a routine with the string xdr_ prepended to the name of the data type. If this routine does not exist in the RPC/XDR library, it must be provided. Providing an undefined data type allows customization of XDR routines.

The following options are available:

−c   Compile into XDR routines.

−D*name*[*=value*]
        Define a symbol *name*. Equivalent to the #define directive in the source. If no *value* is given, *value* is defined as 1. This option may be specified more than once.

−h   Compile into C data-definitions (a header file). −T option can be used in conjunction to produce a header file which supports RPC dispatch tables.

−K *secs*
        By default, services created using rpcgen wait 120 seconds after servicing a request before exiting. That interval can be changed using the −K flag. To create a server that exits immediately upon servicing a request, −K 0 can be used. To create a server that never exits, the appropriate argument is −K −1.

        When monitoring for a server, some portmonitors, like listen(1M), *always* spawn a new process in response to a service request. If it is known that a server will be used with such a monitor, the server should exit immediately on completion. For such servers, rpcgen should be used with −K −1.

−l   Compile into client-side stubs.

−m   Compile into server-side stubs, but do not generate a main routine. This option is useful for doing callback-routines and for users who need to write their own main routine to do initialization.

−n *netid*
        Compile into server-side stubs for the transport specified by *netid*. There should be an entry for *netid* in the netconfig database. This option may be specified more than once, so as to compile a server that serves multiple transports.

−o *outfile*

Specify the name of the output file. If none is specified, standard output is used (−c, −h, −l, −m, −n, −s and −t modes only).

−s *nettype*

Compile into server-side stubs for all the transports belonging to the class *nettype*. The supported classes are netpath, visible, circuit_n, circuit_v, datagram_n, datagram_v, tcp, and udp [see rpc(3N) for the meanings associated with these classes]. This option may be specified more than once. Note: the transports are chosen at run time and not at compile time.

−t   Compile into RPC dispatch table.

−T   Generate the code to support RPC dispatch tables.

The options −c, −h, −l, −m, −s and −t are used exclusively to generate a particular type of file, while the options −D and −T are global and can be used with the other options.

NOTES

The RPC Language does not support nesting of structures. As a work-around, structures can be declared at the top-level, and their name used inside other structures in order to achieve the same effect.

Name clashes can occur when using program definitions, since the apparent scoping does not really apply. Most of these can be avoided by giving unique names for programs, versions, procedures and types.

The server code generated with −n option refers to the transport indicated by *netid* and hence is very site specific.

EXAMPLE

The following example:

        $ rpcgen −T prot.x

generates all the five files: prot.h, prot_clnt.c, prot_svc.c, prot_xdr.c and prot_tbl.i.

The following example sends the C data-definitions (header file) to the standard output.

        $ rpcgen −h prot.x

To send the test version of the −DTEST, server side stubs for all the transport belonging to the class datagram_n to standard output, use:

        $ rpcgen −s datagram_n −DTEST prot.x

To create the server side stubs for the transport indicated by *netid* tcp, use:

        $ rpcgen −n tcp −o prot_svc.c prot.x

SEE ALSO

cc(1).

NAME
rusers – who's logged in on local machines

SYNOPSIS
rusers [–ahilu] *host* ...

DESCRIPTION
The `rusers` command produces output similar to `who`(1), but for remote machines. The listing is in the order that responses are received, but this order can be changed by specifying one of the options listed below.

The default is to print out the names of the users logged in. When the –l flag is given, additional information is printed for each user, including idle time, when user logged in, and tty.

A remote host will only respond if it is running the `rusersd`(1M) daemon, which may be started up from `inetd`(1M) or `listen`(1M).

The following options are available:

–a   Give a report for a machine even if no users are logged on.

–h   Sort alphabetically by host name.

–i   Sort by idle time.

–l   Give a longer listing in the style of `who`(1).

–u   Sort by number of users.

SEE ALSO
`inetd`(1M), `listen`(1M), `pmadm`(1M), `rusersd`(1M), `sacadm`(1M), `who`(1).

NAME
>   ypcat – print values in a YP data base

SYNOPSIS
>   ypcat [–k] [–d *ypdomain*] *mname*

DESCRIPTION
>   The ypcat command prints out values in the YP name service map specified by
>   *mname*, which may be either a map name or a map nickname. Since ypcat uses
>   the YP network services, no YP server is specified.
>
>   Refer to ypfiles(4) and ypserv(1M) for an overview of the YP name service.
>
>   The following options are available:
>
>   –d *ypdomain*
>   >   Specify a domain other that the default domain.
>
>   –k   Display the keys for those maps in which the values are null or the key is
>   not part of the value. None of the maps derived from files that have an
>   ASCII version in /etc fall into this class.

SEE ALSO
>   ypmatch(1), ypserv(1M), ypfiles(4)

NAME

ypmatch – print the value of one or more keys from a YP map

SYNOPSIS

ypmatch [–d *ypdomain*] [–k] *key... mname*

DESCRIPTION

ypmatch prints the values associated with one or more keys from the YPs name services map specified by *mname,* which may be either a *mapname* or an map nickname.

Multiple keys can be specified; the same map will be searched for all keys. The keys must be exact values insofar as capitalization and length are concerned. No pattern matching is available. If a key is not matched, a diagnostic message is produced.

The following options are available:

–d *ypdomain*

Specify a domain other than the default domain.

–k   Before printing the value of a key, print the key itself, followed by a ':' colon . This is useful only if the keys are not duplicated in the values, or so many keys were specified that the output could be confusing.

SEE ALSO

ypcat(1), ypfiles(4)

NAME

ypwhich – return name of YP server or map master

SYNOPSIS

ypwhich [–d [*ypdomain*]] [*hostname*]
ypwhich [–d *ypdomain*] –m [*mname*]

DESCRIPTION

ypwhich tells which YP server supplies the YP name services to a YP client, or which is the master for a map. If invoked without arguments, it gives the YP server for the local machine. If *hostname* is specified, that machine is queried to find out which YP master it is using.

Refer to ypfiles(4) and ypserv(1M) for an overview of the YP name services.

The following options are available:

–d [*ypdomain*]

Use *ypdomain* instead of the default domain.

–m *mname*

Find the master YP server for a map. No *hostname* can be specified with –m. *mname* can be a mapname, or a nickname for a map. When *mname* is omitted, produce a list available maps.

SEE ALSO

ypserv(1M), ypset(1M), ypfiles(4)

NAME

    bootparamd – boot parameter server

SYNOPSIS

    bootparamd [–d]

DESCRIPTION

    bootparamd is a server process that provides information to diskless clients necessary for booting. It obtains its information from the /etc/bootparams file.

    bootparamd can be invoked either by inetd(1M) or by the user.

    The –d option displays the debugging information.

FILES

    /etc/bootparams

SEE ALSO

    inetd(1M)

NAME

domainname – get/set name of current secure RPC domain

SYNOPSIS

domainname [*newname*]

DESCRIPTION

The domainname command is used on secure RPC machines. With no argument, the name of the machine's secure RPC domain is written to standard output.

root privileges are required to use the domainname command with an argument. In this form, the command sets the name of the secure RPC domain to *newname*. *newname* may be up to 255 characters long.

domainname is normally run by the network administrator on all machines using secure RPC to set the name of the secure RPC domain. To use secure RPC, machines must have a secure RPC domain name.

NOTES

Secure RPC domain names are not related to ans should not be confused with RFS domains.

The RPC package expects the *newname* argument to be a valid filename for the underlying file system in use on the networked machines using secure RPC. For example, machines based on the s5 file system should not have domain names longer than 14 characters in length or problems may occur when using secure RPC.

The secure RPC domain name set by domainname will not be remembered across reboots. To give a machine a "permanent" name, set the SRPC_DOMAIN tunable in /etc/master.d/kernel to the secure RPC domain name.

SEE ALSO

RPC Administration in the *Programmer's Guide: Networking Interfaces*.

NAME

inetd – Internet services daemon

SYNOPSIS

inetd [–d] [–s] [*configuration-file*]

DESCRIPTION

inetd, the Internet services daemon, is normally run at boot time by the Service
Access Facility (SAF). When started, inetd reads its configuration information
from *configuration-file*, the default being /etc/inetd.conf. See inetd.conf(4)
for more information on the format of this file. It listens for connections on the
Internet addresses of the services that its configuration file specifies. When a connection is found, it invokes the server daemon specified by that configuration file
for the service requested. Once a server process exits, inetd continues to listen on
the socket.

The –s option allows you to run inetd "stand-alone," outside the Service Access
Facility (SAF).

Rather than having several daemon processes with sparsely distributed requests
each running concurrently, inetd reduces the load on the system by invoking
Internet servers only as they are needed.

inetd itself provides a number of simple TCP-based services. These include
echo, discard, chargen (character generator), daytime (human readable time),
and time (machine readable time, in the form of the number of seconds since
midnight, January 1, 1900). For details of these services, consult the appropriate
RFC, as listed below, from the Network Information Center.

inetd rereads its configuration file whenever it receives a hangup signal, SIGHUP.
New services can be activated, and existing services deleted or modified in
between whenever the file is reread.

SEE ALSO

comsat(1M), ftpd(1M), rexecd(1M), rlogind(1M), rshd(1M), telnetd(1M),
tftpd(1M), inetd.conf(4).

Postel, Jon, "Echo Protocol," RFC 862, Network Information Center, SRI International, Menlo Park, Calif., May 1983.

Postel, Jon, "Discard Protocol," RFC 863, Network Information Center, SRI
International, Menlo Park, Calif., May 1983.

Postel, Jon, "Character Generater Protocol," RFC 864, Network Information
Center,
SRI International, Menlo Park, Calif., May 1983.

Postel, Jon, "Daytime Protocol," RFC 867, Network Information Center, SRI International, Menlo Park, Calif., May 1983.

Postel, Jon, and Ken Harrenstien, "Time Protocol," RFC 868, Network Information Center, SRI International, Menlo Park, Calif., May 1983.

NAME
keyserv – server for storing public and private keys

SYNOPSIS
keyserv [–n]

DESCRIPTION
keyserv is a daemon that is used for storing the private encryption keys of each user logged into the system. These encryption keys are used for accessing secure network services such as secure NFS.

Normally, root's key is read from the file /etc/.rootkey when the daemon is started. This is useful during power-fail reboots when no one is around to type a password.

When the –n option is used, root's key is not read from /etc/.rootkey. Instead, keyserv prompts the user for the password to decrypt root's key stored in the publickey(4) database and then stores the decrypted key in /etc/.rootkey for future use. This option is useful if the /etc/.rootkey file ever gets out of date or corrupted.

FILES
/etc/.rootkey

SEE ALSO
publickey(4).

NAME

makedbm – make a YP dbm file

SYNOPSIS

/usr/sbin/makedbm [–l] [–s] [–i *yp_input_file*] [–o *yp_output_name*]
[–d *yp_domain_name*] [–m *yp_master_name*] *infile outfile*

makedbm [–u *dbmfilename*]

DESCRIPTION

The makedbm command takes *infile* and converts it to a pair of files in dbm(3) format, namely *outfile*.pag and *outfile*.dir. Each line of the input file is converted to a single dbm record. All characters up to the first TAB or SPACE form the key, and the rest of the line is the data. If a line ends with '\', then the data for that record is continued on to the next line. It is left for the clients of the YP name service to interpret '#'; makedbm does not itself treat it as a comment character. *infile* can be '–', in which case the standard input is read.

makedbm is meant to be used in generating dbm files for the YP name service, and it generates a special entry with the key *yp_last_modified*, which is the date of *infile* (or the current time, if *infile* is '–').

The following options are available:

–l   Lowercase. Convert the keys of the given map to lower case, so that host name matches, for example, can work independent of upper or lower case distinctions.

–s   Secure map. Accept connections from secure YP networks only.

–i *yp_input_file*
Create a special entry with the key *yp_input_file*.

–o *yp_output_name*
Create a special entry with the key *yp_output_name*.

–d *yp_domain_name*
Create a special entry with the key *yp_domain_name*.

–m *yp_master_name*
Create a special entry with the key *yp_master_name*. If no master host name is specified, *yp_master_name* will be set to the local host name.

–u *dbmfilename*
Undo a dbm file. That is, print out a dbm file one entry per line, with a single space separating keys from values.

SEE ALSO

dbm(3)

NAME

newkey – create a new key in the publickey database

SYNOPSIS

newkey –h *hostname*

newkey –u *username*

DESCRIPTION

The newkey command is normally run by the network administrator on the machine that contains the publickey(4) database, to establish public keys for users and privileged users on the network. These keys are needed when using secure RPC or secure NFS.

newkey will prompt for a password for the given *username* or *hostname* and then create a new public/secret key pair for the user or host in /etc/publickey, encrypted with the given password.

The following options are available:

–h *hostname*   Create a new public/secret key pair for the privileged user at the given *hostname*. Prompts for a password for the given *hostname*.

–u *username*   Create a new public/secret key pair for the given *username*. Prompts for a password for the given *username*.

SEE ALSO

chkey(1), keylogin(1), keylogout(1), keyserv(1M), publickey(4)

NAME

    pmadm – port monitor administration

SYNOPSIS

    pmadm −a [−p *pmtag* | −t *type*] −s *svctag* −i *id* −m *pmspecific*
        −v *ver* [−f xu] [−y *comment*] [−z *script*]

    pmadm −r −p *pmtag* −s *svctag*

    pmadm −e −p *pmtag* −s *svctag*

    pmadm −d −p *pmtag* −s *svctag*

    pmadm −l [−t *type* | −p *pmtag*] [−s *svctag*]

    pmadm −L [−t *type* | −p *pmtag*] [−s *svctag*]

    pmadm −g −p *pmtag* −s *svctag* [−z *script*]

    pmadm −g −s *svctag* −t *type* −z *script*

DESCRIPTION

    pmadm is the administrative command for the lower level of the Service Access Facility hierarchy, that is, for service administration. A port may have only one service associated with it although the same service may be available through more than one port. In order to uniquely identify an instance of a service the pmadm command must identify both the port monitor or port monitors through which the service is available (−p or −t) and the service (−s). See the option descriptions below.

    pmadm performs the following functions:

> − add or remove a service
> − enable or disable a service
> − install or replace a per-service configuration script
> − print requested service information

    Any user on the system may invoke pmadm to request service status (−l or −L) or to print per-service configuration scripts (−g without the −z option). pmadm with other options may be executed only by a privileged user.

    The options have the following meanings:

    −a   Add a service. pmadm adds an entry for the new service to the port monitor's administrative file. Because of the complexity of the options and arguments that follow the −a option, it may be convenient to use a command script or the menu system to add services. If you use the menu system, enter sysadm ports, then choose the port_services option.

    −d   Disable a service. Add x to the flag field in the entry for the service *svctag* in the port monitor's administrative file. This is the entry used by port monitor *pmtag*. See the −f option, below, for a description of the flags available.

-e   Enable a service. Remove x from the flag field in the entry for the ser-
            vice *svctag* in the port monitor administrative file. This is the entry used
            by port monitor *pmtag*. See the −f option, below, for a description of the
            flags available.

−f xu   The −f option specifies one or both of the following two flags which are
            then included in the flag field of the entry for the new service in the port
            monitor's administrative file. If the −f option is not included, no flags
            are set and the default conditions prevail. By default, a new service is
            enabled and no utmp entry is created for it. A −f option without a fol-
            lowing argument is illegal.

            x   Do not enable the service *svctag* available through
                  port monitor *pmtag*.

            u   Create a utmp entry for service *svctag* available through
                  port monitor *pmtag*.

−g   Print, install, or replace a per-service configuration script. The −g option
            with a −p option and a −s option prints the per-service configuration
            script for service *svctag* available through port monitor *pmtag*. The −g
            option with a −p option, a −s option, and a −z option installs the per-
            service configuration script contained in the file *script* as the per-service
            configuration script for service *svctag* available through port monitor
            pmtag. The −g option with a −s option, a −t option, and a −z option
            installs the file *script* as the per-service configuration script for service
            svctag available through any port monitor of type *type*. Other combina-
            tions of options with −g are invalid.

−i id   id is the identity that is to be assigned to service *svctag* when it is
            started. id must be an entry in /etc/passwd.

−l   The −l option requests service information. Used by itself and with the
            options described below it provides a filter for extracting information in
            several different groupings.

            −l   By itself, the −l option lists all services on the system.

            −l −p *pmtag*   Lists all services available through port monitor *pmtag*.

            −l −s *svctag* Lists all services with tag *svctag*.

            −l −p *pmtag* −s *svctag*
                            Lists service *svctag*.

            −l −t *type*   Lists all services available through port monitors of type
                            type.

            −l −t *type* −s *svctag*
                            Lists all services with tag *svctag* available through a port
                            monitor of type *type*.

            Other combinations of options with −l are invalid.

-L   The -L option is identical to the -l option except that output is printed
          in a condensed format.

-m *pmspecific*
          pmspecific is the port monitor-specific portion of the port monitor admin-
          istrative file entry for the service.

-p *pmtag*
          Specifies the tag associated with the port monitor through which a ser-
          vice (specified as -s *svctag*) is available.

-r   Remove a service. When pmadm removes a service, the entry for the ser-
          vice is removed from the port monitor's administrative file.

-s *svctag*
          Specifies the service tag associated with a given service. The service tag
          is assigned by the system administrator and is part of the entry for the
          service in the port monitor's administrative file.

-t *type* Specifies the the port monitor type.

-v *ver*   Specifies the version number of the port monitor administrative file. The
          version number may be given as

               -v `pmspec -V`

          where *pmspec* is the special administrative command for port monitor
          pmtag. This special command is ttyadm for ttymon and nlsadmin for
          listen. The version stamp of the port monitor is known by the com-
          mand and is returned when *pmspec* is invoked with a -V option.

-y *comment*
          Associate *comment* with the service entry in the port monitor administra-
          tive file.

-z *script*
          Used with the -g option to specify the name of the file that contains the
          per-service configuration script. Modifying a configuration script is a
          three-step procedure. First a copy of the existing script is made (-g
          alone). Then the copy is edited. Finally, the copy is put in place over
          the existing script (-g with -z).

OUTPUT

If successful, pmadm will exit with a status of 0. If it fails for any reason, it will
exit with a nonzero status.

Options that request information write the requested information to the standard
output. A request for information using the -l option prints column headers and
aligns the information under the appropriate headings. In this format, a missing
field is indicated by a hyphen. A request for information in the condensed format using the -L option prints the information in colon-separated fields; missing
fields are indicated by two successive colons. # is the comment character.

EXAMPLES

Add a service to a port monitor with tag pmtag. Give the service the tag svctag.
Port monitor-specific information is generated by specpm The service defined by
svctag will be invoked with identity root.

```
pmadm -a -p pmtag -s svctag -i root -m `specpm -a arg1 -b arg2` \
    -v `specpm -V`
```

Add a service with service tag svctag, identity guest, and port monitor-specific information generated by specpm to all port monitors of type type:

```
pmadm -a -s svctag -i guest -t type -m `specpm -a arg1 -b arg2` \
    -v `specpm -V`
```

Remove the service svctag from port monitor pmtag:

```
pmadm -r -p pmtag -s svctag
```

Enable the service svctag available through port monitor pmtag:

```
pmadm -e -p pmtag -s svctag
```

Disable the service svctag available through port monitor pmtag:

```
pmadm -d -p pmtag -s svctag
```

List status information for all services:

```
pmadm -l
```

List status information for all services available through the port monitor with tag ports:

```
pmadm -l -p ports
```

List the same information in condensed format:

```
pmadm -L -p ports
```

List status information for all services available through port monitors of type listen:

```
pmadm -l -t listen
```

Print the per-service configuration script associated with the service svctag available through port monitor pmtag:

```
pmadm -g -p pmtag -s svctag
```

FILES

```
/etc/saf/pmtag/_config
/etc/saf/pmtag/svctag
/var/saf/pmtag/*
```

SEE ALSO

doconfig(3n), sacadm(1M), sac(1M).

NAME

rpcbind – universal addresses to RPC program number mapper

SYNOPSIS

rpcbind

DESCRIPTION

rpcbind is a server that converts RPC program numbers into universal addresses. It must be running to make RPC calls.

When an RPC service is started, it will tell rpcbind at what address it is listening, and what RPC program numbers it is prepared to serve. When a client wishes to make an RPC call to a given program number, it will first contact rpcbind on the server machine to determine the address where RPC packets should be sent.

Normally, standard RPC servers are started by port monitors, so rpcbind must be started before port monitors are invoked.

rpcbind is restricted to users with appropriate privileges.

NOTES

If rpcbind crashes, all RPC servers must be restarted.

SEE ALSO

rpcinfo(1M).

NAME
    rpcinfo – report RPC information

SYNOPSIS
    rpcinfo [*host*]
    rpcinfo –p [*host*]
    rpcinfo –T *transport host program version*
    rpcinfo [–n *portnum*] –u *host program version*
    rpcinfo [–n *portnum*] –t *host program version*
    rpcinfo –a *serv_address* –T *transport program* [*version*]
    rpcinfo –b [–T *transport*] *program version*
    rpcinfo –d [–T *transport*] *program version*

DESCRIPTION
    rpcinfo makes an RPC call to an RPC server and reports what it finds.

    In the first synopsis, it lists all the registered RPC services with rpcbind on *host*.
    If *host* is not specified, it defaults to the local host.

    In the second synopsis, it lists all the RPC services registered with portmapper.
    Also note that the format of the information is different in the first and the
    second synopsis; this is because in the first case, rpcbind (version 3) is contacted,
    while in the second case portmap (version 2) is contacted for information.

    The third synopsis makes an RPC call to procedure 0 of *program* and *version* on
    the specified *host* and reports whether a response was received. *transport* is the
    transport which has to be used for contacting the given service. The remote
    address of the service is obtained by making a call to remote rpcbind.

    The other ways of using rpcinfo are described below. See EXAMPLES.

    The following options are available:

    –T *transport*   Specify the transport on which the service is required. If this
                        option is not specified, rpcinfo uses the transport specified in
                        the NETPATH environment variable, or if that is unset or null, in
                        the netconfig database. This is a generic option, and can be used
                        in conjunction with any other option, except the –b option.

    –a *serv_address*   Use *serv_address* as the (universal) address for the service on *tran-
                        sport*, to ping procedure 0 of the specified *program* and report
                        whether a response was received. The use of –T option is
                        required with –a option.

                        If version number is not specified, rpcinfo tries to ping all the
                        available version numbers for that program number. This option
                        avoids calls to remote rpcbind to find the address of the service.
                        The *serv_address* is specified in universal address format of the
                        given transport.

    –b   Make an RPC broadcast to procedure 0 of the specified *program*
                        and *version* and report all hosts that respond. If *transport* is
                        specified, it broadcasts its request only on the transport specified
                        through *transport*. If broadcasting is not supported by any tran-
                        sport, an error message is printed. Only UDP transports support
                        broadcasting.

-d   Delete registration for the RPC service of the specified *program* and *version*. If *transport* is specified, unregister the service on only that transport, otherwise unregister the services on all the transports on which it was registered. This option can be exercised only by the privileged user.

-n   Use *portnum* as the port number for the -t and -u options instead of the port number given by the portmapper. Use of this option avoids a call to the remote portmapper to find out the address of the service.

-p   Probe the portmapper on *host*, and print a list of all registered RPC programs. If *host* is not specified, it defaults to the local host.

-t   Make an RPC call to procedure 0 of *program* on the specified *host* using TCP, and report whether a response was received.

-u   Make an RPC call to procedure 0 of *program* on the specified *host* using UDP, and report whether a response was received.

The *program* argument is a number.

If a *version* is specified, rpcinfo attempts to call that version of the specified *program*. Otherwise, rpcinfo attempts to find all the registered version numbers for the specified *program* by calling version 0, which is presumed not to exist; if it does exist, rpcinfo attempts to obtain this information by calling an extremely high version number instead, and attempts to call each registered version. Note: the version number is required for -b and -d options.

EXAMPLES

To show all of the RPC services registered on the local machine use:

$ rpcinfo

To show all of the RPC services registered with rpcbind on the machine named klaxon use:

$ rpcinfo klaxon

To show if the RPC service with program number *prog_no* and version *vers* is registered on the machine named klaxon for the transport tcp use:

$ rpcinfo -T tcp klaxon *prog_no vers*

To show all of the RPC services registered with the portmapper on the local machine use:

$ rpcinfo -p

To ping version 2 of rpcbind (program number 100000) on host sparky:

$ rpcinfo -t sparky 100000 2

To delete the registration for version 1 of the walld (program number 100008) service for all transports use:

```
# rpcinfo -d 100008 1
```

SEE ALSO

rpcbind(1M), rpc(4).

NAME
    rpc.rusersd – network username server

SYNOPSIS
    /usr/lib/netsvc/rusers/rpc.rusersd

DESCRIPTION
    rusersd is a server that returns a list of users on the host. The rusersd daemon
    may be started by inetd(1M) or listen(1M).

SEE ALSO
    inetd(1M), listen(1M), pmadm(1M), sacadm(1M).

NAME

rwall – write to all users over a network

SYNOPSIS

/usr/sbin/rwall *hostname* ...

DESCRIPTION

rwall reads a message from standard input until EOF. It then sends this message, preceded by the line:

Broadcast Message . . .

to all users logged in on the specified host machines.

A machine can only receive such a message if it is running rwalld(1M), which may be started by inetd(1M) or listen(1M).

NOTES

The timeout is fairly short to allow transmission to a large group of machines (some of which may be down) in a reasonable amount of time. Thus the message may not get through to a heavily loaded machine.

SEE ALSO

inetd(1M), listen(1M), pmadm(1M), rwalld(1M), sacadm(1M), wall(1)

NAME
    rpc.rwalld – network rwall server

SYNOPSIS
    /usr/lib/netsvc/rwall/rpc.rwalld

DESCRIPTION
    rwalld is a server that handles rwall(1M) requests. It is implemented by calling
    wall(1M) on all the appropriate network machines. The rwalld daemon may be
    started by inetd(1M) or listen(1M).

SEE ALSO
    inetd(1M), listen(1M), rwall(1M), wall(1M).

NAME

    sac – service access controller

SYNOPSIS

    sac –t *sanity_interval*

DESCRIPTION

The Service Access Controller (SAC) is the overseer of the server machine. It is started when the server machine enters multiuser mode. The SAC performs several important functions as explained below.

Customizing the SAC environment. When sac is invoked, it first looks for the per-system configuration script /etc/saf/_sysconfig. sac interprets _sysconfig to customize its own environment. The modifications made to the SAC environment by _sysconfig are inherited by all the children of the SAC. This inherited environment may be modified by the children.

Starting port monitors. After it has interpreted the _sysconfig file, the sac reads its administrative file /etc/saf/_sactab. _sactab specifies which port monitors are to be started. For each port monitor to be started, sac forks a child [fork(2)] and creates a utmp entry with the *type* field set to LOGIN_PROCESS. Each child then interprets its per-port monitor configuration script /etc/saf/*pmtag*/_config, if the file exists. These modifications to the environment affect the port monitor and will be inherited by all its children. Finally, the child process execs the port monitor, using the command found in the _sactab entry. (See sacadm; this is the command given with the –c option when the port monitor is added to the system.)

Polling port monitors to detect failure. The –t option sets the frequency with which sac polls the port monitors on the system. This time may also be thought of as half of the maximum latency required to detect that a port monitor has failed and that recovery action is necessary.

Administrative functions. The Service Access Controller represents the administrative point of control for port monitors. Its administrative tasks are explained below.

When queried (sacadm with either –l or –L), the Service Access Controller returns the status of the port monitors specified, which sacadm prints on the standard output. A port monitor may be in one of six states:

ENABLED   The port monitor is currently running and is accepting connections. See sacadm(1M) with the –e option.

DISABLED   The port monitor is currently running and is not accepting connections. See sacadm with the –d option, and see NOTRUNNING, below.

STARTING   The port monitor is in the process of starting up. STARTING is an intermediate state on the way to ENABLED or DISABLED.

FAILED   The port monitor was unable to start and remain running.

STOPPING   The port monitor has been manually terminated but has not
                  completed its shutdown procedure. STOPPING is an intermedi-
                  ate state on the way to NOTRUNNING.

NOTRUNNING   The port monitor is not currently running. (See sacadm with
                  −k.) This is the normal "not running" state. When a port mon-
                  itor is killed, all ports it was monitoring are inaccessible. It is
                  not possible for an external user to tell whether a port is not
                  being monitored or the system is down. If the port monitor is
                  not killed but is in the DISABLED state, it may be possible
                  (depending on the port monitor being used) to write a message
                  on the inaccessible port telling the user who is trying to access
                  the port that it is disabled. This is the advantage of having a
                  DISABLED state as well as the NOTRUNNING state.

When a port monitor terminates, the SAC removes the utmp entry for that port
monitor.

The SAC receives all requests to enable, disable, start, or stop port monitors and
takes the appropriate action.

The SAC is responsible for restarting port monitors that terminate. Whether or
not the SAC will restart a given port monitor depends on two things:

- the restart count specified for the port monitor when the port monitor
  was added by sacadm; this information is included in
  /etc/saf/*pmtag*/_sactab
- the number of times the port monitor has already been restarted

SEE ALSO

sacadm(1M), pmadm(1M).

FILES

/etc/saf/_sactab
/etc/saf/_sysconfig
/var/adm/utmp
/var/saf/_log

NAME
sacadm – service access controller administration

SYNOPSIS
sacadm −a −p *pmtag* −t *type* −c *cmd* −v *ver* [−f dx] [−n *count*] \
    [−y *comment*] [−z script]

sacadm −r −p *pmtag*

sacadm −s −p *pmtag*

sacadm −k −p *pmtag*

sacadm −e −p *pmtag*

sacadm −d −p *pmtag*

sacadm −l [−p *pmtag* | −t *type*]

sacadm −L [−p *pmtag* | −t *type*]

sacadm −g −p *pmtag* [−z *script*]

sacadm −G [−z script]

sacadm −x [−p *pmtag*]

DESCRIPTION
sacadm is the administrative command for the upper level of the Service Access Facility hierarchy, that is, for port monitor administration. sacadm performs the following functions:

> − adds or removes a port monitor
> − starts or stops a port monitor
> − enables or disables a port monitor
> − installs or replaces a per-system configuration script
> − installs or replaces a per-port monitor configuration script
> − prints requested port monitor information

Requests about the status of port monitors (−l and −L) and requests to print per-port monitor and per-system configuration scripts (−g and −G without the −z option) may be executed by any user on the system. Other sacadm commands may be executed only by a privileged user.

The options have the following meanings:

−a   Add a port monitor. When adding a port monitor, sacadm creates the supporting directory structure in /etc/saf and /var/saf and adds an entry for the new port monitor to /etc/saf/_sactab. The file _sactab already exists on the delivered system. Initially, it is empty except for a single line, which contains the version number of the Service Access Controller.

        Unless the command line that adds the new port monitor includes a −f option with the argument x, the new port monitor will be started. Because of the complexity of the options and arguments that follow the −a option, it may be convenient to use a command script or the menu system to add port monitors. If you use the menu system, enter **sysadm ports** and then choose the **port_monitors** option.

−c *cmd*   Execute the command string *cmd* to start a port monitor. The −c option may be used only with a −a. A −a option requires a −c.

−d   Disable the port monitor *pmtag*.

−e   Enable the port monitor *pmtag*.

−f dx   The −f option specifies one or both of the following two flags which are then included in the flags field of the _sactab entry for the new port monitor. If the −f option is not included on the command line, no flags are set and the default conditions prevail. By default, a port monitor is started. A −f option with no following argument is illegal.

        d   Do not enable the new port monitor.

        x   Do not start the new port monitor.

−g   The −g option is used to request output or to install or replace the per-port monitor configuration script /etc/saf/*pmtag*/_config. −g requires a −p option. The −g option with only a −p option prints the per-port monitor configuration script for port monitor *pmtag*. The −g option with a −p option and a −z option installs the file **script** as the per-port monitor configuration script for port monitor *pmtag*. Other combinations of options with −g are invalid.

−G   The −G option is used to request output or to install or replace the per-system configuration script /etc/saf/_sysconfig. The −G option by itself prints the per-system configuration script. The −G option in combination with a −z option installs the file **script** as the per-system configuration script. Other combinations of options with a −G option are invalid.

−k   Stop port monitor *pmtag*.

−l   The −l option is used to request port monitor information. The −l by itself lists all port monitors on the system. The −l option in combination with the −p option lists only the port monitor specified by *pmtag*. A −l in combination with the −t option lists all port monitors of type *type*. Any other combination of options with the −l option is invalid.

−L   The −L option is identical to the −l option except that the output appears in a condensed format.

−n *count*

Set the restart count to *count*. If a restart count is not specified, count is set to 0. A count of 0 indicates that the port monitor is not to be restarted if it fails.

−p *pmtag*

Specifies the tag associated with a port monitor.

-r   Remove port monitor *pmtag*. sacadm removes the port monitor entry from /etc/saf/_sactab. If the removed port monitor is not running, then no further action is taken. If the removed port monitor is running, the Service Access Controller (SAC) sends it SIGTERM to indicate that it should shut down. Note that the port monitor's directory structure remains intact.

-s   Start a port monitor. The SAC starts the port monitor *pmtag*.

-t *type*   Specifies the port monitor type.

-v *ver*   Specifies the version number of the port monitor. This version number may be given as

> -v `pmspec -V`

where *pmspec* is the special administrative command for port monitor *pmtag*. This special command is ttyadm for ttymon and nlsadmin for listen. The version stamp of the port monitor is known by the command and is returned when *pmspec* is invoked with a –V option.

-x   The –x option by itself tells the SAC to read its database file (_sactab). The –x option with the –p option tells port monitor *pmtag* to read its administrative file.

-y *comment*
      Include *comment* in the _sactab entry for port monitor *pmtag*.

-z script
      Used with the –g and –G options to specify the name of a file that contains a configuration script. With the –g option, script is a per-port monitor configuration script; with –G it is a per-system configuration script. Modifying a configuration script is a three-step procedure. First a copy of the existing script is made (–g or –G). Then the copy is edited. Finally, the copy is put in place over the existing script (–g or –G with –z).

OUTPUT

If successful, sacadm will exit with a status of 0. If sacadm fails for any reason, it will exit with a nonzero status. Options that request information will write the information on the standard output. In the condensed format (–L), port monitor information is printed as a sequence of colon-separated fields; empty fields are indicated by two successive colons. The standard format (–l) prints a header identifying the columns, and port monitor information is aligned under the appropriate headings. In this format, an empty field is indicated by a hyphen. The comment character is #.

EXAMPLES

The following command line adds a port monitor. The port monitor tag is npack; its type is listen; if necessary, it will restart three times before failing; its administrative command is nlsadmin; and the configuration script to be read is in the file script:

```
sacadm -a -p npack -t listen -c /usr/lib/saf/listen npack \
     -v `nlsadmin -V` -n 3 -z script
```

Remove a port monitor whose tag is pmtag:

    sacadm -r -p pmtag

Start the port monitor whose tag is pmtag:

    sacadm -s -p pmtag

Stop the port monitor whose tag is pmtag:

    sacadm -k -p pmtag

Enable the port monitor whose tag is pmtag:

    sacadm -e -p pmtag

Disable the port monitor whose tag is pmtag:

    sacadm -d -p pmtag

List status information for all port monitors:

    sacadm -l

List status information for the port monitor whose tag is pmtag:

    sacadm -l -p pmtag

List the same information in condensed format:

    sacadm -L -p pmtag

List status information for all port monitors whose type is listen:

    sacadm -l -t listen

Replace the per-port monitor configuration script associated with the port monitor whose tag is pmtag with the contents of the file file.config:

    sacadm -g -p pmtag -z file.config

SEE ALSO

doconfig(3N), pmadm(1M), sac(1M).

FILES

/etc/saf/_sactab
/etc/saf/_sysconfig
/etc/saf/*pmtag*/_config

NAME
spray – spray packets

SYNOPSIS
/usr/sbin/spray [–c count] [–d delay] [–l length] [–t nettype host]

DESCRIPTION
spray sends a one-way stream of packets to *host* using RPC, and reports how many were received, as well as the the transfer rate. The *host* argument can be either a name or an Internet address.

The following options are available:

–c *count*   Specify how many packets to send. The default value of *count* is the number of packets required to make the total stream size 100000 bytes.

–d *delay*   Specify how many microseconds to pause between sending each packet. The default is 0.

–l *length*   The *length* parameter is the numbers of bytes in the Ethernet packet that holds the RPC call message. Since the data is encoded using XDR, and XDR only deals with 32 bit quantities, not all values of *length* are possible, and spray rounds up to the nearest possible value. When *length* is greater than 1514, then the RPC call can no longer be encapsulated in one Ethernet packet, so the *length* field no longer has a simple correspondence to Ethernet packet size. The default value of *length* is 86 bytes (the size of the RPC and UDP headers).

–t *nettype*   Specify clas of transports. Defaults to netpath. See rpc(3N) for a description of supported classes.

SEE ALSO
sprayd(1M), rpc(3N)

NAME
    rpc.sprayd – spray server

SYNOPSIS
    /usr/lib/netsvc/spray/rpc.sprayd

DESCRIPTION
    rpc.sprayd is a server which records the packets sent by spray(1M). The
    rpc.sprayd daemon may be started by inetd(1M) or listen(1M).

SEE ALSO
    inetd(1M) listen(1M), pmadm(1M), sacadm(1M), spray(1M)

NAME

ypinit – build and install YP database

SYNOPSIS

/usr/sbin/ypinit –c
/usr/sbin/ypinit –m
/usr/sbin/ypinit –s *master-name*

DESCRIPTION

ypinit sets up a YP name service database on a YP server. It can be used to set up a master or a slave server, or a client system. You must be the privileged user to run it. It asks a few, self-explanatory questions, and reports success or failure to the terminal.

It sets up a master server using the simple model in which that server is master to all maps in the data base. This is the way to bootstrap the YP system; later if you want you can change the association of maps to masters.

All databases are built from scratch, either from information available to the program at runtime, or from the ASCII data base files in /etc. These files should be in their traditional form, rather than the abbreviated form used on client machines.

A YP database on a slave server is set up by copying an existing database from a running server. The *master-name* argument should be the hostname of a YP server (either the master server for all the maps, or a server on which the data base is up-to-date and stable).

To set up a client, **ypinit** prompts for a list of YP servers to bind the client to, this list should be ordered from closest to farthest server.

Read ypfiles(4) and ypserv(1M) for an overview of the YP name service.

The following options are available:

–c   Set up a client system.

–m   Indicate that the local host is to be the YP master.

–s *master-name*
        Set up a slave database.

SEE ALSO

makedbm(1M), ypmake(1M), yppush(1M), ypserv(1M), ypxfr(1M), ypfiles(4)

FILES

/var/yp/binding/*domainname*/ypservers

NAME
     ypmake – rebuild YP database

SYNOPSIS
     cd /var/yp ; make [*map*]

DESCRIPTION
     The file called Makefile in /var/yp is used by make to build the YP name ser-
     vice database. With no arguments, make creates dbm databases for any YP maps
     that are out-of-date, and then executes yppush(1M) to notify slave databases that
     there has been a change.

     If *map* is supplied on the command line, make will update that map only.

     There are three special variables used by make: DIR, which gives the directory of
     the source files; NOPUSH, which when non-null inhibits doing a yppush of the
     new database files; and DOM, used to construct a domain other than the master's
     default domain. The default for DIR is /etc, and the default for NOPUSH is the
     null string.

     ypmake also creates an entry in /var/yp/aliases.

     Refer to ypfiles(4) and ypserv(1M) for an overview of the YP.

FILES
     /var/yp

SEE ALSO
     make(1), makedbm(1M), yppush(1M), ypserv(1M), ypfiles(4)

NAME

yppoll – return current version of a YP map at a YP server host

SYNOPSIS

/usr/sbin/yppoll [–d *ypdomain*] [–h *host*] *mapname*

DESCRIPTION

The **yppoll** command asks a **ypserv**(1M) process what the order number is, and which host is the master YP server for the named map.

The following options are available:

–d *ypdomain*
    Use *ypdomain* instead of the default domain.

–h *host*
    Ask the **ypserv** process at *host* about the map parameters. If *host* is not specified, the YP server for the local host is used. That is, the default host is the one returned by **ypwhich**(1).

SEE ALSO

ypserv(1M), ypwhich(1), ypfiles(4)

NAME
yppush – force propagation of a changed YP map

SYNOPSIS
/usr/sbin/yppush [–v] [–d ypdomain] mapname

DESCRIPTION
yppush copies a new version of a YP name service map from the master YP server to the slave YP servers. It is normally run only on the master YP server by the Makefile in /var/yp after the master databases are changed. It first constructs a list of YP server hosts by reading the YP map ypservers within the ypdomain, or if the map is not set up, the local file is used. Keys within the map ypservers are the ASCII names of the machines on which the YP servers run.

A transfer map request is sent to the YP server at each host, along with the information needed by the transfer agent (the program which actually moves the map) to call back the yppush . When the attempt has completed (successfully or not), and the transfer agent has sent yppush a status message, the results may be printed to stdout. Messages are also printed when a transfer is not possible; for instance when the request message is undeliverable, or when the timeout period on responses has expired.

Refer to ypfiles(4) and ypserv(1M) for an overview of the YP name service.

The following optionas are available:

–v   Verbose. Print messages when each server is called, and for each response. If this flag is omitted, only error messages are printed.

–d ypdomain
    Specify a ypdomain other than the default domain.

FILES
/var/yp/ypdomain/ypservers.{dir,pag}   local file
/var/yp

SEE ALSO
ypserv(1M), ypxfr(1M), ypfiles(4)

NAME

ypserv, ypbind – YP server and binder processes

SYNOPSIS

/usr/lib/netsvc/yp/ypserv

/usr/lib/netsvc/yp/ypbind [–ypset | –ypsetme]

DESCRIPTION

The YP provides a simple network lookup service consisting of databases and processes. The databases are dbm(3) files in a directory tree rooted at /var/yp. These files are described in ypfiles(4). The processes are /usr/sbin/ypserv, the YP database lookup server, and /usr/sbin/ypbind, the YP binder. The programmatic interface to YP is described in ypclnt(3N). Administrative tools are described in yppush(1M), ypxfr(1M), yppoll(1M), ypwhich(1), and ypset(1M). Tools to see the contents of YP maps are described in ypcat(1), and ypmatch(1). Database generation and maintenance tools are described in ypinit(1M), ypmake(1M), and makedbm(1M).

Both ypserv and ypbind are daemon processes typically activated at system startup time from /etc/rc.local. ypserv runs only on YP server machines with a complete YP database. ypbind runs on all machines using YP services, both YP servers and clients.

The ypserv daemon's primary function is to look up information in its local database of YP maps. Communication to and from ypserv is by means of RPC calls. Lookup functions are described in ypclnt(3N), and are supplied as C-callable functions in the YP library. There are four lookup functions, all of which are performed on a specified map within some YP domain: *Match*, *"Get_first"*, *"Get_next"*, and *"Get_all"*. The *Match* operation takes a key, and returns the associated value. The *"Get_first"* operation returns the first key-value pair from the map, and *"Get_next"* can be used to enumerate the remainder. *"Get_all"* ships the entire map to the requester as the response to a single RPC request.

Two other functions supply information about the map, rather than map entries: *"Get_order_number"*, and *"Get_master_name"*. In fact, both order number and master name exist in the map as key-value pairs, but the server will not return either through the normal lookup functions. If you examine the map with makedbm(1M), however, they will be visible.

The function of ypbind is to remember information that lets client processes on a single node communicate with some ypserv process. ypbind must run on every machine which has YP client processes; ypserv may or may not be running on the same node, but must be running somewhere on the network.

The information ypbind remembers is called a *binding* — the association of a domain name with a YP server.

The process of binding is driven by client requests. As a request for an unbound domain comes in, the ypbind process steps through the ypservers list (last entry first) trying to find a ypserv process that serves maps within that domain. There must be a ypserv process on at least one of the hosts in the ypservers file. Once a domain is bound by a particular ypbind, that same binding is given to every client process on the node. The ypbind process on the local node or a remote node may be queried for the binding of a particular domain by using the ypwhich(1) command.

If ypbind is unable to speak to the ypserv process it is bound to, it marks the domain as unbound, tells the client process that the domain is unbound, and tries to bind the domain once again. Requests received for an unbound domain will wait until the domain requested is bound. In general, a bound domain is marked as unbound when the node running ypserv crashes or gets overloaded. In such a case, ypbind will to bind another YP server listed in /var/yp/binding/*domainname*/ypservers.

ypbind also accepts requests to set its binding for a particular domain. The request is usually generated by the YP subsystem itself. ypset(1M) is a command to access the "*Set_domain*" facility. Note: the *Set Domain* procedure only accepts requests from processes running as root, ant the −ypset or −ypsetme flags must have been set for ypbind.

The following options are available for the ypbind command only:

−ypset   Allow any user to call ypset(1M). By default, no one can call ypset(1M).

−ypsetme   Only allow root on local machines to call ypset(1M). By default, no one can call ypset(1M).

FILES

If the file /var/yp/ypserv.log exists when ypserv starts up, log information will be written to this file when error conditions arise.

/var/yp
/var/yp/binding/*ypdomain*/ypservers

SEE ALSO

makedbm(1M), ypcat(1), ypinit(1M), ypmake(1M), ypmatch(1), yppoll(1M), yppush(1M), ypset(1M), ypwhich(1), ypxfr(1M), dbm(3X), ypclnt(3N), ypfiles(4)

NOTES

Both ypbind and ypserv support multiple domains. The ypserv process determines the domains it serves by looking for directories of the same name in the directory /var/yp. Additionally, the ypbind process can maintain bindings to several domains and their servers.

NAME
ypset – point ypbind at a particular server

SYNOPSIS
/usr/sbin/ypset [–d *ypdomain*] [–h *host*] *server*

DESCRIPTION
In order to run ypset, ypbind must be initiated with the –ypset or –ypsetme options. See ypserv(1M). ypset tells ypbind to get YP services for the specified *ypdomain* from the ypserv process running on *server*. If *server* is down, or is not running ypserv, this is not discovered until a YP client process tries to get a binding for the domain. At this point, the binding set by ypset will be tested by ypbind. If the binding is invalid, ypbind will attempt to rebind for the same domain.

ypset is useful for binding a client node which is not on a broadcast net, or is on a broadcast net which is not running a YP server host. It also is useful for debugging YP client applications, for instance where a YP map only exists at a single YP server host.

In cases where several hosts on the local net are supplying YP services, it is possible for ypbind to rebind to another host even while you attempt to find out if the ypset operation succeeded. For example, you can type:

```
% ypset host1
% ypwhich
host2
```

which can be confusing. This is a function of the YP subsystem's attempt to load-balance among the available YP servers, and occurs when *host1* does not respond to ypbind because it is not running ypserv (or is overloaded), and *host2*, running ypserv, gets the binding.

server indicates the YP server to bind to, and must be specified as a name. This will work only if the node has a current valid binding for the domain in question, and ypbind has been set to allow use of ypset. In most cases, *server* should be specified as an IP address.

ypset tries to bind ypbind over a datagram transport first. Datagram Transports are recommended for higher performance. The YP library calls, yp_enum( ), yp_all( ), yp_next( ), and yp_first( ) use circuit transports regardless of the main transport being used.

Refer to ypfiles(4) and ypserv(1M) for an overview of the YP name service.

The following options are available:

–h *host*   Set ypbind's binding on *host*, instead of locally. *host* must be specified as a name.

–d *ypdomain*   Use *ypdomain* , instead of the default domain.

SEE ALSO
ypserv(1M), ypwhich(1), ypfiles(4)

NAME

ypupdated – server for changing YP information

SYNOPSIS

/usr/lib/netsvc/yp/ypupdated [−is]

DESCRIPTION

ypupdated is a daemon that updates information in the YP name service, normally started up by inetd(1M). ypupdated consults the file updaters(4) in the
directory /var/yp to determine which YP maps should be updated and how to
change them.

By default, the daemon requires the most secure method of authentication available to it, either DES (secure) or UNIX (insecure).

The following options are available:

−i   Accept RPC calls with the insecure AUTH_UNIX credentials. This allows
      programmatic updating of YP maps in all networks.

−s   Only accept calls authenticated using the secure RPC mechanism
      (AUTH_DES authentication). This disables programmatic updating of YP
      maps unless the network supports these calls.

FILES

/var/yp/updaters

SEE ALSO

inetd(1M), keyserv(1M), updaters(4)

NAME

ypxfr – transfer YP map from a YP server to host

SYNOPSIS

/usr/sbin/ypxfr [–c] [–f] [–d *ypdomain*] [–h *host*] [–s *ypdomain*]
    [–C *tid prog server*] *mapname*

DESCRIPTION

The ypxfr command moves a YP map in the default domain for the local host to the local host by making use of normal YP services. It creates a temporary map in the directory /var/yp/*ypdomain* (this directory must already exist; *ypdomain* is the default domain for the local host), fills it by enumerating the map's entries, fetches the map parameters (master and order number), and loads them. It then deletes any old versions of the map and moves the temporary map to the real *mapname*.

If run interactively, ypxfr writes its output to the terminal. However, if it is started without a controlling terminal, and if the log file /var/yp/ypxfr.log exists, it appends all its output to that file. Since ypxfr is most often run from the privileged user's crontab file, or by ypserv, the log file can be used to retain a record of what was attempted, and what the results were.

For consistency between servers, ypxfr should be run periodically for every map in the YP data base. Different maps change at different rates: a map may not change for months at a time, for instance, and may therefore be checked only once a day. Some maps may change several times per day. In such a case, you may want to check hourly for updates. A crontab(1) entry can be used to perform periodic updates automatically. Rather than having a separate crontab entry for each map, you can group comands to update several maps in a shell script. Examples (mnemonically named) are in /usr/sbin/yp: ypxfr_1perday, and ypxfr_1perhour. They can serve as reasonable first cuts.

Refer to ypfiles(4) and ypserv(1M) for an overview of the YP name service.

The following options are available:

–c   Do not send a Clear current map request to the local ypserv process. Use this flag if ypserv is not running locally at the time you are running ypxfr. Otherwise, ypxfr complains that it cannot talk to the local ypserv, and the transfer fails.

–f   Force the transfer to occur even if the version at the master is not more recent than the local version.

–C *tid prog server*

This option is *only* for use by ypserv. When ypserv starts ypxfr, it specifies that ypxfr should call back a yppush process at the host *server*, registered as program number *prog*, and waiting for a response to transaction *tid*.

–d *ypdomain*

Specify a domain other than the default domain.

-h *host*
> Get the map from *host*, regardless of what the map says the master is. If *host* is not specified, ypxfr asks the YP service for the name of the master, and try to get the map from there. *host* must be a name.

-s *ypdomain*
> Specify a source domain from which to transfer a map that should be the same across domains.

FILES

/var/yp/ypxfr.log	log file
/usr/sbin/yp/ypxfr_1perday	script to run one transfer per day, for use with cron(1M)
/usr/sbin/yp/ypxfr_1perhour	script for hourly transfers of volatile maps
/var/yp/*ypdomain*	YP domain
/usr/spool/cron/crontabs/root	privileged user's crontab file

SEE ALSO

cron(1M), crontab(1), ypserv(1M), yppush(1M), ypfiles(4)

NAME

> dbm, dbminit, dbmclose, fetch, store, delete, firstkey, nextkey –
> database subroutines

SYNOPSIS

> ```
> #include <dbm.h>
> typedef struct {
> char *dptr;
> int dsize;
> } datum;
> dbminit(file)
> char *file;
> dbmclose()
> datum fetch(key)
> datum key;
> store(key, content)
> datum key, content;
> delete(key)
> datum key;
> datum firstkey()
> datum nextkey(key)
> datum key;
> ```

DESCRIPTION

> These functions maintain key/content pairs in a database. The functions will
> handle very large (a billion blocks) databases and will access a keyed item in one
> or two file system accesses. The functions are obtained with the loader option
> −lyp.

> *key*s and *content*s are described by the datum typedef. A datum specifies a string
> of *dsize* bytes pointed to by *dptr*. Arbitrary binary data, as well as normal ASCII
> strings, are allowed. The database is stored in two files. One file is a directory
> containing a bit map and has .dir as its suffix. The second file contains all data
> and has .pag as its suffix.

> Before a database can be accessed, it must be opened by dbminit. At the time of
> this call, the files *file*.dir and *file*.pag must exist. An empty database is created
> by creating zero-length .dir and .pag files.

> A database may be closed by calling dbmclose. You must close a database
> before opening a new one.

> Once open, the data stored under a key is accessed by fetch() and data is
> placed under a key by store. A key (and its associated contents) is deleted by
> delete. A linear pass through all keys in a database may be made, in an
> (apparently) random order, by use of firstkey() and nextkey. firstkey()
> will return the first key in the database. With any key nextkey() will return the
> next key in the database. This code will traverse the database:

> > ```
> > for (key = firstkey(); key.dptr != NULL; key = nextkey(key))
> > ```

RETURN VALUE
All functions that return an int indicate errors with negative values. A zero return indicates no error. Routines that return a datum indicate errors with a NULL (0) *dptr*.

NOTES
The .pag file will contain holes so that its apparent size is about four times its actual content. Older versions of the UNIX operating system may create real file blocks for these holes when touched. These files cannot be copied by normal means (cp(1), cat(1), tar(1), ar(1)) without filling in the holes.

dptr pointers returned by these subroutines point into static storage that is changed by subsequent calls.

The sum of the sizes of a key/content pair must not exceed the internal block size (currently 1024 bytes). Moreover all key/content pairs that hash together must fit on a single block. store() will return an error in the event that a disk block fills with inseparable data.

delete() does not physically reclaim file space, although it does make it available for reuse.

The order of keys presented by firstkey() and nextkey() depends on a hashing function, not on anything interesting.

There are no interlocks and no reliable cache flushing; thus concurrent updating and reading is risky.

FILES
/usr/lib/libyp.a

NAME
select – synchronous I/O multiplexing

SYNOPSIS
```
#include <sys/time.h>
#include <sys/types.h>

select(nfds, readfds, writefds, execptfds, timeout)
int nfds;
fd_set *readfds, *writefds, *execptfds;
struct timeval *timeout;

FD_SET(fd, &fdset);
FD_CLR(fd, &fdset);
FD_ISSET(fd, &fdset);
FD_ZERO(&fdset);
int fd;
fd_set fdset;
```

DESCRIPTION
select examines the I/O descriptor sets whose addresses are passed in *readfds*, *writefds*, and *execptfds* to see if any of their descriptors are ready for reading, are ready for writing, or have an exceptional condition pending, respectively. *nfds* is the number of bits to be checked in each bit mask that represents a file descriptor; the descriptors from 0 to −1 in the descriptor sets are examined. On return, select replaces the given descriptor sets with subsets consisting of those descriptors that are ready for the requested operation. The return value from the call to select() is the number of ready descriptors.

The descriptor sets are stored as bit fields in arrays of integers. The following macros are provided for manipulating such descriptor sets: FD_ZERO(&*fdset*) initializes a descriptor set *fdset* to the null set. FD_SET(*fd*, &*fdset*) includes a particular descriptor *fd* in *fdset*. FD_CLR(*fd*, &*fdset*) removes *fd* from *fdset*. FD_ISSET(*fd*, &*fdset*) is nonzero if *fd* is a member of *fdset*, zero otherwise. The behavior of these macros is undefined if a descriptor value is less than zero or greater than or equal to FD_SETSIZE. FD_SETSIZE is a constant defined in sys/select.h and is normally at least equal to the maximum number of descriptors supported by the system.

If *timeout* is not a NULL pointer, it specifies a maximum interval to wait for the selection to complete. If *timeout* is a NULL pointer, the select blocks indefinitely. To affect a poll, the *timeout* argument should be a non-NULL pointer, pointing to a zero-valued timeval structure.

Any of *readfds*, *writefds*, and *execptfds* may be given as NULL pointers if no descriptors are of interest.

RETURN VALUE
select returns the number of ready descriptors contained in the descriptor sets or −1 if an error occurred. If the time limit expires, then select returns 0.

ERRORS

An error return from `select` indicates:

EBADF　One of the I/O descriptor sets specified an invalid I/O descriptor.

EINTR　A signal was delivered before any of the selected events occurred, or the time limit expired.

EINVAL　A component of the pointed-to time limit is outside the acceptable range: t_sec must be between 0 and 10^8, inclusive. t_usec must be greater-than or equal to 0, and less than 10^6.

SEE ALSO

poll(2), read(2), write(2)

NOTES

The default value for FD_SETSIZE (currently 1024) is larger than the default limit on the number of open files. In order to accommodate programs that may use a larger number of open files with `select`, it is possible to increase this size within a program by providing a larger definition of FD_SETSIZE before the inclusion of <sys/types.h>.

In future versions of the system, `select` may return the time remaining from the original timeout, if any, by modifying the time value in place. It is thus unwise to assume that the timeout value will be unmodified by the `select` call.

The descriptor sets are always modified on return, even if the call returns as the result of a timeout.

NAME

accept – accept a connection on a socket

SYNOPSIS

```
#include <sys/types.h>
#include <sys/socket.h>

ns = accept(s, addr, addrlen)
int ns, s;
struct sockaddr *addr;
int *addrlen;
```

DESCRIPTION

The argument *s* is a socket that has been created with socket(3N) and bound to an address with bind(3N), and that is listening for connections after a call to listen(3N). accept() extracts the first connection on the queue of pending connections, creates a new socket with the properties of *s*, and allocates a new file descriptor, *ns*, for the socket. If no pending connections are present on the queue and the socket is not marked as non-blocking, accept() blocks the caller until a connection is present. If the socket is marked as non-blocking and no pending connections are present on the queue, accept() returns an error as described below. accept() uses the netconfig(4) file to determine the STREAMS device file name associated with *s*. This is the device on which the connect indication will be accepted. The accepted socket, *ns*, is used to read and write data to and from the socket that connected to *ns*; it is not used to accept more connections. The original socket (*s*) remains open for accepting further connections.

The argument *addr* is a result parameter that is filled in with the address of the connecting entity as it is known to the communications layer. The exact format of the *addr* parameter is determined by the domain in which the communication occurs.

addrlen is a value-result parameter. Initially, it contains the amount of space pointed to by *addr*; on return it contains the length in bytes of the address returned.

accept() is used with connection-based socket types, currently with SOCK_STREAM.

It is possible to select(3N) a socket for the purpose of an accept() by selecting it for read. However, this will only indicate when a connect indication is pending; it is still necessary to call accept().

RETURN VALUE

accept() returns −1 on error. If it succeeds, it returns a non-negative integer that is a descriptor for the accepted socket.

ERRORS

accept() will fail if:

EBADF	The descriptor is invalid.
ENOTSOCK	The descriptor does not reference a socket.

EOPNOTSUPP	The referenced socket is not of type SOCK_STREAM.
EWOULDBLOCK	The socket is marked as non-blocking and no connections are present to be accepted.
EPROTO	A protocol error has occurred; for example, the STREAMS protocol stack has not been initialized.
ENODEV	The protocol family and type corresponding to s could not be found in the netconfig file.
ENOMEM	There was insufficient user memory available to complete the operation.
ENOSR	There were insufficient STREAMS resources available to complete the operation.

SEE ALSO

bind(3N), connect(3N), listen(3N), socket(3N), netconfig(4).

NAME
bind – bind a name to a socket

SYNOPSIS
```
#include <sys/types.h>
#include <sys/socket.h>

bind(s, name, namelen)
int s;
struct sockaddr *name;
int namelen;
```

DESCRIPTION
bind( ) assigns a name to an unnamed socket. When a socket is created with socket(3N), it exists in a name space (address family) but has no name assigned. bind( ) requests that the name pointed to by *name* be assigned to the socket.

NOTES
Binding a name in the UNIX domain creates a socket in the file system that must be deleted by the caller when it is no longer needed (using unlink(2)).

The rules used in name binding vary between communication domains.

RETURN VALUE
If the bind is successful, a 0 value is returned. A return value of −1 indicates an error, which is further specified in the global errno.

ERRORS
The bind( ) call will fail if:

EBADF	*s* is not a valid descriptor.
ENOTSOCK	*s* is a descriptor for a file, not a socket.
EADDRNOTAVAIL	The specified address is not available on the local machine.
EADDRINUSE	The specified address is already in use.
EINVAL	*namelen* is not the size of a valid address for the specified address family.
EINVAL	The socket is already bound to an address.
EACCES	The requested address is protected and the current user has inadequate permission to access it.
ENOSR	There were insufficient STREAMS resources for the operation to complete.

The following errors are specific to binding names in the UNIX domain:

ENOTDIR	A component of the path prefix of the pathname in *name* is not a directory.
ENOENT	A component of the path prefix of the pathname in *name* does not exist.
EACCES	Search permission is denied for a component of the path prefix of the pathname in *name*.

ELOOP	Too many symbolic links were encountered in translating the pathname in *name*.
EIO	An I/O error occurred while making the directory entry or allocating the inode.
EROFS	The inode would reside on a read-only file system.
EISDIR	A null pathname was specified.

SEE ALSO
unlink(2)

NAME

    byteorder, htonl, htons, ntohl, ntohs – convert values between host and
network byte order

SYNOPSIS

```
#include <sys/types.h>
#include <netinet/in.h>

netlong = htonl(hostlong);
u_long netlong, hostlong;

netshort = htons(hostshort);
u_short netshort, hostshort;

hostlong = ntohl(netlong);
u_long hostlong, netlong;

hostshort = ntohs(netshort);
u_short hostshort, netshort;
```

DESCRIPTION

These routines convert 16 and 32 bit quantities between network byte order and
host byte order. On some architectures these routines are defined as NULL macros
in the include file <netinet/in.h>. On other architectures, if their host byte
order is different from network byte order, these routines are functional.

These routines are most often used in conjunction with Internet addresses and
ports as returned by gethostent(3N) and getservent(3N).

SEE ALSO

    gethostent(3N), getservent(3N)

NAME

connect – initiate a connection on a socket

SYNOPSIS

```
#include <sys/types.h>
#include <sys/socket.h>

connect(s, name, namelen)
int s;
struct sockaddr *name;
int namelen;
```

DESCRIPTION

The parameter s is a socket. If it is of type SOCK_DGRAM, connect() specifies the peer with which the socket is to be associated; this address is the address to which datagrams are to be sent if a receiver is not explicitly designated; it is the only address from which datagrams are to be received. If the socket s is of type SOCK_STREAM, connect() attempts to make a connection to another socket. The other socket is specified by *name*. *name* is an address in the communications space of the socket. Each communications space interprets the *name* parameter in its own way. If s is not bound, then it will be bound to an address selected by the underlying transport provider. Generally, stream sockets may successfully connect() only once; datagram sockets may use connect() multiple times to change their association. Datagram sockets may dissolve the association by connecting to a null address.

RETURN VALUE

If the connection or binding succeeds, then 0 is returned. Otherwise a −1 is returned and a more specific error code is stored in errno.

ERRORS

The call fails if:

EBADF	s is not a valid descriptor.
ENOTSOCK	s is a descriptor for a file, not a socket.
EINVAL	*namelen* is not the size of a valid address for the specified address family.
EADDRNOTAVAIL	The specified address is not available on the remote machine.
EAFNOSUPPORT	Addresses in the specified address family cannot be used with this socket.
EISCONN	The socket is already connected.
ETIMEDOUT	Connection establishment timed out without establishing a connection.
ECONNREFUSED	The attempt to connect was forcefully rejected. The calling program should close(2) the socket descriptor, and issue another socket(3N) call to obtain a new descriptor before attempting another connect() call.

ENETUNREACH	The network is not reachable from this host.
EADDRINUSE	The address is already in use.
EINPROGRESS	The socket is non-blocking and the connection cannot be completed immediately. It is possible to select(3N) for completion by selecting the socket for writing. However, this is only possible if the socket STREAMS module is the topmost module on the protocol stack with a write service procedure. This will be the normal case.
EALREADY	The socket is non-blocking and a previous connection attempt has not yet been completed.
EINTR	The connection attempt was interrupted before any data arrived by the delivery of a signal.
ENOTSOCK	The file referred to by *name* is not a socket.
EPROTOTYPE	The file referred to by *name* is a socket of a type other than type *s* (for example, *s* is a SOCK_DGRAM socket, while *name* refers to a SOCK_STREAM socket).
ENOSR	There were insufficient STREAMS resources available to complete the operation.

The following errors are specific to connecting names in the UNIX domain. These errors may not apply in future versions of the UNIX IPC domain.

ENOTDIR	A component of the path prefix of the pathname in *name* is not a directory.
ENOENT	A component of the path prefix of the pathname in *name* does not exist.
ENOENT	The socket referred to by the pathname in *name* does not exist.
EACCES	Search permission is denied for a component of the path prefix of the pathname in *name*.
ELOOP	Too many symbolic links were encountered in translating the pathname in *name*.
EIO	An I/O error occurred while reading from or writing to the file system.

SEE ALSO
accept(3N), connect(3N), getsockname(3N), socket(3N).

NAME

dial – establish an outgoing terminal line connection

SYNOPSIS

```
#include <dial.h>

int dial (CALL call);

void undial (int fd);
```

DESCRIPTION

dial returns a file-descriptor for a terminal line open for read/write. The argument to dial is a CALL structure (defined in the dial.h header file).

When finished with the terminal line, the calling program must invoke undial to release the semaphore that has been set during the allocation of the terminal device.

The definition of CALL in the dial.h header file is:

```
typedef struct {
        struct termio *attr;    /* pointer to termio attribute struct */
        int           baud;     /* transmission data rate */
        int           speed;    /* 212A modem: low=300, high=1200 */
        char          *line;    /* device name for out-going line */
        char          *telno;   /* pointer to tel-no digits string */
        int           modem;    /* specify modem control for direct lines */
        char          *device;  /* unused */
        int           dev_len;  /* unused */
} CALL;
```

The CALL element speed is intended only for use with an outgoing dialed call, in which case its value should be either 300 or 1200 to identify the 113A modem, or the high- or low-speed setting on the 212A modem. Note that the 113A modem or the low-speed setting of the 212A modem will transmit at any rate between 0 and 300 bits per second. However, the high-speed setting of the 212A modem transmits and receives at 1200 bits per second only. The CALL element baud is for the desired transmission baud rate. For example, one might set baud to 110 and speed to 300 (or 1200). However, if speed is set to 1200, baud must be set to high (1200).

If the desired terminal line is a direct line, a string pointer to its device-name should be placed in the line element in the CALL structure. Legal values for such terminal device names are kept in the Devices file. In this case, the value of the baud element should be set to -1. This value will cause dial to determine the correct value from the Devices file.

The telno element is for a pointer to a character string representing the telephone number to be dialed. Such numbers may consist only of these characters:

0-9	dial 0-9
*	dial *
#	dial #
=	wait for secondary dial tone
–	delay for approximately 4 seconds

The CALL element modem is used to specify modem control for direct lines. This element should be non-zero if modem control is required. The CALL element attr is a pointer to a termio structure, as defined in the termio.h header file. A NULL value for this pointer element may be passed to the dial function, but if such a structure is included, the elements specified in it will be set for the outgoing terminal line before the connection is established. This setting is often important for certain attributes such as parity and baud-rate.

The CALL elements device and dev_len are no longer used. They are retained in the CALL structure for compatibility reasons.

FILES

/etc/uucp/Devices
/etc/uucp/Systems
/var/spool/uucp/LCK. . *tty-device*

SEE ALSO

alarm(2), read(2), write(2).
termio(7) in the *System Administrator's Reference Manual*.
uucp(1C) in the *User's Reference Manual*.

DIAGNOSTICS

On failure, a negative value indicating the reason for the failure will be returned. Mnemonics for these negative indices as listed here are defined in the dial.h header file.

INTRPT	-1	/* interrupt occurred */
D_HUNG	-2	/* dialer hung (no return from write) */
NO_ANS	-3	/* no answer within 10 seconds */
ILL_BD	-4	/* illegal baud-rate */
A_PROB	-5	/* acu problem (open() failure) */
L_PROB	-6	/* line problem (open() failure) */
NO_Ldv	-7	/* can't open Devices file */
DV_NT_A	-8	/* requested device not available */
DV_NT_K	-9	/* requested device not known */
NO_BD_A	-10	/* no device available at requested baud */
NO_BD_K	-11	/* no device known at requested baud */
DV_NT_E	-12	/* requested speed does not match */
BAD_SYS	-13	/* system not in Systems file*/

NOTES

Including the dial.h header file automatically includes the termio.h header file.

An alarm(2) system call for 3600 seconds is made (and caught) within the dial module for the purpose of "touching" the LCK. . file and constitutes the device allocation semaphore for the terminal device. Otherwise, uucp(1C) may simply delete the LCK. . entry on its 90-minute clean-up rounds. The alarm may go off while the user program is in a read(2) or write(2) system call, causing an apparent error return. If the user program expects to be around for an hour or more, error returns from reads should be checked for (errno==EINTR), and the read possibly reissued.

NAME

doconfig – execute a configuration script

SYNOPSIS

include <sac.h> int doconfig(int fd, char *script, long rflag);

DESCRIPTION

doconfig is a Service Access Facility library function that interprets the configuration scripts contained in the files /etc/saf/*pmtag*/_config, /etc/saf/_sysconfig, and /etc/saf/*pmtag*/*svctag*.

script is the name of the configuration script; *fd* is a file descriptor that designates the stream to which stream manipulation operations are to be applied; *rflag* is a bitmask that indicates the mode in which script is to be interpreted. *rflag* may take two values, NORUN and NOASSIGN, which may be or'd. If *rflag* is zero, all commands in the configuration script are eligible to be interpreted. If *rflag* has the NOASSIGN bit set, the assign command is considered illegal and will generate an error return. If *rflag* has the NORUN bit set, the run and runwait commands are considered illegal and will generate error returns.

The configuration language in which script is written consists of a sequence of commands, each of which is interpreted separately. The following reserved keywords are defined: assign, push, pop, runwait, and run. The comment character is #; when a # occurs on a line, everything from that point to the end of the line is ignored. Blank lines are not significant. No line in a command script may exceed 1024 characters.

assign *variable=value*

Used to define environment variables. *variable* is the name of the environment variable and *value* is the value to be assigned to it. The value assigned must be a string constant; no form of parameter substitution is available. *value* may be quoted. The quoting rules are those used by the shell for defining environment variables. assign will fail if space cannot be allocated for the new variable or if any part of the specification is invalid.

push *module1[, module2, module3, . . .]*

Used to push STREAMS modules onto the stream designated by *fd*. *module1* is the name of the first module to be pushed, *module2* is the name of the second module to be pushed, etc. The command will fail if any of the named modules cannot be pushed. If a module cannot be pushed, the subsequent modules on the same command line will be ignored and modules that have already been pushed will be popped.

pop *[module]*

Used to pop STREAMS modules off the designated stream. If pop is invoked with no arguments, the top module on the stream is popped. If an argument is given, modules will be popped one at a time until the named module is at the top of the stream. If the named module is not on the designated stream, the stream is left as it was and the command fails. If *module* is the special keyword ALL, then all modules on the stream will be popped. Note that only modules above the topmost driver are affected.

runwait *command*

>The runwait command runs a command and waits for it to complete. *command* is the pathname of the command to be run. The command is run with /usr/bin/sh −c prepended to it; shell scripts may thus be executed from configuration scripts. The runwait command will fail if *command* cannot be found or cannot be executed, or if *command* exits with a non-zero status.

run *command*

>The run command is identical to runwait except that it does not wait for *command* to complete. *command* is the pathname of the command to be run. run will not fail unless it is unable to create a child process to execute the command.

Although they are syntactically indistinguishable, some of the commands available to run and runwait are interpreter built-in commands. Interpreter built-ins are used when it is necessary to alter the state of a process within the context of that process. The doconfig interpreter built-in commands are similar to the shell special commands and, like these, they do not spawn another process for execution. See sh(1). The initial set of built-in commands is:

>cd
>ulimit
>umask

DIAGNOSTICS

doconfig returns 0 if the script was interpreted successfully. If a command in the script fails, the interpretation of the script ceases at that point and a positive number is returned; this number indicates which line in the script failed. If a system error occurs, a value of −1 is returned. When a script fails, the process whose environment was being established should *not* be started.

SEE ALSO

pmadm(1M), sacadm(1M), sh(1).

NAME

ethers − Ethernet address mapping operations

SYNOPSIS

```
#include <sys/types.h>
#include <sys/socket.h>
#include <net/if.h>
#include <netinet/in.h>
#include <netinet/if_ether.h>

    char *
    ether_ntoa (e)
        struct ether_addr *e;

    struct ether_addr *
    ether_aton (s)
        char *s;

    ether_ntohost (hostname, e)
        char *hostname;
        struct ether_addr *e;

    ether_hostton (hostname, e)
        char *hostname;
        struct ether_addr *e;

    ether_line (l, e, hostname)
        char *l;
        struct ether_addr *e;
        char *hostname;
```

DESCRIPTION

These routines are useful for mapping 48 bit Ethernet numbers to their ASCII representations or their corresponding host names, and vice versa.

The function ether_ntoa () converts a 48 bit Ethernet number pointed to by e to its standard ASCII representation; it returns a pointer to the ASCII string. The representation is of the form *x:x:x:x:x:x* where *x* is a hexadecimal number between 0 and ff. The function ether_aton () converts an ASCII string in the standard representation back to a 48 bit Ethernet number; the function returns NULL if the string cannot be scanned successfully.

The function ether_ntohost () maps an Ethernet number (pointed to by e) to its associated hostname. The string pointed to by hostname must be long enough to hold the hostname and a NULL character. The function returns zero upon success and non-zero upon failure. Inversely, the function ether_hostton () maps a hostname string to its corresponding Ethernet number; the function modifies the Ethernet number pointed to by e. The function also returns zero upon success and non-zero upon failure. The function ether_line () scans a line (pointed to by l) and sets the hostname and the Ethernet number (pointed to by e). The string pointed to by hostname must be long enough to hold the hostname and a NULL character. The function returns zero upon success and non-zero upon failure. The format of the scanned line is described by ethers(4).

FILES

/etc/ethers

SEE ALSO

ethers(4)

NAME
gethostent, gethostbyaddr, gethostbyname, sethostent, endhostent —
get network host entry

SYNOPSIS
```
#include <sys/types.h>
#include <sys/socket.h>
#include <netdb.h>

struct hostent *gethostent()

struct hostent *gethostbyaddr(addr, len, type)
char *addr;
int len, type;

struct hostent *gethostbyname(name)
char *name;

sethostent(stayopen)
int stayopen

endhostent()
```

DESCRIPTION
gethostent(), gethostbyaddr(), and gethostbyname() each return a pointer
to an object with the following structure containing the broken-out fields of a line
in the network host data base, /etc/hosts. In the case of gethostbyaddr(),
addr is a pointer to the binary format address of length *len* (not a character
string).

```
structhostent {
        char   *h_name;    /* official name of host */
        char   **h_aliases;/* alias list */
        int    h_addrtype; /* address type */
        int    h_length;   /* length of address */
        char   **h_addr_list;     /* list of addresses from name server */
};
```

The members of this structure are:

h_name	Official name of the host.
h_aliases	A zero terminated array of alternate names for the host.
h_addrtype	The type of address being returned; currently always **AF_INET**.
h_length	The length, in bytes, of the address.
h_addr_list	A pointer to a list of network addresses for the named host. Host addresses are returned in network byte order.

gethostent() reads the next line of the file, opening the file if necessary.

sethostent() opens and rewinds the file. If the *stayopen* flag is non-zero, the host data base will not be closed after each call to gethostent() (either directly, or indirectly through one of the other gethost calls).

endhostent() closes the file.

gethostbyname() and gethostbyaddr() sequentially search from the beginning of the file until a matching host name or host address is found, or until an EOF is encountered. Host addresses are supplied in network order.

gethostbyaddr() takes a pointer to an address structure. This structure is unique to each type of address. For addres of type **AF_INET** this is in_addr structure. See <netinet/in.h>.

FILES
/etc/hosts

SEE ALSO
hosts(4)

DIAGNOSTICS
A NULL pointer is returned on an EOF or error.

BUGS
All information is contained in a static area so it must be copied if it is to be saved. Only the Internet address format is currently understood.

NAME

getnetconfig – get network configuration database entry

SYNOPSIS

#include <netconfig.h>

void *
setnetconfig ()

struct netconfig *
getnetconfig (handlep)
void * handlep

int
endnetconfig (handlep)
void * handlep

struct netconfig *
getnetconfigent (netid)
        char * netid ;

int
freenetconfigent (netconfigp)
        struct netconfig * netconfigp ;

DESCRIPTION

The five library routines described on this page are part of the UNIX System V Network Selection component. They provide application access to the system network configuration database, /etc/netconfig. In addition to the netconfig database and the routines for accessing it, Network Selection includes the environment variable NETPATH (see environ(5)) and the NETPATH access routines described in getnetpath(3N).

A call to setnetconfig () has the effect of "binding" or "rewinding" the netconfig database. setnetconfig () must be called before the first call to get-netconfig () and may be called at any other time. setnetconfig () need *not* be called before a call to getnetconfigent (). setnetconfig () returns a unique handle to be used by getnetconfig ().

When first called, getnetconfig () returns a pointer to the current entry in the netconfig database, formatted as a struct netconfig. getnetconfig () can thus be used to search the entire netconfig file. getnetconfig () returns NULL at end of file.

endnetconfig () should be called when processing is complete to release resources for reuse. Programmers should be aware, however, that the last call to endnetconfig () frees all memory allocated by getnetconfig () for the struct netconfig data structure. endnetconfig () may not be called before set-netconfig (). endnetconfig () returns 0 on success and −1 on failure (e.g., if setnetconfig () was not called previously).

getnetconfigent (*netid*) returns a pointer to the struct netconfig structure corresponding to *netid*. It returns NULL if *netid* is invalid (i.e., does not name an entry in the netconfig database). It returns NULL and sets *errno* in case of failure (e.g., if setnetconfig () was not called previously).

freenetconfigent (*netconfigp*) frees the netconfig structure pointed to by *netconfigp* (previously returned by getnetconfigent()).

SEE ALSO

netconfig(4), getnetpath(3N), environ(5)
Network Programmer's Guide
System Administrator's Guide

NAME

getnetent, getnetbyaddr, getnetbyname, setnetent, endnetent – get network entry

SYNOPSIS

#include <netdb.h>

struct netent *getnetent ( )

struct netent *getnetbyname (name)
char *name;

struct netent *getnetbyaddr (net, type)
long net;
int type;

setnetent (stayopen)
int stayopen;

endnetent ( )

DESCRIPTION

getnetent ( ), getnetbyname ( ), and getnetbyaddr ( ) each return a pointer to an object with the following structure containing the broken-out fields of a line in the network data base, /etc/networks.

```
struct      netent {
        char *n_name;           /* official name of net */
        char **n_aliases;       /* alias list */
        int  n_addrtype;        /* net number type */
        long n_net;             /* net number */
};
```

The members of this structure are:

n_name   The official name of the network.

n_aliases   A zero terminated list of alternate names for the network.

n_addrtype The type of the network number returned; currently only AF_INET.

n_net   The network number. Network numbers are returned in machine byte order.

getnetent ( ) reads the next line of the file, opening the file if necessary.

setnetent ( ) opens and rewinds the file. If the *stayopen* flag is non-zero, the net data base will not be closed after each call to getnetent ( ) (either directly, or indirectly through one of the other getnet calls).

endnetent ( ) closes the file.

getnetbyname ( ) and getnetbyaddr ( ) sequentially search from the beginning of the file until a matching net name or net address and type is found, or until EOF is encountered. Network numbers are supplied in host order.

FILES

> `/etc/networks`

SEE ALSO

> `networks`(4)

DIAGNOSTICS

> A NULL pointer is returned on EOF or error.

BUGS

> All information is contained in a static area so it must be copied if it is to be saved.
>
> Only Internet network numbers are currently understood.

NAME

getnetpath – get /etc/netconfig entry corresponding to NETPATH component

SYNOPSIS

```
#include <netconfig.h>

void *
setnetpath()

struct netconfig *
getnetpath(handlep);
void * handlep;

int
endnetpath(handlep);
void * handlep;
```

DESCRIPTION

The three routines described on this page are part of the UNIX System V Network Selection component. They provide application access to the system network configuration database, /etc/netconfig, as it is "filtered" by the NETPATH environment variable (see environ(5)). Network Selection also includes routines that access the network configuration database directly (see getnetconfig(3N)).

A call to setnetpath() "binds" or "rewinds" NETPATH. setnetpath() must be called before the first call to getnetpath() and may be called at any other time. It returns a handle that is used by getnetpath. setnetpath() will fail if the netconfig database is not present. If NETPATH is unset, setnetpath() returns the number of "visible" networks in the netconfig file. The set of visible networks constitutes a default NETPATH.

When first called, getnetpath() returns a pointer to the netconfig database entry corresponding to the first valid NETPATH component. The netconfig entry is formatted as a struct netconfig. On each subsequent call, getnetpath returns a pointer to the netconfig entry that corresponds to the next valid NET-PATH component. getnetpath() can thus be used to search the netconfig database for all networks included in the NETPATH variable. When NETPATH has been exhausted, getnetpath() returns NULL.

getnetpath() silently ignores invalid NETPATH components. A NETPATH component is invalid if there is no corresponding entry in the netconfig database.

If the NETPATH variable is *unset*, getnetpath() behaves *as if* NETPATH were set to the sequence of "default" or "visible" networks in the netconfig database, in the order in which they are listed.

endnetpath() may be called to "unbind" NETPATH when processing is complete, releasing resources for reuse. Programmer's should be aware, however, that endnetpath() frees all memory allocated by setnetpath(). endnetpath() returns 0 on success and −1 on failure (e.g., if setnetpath() was not called previously).

SEE ALSO

netconfig(4), getnetconfig(3N), environ(5)
Network Programmer's Guide
System Administrator's Guide

NAME
getpeername – get name of connected peer

SYNOPSIS
```
int getpeername(s, name, namelen)
int s;
struct sockaddr *name;
int *namelen;
```

DESCRIPTION
getpeername() returns the name of the peer connected to socket s. The int pointed to by the *namelen* parameter should be initialized to indicate the amount of space pointed to by *name*. On return it contains the actual size of the name returned(in bytes). The name is truncated if the buffer provided is too small.

RETURN VALUE
0 is returned if the call succeeds, −1 if it fails.

ERRORS
The call succeeds unless:

EBADF	The argument s is not a valid descriptor.
ENOTSOCK	The argument s is a file, not a socket.
ENOTCONN	The socket is not connected.
ENOMEM	There was insufficient user memory for the operation to complete.
ENOSR	There were insufficient STREAMS resources available for the operation to complete.

SEE ALSO
accept(3N), bind(3N), getsockname(3N), socket(3N)

NAME

getprotoent, getprotobynumber, getprotobyname, setprotoent, endpro-
toent – get protocol entry

SYNOPSIS

```
#include <netdb.h>

struct protoent *getprotoent()

struct protoent *getprotobyname(name)
char *name;

struct protoent *getprotobynumber(proto)
int proto;

setprotoent(stayopen)
int stayopen;

endprotoent()
```

DESCRIPTION

getprotoent(), getprotobyname(), and getprotobynumber() each return a
pointer to an object with the following structure containing the broken-out fields
of a line in the network protocol data base, /etc/protocols.

```
struct      protoent {
     char *p_name;        /* official name of protocol */
     char **p_aliases;    /* alias list */
     int  p_proto;        /* protocol number */
};
```

The members of this structure are:

p_name	The official name of the protocol.
p_aliases	A zero terminated list of alternate names for the protocol.
p_proto	The protocol number.

getprotoent() reads the next line of the file, opening the file if necessary.

setprotoent() opens and rewinds the file. If the *stayopen* flag is non-zero, the
net data base will not be closed after each call to getprotoent() (either directly,
or indirectly through one of the other getproto calls).

endprotoent() closes the file.

getprotobyname() and getprotobynumber() sequentially search from the
beginning of the file until a matching protocol name or protocol number is found,
or until an EOF is encountered.

FILES

/etc/protocols

SEE ALSO

protocols(4)

DIAGNOSTICS

A NULL pointer is returned on an EOF or error.

All information is contained in a static area so it must be copied if it is to be saved. Only the Internet protocols are currently understood.

NAME

getservent, getservbyport, getservbyname, setservent, endservent –
get service entry

SYNOPSIS

```
#include <netdb.h>

struct servent *getservent()

struct servent *getservbyname(name, proto)
char *name, *proto;

struct servent *getservbyport(port, proto)
int port;
char *proto;

setservent(stayopen)
int stayopen;

endservent()
```

DESCRIPTION

getservent(), *getservbyname()*, and *getservbyport()* each return a pointer to an
object with the following structure containing the broken-out fields of a line in
the network services data base, /etc/services.

```
struct      servent {
        char *s_name;           /* official name of service */
        char **s_aliases;       /* alias list */
        int  s_port;            /* port service resides at */
        char *s_proto;          /* protocol to use */
};
```

The members of this structure are:

s_name	The official name of the service.
s_aliases	A zero terminated list of alternate names for the service.
s_port	The port number at which the service resides. Port numbers are returned in network short byte order.
s_proto	The name of the protocol to use when contacting the service.

getservent() reads the next line of the file, opening the file if necessary.

setservent() opens and rewinds the file. If the *stayopen* flag is non-zero, the
net data base will not be closed after each call to getservent() (either directly,
or indirectly through one of the other getserv calls).

endservent() closes the file.

getservbyname() and getservbyport() sequentially search from the beginning
of the file until a matching protocol name or port number is found, or until EOF
is encountered. If a protocol name is also supplied (non-NULL), searches must
also match the protocol.

FILES
>   /etc/services

SEE ALSO
>   getprotoent(3N), services(4)

DIAGNOSTICS
>   A NULL pointer is returned on EOF or error.
>
>   All information is contained in a static area so it must be copied if it is to be
>   saved. Expecting port numbers to fit in a 32 bit quantity is probably naive.

NAME
getsockname – get socket name

SYNOPSIS
```
getsockname(s, name, namelen)
int s;
struct sockaddr *name;
int *namelen;
```

DESCRIPTION
getsockname() returns the current *name* for socket *s*. The *namelen* parameter should be initialized to indicate the amount of space pointed to by *name*. On return it contains the actual size of the name returned(in bytes).

RETURN VALUE
0 is returned if the call succeeds; –1 if it fails.

ERRORS
The call succeeds unless:

EBADF	The argument *s* is not a valid descriptor.
ENOTSOCK	The argument *s* is a file, not a socket.
ENOMEM	There was insufficient user memory for the operation to complete.
ENOSR	There were insufficient STREAMS resources available for the operation to complete.

SEE ALSO
bind(3N), getpeername(3N), socket(3N)

NAME

getsockopt, setsockopt – get and set options on sockets

SYNOPSIS

```
#include <sys/types.h>
#include <sys/socket.h>

int getsockopt(s, level, optname, optval, optlen)
int s, level, optname;
char *optval;
int *optlen;

int setsockopt(s, level, optname, optval, optlen)
int s, level, optname;
char *optval;
int optlen;
```

DESCRIPTION

getsockopt() and setsockopt() manipulate *options* associated with a socket. Options may exist at multiple protocol levels; they are always present at the uppermost socket level.

When manipulating socket options, the level at which the option resides and the name of the option must be specified. To manipulate options at the socket level, *level* is specified as SOL_SOCKET. To manipulate options at any other level, *level* is the protocol number of the protocol that controls the option. For example, to indicate that an option is to be interpreted by the TCP protocol, *level* is set to the TCP protocol number [see getprotoent(3N)].

The parameters *optval* and *optlen* are used to access option values for set‐sockopt(). For getsockopt(), they identify a buffer in which the value(s) for the requested option(s) are to be returned. For getsockopt(), *optlen* is a value-result parameter, initially containing the size of the buffer pointed to by *optval*, and modified on return to indicate the actual size of the value returned. If no option value is to be supplied or returned, a 0 *optval* may be supplied.

optname and any specified options are passed uninterpreted to the appropriate protocol module for interpretation. The include file /usr/include/sys/socket.h contains definitions for the socket-level options described below. Options at other protocol levels vary in format and name.

Most socket-level options take an *int* for *optval*. For setsockopt(), the *optval* parameter should be non-zero to enable a boolean option, or zero if the option is to be disabled. SO_LINGER uses a struct linger parameter that specifies the desired state of the option and the linger interval (see below). struct linger is defined in /usr/include/sys/socket.h.

The following options are recognized at the socket level. Except as noted, each may be examined with getsockopt() and set with setsockopt().

SO_DEBUG	toggle recording of debugging information
SO_REUSEADDR	toggle local address reuse

SO_KEEPALIVE	toggle keep connections alive
SO_DONTROUTE	toggle routing bypass for outgoing messages
SO_LINGER	linger on close if data is present
SO_BROADCAST	toggle permission to transmit broadcast messages
SO_OOBINLINE	toggle reception of out-of-band data in band
SO_SNDBUF	set buffer size for output
SO_RCVBUF	set buffer size for input
SO_TYPE	get the type of the socket(get only)
SO_ERROR	get and clear error on the socket(get only)

SO_DEBUG enables debugging in the underlying protocol modules. SO_REUSEADDR indicates that the rules used in validating addresses supplied in a bind(3N) call should allow reuse of local addresses. SO_KEEPALIVE enables the periodic transmission of messages on a connected socket. If the connected party fails to respond to these messages, the connection is considered broken and processes using the socket are notified using a SIGPIPE signal. SO_DONTROUTE indicates that outgoing messages should bypass the standard routing facilities. Instead, messages are directed to the appropriate network interface according to the network portion of the destination address.

SO_LINGER controls the action taken when unsent messages are queued on a socket and a close(2) is performed. If the socket promises reliable delivery of data and SO_LINGER is set, the system will block the process on the close() attempt until it is able to transmit the data or until it decides it is unable to deliver the information (a timeout period, termed the linger interval, is specified in the setsockopt() call when SO_LINGER is requested). If SO_LINGER is disabled and a close() is issued, the system will process the close() in a manner that allows the process to continue as quickly as possible.

The option SO_BROADCAST requests permission to send broadcast datagrams on the socket. With protocols that support out-of-band data, the SO_OOBINLINE option requests that out-of-band data be placed in the normal data input queue as received; it will then be accessible with recv() or read() calls without the MSG_OOB flag. SO_SNDBUF and SO_RCVBUF are options that adjust the normal buffer sizes allocated for output and input buffers, respectively. The buffer size may be increased for high-volume connections or may be decreased to limit the possible backlog of incoming data. The system places an absolute limit on these values. Finally, SO_TYPE and SO_ERROR are options used only with getsockopt(). SO_TYPE returns the type of the socket (for example, SOCK_STREAM). It is useful for servers that inherit sockets on startup. SO_ERROR returns any pending error on the socket and clears the error status. It may be used to check for asynchronous errors on connected datagram sockets or for other asynchronous errors.

RETURN VALUE

A 0 is returned if the call succeeds, −1 if it fails.

ERRORS

The call succeeds unless:

EBADF	The argument *s* is not a valid descriptor.
ENOTSOCK	The argument *s* is a file, not a socket.
ENOPROTOOPT	The option is unknown at the level indicated.
ENOMEM	There was insufficient user memory available for the operation to complete.
ENOSR	There were insufficient STREAMS resources available for the operation to complete.

SEE ALSO

ioctl(2), socket(3N), getprotoent(3N).

NAME

inet: inet_addr, inet_network, inet_makeaddr, inet_lnaof, inet_netof, inet_ntoa − Internet address manipulation

SYNOPSIS

```
#include <sys/types.h>
#include <sys/socket.h>
#include <netinet/in.h>
#include <arpa/inet.h>

unsigned long
inet_addr(cp)
char *cp;

inet_network(cp)
char *cp;

struct in_addr
inet_makeaddr(net, lna)
int net, lna;

inet_lnaof(in)
struct in_addr in;

inet_netof(in)
struct in_addr in;

char *
inet_ntoa(in)
struct in_addr in;
```

DESCRIPTION

The routines inet_addr() and inet_network() each interpret character strings representing numbers expressed in the Internet standard '.' notation, returning numbers suitable for use as Internet addresses and Internet network numbers, respectively. The routine inet_makeaddr() takes an Internet network number and a local network address and constructs an Internet address from it. The routines inet_netof() and inet_lnaof() break apart Internet host addresses, returning the network number and local network address part, respectively.

The routine inet_ntoa() returns a pointer to a string in the base 256 notation d.d.d.d described below.

All Internet addresses are returned in network order (bytes ordered from left to right). All network numbers and local address parts are returned as machine format integer values.

INTERNET ADDRESSES

Values specified using the '.' notation take one of the following forms:

```
a.b.c.d
a.b.c
a.b
a
```

When four parts are specified, each is interpreted as a byte of data and assigned, from left to right, to the four bytes of an Internet address.

When a three part address is specified, the last part is interpreted as a 16-bit quantity and placed in the right most two bytes of the network address. This makes the three part address format convenient for specifying Class B network addresses as 128.net.host.

When a two part address is supplied, the last part is interpreted as a 24-bit quantity and placed in the right most three bytes of the network address. This makes the two part address format convenient for specifying Class A network addresses as net.host.

When only one part is given, the value is stored directly in the network address without any byte rearrangement.

All numbers supplied as parts in a '.' notation may be decimal, octal, or hexadecimal, as specified in the C language (that is, a leading 0x or 0X implies hexadecimal; otherwise, a leading 0 implies octal; otherwise, the number is interpreted as decimal).

SEE ALSO
gethostent(3N), getnetent(3N), hosts(4), networks(4)

DIAGNOSTICS
The value −1 is returned by inet_addr() and inet_network() for malformed requests.

BUGS
The problem of host byte ordering versus network byte ordering is confusing. A simple way to specify Class C network addresses in a manner similar to that for Class B and Class A is needed.

The return value from inet_ntoa() points to static information which is overwritten in each call.

NAME
listen – listen for connections on a socket

SYNOPSIS
listen(s, backlog)
int s, backlog;

DESCRIPTION
To accept connections, a socket is first created with socket(2), a backlog for incoming connections is specified with listen() and then the connections are accepted with accept(2). The listen() call applies only to sockets of type SOCK_STREAM or SOCK_SEQPACKET.

The *backlog* parameter defines the maximum length the queue of pending connections may grow to. If a connection request arrives with the queue full, the client will receive an error with an indication of ECONNREFUSED.

RETURN VALUE
A 0 return value indicates success; −1 indicates an error.

ERRORS
The call fails if:

EBADF	The argument *s* is not a valid descriptor.
ENOTSOCK	The argument *s* is not a socket.
EOPNOTSUPP	The socket is not of a type that supports the operation listen.

NOTES
There is currently no *backlog* limit.

NAME

netdir_getbyname, netdir_getbyaddr, netdir_free, netdir_mergeaddr, taddr2uaddr, uaddr2taddr, netdir_perror, netdir_sperror − generic transport name-to-address translation

SYNOPSIS

```
#include <netdir.h>

int
netdir_getbyname(config, service, addrs)
     struct netconfig  *config;
     struct nd_hostserv  *service;
     struct nd_addrlist  **addrs;

int
netdir_getbyaddr(config, service, netaddr)
     struct netconfig  *config;
     struct nd_hostservlist  **service;
     struct netbuf  *netaddr;

void
netdir_free(ptr, ident)
     void *ptr;
     int ident;

int
netdir_mergeaddr(config, mrg_uaddr, s_uaddr, c_uaddr)
     struct netconfig  *config;
     char  **mrg_uaddr, *s_uaddr, *c_uaddr;

char *
taddr2uaddr(config, addr)
     struct netconfig  *config;
     struct netbuf  *addr;

struct netbuf *
uaddr2taddr(config, uaddr)
     struct netconfig  *config;
     char  *uaddr;

int
netdir_options(netconfig, option, fd, pointer_to_args)
     struct netconfig  *netconfig;
     int  option;
     int fd;
     char  *point_to_args;

void
netdir_perror(s)
char  *s;

char *
netdir_sperror()
```

DESCRIPTION

These routines provide a generic interface for name-to-address mapping that will work with a all transport protocols. This interface provides a generic way for programs to convert transport specific addresses into common structures and back again.

The `netdir_getbyname()` routine maps the machine name and service name in the `nd_hostserv` structure to a collection of addresses of the type understood by the transport identified in the `netconfig` structure. This routine returns all addresses that are valid for that transport in the `nd_addrlist` structure. The `nd_hostserv` and `nd_addrlist` structures have the following elements. The `netconfig` structure is described on the `netconfig`(4) manual page.

```
struct nd_addrlist
      int n_cnt
      struct netbuf   *n_addrs;
struct nd_hostserv
      char   *h_host;
      char   *h_serv;
```

`netdir_getbyname()` accepts some special-case host names. These host names are hints to the underlying mapping routines that define the intent of the request. This information is required for some transport provider developers to provide the correct information back to the caller. The host names are defined in `/usr/include/netdir.h`. The currently defined host names are:

HOST_SELF   Represents the address to which local programs will bind their endpoints. HOST_SELF differs from the host name provided by gethostname(3), which represents the address to which *remote* programs will bind their endpoints.

HOST_ANY   Represents any host accessible by this transport provider. HOST_ANY allows applications to specify a required service without specifying a particular host name.

HOST_BROADCAST
             Represents the address for all hosts accessible by this transport provider. Network requests to this address will be received by all machines.

All fields of the nd_hostserv structure must be initialized.

To find all available transports, call the `netdir_getbyname()` routine with each `struct netconfig` structure returned by the getnetpath(3N) call.

The `netdir_getbyaddr()` routine maps addresses to service names. This routine returns a list of host and service pairs that would yield this address. If more than one tuple of host and service name is returned then the first tuple contains the preferred host and service names.

```
struct nd_hostservlist
      int   *h_cnt;
      struct hostserv   *h_hostservs;
```

The `netdir_free()` structure is used to free the structures allocated by the name to address translation routines.

The `netdir_mergeaddr()` routine is used by a network service to return an optimized network addresses to a client. This routine takes the universal address of the endpoint that the service has bound to, which is pointed to by the *s_uaddr* parameter, and the address of the endpoint that a request came in on, which is pointed to by the *c_uaddr* paramter, to create an optimized address for communication with the service. The service address should be an address returned by the `netdir_getbyname()` call, specified with the special host name HOST_SELF.

The `taddr2uaddr()` and `uaddr2taddr()` routines support translation between universal addresses and TLI type netbufs. The take and return character string pointers. The `taddr2uaddr()` routine returns a pointer to a string that contains the universal address and returns NULL if the conversion is not possible. This is not a fatal condition as some transports may not suppose a universal address form.

option, *fd*, and *pointer_to_args* are passed to the `netdir_options` routine for the transport specified in `netconfigp`. There are four values for *option*:

          ND_SET_BROADCAST
          ND_SET_RESERVEDPORT
          ND_CHECK_RESERVEDPORT
          ND_MERGEADDR

If a transport provider does not support an option, `netdir_options` returns −1 and sets `_nderror` to ND_NOCTRL.

The specific actions of each option follow.

ND_SET_BROADCAST   Sets the transport provider up to allow broadcast, if the transport supports broadcast. *fd* is a file descriptor into the transport (i.e., the result of a t_open of /dev/udp). *pointer_to_args* is not used. If this completes, broadcast operations may be performed on file descriptor *fd*.

ND_SET_RESERVEDPORT
                    Allows the application to bind to a reserved port, if that concept exists for the transport provider. *fd* is a file descriptor into the transport (it must not be bound to an address). If *pointer_to_args* is NULL, *fd* will be bound to a reserved port. If *pointer_to_args* is a pointer to a netbuf structure, an attempt will be made to bind to a reserved port on the specified address.

ND_CHECK_RESERVEDPORT
                    Used to verify that an address corresponds to a reserved port, if that concept exists for the transport provider. *fd* is not used. *pointer_to_args* is a pointer to a netbuf structure that contains an address. This option returns 0 only if the address specified in *pointer_to_args* is reserved.

ND_MERGEADDR   Used to take a "local address" (like the 0.0.0.0 address that TCP uses) and return a "real address" that client machines can connect to. *fd* is not used. *pointer_to_args* is a pointer to a **struct** nd_mergearg, which has the following form:

```
struct nd_mergearg {
        char *s_uaddr;   /* server's universal address */
        char *c_uaddr;   /* client's universal address */
        char *m_uaddr;   /* the result */
}
```

s_uaddr is something like 0.0.0.0.1.12, and, if the call is successful, m_uaddr will be set to something like 192.11.109.89.1.12. For most transports, m_uaddr is exactly what s_uaddr is.

The netdir_perror() routine prints an error message on the standard output stating why one of the name-to-address mapping routines failed. The error message is preceded by the string given as an argument.

The netdir_sperror() routine returns a string containing an error message stating why one of the name-to-address mapping routines failed.

SEE ALSO
getnetpath(3N)

NAME
nlsgetcall – get client's data passed via the listener

SYNOPSIS
#include <sys/tiuser.h>

struct t_call *nlsgetcall (int fd);

DESCRIPTION
nlsgetcall allows server processes started by the listener process to access the client's t_call structure, that is, the *sndcall* argument of t_connect(3N).

The t_call structure returned by nlsgetcall can be released using t_free(3N).

nlsgetcall returns the address of an allocated t_call structure or NULL if a t_call structure cannot be allocated. If the t_alloc succeeds, undefined environment variables are indicated by a negative *len* field in the appropriate netbuf structure. A *len* field of zero in the netbuf structure is valid and means that the original buffer in the listener's t_call structure was NULL.

WARNING
The *len* field in the netbuf structure is defined as being unsigned. In order to check for error returns, it should first be cast to an int.

The listener process limits the amount of user data (*udata*) and options data (*opt*) to 128 bytes each. Address data *addr* is limited to 64 bytes. If the original data was longer, no indication of overflow is given.

DIAGNOSTICS
A NULL pointer is returned if a t_call structure cannot be allocated by t_alloc. t_errno can be inspected for further error information. Undefined environment variables are indicated by a negative length field (*len*) in the appropriate netbuf structure.

FILES
/usr/lib/libnsl_s.a
/usr/lib/libslan.a
/usr/lib/libnls.a

SEE ALSO
nlsadmin(1), getenv(3), t_connect(3N), t_alloc(3N), t_free(3N), t_error(3N).

NOTES
Server processes must call t_sync(3N) before calling this routine.

NAME
       nlsprovider – get name of transport provider

SYNOPSIS
       char *nlsprovider();

DESCRIPTION
       nlsprovider returns a pointer to a null terminated character string which con-
       tains the name of the transport provider as placed in the environment by the
       listener process. If the variable is not defined in the environment, a NULL pointer
       is returned.

       The environment variable is only available to server processes started by the
       listener process.

SEE ALSO
       nlsadmin(1M).

DIAGNOSTICS
       If the variable is not defined in the environment, a NULL pointer is returned.

FILES
       /usr/lib/libslan.a (7300)
       /usr/lib/libnls.a (3B2 Computer)
       /usr/lib/libnsl_s.a

NAME
nlsrequest – format and send listener service request message

SYNOPSIS
#include <listen.h>

int nlsrequest (int fd, char *service_code);

extern int _nlslog, t_errno;
extern char *_nlsrmsg;

DESCRIPTION
Given a virtual circuit to a listener process (*fd*) and a service code of a server process, nlsrequest formats and sends a *service request message* to the remote listener
process requesting that it start the given service. nlsrequest waits for the remote
listener process to return a *service request response message*, which is made available
to the caller in the static, null terminated data buffer pointed to by _nlsrmsg.
The *service request response message* includes a success or failure code and a text
message. The entire message is printable.

SEE ALSO
nlsadmin(1), t_error(3).

FILES
/usr/lib/libnls.a
/usr/lib/libslan.a
/usr/lib/libnsl_s.a

DIAGNOSTICS
The success or failure code is the integer return code from nlsrequest. Zero
indicates success, other negative values indicate nlsrequest failures as follows:

-1: Error encountered by nlsrequest, see t_errno.

Postive values are error return codes from the *listener* process. Mnemonics for
these codes are defined in <listen.h>.

2: Request message not interpretable.
3: Request service code unknown.
4: Service code known, but currently disabled.

If non-null, _nlsrmsg contains a pointer to a static, null terminated character
buffer containing the *service request response message*. Note that both _nlsrmsg
and the data buffer are overwritten by each call to nlsrequest.

If _nlslog is non-zero, nlsrequest prints error messages on stderr. Initially,
_nlslog is zero.

WARNING
nlsrequest cannot always be certain that the remote server process has been
successfully started. In this case, nlsrequest returns with no indication of an
error and the caller will receive notification of a disconnect event via a T_LOOK
error before or during the first t_snd or t_rcv call.

NAME
publickey: getpublickey, getsecretkey – retrieve public or secret key

SYNOPSIS
```
#include <rpc/rpc.h>
#include <rpc/key_prot.h>

getpublickey(const char netname[MAXNETNAMELEN],
    char publickey[HEXKEYBYTES]);

getsecretkey(const char netname[MAXNETNAMELEN],
    char secretkey[HEXKEYBYTES], const char *passwd);
```

DESCRIPTION
getpublickey and getsecretkey get public and secret keys for *netname* from the publickey(4) database.

getsecretkey has an extra argument, *passwd*, used to decrypt the encrypted secret key stored in the database.

Both routines return 1 if they are successful in finding the key, 0 otherwise. The keys are returned as NULL-terminated, hexadecimal strings. If the password supplied to getsecretkey fails to decrypt the secret key, the routine will return 1 but the *secretkey* argument will be a NULL string.

SEE ALSO
publickey(4).

NAME

recv, recvfrom, recvmsg – receive a message from a socket

SYNOPSIS

```
#include <sys/types.h>
#include <sys/socket.h>

int recv(s, buf, len, flags)
int s;
char *buf;
int len, flags;

int recvfrom(s, buf, len, flags, from, fromlen)
int s;
char *buf;
int len, flags;
struct sockaddr *from;
int *fromlen;

int recvmsg(s, msg, flags)
int s;
struct msghdr *msg;
int flags;
```

DESCRIPTION

s is a socket created with socket(3N). recv(), recvfrom(), and recvmsg() are used to receive messages from another socket. recv() may be used only on a *connected* socket (see connect(3N)), while recvfrom() and recvmsg() may be used to receive data on a socket whether it is in a connected state or not.

If *from* is not a NULL pointer, the source address of the message is filled in. *fromlen* is a value-result parameter, initialized to the size of the buffer associated with *from*, and modified on return to indicate the actual size of the address stored there. The length of the message is returned. If a message is too long to fit in the supplied buffer, excess bytes may be discarded depending on the type of socket the message is received from (see socket(3N)).

If no messages are available at the socket, the receive call waits for a message to arrive, unless the socket is nonblocking (see fcntl(2)) in which case −1 is returned with the external variable errno set to EWOULDBLOCK.

The select() call may be used to determine when more data arrives.

The *flags* parameter is formed by ORing one or more of the following:

MSG_OOB   Read any out-of-band data present on the socket rather than the regular in-band data.

MSG_PEEK   Peek at the data present on the socket; the data is returned, but not consumed, so that a subsequent receive operation will see the same data.

The recvmsg() call uses a msghdr structure to minimize the number of directly supplied parameters. This structure is defined in /usr/include/sys/socket.h and includes the following members:

```
caddr_t        msg_name;            /* optional address */
int            msg_namelen;         /* size of address */
struct iovec   *msg_iov;            /* scatter/gather array */
int            msg_iovlen;          /* # elements in msg_iov */
caddr_t        msg_accrights;       /* access rights sent/received */
int            msg_accrightslen;
```

Here msg_name and msg_namelen specify the destination address if the socket is unconnected; msg_name may be given as a NULL pointer if no names are desired or required. The msg_iov and msg_iovlen describe the scatter-gather locations, as described in read(2). A buffer to receive any access rights sent along with the message is specified in msg_accrights, which has length msg_accrightslen.

RETURN VALUE

These calls return the number of bytes received, or −1 if an error occurred.

ERRORS

The calls fail if:

EBADF   s is an invalid descriptor.

ENOTSOCK   s is a descriptor for a file, not a socket.

EINTR   The operation was interrupted by delivery of a signal before any data was available to be received.

EWOULDBLOCK   The socket is marked non-blocking and the requested operation would block.

ENOMEM   There was insufficient user memory available for the operation to complete.

ENOSR   There were insufficient STREAMS resouces available for the operation to complete.

SEE ALSO

connect(3N),   fcntl(2),   getsockopt(3N),   ioctl(2),   read(2),   send(3N), socket(3N).

NAME

resolver, res_mkquery, res_send, res_init, dn_comp, dn_expand – resolver routines

SYNOPSIS

```
#include <sys/types.h>
#include <netinet/in.h>
#include <arpa/nameser.h>
#include <resolv.h>

res_mkquery(op, dname, class, type, data, datalen, newrr, buf, buflen)
int op;
char *dname;
int class, type;
char *data;
int datalen;
struct rrec *newrr;
char *buf;
int buflen;

res_send(msg, msglen, answer, anslen)
char *msg;
int msglen;
char *answer;
int anslen;

res_init

dn_comp(exp_dn, comp_dn, length, dnptrs, lastdnptr)
char *exp_dn, *comp_dn;
int length;
char **dnptrs, **lastdnptr;

dn_expand(msg, msglen, comp_dn, exp_dn, length)
char *msg, *comp_dn, exp_dn;
int  msglen, length;
```

DESCRIPTION

These routines are used for making, sending and interpreting packets to Internet domain name servers. Global information that is used by the resolver routines is kept in the variable _res. Most of the values have reasonable defaults and can be ignored. Options are a simple bit mask and are OR'ed in to enable. Options stored in _res.options are defined in /usr/include/resolv.h and are as follows.

RES_INIT   True if the initial name server address and default domain name are initialized (that is, res_init has been called).

RES_DEBUG   Print debugging messages.

RES_AAONLY   Accept authoritative answers only. res_send will continue until it finds an authoritative answer or finds an error. Currently this is not implemented.

| RES_USEVC | Use TCP connections for queries instead of UDP. |

RES_STAYOPEN — Used with RES_USEVC to keep the TCP connection open between queries. This is useful only in programs that regularly do many queries. UDP should be the normal mode used.

RES_IGNTC — Unused currently (ignore truncation errors, that is, do not retry with TCP).

RES_RECURSE — Set the recursion desired bit in queries. This is the default. **res_send** does not do iterative queries and expects the name server to handle recursion.

RES_DEFNAMES — Append the default domain name to single label queries. This is the default.

res_init reads the initialization file to get the default domain name and the Internet address of the initial hosts running the name server. If this line does not exist, the host running the resolver is tried. **res_mkquery** makes a standard query message and places it in *buf*. **res_mkquery** will return the size of the query or −1 if the query is larger than *buflen*. *op* is usually QUERY but can be any of the query types defined in /usr/include/arpa/nameser.h. *dname* is the domain name. If *dname* consists of a single label and the RES_DEFNAMES flag is enabled (the default), *dname* will be appended with the current domain name. The current domain name is defined in a system file and can be overridden by the environment variable LOCALDOMAIN. *newrr* is currently unused but is intended for making update messages.

res_send sends a query to name servers and returns an answer. It will call **res_init** if RES_INIT is not set, send the query to the local name server, and handle timeouts and retries. The length of the message is returned or −1 if there were errors.

dn_expand expands the compressed domain name *comp_dn* to a full domain name. Expanded names are converted to upper case. *msg* is a pointer to the beginning of the message, *exp_dn* is a pointer to a buffer of size *length* for the result. The size of compressed name is returned or −1 if there was an error.

dn_comp compresses the domain name *exp_dn* and stores it in *comp_dn*. The size of the compressed name is returned or −1 if there were errors. *length* is the size of the array pointed to by *comp_dn*. *dnptrs* is a list of pointers to previously compressed names in the current message. The first pointer points to to the beginning of the message and the list ends with NULL. *lastdnptr* is a pointer to the end of the array pointed to *dnptrs*. A side effect is to update the list of pointers for labels inserted into the message by **dn_comp** as the name is compressed. If *dnptr* is NULL, do not try to compress names. If *lastdnptr* is NULL, do not update the list.

FILES

/usr/include/arpa/nameserv.h
/usr/include/netinet/in.h

```
/usr/include/resolv.h
/usr/include/sys/types.h
/etc/resolv.conf
/usr/lib/libresolv.a
```

SEE ALSO

named(1M), resolv.conf(4).

NOTES

/usr/lib/libresolv.a is necessary for compiling programs.

Programs must be loaded with the option −lresolv.

NAME

rexec – return stream to a remote command

SYNOPSIS

```
rem = rexec(ahost, inport, user, passwd, cmd, fd2p);
char **ahost;
u_short inport;
char *user, *passwd, *cmd;
int *fd2p;
```

DESCRIPTION

rexec( ) looks up the host *ahost* using **gethostbyname** [see **gethostent**(3N)], returning −1 if the host does not exist. Otherwise *ahost* is set to the standard name of the host. If a username and password are both specified, then these are used to authenticate to the foreign host; otherwise the environment and then the user's .netrc file in his home directory are searched for appropriate information. If all this fails, the user is prompted for the information.

The port inport specifies which well-known DARPA Internet port to use for the connection. The protocol for connection is described in detail in **rexecd**(1M).

If the call succeeds, a socket of type SOCK_STREAM is returned to the caller, and given to the remote command as its standard input and standard output. If *fd2p* is non-zero, then a auxiliary channel to a control process will be setup, and a descriptor for it will be placed in *fd2p*. The control process will return diagnostic output from the command (unit 2) on this channel, and will also accept bytes on this channel as signal numbers, to be forwarded to the process group of the command. If *fd2p* is 0, then the standard error (unit 2 of the remote command) will be made the same as its standard output and no provision is made for sending arbitrary signals to the remote process, although you may be able to get its attention by using out-of-band data.

SEE ALSO

gethostent(3N), getservent(3N), rcmd(3N), rexecd(1M).

NOTES

There is no way to specify options to the socket( ) call that rexec( ) makes.

NAME

rpc – library routines for remote procedure calls

DESCRIPTION

RPC routines allow C language programs to make procedure calls on other machines across a network. First, the client calls a procedure to send a data packet to the server. On receipt of the packet, the server calls a dispatch routine to perform the requested service, and then sends back a reply.

The following sections describe data objects use by the RPC package.

Nettype

Some of the high-level RPC interface routines take a *nettype* string as one of the parameters [for example, clnt_create, svc_create, rpc_reg, rpc_call]. This string defines a class of transports which can be used for a particular application. The transports are tried in left to right order in the **NETPATH** variable or in top to down order in the /etc/netconfig file.

nettype can be one of the following:

netpath   Choose from the transports which have been indicated by their token names in the **NETPATH** variable. If **NETPATH** is unset or **NULL**, it defaults to visible. netpath is the default *nettype*.

visible   Choose the transports which have the visible flag (v) set in the /etc/netconfig file.

circuit_v   This is same as visible except that it chooses only the connection oriented transports from the entries in /etc/netconfig file.

datagram_v   This is same as visible except that it chooses only the connectionless datagram transports from the entries in /etc/netconfig file.

circuit_n   This is same as netpath except that it chooses only the connection oriented datagram transports

datagram_n   This is same as netpath except that it chooses only the connectionless datagram transports.

udp   It refers to Internet UDP.

tcp   It refers to Internet TCP.

raw   This is for memory based RPC, mainly for performance evaluation.

If *nettype* is **NULL**, it defaults to netpath.

Data Structures
Some of the data structures used by the RPC package are shown below.

The AUTH Structure
```
union des_block {
    struct {
        u_int32 high;
        u_int32 low;
    } key;
    char c[8];
};
typedef union des_block des_block;
extern bool_t xdr_des_block();

/*
 * Authentication info. Opaque to client.
 */
struct opaque_auth {
    enum_t  oa_flavor;  /* flavor of auth */
    caddr_t oa_base;    /* address of more auth stuff */
    u_int   oa_length;  /* not to exceed MAX_AUTH_BYTES */
};

/*
 * Auth handle, interface to client side authenticators.
 */
typedef struct {
    struct  opaque_auth  ah_cred;
    struct  opaque_auth  ah_verf;
    union   des_block    ah_key;
    struct auth_ops {
        void (*ah_nextverf)();
        int  (*ah_marshal)();   /* nextverf & serialize */
        int  (*ah_validate)();  /* validate varifier */
        int  (*ah_refresh)();   /* refresh credentials */
        void (*ah_destroy)();   /* destroy this structure */
    } *ah_ops;
    caddr_t ah_private;
} AUTH;
```

The CLIENT Structure
```
/*
 * Client rpc handle.
 * Created by individual implementations
 * Client is responsible for initializing auth, see e.g. auth_none.c.
 */
typedef struct {
    AUTH            *cl_auth;            /* authenticator */
    struct clnt_ops {
        enum clnt_stat  (*cl_call)();   /* call remote procedure */
        void            (*cl_abort)();  /* abort a call */
        void            (*cl_geterr)(); /* get specific error code */
        bool_t          (*cl_freeres)();/* frees results */
        void            (*cl_destroy)();/* destroy this structure */
        bool_t          (*cl_control)();/* the ioctl() of rpc */
```

```
          } *cl_ops;
          caddr_t           cl_private;              /* private stuff */
          char              *cl_netid;               /* network token */
          char              *cl_tp;                  /* device name */
     } CLIENT;
```

The SVCXPRT Structure

```
     enum xprt_stat {
         XPRT_DIED,
         XPRT_MOREREQS,
         XPRT_IDLE
     };

     /*
      * Server side transport handle
      */
     typedef struct {
         int               xp_fd;
#define xp_sock               xp_fd
#endif
         u_short           xp_port;                  /* associated port number.
                                                       * Obsolete, but still used to
                                                       * specify whether rendezvouser
                                                       * or normal connection
                                                       */

         struct xp_ops {
             bool_t        (*xp_recv)();             /* receive incoming requests */
             enum xprt_stat (*xp_stat)();            /* get transport status */
             bool_t        (*xp_getargs)();          /* get arguments */
             bool_t        (*xp_reply)();            /* send reply */
             bool_t        (*xp_freeargs)();         /* free mem allocated for args */
             void          (*xp_destroy)();          /* destroy this struct */
         } *xp_ops;
         int          xp_addrlen;                    /* length of remote addr. Obsolete */
         char         *xp_tp;                        /* transport provider device name */
         char         *xp_netid;                     /* network token */
         struct netbuf     xp_ltaddr;                /* local transport address */
         struct netbuf     xp_rtaddr;                /* remote transport address */
         char              xp_raddr[16];             /* remote address. Obsolete */
         struct opaque_auth xp_verf;                 /* raw response verifier */
         caddr_t           xp_p1;                    /* private: for use by svc ops */
         caddr_t           xp_p2;                    /* private: for use by svc ops */
         caddr_t           xp_p3;                    /* private: for use by svc lib */
     } SVCXPRT;
```

The XDR Structure

```
     /*
      * Xdr operations.  XDR_ENCODE causes the type to be encoded into the
      * stream.  XDR_DECODE causes the type to be extracted from the stream.
      * XDR_FREE can be used to release the space allocated by an XDR_DECODE
      * request.
      */
     enum xdr_op {
         XDR_ENCODE=0,
         XDR_DECODE=1,
```

```
    XDR_FREE=2
};

/*
 * This is the number of bytes per unit of external data.
 */
#define BYTES_PER_XDR_UNIT      (4)
#define RNDUP(x)   ((((x) + BYTES_PER_XDR_UNIT - 1) / BYTES_PER_XDR_UNIT) \
            * BYTES_PER_XDR_UNIT)

/*
 * A xdrproc_t exists for each data type which is to be encoded or decoded.
 *
 * The second argument to the xdrproc_t is a pointer to an opaque pointer.
 * The opaque pointer generally points to a structure of the data type
 * to be decoded.  If this pointer is 0, then the type routines should
 * allocate dynamic storage of the appropriate size and return it.
 * bool_t    (*xdrproc_t)(XDR *, caddr_t *);
 */
typedef        bool_t (*xdrproc_t)();

/*
 * The XDR handle.
 * Contains operation which is being applied to the stream,
 * an operations vector for the paticular implementation (e.g. see xdr_mem.c),
 * and two private fields for the use of the particular impelementation.
 */
typedef struct {
    enum xdr_op x_op;                  /* operation; fast additional param */
    struct xdr_ops {
        bool_t  (*x_getlong)();  /* get a long from underlying stream */
        bool_t  (*x_putlong)();  /* put a long to " */
        bool_t  (*x_getbytes)(); /* get some bytes from " */
        bool_t  (*x_putbytes)(); /* put some bytes to " */
        u_int   (*x_getpostn)(); /* returns bytes off from beginning */
        bool_t  (*x_setpostn)(); /* lets you reposition the stream */
        long *  (*x_inline)();   /* buf quick ptr to buffered data */
        void    (*x_destroy)();  /* free privates of this xdr_stream */
    } *x_ops;
    caddr_t    x_public;    /* users' data */
    caddr_t    x_private;   /* pointer to private data */
    caddr_t    x_base;      /* private used for position info */
    int        x_handy;     /* extra private word */
} XDR;
```

Index to Routines

The following table lists RPC routines and the manual reference pages on which they are described:

RPC Routine	Manual Reference Page
auth_destroy	rpc_clnt_auth(3N)
authdes_getucred	secure_rpc(3N)
authdes_seccreate	secure_rpc(3N)
authnone_create	rpc_clnt_auth(3N)
authsys_create	rpc_clnt_auth(3N)
authsys_create_default	rpc_clnt_auth(3N)
clnt_call	rpc_clnt_calls(3N)
clnt_control	rpc_clnt_create(3N)
clnt_create	rpc_clnt_create(3N)
clnt_destroy	rpc_clnt_create(3N)
clnt_dg_create	rpc_clnt_create(3N)
clnt_freeres	rpc_clnt_calls(3N)
clnt_geterr	rpc_clnt_calls(3N)
clnt_pcreateerror	rpc_clnt_create(3N)
clnt_perrno	rpc_clnt_calls(3N)
clnt_perror	rpc_clnt_calls(3N)
clnt_raw_create	rpc_clnt_create(3N)
clnt_spcreateerror	rpc_clnt_create(3N)
clnt_sperrno	rpc_clnt_calls(3N)
clnt_sperror	rpc_clnt_calls(3N)
clnt_tli_create	rpc_clnt_create(3N)
clnt_tp_create	rpc_clnt_create(3N)
clnt_vc_create	rpc_clnt_create(3N)
getnetname	secure_rpc(3N)
host2netname	secure_rpc(3N)
key_decryptsession	secure_rpc(3N)
key_encryptsession	secure_rpc(3N)
key_gendes	secure_rpc(3N)
key_setsecret	secure_rpc(3N)
netname2host	secure_rpc(3N)
netname2user	secure_rpc(3N)
rpc_broadcast	rpc_clnt_calls(3N)
rpc_call	rpc_clnt_calls(3N)
rpc_reg	rpc_svc_calls(3N)
svc_create	rpc_svc_create(3N)
svc_destroy	rpc_svc_create(3N)
svc_dg_create	rpc_svc_create(3N)
svc_fd_create	rpc_svc_create(3N)
svc_freeargs	rpc_svc_reg(3N)
svc_getargs	rpc_svc_reg(3N)
svc_getreqset	rpc_svc_reg(3N)
svc_getrpccaller	rpc_svc_reg(3N)
svc_raw_create	rpc_svc_create(3N)
svc_reg	rpc_svc_calls(3N)
svc_run	rpc_svc_reg(3N)
svc_sendreply	rpc_svc_reg(3N)

svc_tli_create	rpc_svc_create(3N)
svc_tp_create	rpc_svc_create(3N)
svc_unreg	rpc_svc_calls(3N)
svc_vc_create	rpc_svc_create(3N)
svcerr_auth	rpc_svc_err(3N)
svcerr_decode	rpc_svc_err(3N)
svcerr_noproc	rpc_svc_err(3N)
svcerr_noprog	rpc_svc_err(3N)
svcerr_progvers	rpc_svc_err(3N)
svcerr_systemerr	rpc_svc_err(3N)
svcerr_weakauth	rpc_svc_err(3N)
user2netname	secure_rpc(3N)
xdr_accepted_reply	rpc_xdr(3N)
xdr_authsys_parms	rpc_xdr(3N)
xdr_callhdr	rpc_xdr(3N)
xdr_callmsg	rpc_xdr(3N)
xdr_opaque_auth	rpc_xdr(3N)
xdr_rejected_reply	rpc_xdr(3N)
xdr_replymsg	rpc_xdr(3N)
xprt_register	rpc_svc_calls(3N)
xprt_unregister	rpc_svc_calls(3N)

FILES

/etc/netconfig

SEE ALSO

environ(5), getnetconfig(3N), getnetpath(3N), rpc_clnt_auth(3N),
rpc_clnt_calls(3N), rpc_clnt_create(3N), rpc_svc_calls(3N),
rpc_svc_create(3N), rpc_svc_err(3N), rpc_svc_reg(3N), rpc_xdr(3N),
rpcbind(3N), secure_rpc(3N), xdr(3N), netconfig(4).

NAME
rpc_clnt_auth: auth_destroy,   authnone_create,   authsys_create,
authsys_create_default – library routines for client side remote procedure call
authentication

DESCRIPTION
These routines are part of the RPC library that allows C language programs to
make procedure calls on other machines across the network, with desired authentication. First, the client calls a procedure to send a data packet to the server.
Upon receipt of the packet, the server calls a dispatch routine to perform the
requested service, and then sends back a reply.

These routines are normally called after creating the CLIENT handle. The client's
authentication information is passed to the server when the RPC call is made.

Routines
The following routines require that the header rpc.h be included [see rpc(3N)
for the definition of the AUTH data structure].

```
#include <rpc/rpc.h>

void
auth_destroy(AUTH *auth);
```

A function macro that destroys the authentication information associated
with *auth*. Destruction usually involves deallocation of private data structures. The use of *auth* is undefined after calling auth_destroy.

```
AUTH *
authnone_create(void);
```

Create and return an RPC authentication handle that passes nonusable
authentication information with each remote procedure call. This is the
default authentication used by RPC.

```
AUTH *
authsys_create(const char *host, const uid_t uid, const gid_t gid,
      const int len, const gid_t *aup_gids);
```

Create and return an RPC authentication handle that contains AUTH_SYS
authentication information. The parameter *host* is the name of the
machine on which the information was created; *uid* is the user's user ID;
gid is the user's current group ID; *len* and *aup_gids* refer to a counted array
of groups to which the user belongs.

```
AUTH *
authsys_create_default(void);
```

Call authsys_create with the appropriate parameters.

SEE ALSO
rpc(3N), rpc_clnt_create(3N), rpc_clnt_calls(3N).

NAME

rpc_clnt_calls: clnt_call, clnt_freeres, clnt_geterr, clnt_perrno, clnt_perror, clnt_sperrno, clnt_sperror, rpc_broadcast, rpc_call – library routines for client side calls

DESCRIPTION

RPC library routines allow C language programs to make procedure calls on other machines across the network. First, the client calls a procedure to send a data packet to the server. Upon receipt of the packet, the server calls a dispatch routine to perform the requested service, and then sends back a reply.

The clnt_call, rpc_call and rpc_broadcast routines handle the client side of the procedure call. The remaining routines deal with error handling in the case of errors.

Routines

See rpc(3N) for the definition of the CLIENT data structure.

```
#include <rpc/rpc.h>
```

```
enum clnt_stat
clnt_call(CLIENT *clnt, const u_long procnum, const xdrproc_t inproc,
        caddr_t in, const xdrproc_t outproc, caddr_t out,
        const struct timeval tout);
```

A function macro that calls the remote procedure *procnum* associated with the client handle, *clnt*, which is obtained with an RPC client creation routine such as clnt_create [see rpc_clnt_create(3N)]. The parameter *in* is the address of the procedure's argument(s), and *out* is the address of where to place the result(s); *inproc* is used to encode the procedure's parameters, and *outproc* is used to decode the procedure's results; *tout* is the time allowed for results to be returned.

If the remote call succeeds, the status is returned in RPC_SUCCESS, otherwise an appropriate status is returned.

```
int clnt_freeres(CLIENT *clnt, const xdrproc_t outproc, caddr_t out);
```

A function macro that frees any data allocated by the RPC/XDR system when it decoded the results of an RPC call. The parameter *out* is the address of the results, and *outproc* is the XDR routine describing the results. This routine returns 1 if the results were successfully freed, and 0 otherwise.

```
void
clnt_geterr(const CLIENT *clnt, struct rpc_err *errp);
```

A function macro that copies the error structure out of the client handle to the structure at address *errp*.

```
void
clnt_perrno(const enum clnt_stat stat);
```

Print a message to standard error corresponding to the condition indicated by *stat*. A newline is appended at the end of the message. Normally used after a procedure call fails, for instance rpc_call.

```
void
clnt_perror(const CLIENT *clnt, const char *s);
```

Print a message to standard error indicating why an RPC call failed; *clnt* is the handle used to do the call. The message is prepended with string *s* and a colon. A newline is appended at the end of the message. Normally used after a procedure call fails, for instance clnt_call.

```
char *
clnt_sperrno(const enum clnt_stat stat);
```

Take the same arguments as clnt_perrno, but instead of sending a message to the standard error indicating why an RPC call failed, return a pointer to a string which contains the message.

clnt_sperrno is normally used instead of clnt_perrno when the program does not have a standard error (as a program running as a server quite likely does not), or if the programmer does not want the message to be output with printf [see printf(3S)], or if a message format different than that supported by clnt_perrno is to be used. Note: unlike clnt_sperror and clnt_spcreaterror [see rpc_clnt_create(3N)], clnt_sperrno does not return pointer to static data so the result will not get overwritten on each call.

```
char *
clnt_sperror(const CLIENT *clnt, const char *s);
```

Like clnt_perror, except that (like clnt_sperrno) it returns a string instead of printing to standard error. However, clnt_sperror does not append a newline at the end of the message.

Warning: returns pointer to static data that is overwritten on each call.

```
enum clnt_stat
rpc_broadcast(const u_long prognum, const u_long versnum,
     const u_long procnum, const xdrproc_t inproc, caddr_t in,
     const xdrproc_t outproc, caddr_t out, const resultproc_t eachresult,
     const char *nettype);
```

Like rpc_call, except the call message is broadcast to the connectionless
network specified by *nettype*. If *nettype* is NULL, it defaults to netpath.
Each time it receives a response, this routine calls eachresult, whose
form is:

```
bool_t
eachresult(const caddr_t out, const struct netbuf *addr,
     struct netconfig *netconf);
```

where *out* is the same as *out* passed to rpc_broadcast, except that the
remote procedure's output is decoded there; *addr* points to the address of
the machine that sent the results, and *netconf* is the netconfig structure of
the transport on which the remote server responded. If eachresult
returns 0, rpc_broadcast waits for more replies; otherwise it returns
with appropriate status.

Warning: broadcast file descriptors are limited in size to the maximum
transfer size of that transport. For Ethernet, this value is 1500 bytes.

```
enum clnt_stat
rpc_call(const char *host, const u_long prognum,
     const u_long versnum, const u_long procnum,
     const xdrproc_t inproc, const xdrproc_t outproc,
     const char *in, char *out, const char *nettype);
```

Call the remote procedure associated with *prognum*, *versnum*, and *procnum*
on the machine, *host*. The parameter *in* is the address of the procedure's
argument(s), and *out* is the address of where to place the result(s); *inproc* is
used to encode the procedure's parameters, and *outproc* is used to decode
the procedure's results. *nettype* can be any of the values listed on
rpc(3N). If *nettype* is NULL, it defaults to netpath. This routine returns 0
if it succeeds, or the value of enum clnt_stat cast to an integer if it fails.
Use the clnt_perrno routine to translate failure statuses into messages.

Warning: rpc_call uses the first available transport belonging to the class
nettype, on which it can create a connection. You do not have control of
timeouts or authentication using this routine. There is also no way to destroy the client handle.

SEE ALSO

printf(3S), rpc(3N), rpc_clnt_auth(3N), rpc_clnt_create(3N).

NAME

rpc_clnt_create: clnt_control, clnt_create, clnt_destroy,
clnt_dg_create, clnt_pcreateerror, clnt_raw_create,
clnt_spcreateerror, clnt_tli_create, clnt_tp_create, clnt_vc_create –
library routines for dealing with creation and manipulation of CLIENT handles

DESCRIPTION

RPC library routines allow C language programs to make procedure calls on
other machines across the network. First a CLIENT handle is created and then the
client calls a procedure to send a data packet to the server. Upon receipt of the
packet, the server calls a dispatch routine to perform the requested service, and
then sends back a reply.

Routines

See rpc(3N) for the definition of the CLIENT data structure.

```
#include <rpc/rpc.h>

bool_t
clnt_control(CLIENT *clnt, const u_int req, char *info);
```

A function macro used to change or retrieve various information about a
client object. *req* indicates the type of operation, and *info* is a pointer to
the information. For both connectionless and connection-oriented transports, the supported values of *req* and their argument types and what
they do are:

CLSET_TIMEOUT	struct timeval	set total timeout
CLGET_TIMEOUT	struct timeval	get total timeout

Note: if you set the timeout using clnt_control, the timeout parameter
passed to clnt_call will be ignored in all future calls.

CLGET_FD	int	get the associated file descriptor
CLGET_SVC_ADDR	struct netbuf	get servers address
CLSET_FD_CLOSE	int	close the file descriptor when destroying the client handle [see clnt_destroy]
CLSET_FD_NCLOSE	int	do not close the file descriptor when destroying the client handle

The following operations are valid for connectionless transports only:

CLSET_RETRY_TIMEOUT	struct timeval	set the retry timeout
CLGET_RETRY_TIMEOUT	struct timeval	get the retry timeout

The retry timeout is the time that RPC waits for the server to reply before
retransmitting the request.

clnt_control returns 1 on success and 0 on failure.

```
CLIENT *
clnt_create(const char *host, const u_long prognum,
        const u_long versnum, const char *nettype);
```

Generic client creation routine for program *prognum* and version *versnum*. *host* identifies the name of the remote host where the server is located. *nettype* indicates the class of transport protocol to use. The transports are tried in left to right order in NETPATH variable or in top to down order in the netconfig database.

clnt_create tries all the transports of the *nettype* class available from the NETPATH environment variable and the the netconfig database, and chooses the first successful one. Default timeouts are set, but can be modified using clnt_control.

```
void
clnt_destroy(CLIENT *clnt);
```

A function macro that destroys the client's RPC handle. Destruction usually involves deallocation of private data structures, including *clnt* itself. Use of *clnt* is undefined after calling clnt_destroy. If the RPC library opened the associated file descriptor, or CLSET_FD_CLOSE was set using clnt_control, it will be closed.

```
CLIENT *
clnt_dg_create(const int fd, const struct netbuf *svcaddr,
        const u_long prognum, const u_long versnum,
        const u_int sendsz, const u_int recvsz);
```

This routine creates an RPC client for the remote program *prognum* and version *versnum*; the client uses a connectionless transport. The remote program is located at address *svcaddr*. The parameter *fd* is an open and bound file descriptor. This routine will resend the call message in intervals of 15 seconds until a response is received or until the call times out. The total time for the call to time out is specified by clnt_call [see clnt_call in rpc_clnt_calls(3N)]. This routine returns NULL if it fails. The retry time out and the total time out periods can be changed using clnt_control. The user may set the size of the send and receive buffers with the parameters *sendsz* and *recvsz*; values of 0 choose suitable defaults.

```
void
clnt_pcreateerror(const char *s);
```

Print a message to standard error indicating why a client RPC handle could not be created. The message is prepended with the string *s* and a colon, and appended with a newline.

```
CLIENT *
clnt_raw_create(const u_long prognum, const u_long versnum);
```

This routine creates a toy RPC client for the remote program *prognum* and version *versnum*. The transport used to pass messages to the service is a buffer within the process's address space, so the corresponding RPC server should live in the same address space; [see `svc_raw_create` in `rpc_clnt_calls`(3N)]. This allows simulation of RPC and acquisition of RPC overheads, such as round trip times, without any kernel interference. This routine returns `NULL` if it fails. `clnt_raw_create` should be called after `svc_raw_create`.

```
char *
clnt_spcreateerror(const char *s);
```

Like `clnt_pcreateerror`, except that it returns a string instead of printing to the standard error. A newline is not appended to the message in this case.

Warning: returns a pointer to static data that is overwritten on each call.

```
CLIENT *
clnt_tli_create(const int fd, const struct netconfig *netconf,
     const struct netbuf *svcaddr, u const_long prognum,
     const u_long versnum, const u_int sendsz,
     const u_int recvsz);
```

This routine creates an RPC client handle for the remote program *prognum* and version *versnum*. The remote program is located at address *svcaddr*. If *svcaddr* is `NULL` and it is connection-oriented, it is assumed that the file descriptor is connected. For connectionless transports, if *svcaddr* is `NULL`, `RPC_UNKNOWNADDR` error is set. *fd* is a file descriptor which may be open, bound and connected. If it is `RPC_ANYFD`, it opens a file descriptor on the transport specified by *netconf*. If *netconf* is `NULL`, a `RPC_UNKNOWNPROTO` error is set. If *fd* is unbound, then it will attempt to bind the descriptor. The user may specify the size of the buffers with the parameters *sendsz* and *recvsz*; values of 0 choose suitable defaults. Depending upon the type of the transport (connection-oriented or connectionless), `clnt_tli_create` calls appropriate client creation routines. This routine returns `NULL` if it fails. The `clnt_pcreaterror` routine can be used to print the reason for failure. The remote rpcbind service [see rpcbind(1M)] will not be consulted for the address of the remote service.

```
CLIENT *
clnt_tp_create(const char *host, const u_long prognum,
     const u_long versnum, const struct netconfig *netconf);
```

`clnt_tp_create` creates a client handle for the transport specified by *netconf*. Default options are set, which can be changed using `clnt_control` calls. The remote rpcbind service on the host *host* is consulted for the address of the remote service. This routine returns `NULL` if it fails. The `clnt_pcreaterror` routine can be used to print the reason for failure.

```
CLIENT *
clnt_vc_create(const int fd, const struct netbuf *svcaddr,
     const u_long prognum, const u_long versnum,
     const u_int sendsz, const u_int recvsz);
```

This routine creates an RPC client for the remote program *prognum* and version *versnum*; the client uses a connection-oriented transport. The remote program is located at address *svcaddr*. The parameter *fd* is an open and bound file descriptor. The user may specify the size of the send and receive buffers with the parameters *sendsz* and *recvsz*; values of 0 choose suitable defaults. This routine returns NULL if it fails.

The address *svcaddr* should not be NULL and should point to the actual address of the remote program. clnt_vc_create will not consult the remote rpcbind service for this information.

SEE ALSO

rpcbind(1M), rpc(3N), rpc_clnt_auth(3N), rpc_clnt_calls(3N).

NAME

rpc_svc_calls: rpc_reg, svc_reg, svc_unreg, xprt_register, xprt_unregister – library routines for registering servers

DESCRIPTION

These routines are a part of the RPC library which allows the RPC servers to register themselves with rpcbind [see rpcbind(1M)], and it associates the given program and version number with the dispatch function.

Routines

See rpc(3N) for the definition of the SVCXPRT data structure.

```
#include <rpc/rpc.h>

int
rpc_reg(const u_long prognum, const u_long versnum,
    const u_long procnum, const char *(*procname),
    const xdrproc_t inproc, const xdrproc_t outproc,
    const char *nettype);
```

Register program *prognum*, procedure *procname*, and version *versnum* with the RPC service package. If a request arrives for program *prognum*, version *versnum*, and procedure *procnum*, *procname* is called with a pointer to its parameter(s); *procname* should return a pointer to its static result(s); *inproc* is used to decode the parameters while *outproc* is used to encode the results. Procedures are registered on all available transports of the class *nettype*. *nettype* defines a class of transports which can be used for a particular application. If *nettype* is NULL, it defaults to netpath. This routine returns 0 if the registration succeeded, −1 otherwise.

```
int
svc_reg(const SVCXPRT *xprt, const u_long prognum, const u_long versnum,
    const void (*dispatch), const struct netconfig *netconf);
```

Associates *prognum* and *versnum* with the service dispatch procedure, *dispatch*. If *netconf* is NULL, the service is not registered with the rpcbind service. If *netconf* is non-zero, then a mapping of the triple [*prognum, versnum, netconf->nc_netid*] to *xprt->xp_ltaddr* is established with the local rpcbind service.

The svc_reg routine returns 1 if it succeeds, and 0 otherwise

```
void
svc_unreg(const u_long prognum, const u_long versnum);
```

Remove, from the rpcbind service, all mappings of the double [*prognum, versnum*] to dispatch routines, and of the triple [*prognum, versnum, ***] to network address.

```
void
xprt_register(const SVCXPRT *xprt);
```

> After RPC service transport handle *xprt* is created, it is registered with the RPC service package. This routine modifies the global variable **svc_fds**. Service implementors usually do not need this routine.

```
void
xprt_unregister(const SVCXPRT *xprt);
```

> Before an RPC service transport handle *xprt* is destroyed, it unregisters itself with the RPC service package. This routine modifies the global variable **svc_fds**. Service implementors usually do not need this routine.

SEE ALSO

rpcbind(1M), rpcbind(3N), rpc(3N), rpc_svc_err(3N), rpc_svc_create(3N), rpc_svc_reg(3N).

NAME

rpc_svc_create: svc_create, svc_destroy, svc_dg_create, svc_fd_create, svc_raw_create, svc_tli_create, svc_tp_create, svc_vc_create – library routines for dealing with the creation of server handles

DESCRIPTION

These routines are part of the RPC library which allows C language programs to make procedure calls on servers across the network. These routines deal with the creation of service handles. Once the handle is created, the server can be invoked by calling svc_run.

Routines

See rpc(3N) for the definition of the SVCXPRT data structure.

```
#include <rpc/rpc.h>

int
svc_create(
     const void (*dispatch)(const struct svc_req *, const SVCXPRT *),
     const u_long prognum, const u_long versnum,
     const char *nettype);
```

svc_create creates server handles for all the transports belonging to the class *nettype*.

nettype defines a class of transports which can be used for a particular application. The transports are tried in left to right order in NETPATH variable or in top to down order in the netconfig database.

If *nettype* is NULL, it defaults to netpath. svc_create registers itself with the rpcbind service [see rpcbind(1M)]. *dispatch* is called when there is a remote procedure call for the given *prognum* and *versnum*; this requires calling svc_run [see svc_run in rpc_svc_reg(3N)]. If it succeeds, svc_create returns the number of server handles it created, otherwise it returns 0 and the error message is logged.

```
void
svc_destroy(SVCXPRT *xprt);
```

A function macro that destroys the RPC service transport handle *xprt*. Destruction usually involves deallocation of private data structures, including *xprt* itself. Use of *xprt* is undefined after calling this routine.

```
SVCXPRT *
svc_dg_create(const int fd, const u_int sendsz, const u_int recvsz);
```

This routine creates a connectionless RPC service handle, and returns a pointer to it. This routine returns NULL if it fails, and an error message is logged. *sendsz* and *recvsz* are parameters used to specify the size of the buffers. If they are 0, suitable defaults are chosen. The file descriptor *fd* should be open and bound.

Warning: since connectionless-based RPC messages can only hold limited amount of encoded data, this transport cannot be used for procedures that take large arguments or return huge results.

```
SVCXPRT *
svc_fd_create(const int fd, const u_int sendsz, const u_int recvsz);
```
This routine creates a service on top of any open and bound descriptor, and returns the handle to it. Typically, this descriptor is a connected file descriptor for a connection-oriented transport. *sendsz* and *recvsz* indicate sizes for the send and receive buffers. If they are 0, a reasonable default is chosen. This routine returns NULL, if it fails, and an error message is logged.

```
SVCXPRT *
svc_raw_create(void);
```
This routine creates a toy RPC service transport, to which it returns a pointer. The transport is really a buffer within the process's address space, so the corresponding RPC client should live in the same address space; [see clnt_raw_create in rpc_clnt_create]. This routine allows simulation of RPC and acquisition of RPC overheads (such as round trip times), without any kernel interference. This routine returns NULL if it fails, and an error message is logged.

```
SVCXPRT *
svc_tli_create(const int fd, const struct netconfig *netconf,
      const struct t_bind *bindaddr, const u_int sendsz,
      const u_int recvsz);
```
This routine creates an RPC server handle, and returns a pointer to it. *fd* is the file descriptor on which the service is listening. If *fd* is RPC_ANYFD, it opens a file descriptor on the transport specified by *netconf*. If the file descriptor is unbound, it is bound to the address specified by *bindaddr*, if *bindaddr* is non-null, otherwise it is bound to a default address chosen by the transport. In the case where the default address is chosen, the number of outstanding connect requests is set to 8 for connection-oriented transports. The user may specify the size of the send and receive buffers with the parameters *sendsz* and *recvsz*; values of 0 choose suitable defaults. This routine returns NULL if it fails, and an error message is logged.

```
SVCPRT *
svc_tp_create(const void (*dispatch)(const RQSTP *, const SVCXPRT *),
      const u_long prognum, const u_long versnum,
      const struct netconfig *netconf);
```
svc_tp_create creates a server handle for the network specified by *netconf*, and registers itself with the rpcbind service. *dispatch* is called when there is a remote procedure call for the given *prognum* and *versnum*; this requires calling svc_run. svc_tp_create returns the service handle if it succeeds, otherwise a NULL is returned, and an error message is logged.

```
SVCXPRT *
svc_vc_create(const int fd, const u_int sendsz, const u_int recvsz);
```
This routine creates a connection-oriented RPC service and returns a pointer to it. This routine returns **NULL** if it fails, and an error message is logged. The users may specify the size of the send and receive buffers with the parameters *sendsz* and *recvsz*; values of 0 choose suitable defaults. The file descriptor *fd* should be open and bound.

SEE ALSO
rpcbind(1M), rpc(3N), rpc_svc_calls(3N), rpc_svc_err(3N), rpc_svc_reg(3N).

NAME

rpc_svc_err: svcerr_auth, svcerr_decode, svcerr_noproc,
svcerr_noprog, svcerr_progvers, svcerr_systemerr, svcerr_weakauth –
library routines for server side remote procedure call errors

DESCRIPTION

These routines are part of the RPC library which allows C language programs to
make procedure calls on other machines across the network.

These routines can be called by the server side dispatch function if there is any
error in the transaction with the client.

Routines

See rpc(3N) for the definition of the SVCXPRT data structure.

```
#include <rpc/rpc.h>
```

```
void
svcerr_auth(const SVCXPRT *xprt, const enum auth_stat why);
```

Called by a service dispatch routine that refuses to perform a remote procedure call due to an authentication error.

```
void
svcerr_decode(const SVCXPRT *xprt);
```

Called by a service dispatch routine that cannot successfully decode the
remote parameters [see svc_getargs in rpc_svc_reg(3N)].

```
void
svcerr_noproc(const SVCXPRT *xprt);
```

Called by a service dispatch routine that does not implement the procedure number that the caller requests.

```
void
svcerr_noprog(const SVCXPRT *xprt);
```

Called when the desired program is not registered with the RPC package.
Service implementors usually do not need this routine.

```
void
svcerr_progvers(const SVCXPRT *xprt);
```

Called when the desired version of a program is not registered with the
RPC package. Service implementors usually do not need this routine.

```
void
svcerr_systemerr(const SVCXPRT *xprt);
```

Called by a service dispatch routine when it detects a system error not
covered by any particular protocol. For example, if a service can no
longer allocate storage, it may call this routine.

void
svcerr_weakauth(const SVCXPRT *xprt);

Called by a service dispatch routine that refuses to perform a remote procedure call due to insufficient (but correct) authentication parameters. The
routine calls svcerr_auth(xprt, AUTH_TOOWEAK).

SEE ALSO

rpc(3N), rpc_svc_calls(3N), rpc_svc_create(3N), rpc_svc_reg(3N).

NAME

rpc_svc_reg: svc_freeargs, svc_getargs, svc_getreqset,
svc_getrpccaller, svc_run, svc_sendreply – library routines for RPC servers

DESCRIPTION

These routines are part of the RPC library which allows C language programs to
make procedure calls on other machines across the network.

These routines are associated with the server side of the RPC mechanism. Some
of them are called by the server side dispatch function, while others [such as
svc_run] are called when the server is initiated.

Routines

```
#include <rpc/rpc.h>

int
svc_freeargs(const SVCXPRT *xprt, const xdrproc_t inproc, char *in);
```

A function macro that frees any data allocated by the RPC/XDR system
when it decoded the arguments to a service procedure using
svc_getargs. This routine returns 1 if the results were successfully freed,
and 0 otherwise.

```
int
svc_getargs(const SVCXPRT *xprt, const xdrproc_t inproc, caddr_t *in);
```

A function macro that decodes the arguments of an RPC request associated with the RPC service transport handle *xprt*. The parameter *in* is the
address where the arguments will be placed; *inproc* is the XDR routine
used to decode the arguments. This routine returns 1 if decoding
succeeds, and 0 otherwise.

```
void
svc_getreqset(fd_set *rdfds);
```

This routine is only of interest if a service implementor does not call
svc_run, but instead implements custom asynchronous event processing.
It is called when poll has determined that an RPC request has arrived on
some RPC file descriptors; *rdfds* is the resultant read file descriptor bit
mask. The routine returns when all file descriptors associated with the
value of *rdfds* have been serviced

```
struct netbuf *
svc_getrpccaller(const SVCXPRT *xprt);
```

The approved way of getting the network address of the caller of a procedure associated with the RPC service transport handle *xprt*.

```
void
svc_run(void);
```

This routine never returns. It waits for RPC requests to arrive, and calls
the appropriate service procedure using svc_getreqset when one
arrives. This procedure is usually waiting for a poll library call to return.

```
int
svc_sendreply(const SVCXPRT *xprt, const xdrproc_t outproc,
    const caddr_t *out);
```

Called by an RPC service's dispatch routine to send the results of a remote procedure call. The parameter *xprt* is the request's associated transport handle; *outproc* is the XDR routine which is used to encode the results; and *out* is the address of the results. This routine returns 1 if it succeeds, 0 otherwise.

SEE ALSO

poll(2), rpc(3N), rpc_svc_calls(3N), rpc_svc_create(3N), rpc_svc_err(3N).

NAME

rpc_xdr: xdr_accepted_reply, xdr_authsys_parms, xdr_callhdr,
xdr_callmsg, xdr_opaque_auth, xdr_rejected_reply, xdr_replymsg – XDR
library routines for remote procedure calls

DESCRIPTION

These routines are used for describing the RPC messages in XDR language. They
should normally be used by those who do not want to use the RPC package.

Routines

See rpc(3N) for the definition of the XDR data structure.

```
#include <rpc/rpc.h>
```

```
bool_t
xdr_accepted_reply(XDR *xdrs, const struct accepted_reply *ar);
```

Used for encoding RPC reply messages. It encodes the status of the RPC
call in the XDR language format, and in the case of success, it encodes the
call results also.

```
bool_t
xdr_authsys_parms(XDR *xdrs, const struct authsys_parms *aupp);
```

Used for describing operating system credentials. It includes machinename, uid, gid list, etc.

```
void
xdr_callhdr(XDR *xdrs, const struct rpc_msg *chdr);
```

Used for describing RPC call header messages. It encodes the static part
of the call message header in the XDR language format. It includes information such as transaction ID, RPC version number, program and version
number.

```
bool_t
xdr_callmsg(XDR *xdrs, const struct rpc_msg *cmsg);
```

Used for describing RPC call messages. This includes all the RPC call
information such as transaction ID, RPC version number, program
number, version number, authentication information, etc. This is normally
used by servers to determine information about the client RPC call.

```
bool_t
xdr_opaque_auth(XDR *xdrs, const struct opaque_auth *ap);
```

Used for describing RPC opaque authentication information messages.

```
bool_t
xdr_rejected_reply(XDR *xdrs, const struct rejected_reply *rr);
```

Used for describing RPC reply messages. It encodes the rejected RPC
message in the XDR language format. The message could be rejected
either because of version number mis-match or because of authentication
errors.

```
bool_t
xdr_replymsg(XDR *xdrs, const struct rpc_msg *rmsg);
```
> Used for describing RPC reply messages. It encodes all the RPC reply message in the XDR language format This reply could be either an acceptance, rejection or NULL.

SEE ALSO
> rpc(3N).

NAME

    rpcbind: rpcb_getmaps, rpcb_getaddr, rpcb_gettime, rpcb_rmtcall,
    rpcb_set, rpcb_unset − library routines for RPC bind service

DESCRIPTION

    These routines allow client C programs to make procedure calls to the RPC
    binder service. rpcbind [see rpcbind(1M)] maintains a list of mappings between
    programs and their universal addresses.

Routines

    #include <rpc/rpc.h>

    struct rpcblist *
    rpcb_getmaps(const struct netconfig *netconf, const char *host);

        A user interface to the rpcbind service, which returns a list of the current
        RPC program-to-address mappings on the host named. It uses the tran-
        sport specified through *netconf* to contact the remote rpcbind service on
        host *host*. This routine will return NULL, if the remote rpcbind could not
        be contacted.

    bool_t
    rpcb_getaddr(const u_long prognum, const u_long versnum,
        const struct netconfig *netconf, struct netbuf *svcaddr,
        const char *host);

        A user interface to the rpcbind service, which finds the address of the
        service on *host* that is registered with program number *prognum*, version
        versnum, and speaks the transport protocol associated with *netconf*. The
        address found is returned in *svcaddr*. *svcaddr* should be preallocated. This
        routine returns 1 if it succeeds. A return value of 0 means that the map-
        ping does not exist or that the RPC system failed to contact the remote
        rpcbind service. In the latter case, the global variable rpc_createerr
        contains the RPC status.

    bool_t
    rpcb_gettime(const char *host, time_t *timep);

        This routine returns the time on *host* in *timep*. If *host* is NULL,
        rpcb_gettime returns the time on its own machine. This routine returns
        1 if it succeeds, 0 if it fails. rpcb_gettime can be used to synchronize the
        time between the client and the remote server. This routine is particularly
        useful for secure RPC.

```
enum clnt_stat
rpcb_rmtcall(const struct netconfig *netconf, const char *host,
      const u_long prognum, const u_long versnum, const u_long procnum,
      const xdrproc_t inproc, const caddr_t in,
      const xdrproc_t outproc, const caddr_t out,
      const struct timeval tout, struct netbuf *svcaddr);
```

A user interface to the rpcbind service, which instructs rpcbind on *host* to make an RPC call on your behalf to a procedure on that host. The parameter *svcaddr* will be modified to the server's address if the procedure succeeds [see rpc_call and clnt_call in rpc_clnt_calls(3N) for the definitions of other parameters]. This procedure should normally be used for a ping and nothing else [see rpc_broadcast in rpc_clnt_calls(3N)]. This routine allows programs to do lookup and call, all in one step.

```
bool_t
rpcb_set(const u_long prognum, const u_long versnum,
      const struct netconfig *netconf, const struct netbuf *svcaddr);
```

A user interface to the rpcbind service, which establishes a mapping between the triple [*prognum, versnum, netconf*->nc_netid] and *svcaddr* on the machine's rpcbind service. The value of *transport* must correspond to a network token that is defined by the netconfig database. This routine returns 1 if it succeeds, 0 otherwise. [See also svc_reg in rpc_svc_calls(3N)].

```
bool_t
rpcb_unset(const u_long prognum, const u_long versnum,
      const struct netconfig *netconf);
```

A user interface to the rpcbind service, which destroys all mapping between the triple [*prognum, versnum, netconf*->nc_netid] and the address on the machine's rpcbind service. If *netconf* is NULL, rpcb_unset destroys all mapping between the triple [*prognum, versnum, *] and the addresses on the machine's rpcbind service. This routine returns 1 if it succeeds, 0 otherwise. [See also svc_unreg in rpc_svc_calls(3N)].

SEE ALSO

rpc_clnt_calls(3N), rpc_svc_calls(3N), rpcbind(1M), rpcinfo(1M).

NAME
rusers – return information about users on remote machines

SYNOPSIS
#include <rpcsvc/rusers.h>

int rusers(char *_host_, struct utmpidlearr *_up_);

rusers fills the utmpidlearr structure with data about _host_, and returns 0 if successful. The function will fail if the underlying transport does not support broadcast mode.

SEE ALSO
rusers(1).

NAME
rwall – write to specified remote machines

SYNOPSIS
#include <rpcsvc/rwall.h>

rwall(char *host, char *msg);

DESCRIPTION
rwall executes wall(1M) on *host*. *host* prints the string *msg* to all its users. It returns 0 if successful.

SEE ALSO
rwall(1M), rwalld(1M).

NAME

secure_rpc: authdes_seccreate, authdes_getucred, getnetname, host2netname, key_decryptsession, key_encryptsession, key_gendes, key_setsecret, netname2host, netname2user, user2netname – library routines for secure remote procedure calls

DESCRIPTION

RPC library routines allow C programs to make procedure calls on other machines across the network. First, the client calls a procedure to send a data packet to the server. Upon receipt of the packet, the server calls a dispatch routine to perform the requested service, and then sends back a reply.

RPC supports various authentication flavors. Among them are:

AUTH_NONE	(none) no authentication.
AUTH_SYS	Traditional UNIX®-style authentication.
AUTH_DES	DES encryption-based authentication.

The authdes_getucred and authdes_seccreate routines implement the AUTH_DES authentication flavor. The keyserver daemon keyserv [see keyserv(1M)] must be running for the AUTH_DES authentication system to work.

Routines

See rpc(3N) for the definition of the AUTH data structure.

```
#include <rpc/rpc.h>
```

```
int
authdes_getucred(const struct authdes_cred *adc, uid_t *uidp,
        gid_t *gidp, short *gidlenp, gid_t *gidlist);
```

authdes_getucred is the first of the two routines which interface to the RPC secure authentication system known as AUTH_DES. The second is authdes_seccreate, below. authdes_getucred is used on the server side for converting an AUTH_DES credential, which is operating system independent, into an AUTH_SYS credential. This routine returns 1 if it succeeds, 0 if it fails.

uidp is set to the user's numerical ID associated with *adc*. *gidp* is set to the numerical ID of the group to which the user belongs. *gidlist* contains the numerical IDs of the other groups to which the user belongs. *gidlenp* is set to the number of valid group ID entries in *gidlist* [see netname2user, below].

```
AUTH *
authdes_seccreate(const char *name, const unsigned int window,
     const char *timehost, const des_block *ckey);
```

> authdes_seccreate, the second of two AUTH_DES authentication routines,
> is used on the client side to return an authentication handle that will
> enable the use of the secure authentication system. The first parameter
> *name* is the network name, or *netname*, of the owner of the server process.
> This field usually represents a hostname derived from the utility routine
> host2netname, but could also represent a user name using
> user2netname, described below. The second field is window on the vali-
> dity of the client credential, given in seconds. A small window is more
> secure than a large one, but choosing too small of a window will increase
> the frequency of resynchronizations because of clock drift. The third
> parameter, *timehost*, the host's name, is optional. If it is NULL, then the
> authentication system will assume that the local clock is always in sync
> with the *timehost* clock, and will not attempt resynchronizations. If a
> timehost is supplied, however, then the system will consult with the
> remote time service whenever resynchronization is required. This parame-
> ter is usually the name of the RPC server itself. The final parameter *ckey*
> is also optional. If it is NULL, then the authentication system will generate
> a random DES key to be used for the encryption of credentials. If *ckey* is
> supplied, then it will be used instead.

```
int
getnetname(char name[MAXNETNAMELEN+1]);
```

> getnetname installs the unique, operating-system independent netname of
> the caller in the fixed-length array *name*. Returns 1 if it succeeds, and 0 if
> it fails.

```
int
host2netname(char name[MAXNETNAMELEN+1], const char *host,
     const char *domain);
```

> Convert from a domain-specific hostname *host* to an operating-system
> independent netname. Return 1 if it succeeds, and 0 if it fails. Inverse of
> netname2host. If *domain* is NULL, host2netname uses the default domain
> name of the machine. If *host* is NULL, it defaults to that machine itself.

```
int
key_decryptsession(const char *remotename, des_block *deskey);
```

> key_decryptsession is an interface to the keyserver daemon, which is
> associated with RPC's secure authentication system (AUTH_DES authentica-
> tion). User programs rarely need to call it, or its associated routines
> key_encryptsession, key_gendes and key_setsecret.

> key_decryptsession takes a server netname *remotename* and a DES key
> *deskey*, and decrypts the key by using the the public key of the the server
> and the secret key associated with the effective UID of the calling process.
> It is the inverse of key_encryptsession.

```
int
key_encryptsession(const char *remotename, des_block *deskey);
```

> key_encryptsession is a keyserver interface routine. It takes a server
> netname *remotename* and a DES key *deskey*, and encrypts it using the pub-
> lic key of the the server and the secret key associated with the effective
> UID of the calling process. It is the inverse of key_decryptsession. This
> routine returns 0 if it succeeds, −1 if it fails.

```
int
key_gendes(des_block *deskey);
```

> key_gendes is a keyserver interface routine. It is used to ask the
> keyserver for a secure conversation key. Choosing one at random is usu-
> ally not good enough, because the common ways of choosing random
> numbers, such as using the current time, are very easy to guess.

```
int
key_setsecret(const char *key);
```

> key_setsecret is a keyserver interface routine. It is used to set the key
> for the effective UID of the calling process. this routine returns 0 if it
> succeeds, −1 if it fails.

```
int
netname2host(const char *name, char *host, const int hostlen);
```

> Convert from an operating-system independent netname *name* to a
> domain-specific hostname *host*. *hostlen* is the maximum size of *host*.
> Returns 1 if it succeeds, and 0 if it fails. Inverse of host2netname.

```
int
netname2user(const char *name, uid_t *uidp, gid_t *gidp,
    int *gidlenp, gid_t gidlist[NGROUPS]);
```

> Convert from an operating-system independent netname to a domain-
> specific user ID. Returns 1 if it succeeds, and 0 if it fails. Inverse of
> user2netname.
>
> **gidp* is set to the user's numerical ID associated with *name*. **gidp* is set to
> the numerical ID of the group to which the user belongs. *gidlist* contains
> the numerical IDs of the other groups to which the user belongs. **gidlenp*
> is set to the number of valid group ID entries in *gidlist*.

```
int
user2netname(char name[MAXNETNAMELEN+1], const uid_t uid,
    const char *domain);
```

> Convert from a domain-specific username to an operating-system indepen-
> dent netname. Returns 1 if it succeeds, and 0 if it fails. Inverse of
> netname2user.

SEE ALSO
  chkey(1), keyserv(1M), newkey(1M), rpc(3N), rpc_clnt_auth(3N).

NAME

send, sendto, sendmsg – send a message from a socket

SYNOPSIS

```
#include <sys/types.h>
#include <sys/socket.h>

int send(s, msg, len, flags)
int s;
char *msg;
int len, flags;

int sendto(s, msg, len, flags, to, tolen)
int s;
char *msg;
int len, flags;
struct sockaddr *to;
int tolen;

int sendmsg(s, msg, flags)
int s;
struct msghdr *msg;
int flags;
```

DESCRIPTION

s is a socket created with socket(3N). send(), sendto(), and sendmsg() are used to transmit a message to another socket. send() may be used only when the socket is in a *connected* state, while sendto() and sendmsg() may be used at any time.

The address of the target is given by *to* with *tolen* specifying its size. The length of the message is given by *len*. If the message is too long to pass atomically through the underlying protocol, then the error EMSGSIZE is returned, and the message is not transmitted.

No indication of failure to deliver is implicit in a send(). Return values of −1 indicate some locally detected errors.

If no buffer space is available at the socket to hold the message to be transmitted, then send() normally blocks, unless the socket has been placed in non-blocking I/O mode (see fcntl(2)). The select() call may be used to determine when it is possible to send more data.

The *flags* parameter is formed by ORing one or more of the following:

MSG_OOB   Send out-of-band data on sockets that support this notion. The underlying protocol must also support out-of-band data. Currently, only SOCK_STREAM sockets created in the AF_INET address family support out-of-band data.

MSG_DONTROUTE   The SO_DONTROUTE option is turned on for the duration of the operation. It is used only by diagnostic or routing programs.

See recv(3N) for a description of the msghdr structure.

RETURN VALUE

These calls return the number of bytes sent, or −1 if an error occurred.

ERRORS

The calls fail if:

EBADF	s is an invalid descriptor.
ENOTSOCK	s is a descriptor for a file, not a socket.
EINVAL	*tolen* is not the size of a valid address for the specified address family.
EINTR	The operation was interrupted by delivery of a signal before any data could be buffered to be sent.
EMSGSIZE	The socket requires that message be sent atomically, and the message was too long.
EWOULDBLOCK	The socket is marked non-blocking and the requested operation would block.
ENOMEM	There was insufficient user memory available for the operation to complete.
ENOSR	There were insufficient STREAMS resources available for the operation to complete.

SEE ALSO

connect(3N), fcntl(2), getsockopt(3N), recv(3N), socket(3N), write(2).

NAME
shutdown – shut down part of a full-duplex connection

SYNOPSIS
```
shutdown(s, how)
int s, how;
```

DESCRIPTION
The shutdown() call shuts down all or part of a full-duplex connection on the socket associated with s. If *how* is 0, then further receives will be disallowed. If *how* is 1, then further sends will be disallowed. If *how* is 2, then further sends and receives will be disallowed.

RETURN VALUE
A 0 is returned if the call succeeds, −1 if it fails.

ERRORS
The call succeeds unless:

EBADF	*s* is not a valid descriptor.
ENOTSOCK	*s* is a file, not a socket.
ENOTCONN	The specified socket is not connected.
ENOMEM	There was insufficient user memory available for the operation to complete.
ENOSR	There were insufficient STREAMS resources available for the operation to complete.

SEE ALSO
connect(3N), socket(3N).

NOTES
The *how* values should be defined constants.

NAME

socket – create an endpoint for communication

SYNOPSIS

```
#include <sys/types.h>
#include <sys/socket.h>

int socket(domain, type, protocol)
int domain, type, protocol;
```

DESCRIPTION

socket() creates an endpoint for communication and returns a descriptor.

The *domain* parameter specifies a communications domain within which communication will take place; this selects the protocol family which should be used. The protocol family generally is the same as the address family for the addresses supplied in later operations on the socket. These families are defined in the include file /usr/include/sys/socket.h. There must be an entry in the netconfig(4) file for at least each protocol family and type required. If *protocol* has been specified, but no exact match for the tuplet family, type, protocol is found, then the first entry containing the specified family and type with zero for protocol will be used. The currently understood formats are:

PF_UNIX   UNIX system internal protocols

PF_INET   ARPA Internet protocols

The socket has the indicated *type*, which specifies the communication semantics. Currently defined types are:

```
SOCK_STREAM
SOCK_DGRAM
SOCK_RAW
SOCK_SEQPACKET
SOCK_RDM
```

A SOCK_STREAM type provides sequenced, reliable, two-way connection-based byte streams. An out-of-band data transmission mechanism may be supported. A SOCK_DGRAM socket supports datagrams (connectionless, unreliable messages of a fixed (typically small) maximum length). A SOCK_SEQPACKET socket may provide a sequenced, reliable, two-way connection-based data transmission path for datagrams of fixed maximum length; a consumer may be required to read an entire packet with each read system call. This facility is protocol specific, and presently not implemented for any protocol family. SOCK_RAW sockets provide access to internal network interfaces. The types SOCK_RAW, which is available only to the super-user, and SOCK_RDM, for which no implementation currently exists, are not described here.

protocol specifies a particular protocol to be used with the socket. Normally only a single protocol exists to support a particular socket type within a given protocol family. However, multiple protocols may exist, in which case a particular protocol must be specified in this manner. The protocol number to use is particular to the communication domain in which communication is to take place. If a protocol is specified by the caller, then it will be packaged into a socket level option request and sent to the underlying protocol layers.

Sockets of type SOCK_STREAM are full-duplex byte streams, similar to pipes. A stream socket must be in a *connected* state before any data may be sent or received on it. A connection to another socket is created with a connect(3N) call. Once connected, data may be transferred using read(2) and write(2) calls or some variant of the send(3N) and recv(3N) calls. When a session has been completed, a close(2) may be performed. Out-of-band data may also be transmitted as described on the send(3N) manual page and received as described on the recv(3N) manual page.

The communications protocols used to implement a SOCK_STREAM insure that data is not lost or duplicated. If a piece of data for which the peer protocol has buffer space cannot be successfully transmitted within a reasonable length of time, then the connection is considered broken and calls will indicate an error with −1 returns and with ETIMEDOUT as the specific code in the global variable errno. The protocols optionally keep sockets warm by forcing transmissions roughly every minute in the absence of other activity. An error is then indicated if no response can be elicited on an otherwise idle connection for a extended period (for instance 5 minutes). A SIGPIPE signal is raised if a process sends on a broken stream; this causes naive processes, which do not handle the signal, to exit.

SOCK_SEQPACKET sockets employ the same system calls as SOCK_STREAM sockets. The only difference is that read calls will return only the amount of data requested, and any remaining in the arriving packet will be discarded.

SOCK_DGRAM and SOCK_RAW sockets allow datagrams to be sent to correspondents named in sendto calls. Datagrams are generally received with recvfrom, which returns the next datagram with its return address.

An fcntl(2) call can be used to specify a process group to receive a SIGURG signal when the out-of-band data arrives. It may also enable non-blocking I/O and asynchronous notification of I/O events with SIGIO signals.

The operation of sockets is controlled by socket level *options*. These options are defined in the file /usr/include/sys/socket.h. setsockopt(3N) and getsockopt(3N) are used to set and get options, respectively.

RETURN VALUE

A −1 is returned if an error occurs. Otherwise the return value is a descriptor referencing the socket.

ERRORS

The socket() call fails if:

EPROTONOSUPPORT	The protocol type or the specified protocol is not supported within this domain.
EMFILE	The per-process descriptor table is full.
EACCESS	Permission to create a socket of the specified type and/or protocol is denied.
ENOMEM	Insufficient user memory is available.

ENOSR   There were insufficient STREAMS resources available to
                         complete the operation.

SEE ALSO
   close(2), fcntl(2), ioctl(2), read(2), write(2), accept(3N), bind(3N),
   connect(3N), getsockname(3N), getsockopt(3N), listen(3N), recv(3N),
   send(3N), shutdown(3N), socketpair(3N).

NAME
socketpair – create a pair of connected sockets

SYNOPSIS
#include <sys/types.h>
#include <sys/socket.h>

socketpair(d, type, protocol, sv)
int d, type, protocol;
int sv[2];

DESCRIPTION
The socketpair() library call creates an unnamed pair of connected sockets in the specified address family *d*, of the specified *type* , and using the optionally specified *protocol*. The descriptors used in referencing the new sockets are returned in *sv*[0] and *sv*[1]. The two sockets are indistinguishable.

RETURN VALUE
socketpair() returns a −1 on failure, otherwise it returns the number of the second file descriptor it creates.

ERRORS
The call succeeds unless:

EMFILE	Too many descriptors are in use by this process.
EAFNOSUPPORT	The specified address family is not supported on this machine.
EPROTONOSUPPORT	The specified protocol is not supported on this machine.
EOPNOSUPPORT	The specified protocol does not support creation of socket pairs.
ENOMEM	There was insufficient user memory for the operation to complete.
ENOSR	There were insufficient STREAMS resources for the operation to complete.

SEE ALSO
pipe(2), read(2), write(2)

NOTES
This call is currently implemented only for the AF_UNIX address family.

NAME
spray – scatter data in order to check the network

SYNOPSIS
#include <rpcsvc/spray.h>

DESCRIPTION
The spray protocol sends packets to a given machine to test the speed and reliability of communications with that machine.

The spray protocol is not a C function interface, per se, but can be accessed using
the generic remote procedure calling interface clnt_call() [see
rpc_clnt_calls(3N)]. The protocol sends a packet to the called host. The host
acknowledges receipt of the packet. The protocol counts the number of ack-
nowledgments and can return that count.

The spray protocol currently supports the following procedures, which should be
called in the order given:

SPRAYPROC_CLEAR
    This procedure clears the counter.

SPRAYPROC_SPRAY
    This procedure sends the packet.

SPRAYPROC_GET
    This procedure returns the count and the amount of time since the last
    SPRAYPROC_CLEAR.

The following XDR routines are available in librpcsvc:

xdr_sprayarr
xdr_spraycumul

EXAMPLE
The following code fragment demonstrates how the spray protocol is used:

```
#include <rpc/rpc.h>
#include <rpcsvc/spray.h>

    .   .   .
        spraycumul spray_result;
        sprayarr   spray_data;
        char       buf[100];        /* arbitrary data */
        int        loop = 1000;
        CLIENT     *clnt;
        struct timeval timeout0 = {0, 0};
        struct timeval timeout25 = {25, 0};

        spray_data.sprayarr_len = (u_int)100;
        spray_data.sprayarr_val = buf;

        clnt = clnt_create("somehost", SPRAYPROG, SPRAYVERS, "netpath");
        if (clnt == (CLIENT *)NULL) {
            /* handle this error */
        }
```

```
        if (clnt_call(clnt, SPRAYPROC_CLEAR,
            xdr_void, NULL, xdr_void, NULL, timeout25)) {
                /* handle this error */
        }
        while (loop-- > 0) {
            if (clnt_call(clnt, SPRAYPROC_SPRAY,
                    xdr_sprayarr, &spray_data, xdr_void, NULL, timeout0)) {
                    /* handle this error */
            }
        }
        if (clnt_call(clnt, SPRAYPROC_GET,
            xdr_void, NULL, xdr_spraycumul, &spray_result, timeout25)) {
                /* handle this error */
        }
        printf("Acknowledged %ld of 1000 packets in %d secs %d usecs\n",
            spray_result.counter,
            spray_result.clock.sec,
            spray_result.clock.usec);
```

SEE ALSO

rpc_clnt_calls(3N), spray(1M), sprayd(1M).

NAME

t_accept – accept a connect request

SYNOPSIS

#include <tiuser.h>

int t_accept (int fd, int resfd, struct t_call *call);

DESCRIPTION

This function is issued by a transport user to accept a connect request. fd
identifies the local transport endpoint where the connect indication arrived,
resfd specifies the local transport endpoint where the connection is to be established, and call contains information required by the transport provider to
complete the connection. call points to a t_call structure that contains the following members:

```
struct netbuf addr;
struct netbuf opt;
struct netbuf udata;
int sequence;
```

netbuf is described in intro(3). In call, addr is the address of the caller, opt
indicates any protocol-specific parameters associated with the connection, udata
points to any user data to be returned to the caller, and sequence is the value
returned by t_listen that uniquely associates the response with a previously
received connect indication.

A transport user may accept a connection on either the same, or on a different,
local transport endpoint from the one on which the connect indication arrived. If
the same endpoint is specified (i.e., resfd=fd), the connection can be accepted
unless the following condition is true: The user has received other indications on
that endpoint but has not responded to them (with t_accept or t_snddis). For
this condition, t_accept will fail and set t_errno to TBADF.

If a different transport endpoint is specified (resfd!=fd), the endpoint must be
bound to a protocol address and must be in the T_IDLE state [see
t_getstate(3N)] before the t_accept is issued.

For both types of endpoints, t_accept will fail and set t_errno to TLOOK if there
are indications (e.g., a connect or disconnect) waiting to be received on that endpoint.

The values of parameters specified by opt and the syntax of those values are protocol specific. The udata argument enables the called transport user to send user
data to the caller and the amount of user data must not exceed the limits supported by the transport provider as returned in the connect field of the info
argument of t_open or t_getinfo. If the len [see netbuf in intro(3)] field of
udata is zero, no data will be sent to the caller.

On failure, t_errno may be set to one of the following:

[TBADF]   The specified file descriptor does not refer to a transport
                           endpoint, or the user is illegally accepting a connection on
                           the same transport endpoint on which the connect indication
                           arrived.

[TOUTSTATE]	The function was issued in the wrong sequence on the transport endpoint referenced by fd, or the transport endpoint referred to by resfd is not in the T_IDLE state.
[TACCES]	The user does not have permission to accept a connection on the responding transport endpoint or use the specified options.
[TBADOPT]	The specified options were in an incorrect format or contained illegal information.
[TBADDATA]	The amount of user data specified was not within the bounds allowed by the transport provider.
[TBADSEQ]	An invalid sequence number was specified.
[TLOOK]	An asynchronous event has occurred on the transport endpoint referenced by fd and requires immediate attention.
[TNOTSUPPORT]	This function is not supported by the underlying transport provider.
[TSYSERR]	A system error has occurred during execution of this function.

SEE ALSO

intro(3), t_connect(3N), t_getstate(3N), t_listen(3N), t_open(3N),
t_rcvconnect(3N).

UNIX System V Network Programmer's Guide.

DIAGNOSTICS

Upon successful completion, a value of 0 is returned. Otherwise, a value of −1 is
returned and t_errno is set to indicate the error.

NAME

t_alloc − allocate a library structure

SYNOPSIS

```
#include <tiuser.h>

char *t_alloc(fd, struct_type, fields)
int fd;
int struct_type;
int fields;
```

DESCRIPTION

The t_alloc function dynamically allocates memory for the various transport function argument structures as specified below. This function will allocate memory for the specified structure, and will also allocate memory for buffers referenced by the structure.

The structure to allocate is specified by struct_type, and can be one of the following:

T_BIND	struct t_bind
T_CALL	struct t_call
T_OPTMGMT	struct t_optmgmt
T_DIS	struct t_discon
T_UNITDATA	struct t_unitdata
T_UDERROR	struct t_uderr
T_INFO	struct t_info

where each of these structures may subsequently be used as an argument to one or more transport functions.

Each of the above structures, except T_INFO, contains at least one field of type struct netbuf. netbuf is described in intro(3). For each field of this type, the user may specify that the buffer for that field should be allocated as well. The fields argument specifies this option, where the argument is the bitwise-OR of any of the following:

T_ADDR	The addr field of the t_bind, t_call, t_unitdata, or t_uderr structures.
T_OPT	The opt field of the t_optmgmt, t_call, t_unitdata, or t_uderr structures.
T_UDATA	The udata field of the t_call, t_discon, or t_unitdata structures.
T_ALL	All relevant fields of the given structure.

For each field specified in fields, t_alloc will allocate memory for the buffer associated with the field, and initialize the buf pointer and maxlen [see netbuf in intro(3) for description of buf and maxlen] field accordingly. The length of the buffer allocated will be based on the same size information that is returned to the user on t_open and t_getinfo. Thus, fd must refer to the transport endpoint through which the newly allocated structure will be passed, so that the appropriate size information can be accessed. If the size value associated with any specified field is −1 or −2 (see t_open or t_getinfo), t_alloc will be unable to determine the size of the buffer to allocate and will fail, setting t_errno to TSYSERR and errno to EINVAL. For any field not specified in fields, buf will be set to NULL and maxlen will be set to zero.

Use of t_alloc to allocate structures will help ensure the compatibility of user programs with future releases of the transport interface.

On failure, t_errno may be set to one of the following:

[TBADF]   The specified file descriptor does not refer to a transport end-point.

[TSYSERR]   A system error has occurred during execution of this function.

SEE ALSO
intro(3), t_free(3N), t_getinfo(3N), t_open(3N).
UNIX System V Network Programmer's Guide.

DIAGNOSTICS
On successful completion, t_alloc returns a pointer to the newly allocated structure. On failure, NULL is returned.

NAME

    t_bind – bind an address to a transport endpoint

SYNOPSIS

    #include <tiuser.h>

    int t_bind (fd, req, ret)
    int fd;
    struct t_bind *req;
    struct t_bind *ret;

DESCRIPTION

    This function associates a protocol address with the transport endpoint specified by fd and activates that transport endpoint. In connection mode, the transport provider may begin accepting or requesting connections on the transport endpoint. In connectionless mode, the transport user may send or receive data units through the transport endpoint.

    The req and ret arguments point to a t_bind structure containing the following members:

    struct netbuf addr;
    unsigned qlen;

    netbuf is described in intro(3). The addr field of the t_bind structure specifies a protocol address and the qlen field is used to indicate the maximum number of outstanding connect indications.

    req is used to request that an address, represented by the netbuf structure, be bound to the given transport endpoint. len [see netbuf in intro(3); also for buf and maxlen] specifies the number of bytes in the address and buf points to the address buffer. maxlen has no meaning for the req argument. On return, ret contains the address that the transport provider actually bound to the transport endpoint; this may be different from the address specified by the user in req. In ret, the user specifies maxlen, which is the maximum size of the address buffer, and buf, which points to the buffer where the address is to be placed. On return, len specifies the number of bytes in the bound address and buf points to the bound address. If maxlen is not large enough to hold the returned address, an error will result.

    If the requested address is not available, or if no address is specified in req (the len field of addr in req is zero) the transport provider may assign an appropriate address to be bound, and will return that address in the addr field of ret. The user can compare the addresses in req and ret to determine whether the transport provider bound the transport endpoint to a different address than that requested.

    req may be NULL if the user does not wish to specify an address to be bound. Here, the value of qlen is assumed to be zero, and the transport provider must assign an address to the transport endpoint. Similarly, ret may be NULL if the user does not care what address was bound by the provider and is not interested in the negotiated value of qlen. It is valid to set req and ret to NULL for the same call, in which case the provider chooses the address to bind to the transport endpoint and does not return that information to the user.

The qlen field has meaning only when initializing a connection-mode service. It specifies the number of outstanding connect indications the transport provider should support for the given transport endpoint. An outstanding connect indication is one that has been passed to the transport user by the transport provider. A value of qlen greater than zero is only meaningful when issued by a passive transport user that expects other users to call it. The value of qlen will be negotiated by the transport provider and may be changed if the transport provider cannot support the specified number of outstanding connect indications. On return, the qlen field in ret will contain the negotiated value.

This function allows more than one transport endpoint to be bound to the same protocol address (however, the transport provider must support this capability also), but it is not allowable to bind more than one protocol address to the same transport endpoint. If a user binds more than one transport endpoint to the same protocol address, only one endpoint can be used to listen for connect indications associated with that protocol address. In other words, only one t_bind for a given protocol address may specify a value of qlen greater than zero. In this way, the transport provider can identify which transport endpoint should be notified of an incoming connect indication. If a user attempts to bind a protocol address to a second transport endpoint with a value of qlen greater than zero, the transport provider will assign another address to be bound to that endpoint. If a user accepts a connection on the transport endpoint that is being used as the listening endpoint, the bound protocol address will be found to be busy for the duration of that connection. No other transport endpoints may be bound for listening while that initial listening endpoint is in the data transfer phase. This will prevent more than one transport endpoint bound to the same protocol address from accepting connect indications.

On failure, t_errno may be set to one of the following:

[TBADF]	The specified file descriptor does not refer to a transport endpoint.
[TOUTSTATE]	The function was issued in the wrong sequence.
[TBADADDR]	The specified protocol address was in an incorrect format or contained illegal information.
[TNOADDR]	The transport provider could not allocate an address.
[TACCES]	The user does not have permission to use the specified address.
[TBUFOVFLW]	The number of bytes allowed for an incoming argument is not sufficient to store the value of that argument. The provider's state will change to T_IDLE and the information to be returned in ret will be discarded.
[TSYSERR]	A system error has occurred during execution of this function.

SEE ALSO

    intro(3), t_open(3N), t_optmgmt(3N), t_unbind(3N).
    UNIX System V Network Programmer's Guide.

DIAGNOSTICS

    t_bind returns 0 on success and −1 on failure and t_errno is set to indicate the
    error.

NAME

t_close – close a transport endpoint

SYNOPSIS

```
#include <tiuser.h>

int t_close(fd)
int fd;
```

DESCRIPTION

The **t_close** function informs the transport provider that the user is finished with the transport endpoint specified by **fd**, and frees any local library resources associated with the endpoint. In addition, **t_close** closes the file associated with the transport endpoint.

t_close should be called from the **T_UNBND** state [see **t_getstate**(3N)]. However, this function does not check state information, so it may be called from any state to close a transport endpoint. If this occurs, the local library resources associated with the endpoint will be freed automatically. In addition, **close**(2) will be issued for that file descriptor; the close will be abortive if no other process has that file open, and will break any transport connection that may be associated with that endpoint.

On failure, **t_errno** may be set to the following:

[TBADF]   The specified file descriptor does not refer to a transport endpoint.

SEE ALSO

t_getstate(3N), t_open(3N), t_unbind(3N).
UNIX System V Network Programmer's Guide.

DIAGNOSTICS

t_close returns 0 on success and −1 on failure and **t_errno** is set to indicate the error.

NAME
        t_connect – establish a connection with another transport user

SYNOPSIS
        #include <tiuser.h>

        int t_connect(fd, sndcall, rcvcall)
        int fd;
        struct t_call *sndcall;
        struct t_call *rcvcall;

DESCRIPTION
        This function enables a transport user to request a connection to the specified
        destination transport user. fd identifies the local transport endpoint where com-
        munication will be established, while sndcall and rcvcall point to a t_call
        structure that contains the following members:

                struct netbuf addr;
                struct netbuf opt;
                struct netbuf udata;
                int sequence;

        sndcall specifies information needed by the transport provider to establish a
        connection and rcvcall specifies information that is associated with the newly
        established connection.

        netbuf is described in intro(3). In sndcall, addr specifies the protocol address
        of the destination transport user, opt presents any protocol-specific information
        that might be needed by the transport provider, udata points to optional user
        data that may be passed to the destination transport user during connection
        establishment, and sequence has no meaning for this function.

        On return in rcvcall, addr returns the protocol address associated with the
        responding transport endpoint, opt presents any protocol-specific information
        associated with the connection, udata points to optional user data that may be
        returned by the destination transport user during connection establishment, and
        sequence has no meaning for this function.

        The opt argument implies no structure on the options that may be passed to the
        transport provider. The transport provider is free to specify the structure of any
        options passed to it. These options are specific to the underlying protocol of the
        transport provider. The user may choose not to negotiate protocol options by
        setting the len field of opt to zero. In this case, the provider may use default
        options.

        The udata argument enables the caller to pass user data to the destination tran-
        sport user and receive user data from the destination user during connection
        establishment. However, the amount of user data must not exceed the limits sup-
        ported by the transport provider as returned in the connect field of the info
        argument of t_open(3N) or t_getinfo(3N). If the len [see netbuf in intro(3)]
        field of udata is zero in sndcall, no data will be sent to the destination transport
        user.

On return, the **addr**, **opt**, and **udata** fields of **rcvcall** will be updated to reflect values associated with the connection. Thus, the **maxlen** [see netbuf in intro(3)] field of each argument must be set before issuing this function to indicate the maximum size of the buffer for each. However, **rcvcall** may be NULL, in which case no information is given to the user on return from t_connect.

By default, **t_connect** executes in synchronous mode, and will wait for the destination user's response before returning control to the local user. A successful return (i.e., return value of zero) indicates that the requested connection has been established. However, if O_NDELAY or O_NONBLOCK is set (via t_open or fcntl), **t_connect** executes in asynchronous mode. In this case, the call will not wait for the remote user's response, but will return control immediately to the local user and return -1 with t_errno set to TNODATA to indicate that the connection has not yet been established. In this way, the function simply initiates the connection establishment procedure by sending a connect request to the destination transport user.

On failure, t_errno may be set to one of the following:

[TBADF]   The specified file descriptor does not refer to a transport endpoint.

[TOUTSTATE]   The function was issued in the wrong sequence.

[TNODATA]   O_NDELAY or O_NONBLOCK was set, so the function successfully initiated the connection establishment procedure, but did not wait for a response from the remote user.

[TBADADDR]   The specified protocol address was in an incorrect format or contained illegal information.

[TBADOPT]   The specified protocol options were in an incorrect format or contained illegal information.

[TBADDATA]   The amount of user data specified was not within the bounds allowed by the transport provider.

[TACCES]   The user does not have permission to use the specified address or options.

[TBUFOVFLW]   The number of bytes allocated for an incoming argument is not sufficient to store the value of that argument. If executed in synchronous mode, the provider's state, as seen by the user, changes to T_DATAXFER, and the connect indication information to be returned in rcvcall is discarded.

[TLOOK]   An asynchronous event has occurred on this transport endpoint and requires immediate attention.

[TNOTSUPPORT]   This function is not supported by the underlying transport provider.

[TSYSERR]   A system error has occurred during execution of this function.

SEE ALSO

intro(3), t_accept(3N), t_getinfo(3N), t_listen(3N), t_open(3N),
t_optmgmt(3N), t_rcvconnect(3N).
UNIX System V Network Programmer's Guide.

DIAGNOSTICS

t_connect returns 0 on success and −1 on failure and t_errno is set to indicate
the error.

NAME

t_error – produce error message

SYNOPSIS

```
#include <tiuser.h>

void t_error(errmsg)
char *errmsg;
extern int t_errno;
extern char *t_errlist[];
extern int t_nerr;
```

DESCRIPTION

t_error produces a message on the standard error output which describes the last error encountered during a call to a transport function. The argument string errmsg is a user-supplied error message that gives context to the error.

t_error prints the user-supplied error message followed by a colon and the standard transport function error message for the current value contained in t_errno. If t_errno is TSYSERR, t_error will also print the standard error message for the current value contained in errno [see intro(2)].

t_errlist is the array of message strings, to allow user message formatting. t_errno can be used as an index into this array to retrieve the error message string (without a terminating newline). t_nerr is the maximum index value for the t_errlist array.

t_errno is set when an error occurs and is not cleared on subsequent successful calls.

EXAMPLE

If a t_connect function fails on transport endpoint fd2 because a bad address was given, the following call might follow the failure:

t_error("t_connect failed on fd2");

The diagnostic message would print as:

t_connect failed on fd2: Incorrect transport address format

where "t_connect failed on fd2" tells the user which function failed on which transport endpoint, and "Incorrect transport address format" identifies the specific error that occurred.

SEE ALSO

UNIX System V Network Programmer's Guide.

NAME

    t_free – free a library structure

SYNOPSIS

    #include <tiuser.h>

    int t_free (ptr, struct_type)
    char *ptr;
    int struct_type;

DESCRIPTION

    The **t_free** function frees memory previously allocated by **t_alloc**. This function will free memory for the specified structure, and will also free memory for buffers referenced by the structure.

    ptr points to one of the six structure types described for **t_alloc**, and **struct_type** identifies the type of that structure, which can be one of the following:

T_BIND	struct t_bind
T_CALL	struct t_call
T_OPTMGMT	struct t_optmgmt
T_DIS	struct t_discon
T_UNITDATA	struct t_unitdata
T_UDERROR	struct t_uderr
T_INFO	struct t_info

    where each of these structures is used as an argument to one or more transport functions.

    t_free will check the **addr**, **opt**, and **udata** fields of the given structure (as appropriate), and free the buffers pointed to by the **buf** field of the **netbuf** [see intro(3)] structure. If **buf** is NULL, **t_free** will not attempt to free memory. After all buffers are freed, **t_free** will free the memory associated with the structure pointed to by **ptr**.

    Undefined results will occur if **ptr** or any of the **buf** pointers points to a block of memory that was not previously allocated by **t_alloc**.

    On failure, **t_errno** may be set to the following:

    [TSYSERR]   A system error has occurred during execution of this function.

SEE ALSO

    intro(3), t_alloc(3N).
    UNIX System V Network Programmer's Guide.

DIAGNOSTICS

    t_free returns 0 on success and −1 on failure and **t_errno** is set to indicate the error.

NAME
     t_getinfo – get protocol-specific service information
SYNOPSIS
     #include <tiuser.h>

     int t_getinfo(fd, info)
     int fd;
     struct t_info *info;
DESCRIPTION
     This function returns the current characteristics of the underlying transport proto-
     col associated with file descriptor fd. The info structure is used to return the
     same information returned by t_open. This function enables a transport user to
     access this information during any phase of communication.

     This argument points to a t_info structure, which contains the following
     members:

     long addr;   /* max size of the transport protocol address */
     long options;   /* max number of bytes of protocol-specific options */
     long tsdu;   /* max size of a transport service data unit (TSDU) */
     long etsdu;   /* max size of an expedited transport service data unit (ETSDU) */
     long connect;   /* max amount of data allowed on connection establishment functions */
     long discon;   /* max amount of data allowed on t_snddis and t_rcvdis functions */
     long servtype;   /* service type supported by the transport provider */

     The values of the fields have the following meanings:

     addr   A value greater than or equal to zero indicates the maximum size
                 of a transport protocol address; a value of −1 specifies that there
                 is no limit on the address size; and a value of −2 specifies that the
                 transport provider does not provide user access to transport pro-
                 tocol addresses.

     options   A value greater than or equal to zero indicates the maximum
                 number of bytes of protocol-specific options supported by the pro-
                 vider; a value of −1 specifies that there is no limit on the option
                 size; and a value of −2 specifies that the transport provider does
                 not support user-settable options.

     tsdu   A value greater than zero specifies the maximum size of a tran-
                 sport service data unit (TSDU); a value of zero specifies that the
                 transport provider does not support the concept of TSDU, although
                 it does support the sending of a data stream with no logical boun-
                 daries preserved across a connection; a value of −1 specifies that
                 there is no limit on the size of a TSDU; and a value of −2 specifies
                 that the transfer of normal data is not supported by the transport
                 provider.

     etsdu   A value greater than zero specifies the maximum size of an
                 expedited transport service data unit (ETSDU); a value of zero
                 specifies that the transport provider does not support the concept
                 of ETSDU, although it does support the sending of an expedited
                 data stream with no logical boundaries preserved across a

connection; a value of −1 specifies that there is no limit on the size of an ETSDU; and a value of −2 specifies that the transfer of expedited data is not supported by the transport provider.

connect   A value greater than or equal to zero specifies the maximum amount of data that may be associated with connection establishment functions; a value of −1 specifies that there is no limit on the amount of data sent during connection establishment; and a value of −2 specifies that the transport provider does not allow data to be sent with connection establishment functions.

discon   A value greater than or equal to zero specifies the maximum amount of data that may be associated with the t_snddis and t_rcvdis functions; a value of −1 specifies that there is no limit on the amount of data sent with these abortive release functions; and a value of −2 specifies that the transport provider does not allow data to be sent with the abortive release functions.

servtype   This field specifies the service type supported by the transport provider, as described below.

If a transport user is concerned with protocol independence, the above sizes may be accessed to determine how large the buffers must be to hold each piece of information. Alternatively, the t_alloc function may be used to allocate these buffers. An error will result if a transport user exceeds the allowed data size on any function. The value of each field may change as a result of option negotiation, and t_getinfo enables a user to retrieve the current characteristics.

The servtype field of info may specify one of the following values on return:

T_COTS   The transport provider supports a connection-mode service but does not support the optional orderly release facility.

T_COTS_ORD The transport provider supports a connection-mode service with the optional orderly release facility.

T_CLTS   The transport provider supports a connectionless-mode service. For this service type, t_open will return −2 for etsdu, connect, and discon.

On failure, t_errno may be set to one of the following:

[TBADF]   The specified file descriptor does not refer to a transport endpoint.

[TSYSERR] A system error has occurred during execution of this function.

SEE ALSO

t_open(3N).

UNIX System V Network Programmer's Guide.

DIAGNOSTICS

t_getinfo returns 0 on success and −1 on failure and t_errno is set to indicate the error.

NAME

t_getstate – get the current state

SYNOPSIS

#include <tiuser.h>

int t_getstate(fd)
int fd;

DESCRIPTION

The t_getstate function returns the current state of the provider associated with the transport endpoint specified by fd.

On failure, t_errno may be set to one of the following:

[TBADF]	The specified file descriptor does not refer to a transport endpoint.
[TSTATECHNG]	The transport provider is undergoing a state change.
[TSYSERR]	A system error has occurred during execution of this function.

SEE ALSO

t_open(3N).

UNIX System V Network Programmer's Guide.

DIAGNOSTICS

t_getstate returns the current state on successful completion and −1 on failure and t_errno is set to indicate the error. The current state may be one of the following:

T_UNBND	unbound
T_IDLE	idle
T_OUTCON	outgoing connection pending
T_INCON	incoming connection pending
T_DATAXFER	data transfer
T_OUTREL	outgoing orderly release (waiting for an orderly release indication)
T_INREL	incoming orderly release (waiting for an orderly release request)

If the provider is undergoing a state transition when t_getstate is called, the function will fail.

NAME

t_listen – listen for a connect request

SYNOPSIS

#include <tiuser.h>

int t_listen(fd, call)
int fd;
struct t_call *call;

DESCRIPTION

This function listens for a connect request from a calling transport user. fd identifies the local transport endpoint where connect indications arrive, and on return, call contains information describing the connect indication. call points to a t_call structure, which contains the following members:

struct netbuf addr;
truct netbuf opt;
struct netbuf udata;
int sequence;

netbuf is described in intro(3). In call, addr returns the protocol address of the calling transport user, opt returns protocol-specific parameters associated with the connect request, udata returns any user data sent by the caller on the connect request, and sequence is a number that uniquely identifies the returned connect indication. The value of sequence enables the user to listen for multiple connect indications before responding to any of them.

Since this function returns values for the addr, opt, and udata fields of call, the maxlen [see netbuf in intro(3)] field of each must be set before issuing t_listen to indicate the maximum size of the buffer for each.

By default, t_listen executes in synchronous mode and waits for a connect indication to arrive before returning to the user. However, if O_NDELAY or O_NONBLOCK is set (via t_open or fcntl), t_listen executes asynchronously, reducing to a poll for existing connect indications. If none are available, it returns −1 and sets t_errno to TNODATA.

On failure, t_errno may be set to one of the following:

[TBADF]   The specified file descriptor does not refer to a transport endpoint.

[TBUFOVFLW]   The number of bytes allocated for an incoming argument is not sufficient to store the value of that argument. The provider's state, as seen by the user, changes to T_INCON, and the connect indication information to be returned in call is discarded.

[TNODATA]   O_NDELAY or O_NONBLOCK was set, but no connect indications had been queued.

[TLOOK]   An asynchronous event has occurred on this transport endpoint and requires immediate attention.

[TNOTSUPPORT]	This function is not supported by the underlying transport provider.
[TSYSERR]	A system error has occurred during execution of this function.

CAVEATS

If a user issues t_listen in synchronous mode on a transport endpoint that was not bound for listening (i.e., qlen was zero on t_bind), the call will wait forever because no connect indications will arrive on that endpoint.

SEE ALSO

intro(3), t_accept(3N), t_bind(3N), t_connect(3N), t_open(3N), t_rcvconnect(3N).

UNIX System V Network Programmer's Guide.

DIAGNOSTICS

t_listen returns 0 on success and −1 on failure and t_errno is set to indicate the error.

NAME

t_look – look at the current event on a transport endpoint

SYNOPSIS

#include <tiuser.h>

int t_look(fd)
int fd;

DESCRIPTION

This function returns the current event on the transport endpoint specified by fd. This function enables a transport provider to notify a transport user of an asynchronous event when the user is issuing functions in synchronous mode. Certain events require immediate notification of the user and are indicated by a specific error, TLOOK, on the current or next function to be executed.

This function also enables a transport user to poll a transport endpoint periodically for asynchronous events.

On failure, t_errno may be set to one of the following:

[TBADF]   The specified file descriptor does not refer to a transport endpoint.

[TSYSERR]   A system error has occurred during execution of this function.

SEE ALSO

t_open(3N).
UNIX System V Network Programmer's Guide.

DIAGNOSTICS

Upon success, t_look returns a value that indicates which of the allowable events has occurred, or returns zero if no event exists. One of the following events is returned:

T_LISTEN   connection indication received

T_CONNECT   connect confirmation received

T_DATA   normal data received

T_EXDATA   expedited data received

T_DISCONNECT   disconnect received

T_UDERR   datagram error indication

T_ORDREL   orderly release indication

On failure, −1 is returned and t_errno is set to indicate the error.

NAME

   t_open – establish a transport endpoint

SYNOPSIS

   #include <tiuser.h>

   #include <fcntl.h>

   int t_open (char path, int oflag, struct t_info *info);

DESCRIPTION

   t_open must be called as the first step in the initialization of a transport endpoint. This function establishes a transport endpoint by opening a UNIX file that
   identifies a particular transport provider (i.e., transport protocol) and returning a
   file descriptor that identifies that endpoint. For example, opening the file
   /dev/iso_cots identifies an OSI connection-oriented transport layer protocol as
   the transport provider.

   path points to the path name of the file to open, and oflag identifies any open
   flags [as in open(2)]. oflag may be constructed from O_NDELAY or O_NONBLOCK
   OR-ed with O_RDWR. These flags are defined in the header file <fcntl.h>.
   t_open returns a file descriptor that will be used by all subsequent functions to
   identify the particular local transport endpoint.

   This function also returns various default characteristics of the underlying transport protocol by setting fields in the t_info structure. This argument points to
   a t_info which contains the following members:

   long addr;   /* max size of the transport protocol address */
   long options;   /* max number of bytes of protocol-specific options */
   long tsdu;   /* max size of a transport service data unit (TSDU) */
   long etsdu;   /* max size of an expedited transport service data unit (ETSDU) */
   long connect;   /* max amount of data allowed on connection establishment functions */
   long discon;   /* max amount of data allowed on t_snddis and t_rcvdis functions */
   long servtype;   /* service type supported by the transport provider */

   The values of the fields have the following meanings:

   addr   A value greater than or equal to zero indicates the maximum size
                of a transport protocol address; a value of −1 specifies that there
                is no limit on the address size; and a value of -2 specifies that the
                transport provider does not provide user access to transport pro-
                tocol addresses.

   options   A value greater than or equal to zero indicates the maximum
                number of bytes of protocol-specific options supported by the pro-
                vider; a value of −1 specifies that there is no limit on the option
                size; and a value of −2 specifies that the transport provider does
                not support user-settable options.

   tsdu   A value greater than zero specifies the maximum size of a tran-
                sport service data unit (TSDU); a value of zero specifies that the
                transport provider does not support the concept of TSDU, although
                it does support the sending of a data stream with no logical boun-
                daries preserved across a connection; a value of −1 specifies that
                there is no limit on the size of a TSDU; and a value of −2 specifies

that the transfer of normal data is not supported by the transport provider.

etsdu   A value greater than zero specifies the maximum size of an expedited transport service data unit (ETSDU); a value of zero specifies that the transport provider does not support the concept of ETSDU, although it does support the sending of an expedited data stream with no logical boundaries preserved across a connection; a value of −1 specifies that there is no limit on the size of an ETSDU; and a value of −2 specifies that the transfer of expedited data is not supported by the transport provider.

connect   A value greater than or equal to zero specifies the maximum amount of data that may be associated with connection establishment functions; a value of −1 specifies that there is no limit on the amount of data sent during connection establishment; and a value of −2 specifies that the transport provider does not allow data to be sent with connection establishment functions.

discon   A value greater than or equal to zero specifies the maximum amount of data that may be associated with the t_snddis and t_rcvdis functions; a value of −1 specifies that there is no limit on the amount of data sent with these abortive release functions; and a value of −2 specifies that the transport provider does not allow data to be sent with the abortive release functions.

servtype   This field specifies the service type supported by the transport provider, as described below.

If a transport user is concerned with protocol independence, the above sizes may be accessed to determine how large the buffers must be to hold each piece of information. Alternatively, the t_alloc function may be used to allocate these buffers. An error will result if a transport user exceeds the allowed data size on any function.

The servtype field of info may specify one of the following values on return:

T_COTS   The transport provider supports a connection-mode service but does not support the optional orderly release facility.

T_COTS_ORD   The transport provider supports a connection-mode service with the optional orderly release facility.

T_CLTS   The transport provider supports a connectionless-mode service. For this service type, t_open will return −2 for etsdu, connect, and discon.

A single transport endpoint may support only one of the above services at one time.

If info is set to uu by the transport user, no protocol information is returned by t_open.

On failure, t_errno may be set to the following:

[TSYSERR]   A system error has occurred during execution of this func-
                   tion.

[TBADFLAG]   An invalid flag is specified.

DIAGNOSTICS

t_open returns a valid file descriptor on success and −1 on failure and t_errno
is set to indicate the error.

NOTES

If t_open is used on a non-TLI-conforming STREAMS device, unpredictable events
may occur.

SEE ALSO

open(2).

UNIX System V Network Programmer's Guide.

NAME

t_optmgmt – manage options for a transport endpoint

SYNOPSIS

#include <tiuser.h>

int t_optmgmt (int fd, struct t_optmgmt *req, struct t_optmgmt *ret);

DESCRIPTION

The t_optmgmt function enables a transport user to retrieve, verify, or negotiate protocol options with the transport provider. fd identifies a bound transport endpoint.

The req and ret arguments point to a t_optmgmt structure containing the following members:

```
struct netbuf opt;
long flags;
```

The opt field identifies protocol options and the flags field is used to specify the action to take with those options.

The options are represented by a netbuf [see intro(3); also for len, buf, and maxlen] structure in a manner similar to the address in t_bind. req is used to request a specific action of the provider and to send options to the provider. len specifies the number of bytes in the options, buf points to the options buffer, and maxlen has no meaning for the req argument. The transport provider may return options and flag values to the user through ret. For ret, maxlen specifies the maximum size of the options buffer and buf points to the buffer where the options are to be placed. On return, len specifies the number of bytes of options returned. maxlen has no meaning for the req argument, but must be set in the ret argument to specify the maximum number of bytes the options buffer can hold. The actual structure and content of the options is imposed by the transport provider.

The flags field of req can specify one of the following actions:

T_NEGOTIATE   This action enables the user to negotiate the values of the options specified in req with the transport provider. The provider will evaluate the requested options and negotiate the values, returning the negotiated values through ret.

T_CHECK   This action enables the user to verify whether the options specified in req are supported by the transport provider. On return, the flags field of ret will have either T_SUCCESS or T_FAILURE set to indicate to the user whether the options are supported. These flags are only meaningful for the T_CHECK request.

T_DEFAULT   This action enables a user to retrieve the default options supported by the transport provider into the opt field of ret. In req, the len field of opt must be zero and the buf field may be NULL.

If issued as part of the connectionless-mode service, t_optmgmt may block due to flow control constraints. The function will not complete until the transport provider has processed all previously sent data units.

On failure, t_errno may be set to one of the following:

[TBADF]	The specified file descriptor does not refer to a transport endpoint.
[TOUTSTATE]	The function was issued in the wrong sequence.
[TACCES]	The user does not have permission to negotiate the specified options.
[TBADOPT]	The specified protocol options were in an incorrect format or contained illegal information.
[TBADFLAG]	An invalid flag was specified.
[TBUFOVFLW]	The number of bytes allowed for an incoming argument is not sufficient to store the value of that argument. The information to be returned in ret will be discarded.
[TSYSERR]	A system error has occurred during execution of this function.

SEE ALSO

intro(3), t_getinfo(3N), t_open(3N).

UNIX System V Network Programmer's Guide.

DIAGNOSTICS

t_optmgmt returns 0 on success and −1 on failure and t_errno is set to indicate the error.

NAME

t_rcv – receive data or expedited data sent over a connection

SYNOPSIS

`int t_rcv (int fd, char *buf, unsigned nbytes, int *flags);`

DESCRIPTION

This function receives either normal or expedited data. fd identifies the local transport endpoint through which data will arrive, buf points to a receive buffer where user data will be placed, and nbytes specifies the size of the receive buffer. flags may be set on return from t_rcv and specifies optional flags as described below.

By default, t_rcv operates in synchronous mode and will wait for data to arrive if none is currently available. However, if O_NDELAY or O_NONBLOCK is set (via t_open or fcntl), t_rcv will execute in asynchronous mode and will fail if no data is available. (See TNODATA below.)

On return from the call, if T_MORE is set in flags, this indicates that there is more data and the current transport service data unit (TSDU) or expedited transport service data unit (ETSDU) must be received in multiple t_rcv calls. Each t_rcv with the T_MORE flag set indicates that another t_rcv must follow to get more data for the current TSDU. The end of the TSDU is identified by the return of a t_rcv call with the T_MORE flag not set. If the transport provider does not support the concept of a TSDU as indicated in the info argument on return from t_open or t_getinfo, the T_MORE flag is not meaningful and should be ignored.

On return, the data returned is expedited data if T_EXPEDITED is set in flags. If the number of bytes of expedited data exceeds nbytes, t_rcv will set T_EXPEDITED and T_MORE on return from the initial call. Subsequent calls to retrieve the remaining ETSDU will have T_EXPEDITED set on return. The end of the ETSDU is identified by the return of a t_rcv call with the T_MORE flag not set.

If expedited data arrives after part of a TSDU has been retrieved, receipt of the remainder of the TSDU will be suspended until the ETSDU has been processed. Only after the full ETSDU has been retrieved (T_MORE not set) will the remainder of the TSDU be available to the user.

On failure, t_errno may be set to one of the following:

[TBADF]	The specified file descriptor does not refer to a transport endpoint.
[TNODATA]	O_NDELAY or O_NONBLOCK was set, but no data is currently available from the transport provider.
[TLOOK]	An asynchronous event has occurred on this transport endpoint and requires immediate attention.
[TNOTSUPPORT]	This function is not supported by the underlying transport provider.
[TSYSERR]	A system error has occurred during execution of this function.

SEE ALSO
>   t_open(3N), t_snd(3N).
>   *UNIX System V Network Programmer's Guide.*

DIAGNOSTICS
>   On successful completion, t_rcv returns the number of bytes received, and it
>   returns −1 on failure and t_errno is set to indicate the error.

NAME

t_rcvconnect – receive the confirmation from a connect request

SYNOPSIS

#include <tiuser.h>

int t_rcvconnect (int fd, struct t_call *call);

DESCRIPTION

This function enables a calling transport user to determine the status of a previously sent connect request and is used in conjunction with t_connect to establish a connection in asynchronous mode. The connection will be established on successful completion of this function.

fd identifies the local transport endpoint where communication will be established, and call contains information associated with the newly established connection. call points to a t_call structure which contains the following members:

```
struct netbuf addr;
struct netbuf opt;
struct netbuf udata;
int sequence;
```

netbuf is described in intro(3). In call, addr returns the protocol address associated with the responding transport endpoint, opt presents any protocol-specific information associated with the connection, udata points to optional user data that may be returned by the destination transport user during connection establishment, and sequence has no meaning for this function.

The maxlen [see netbuf in intro(3)] field of each argument must be set before issuing this function to indicate the maximum size of the buffer for each. However, call may be NULL, in which case no information is given to the user on return from t_rcvconnect. By default, t_rcvconnect executes in synchronous mode and waits for the connection to be established before returning. On return, the addr, opt, and udata fields reflect values associated with the connection.

If O_NDELAY or O_NONBLOCK is set (via t_open or fcntl), t_rcvconnect executes in asynchronous mode, and reduces to a poll for existing connect confirmations. If none are available, t_rcvconnect fails and returns immediately without waiting for the connection to be established. (See TNODATA below.) t_rcvconnect must be re-issued at a later time to complete the connection establishment phase and retrieve the information returned in call.

On failure, t_errno may be set to one of the following:

[TBADF]	The specified file descriptor does not refer to a transport endpoint.
[TBUFOVFLW]	The number of bytes allocated for an incoming argument is not sufficient to store the value of that argument and the connect information to be returned in call will be discarded. The provider's state, as seen by the user, will be changed to DATAXFER.

[TNODATA]	O_NDELAY or O_NONBLOCK was set, but a connect confirmation has not yet arrived.
[TLOOK]	An asynchronous event has occurred on this transport connection and requires immediate attention.
[TNOTSUPPORT]	This function is not supported by the underlying transport provider.
[TSYSERR]	A system error has occurred during execution of this function.

SEE ALSO

intro(3), t_accept(3N), t_bind(3N), t_connect(3N), t_listen(3N), t_open(3N).

UNIX System V Network Programmer's Guide.

DIAGNOSTICS

t_rcvconnect returns 0 on success and −1 on failure and t_errno is set to indicate the error.

NAME

t_rcvdis – retrieve information from disconnect

SYNOPSIS

#include <tiuser.h>

t_rcvdis (int fd, struct t_discon *discon);

DESCRIPTION

This function is used to identify the cause of a disconnect, and to retrieve any user data sent with the disconnect. fd identifies the local transport endpoint where the connection existed, and discon points to a t_discon structure containing the following members:

```
struct netbuf udata;
int reason;
int sequence;
```

netbuf is described in intro(3). reason specifies the reason for the disconnect through a protocol-dependent reason code, udata identifies any user data that was sent with the disconnect, and sequence may identify an outstanding connect indication with which the disconnect is associated. sequence is only meaningful when t_rcvdis is issued by a passive transport user who has executed one or more t_listen functions and is processing the resulting connect indications. If a disconnect indication occurs, sequence can be used to identify which of the outstanding connect indications is associated with the disconnect.

If a user does not care if there is incoming data and does not need to know the value of reason or sequence, discon may be NULL and any user data associated with the disconnect will be discarded. However, if a user has retrieved more than one outstanding connect indication (via t_listen) and discon is NULL, the user will be unable to identify which connect indication the disconnect is associated with.

On failure, t_errno may be set to one of the following:

[TBADF]	The specified file descriptor does not refer to a transport endpoint.
[TNODIS]	No disconnect indication currently exists on the specified transport endpoint.
[TBUFOVFLW]	The number of bytes allocated for incoming data is not sufficient to store the data. The provider's state, as seen by the user, will change to T_IDLE, and the disconnect indication information to be returned in discon will be discarded.
[TNOTSUPPORT]	This function is not supported by the underlying transport provider.
[TSYSERR]	A system error has occurred during execution of this function.

SEE ALSO

    intro(3), t_connect(3N), t_listen(3N), t_open(3N), t_snddis(3N).
    UNIX System V Network Programmer's Guide.

DIAGNOSTICS

    t_rcvdis returns 0 on success and −1 on failure and t_errno is set to indicate
    the error.

NAME

t_rcvrel – acknowledge receipt of an orderly release indication

SYNOPSIS

#include <tiuser.h>

t_rcvrel (int fd);

DESCRIPTION

This function is used to acknowledge receipt of an orderly release indication. fd identifies the local transport endpoint where the connection exists. After receipt of this indication, the user should not attempt to receive more data because such an attempt will block forever. However, the user may continue to send data over the connection if t_sndrel has not been issued by the user.

This function is an optional service of the transport provider, and is only supported if the transport provider returned service type T_COTS_ORD on t_open or t_getinfo.

On failure, t_errno may be set to one of the following:

[TBADF]   The specified file descriptor does not refer to a transport endpoint.

[TNOREL]   No orderly release indication currently exists on the specified transport endpoint.

[TLOOK]   An asynchronous event has occurred on this transport endpoint and requires immediate attention.

[TNOTSUPPORT]   This function is not supported by the underlying transport provider.

[TSYSERR]   A system error has occurred during execution of this function.

SEE ALSO

t_open(3N), t_sndrel(3N).

UNIX System V Network Programmer's Guide.

DIAGNOSTICS

t_rcvrel returns 0 on success and −1 on failure t_errno is set to indicate the error.

NAME

t_rcvudata – receive a data unit

SYNOPSIS

#include <tiuser.h>

int t_rcvudata (int fd, struct t_unitdata *unitdata, int *flags);

DESCRIPTION

This function is used in connectionless mode to receive a data unit from another transport user. fd identifies the local transport endpoint through which data will be received, unitdata holds information associated with the received data unit, and flags is set on return to indicate that the complete data unit was not received. unitdata points to a t_unitdata structure containing the following members:

        struct netbuf addr;
        struct netbuf opt;
        struct netbuf udata;

The maxlen [see netbuf in intro(3)] field of addr, opt, and udata must be set before issuing this function to indicate the maximum size of the buffer for each.

On return from this call, addr specifies the protocol address of the sending user, opt identifies protocol-specific options that were associated with this data unit, and udata specifies the user data that was received.

By default, t_rcvudata operates in synchronous mode and will wait for a data unit to arrive if none is currently available. However, if O_NDELAY or O_NONBLOCK is set (via t_open or fcntl), t_rcvudata will execute in asynchronous mode and will fail if no data units are available.

If the buffer defined in the udata field of unitdata is not large enough to hold the current data unit, the buffer will be filled and T_MORE will be set in flags on return to indicate that another t_rcvudata should be issued to retrieve the rest of the data unit. Subsequent t_rcvudata call(s) will return zero for the length of the address and options until the full data unit has been received.

On failure, t_errno may be set to one of the following:

[TBADF]	The specified file descriptor does not refer to a transport endpoint.
[TNODATA]	O_NDELAY or O_NONBLOCK was set, but no data units are currently available from the transport provider.
[TBUFOVFLW]	The number of bytes allocated for the incoming protocol address or options is not sufficient to store the information. The unit data information to be returned in unitdata will be discarded.
[TLOOK]	An asynchronous event has occurred on this transport endpoint and requires immediate attention.
[TNOTSUPPORT]	This function is not supported by the underlying transport provider.

    [TSYSERR]   A system error has occurred during execution of this function.

SEE ALSO

    intro(3), t_rcvuderr(3N), t_sndudata(3N).

    UNIX System V Network Programmer's Guide.

DIAGNOSTICS

    t_rcvudata returns 0 on successful completion and −1 on failure and t_errno is set to indicate the error.

NAME
t_rcvuderr – receive a unit data error indication

SYNOPSIS
```
#include <tiuser.h>

int t_rcvuderr (int fd, struct t_uderr *uderr);
```

DESCRIPTION
This function is used in connectionless mode to receive information concerning an error on a previously sent data unit, and should be issued only after a unit data error indication. It informs the transport user that a data unit with a specific destination address and protocol options produced an error. fd identifies the local transport endpoint through which the error report will be received, and uderr points to a t_uderr structure containing the following members:

```
struct netbuf addr;
struct netbuf opt;
long error;
```

netbuf is described in intro(3). The maxlen [see netbuf in intro(3)] field of addr and opt must be set before issuing this function to indicate the maximum size of the buffer for each.

On return from this call, the addr structure specifies the destination protocol address of the erroneous data unit, the opt structure identifies protocol-specific options that were associated with the data unit, and error specifies a protocol-dependent error code.

If the user does not care to identify the data unit that produced an error, uderr may be set to NULL and t_rcvuderr will simply clear the error indication without reporting any information to the user.

On failure, t_errno may be set to one of the following:

[TBADF]   The specified file descriptor does not refer to a transport endpoint.

[TNOUDERR]   No unit data error indication currently exists on the specified transport endpoint.

[TBUFOVFLW]   The number of bytes allocated for the incoming protocol address or options is not sufficient to store the information. The unit data error information to be returned in uderr will be discarded.

[TNOTSUPPORT]   This function is not supported by the underlying transport provider.

[TSYSERR]   A system error has occurred during execution of this function.

SEE ALSO
intro(3), t_rcvudata(3N), t_sndudata(3N).
UNIX System V Network Programmer's Guide.

DIAGNOSTICS

t_rcvuderr returns 0 on successful completion and −1 on failure and t_errno is set to indicate the error.

NAME

t_snd – send data or expedited data over a connection

SYNOPSIS

```
#include <tiuser.h>

int t_snd (int fd, char *buf, unsigned nbytes, int flags);
```

DESCRIPTION

This function is used to send either normal or expedited data. fd identifies the local transport endpoint over which data should be sent, buf points to the user data, nbytes specifies the number of bytes of user data to be sent, and flags specifies any optional flags described below.

By default, t_snd operates in synchronous mode and may wait if flow control restrictions prevent the data from being accepted by the local transport provider at the time the call is made. However, if O_NDELAY or O_NONBLOCK is set (via t_open or fcntl), t_snd will execute in asynchronous mode, and will fail immediately if there are flow control restrictions.

Even when there are no flow control restrictions, t_snd will wait if STREAMS internal resources are not available, regardless of the state of O_NDELAY or O_NONBLOCK.

On successful completion, t_snd returns the number of bytes accepted by the transport provider. Normally this will equal the number of bytes specified in nbytes. However, if O_NDELAY or O_NONBLOCK is set, it is possible that only part of the data will be accepted by the transport provider. In this case, t_snd will set T_MORE for the data that was sent (see below) and will return a value less than nbytes. If nbytes is zero and sending of zero bytes is not supported by the underlying transport provider, t_snd() will return −1 with t_errno set to TBAD-DATA. A return value of zero indicates that the request to send a zero-length data message was sent to the provider.

If T_EXPEDITED is set in flags, the data will be sent as expedited data, and will be subject to the interpretations of the transport provider.

If T_MORE is set in flags, or is set as described above, an indication is sent to the transport provider that the transport service data unit (TSDU) or expedited transport service data unit (ETSDU) is being sent through multiple t_snd calls. Each t_snd with the T_MORE flag set indicates that another t_snd will follow with more data for the current TSDU. The end of the TSDU (or ETSDU) is identified by a t_snd call with the T_MORE flag not set. Use of T_MORE enables a user to break up large logical data units without losing the boundaries of those units at the other end of the connection. The flag implies nothing about how the data is packaged for transfer below the transport interface. If the transport provider does not support the concept of a TSDU as indicated in the info argument on return from t_open or t_getinfo, the T_MORE flag is not meaningful and should be ignored.

The size of each TSDU or ETSDU must not exceed the limits of the transport provider as returned by t_open or t_getinfo. If the size is exceeded, a TSYSERR with system error EPROTO will occur. However, the t_snd may not fail because EPROTO errors may not be reported immediately. In this case, a subsequent call that accesses the transport endpoint will fail with the associated TSYSERR.

If t_snd is issued from the T_IDLE state, the provider may silently discard the data. If t_snd is issued from any state other than T_DATAXFER, T_INREL or T_IDLE, the provider will generate a TSYSERR with system error EPROTO (which may be reported in the manner described above).

On failure, t_errno may be set to one of the following:

[TBADF]   The specified file descriptor does not refer to a transport endpoint.

[TFLOW]   O_NDELAY or O_NONBLOCK was set, but the flow control mechanism prevented the transport provider from accepting data at this time.

[TNOTSUPPORT]   This function is not supported by the underlying transport provider.

[TSYSERR]   A system error [see intro(2)] has been detected during execution of this function.

[TBADDATA]   nbytes is zero and sending zero bytes is not supported by the transport provider.

SEE ALSO

t_open(3N), t_rcv(3N).
UNIX System V Network Programmer's Guide.

DIAGNOSTICS

On successful completion, t_snd returns the number of bytes accepted by the transport provider, and it returns −1 on failure and t_errno is set to indicate the error.

NAME

t_snddis – send user-initiated disconnect request

SYNOPSIS

#include <tiuser.h>

int t_snddis (int fd, struct t_call *call):

DESCRIPTION

This function is used to initiate an abortive release on an already established connection or to reject a connect request. fd identifies the local transport endpoint of the connection, and call specifies information associated with the abortive release. call points to a t_call structure that contains the following members:

        struct netbuf addr;
        struct netbuf opt;
        struct netbuf udata;
        int sequence;

netbuf is described in intro(3). The values in call have different semantics, depending on the context of the call to t_snddis. When rejecting a connect request, call must be non-NULL and contain a valid value of sequence to identify uniquely the rejected connect indication to the transport provider. The addr and opt fields of call are ignored. In all other cases, call need only be used when data is being sent with the disconnect request. The addr, opt, and sequence fields of the t_call structure are ignored. If the user does not wish to send data to the remote user, the value of call may be NULL.

udata specifies the user data to be sent to the remote user. The amount of user data must not exceed the limits supported by the transport provider as returned in the discon field of the info argument of t_open or t_getinfo. If the len field of udata is zero, no data will be sent to the remote user.

On failure, t_errno may be set to one of the following:

[TBADF]   The specified file descriptor does not refer to a transport endpoint.

[TOUTSTATE]   The function was issued in the wrong sequence. The transport provider's outgoing queue may be flushed, so data may be lost.

[TBADDATA]   The amount of user data specified was not within the bounds allowed by the transport provider. The transport provider's outgoing queue will be flushed, so data may be lost.

[TBADSEQ]   An invalid sequence number was specified, or a NULL call structure was specified when rejecting a connect request. The transport provider's outgoing queue will be flushed, so data may be lost.

[TLOOK]   An asynchronous event has occurred on this transport endpoint and requires immediate attention.

[TNOTSUPPORT]   This function is not supported by the underlying transport provider.

[TSYSERR]   A system error has occurred during execution of this function.

SEE ALSO

intro(3), t_connect(3N), t_getinfo(3N), t_listen(3N), t_open(3N).

UNIX System V Network Programmer's Guide.

DIAGNOSTICS

t_snddis returns 0 on success and −1 on failure and **t_errno** is set to indicate the error.

NAME
  t_sndrel – initiate an orderly release

SYNOPSIS
  #include <tiuser.h>

  int t_sndrel (int fd);

DESCRIPTION
  This function is used to initiate an orderly release of a transport connection and indicates to the transport provider that the transport user has no more data to send. fd identifies the local transport endpoint where the connection exists. After issuing t_sndrel, the user may not send any more data over the connection. However, a user may continue to receive data if an orderly release indication has not been received.

  This function is an optional service of the transport provider, and is only supported if the transport provider returned service type T_COTS_ORD on t_open or t_getinfo.

  If t_sndrel is issued from an invalid state, the provider will generate an EPROTO protocol error; however, this error may not occur until a subsequent reference to the transport endpoint.

  On failure, t_errno may be set to one of the following:

  [TBADF]   The specified file descriptor does not refer to a transport endpoint.

  [TFLOW]   O_NDELAY or O_NONBLOCK was set, but the flow control mechanism prevented the transport provider from accepting the function at this time.

  [TNOTSUPPORT]   This function is not supported by the underlying transport provider.

  [TSYSERR]   A system error has occurred during execution of this function.

SEE ALSO
  t_open(3N), t_rcvrel(3N).
  UNIX System V Network Programmer's Guide.

DIAGNOSTICS
  t_sndrel returns 0 on success and −1 on failure and t_errno is set to indicate the error.

NAME
    t_sndudata – send a data unit
SYNOPSIS
    #include <tiuser.h>

    int t_sndudata (int fd, struct t_unitdata *unitdata);
DESCRIPTION
    This function is used in connectionless mode to send a data unit to another tran-
    sport user. fd identifies the local transport endpoint through which data will be
    sent, and unitdata points to a t_unitdata structure containing the following
    members:

        struct netbuf addr;
        struct netbuf opt;
        struct netbuf udata;

    netbuf is described in intro(3). In unitdata, addr specifies the protocol
    address of the destination user, opt identifies protocol-specific options that the
    user wants associated with this request, and udata specifies the user data to be
    sent. The user may choose not to specify what protocol options are associated
    with the transfer by setting the len field of opt to zero. In this case, the provider
    may use default options.

    If the len field of udata is zero, and the sending of zero bytes is not supported
    by the underlying transport provider, t_sndudata will return −1 with t_errno
    set to TBADDATA.

    By default, t_sndudata operates in synchronous mode and may wait if flow con-
    trol restrictions prevent the data from being accepted by the local transport pro-
    vider at the time the call is made. However, if O_NDELAY or O_NONBLOCK is set
    (via t_open or fcntl), t_sndudata will execute in asynchronous mode and will
    fail under such conditions.

    If t_sndudata is issued from an invalid state, or if the amount of data specified
    in udata exceeds the TSDU size as returned in the tsdu field of the info argu-
    ment of t_open or t_getinfo, the provider will generate an EPROTO protocol
    error. (See TSYSERR below.) If the state is invalid, this error may not occur until
    a subsequent reference is made to the transport endpoint.

    On failure, t_errno may be set to one of the following:

    [TBADF]   The specified file descriptor does not refer to a transport end-
                       point.

    [TFLOW]   O_NDELAY or O_NONBLOCK was set, but the flow control
                       mechanism prevented the transport provider from accepting
                       data at this time.

    [TNOTSUPPORT]   This function is not supported by the underlying transport
                       provider.

    [TSYSERR]   A system error has occurred during execution of this func-
                       tion.

[TBADDATA]   **nbytes** is zero and sending zero bytes is not supported by
                  the transport provider.

SEE ALSO

intro(3), t_rcvudata(3N), t_rcvuderr(3N).

UNIX System V Network Programmer's Guide.

DIAGNOSTICS

t_sndudata returns 0 on successful completion and −1 on failure t_errno is set
to indicate the error.

NAME

t_sync – synchronize transport library

SYNOPSIS

#include <tiuser.h>

int t_sync (int fd);

DESCRIPTION

For the transport endpoint specified by **fd**, **t_sync** synchronizes the data structures managed by the transport library with information from the underlying transport provider. In doing so, it can convert a raw file descriptor [obtained via **open**(2), **dup**(2), or as a result of a **fork**(2) and **exec**(2)] to an initialized transport endpoint, assuming that file descriptor referenced a transport provider. This function also allows two cooperating processes to synchronize their interaction with a transport provider.

For example, if a process **forks** a new process and issues an **exec**, the new process must issue a **t_sync** to build the private library data structure associated with a transport endpoint and to synchronize the data structure with the relevant provider information.

It is important to remember that the transport provider treats all users of a transport endpoint as a single user. If multiple processes are using the same endpoint, they should coordinate their activities so as not to violate the state of the provider. **t_sync** returns the current state of the provider to the user, thereby enabling the user to verify the state before taking further action. This coordination is only valid among cooperating processes; it is possible that a process or an incoming event could change the provider's state *after* a **t_sync** is issued.

If the provider is undergoing a state transition when **t_sync** is called, the function will fail.

On failure, **t_errno** may be set to one of the following:

[TBADF]	The specified file descriptor does not refer to a transport endpoint.
[TSTATECHNG]	The transport provider is undergoing a state change.
[TSYSERR]	A system error has occurred during execution of this function.

SEE ALSO

dup(2), exec(2), fork(2), open(2).

UNIX System V Network Programmer's Guide.

DIAGNOSTICS

t_sync returns the state of the transport provider on successful completion and -1 on failure and **t_errno** is set to indicate the error. The state returned may be one of the following:

T_UNBND   unbound

T_IDLE	idle
T_OUTCON	outgoing connection pending
T_INCON	incoming connection pending
T_DATAXFER	data transfer
T_OUTREL	outgoing orderly release (waiting for an orderly release indication)
T_INREL	incoming orderly release (waiting for an orderly release request)

NAME
t_unbind – disable a transport endpoint

SYNOPSIS
#include <tiuser.h>

int t_unbind (int fd);

DESCRIPTION
The t_unbind function disables the transport endpoint specified by fd which was previously bound by t_bind(3N). On completion of this call, no further data or events destined for this transport endpoint will be accepted by the transport provider.

On failure, t_errno may be set to one of the following:

[TBADF]	The specified file descriptor does not refer to a transport endpoint.
[TOUTSTATE]	The function was issued in the wrong sequence.
[TLOOK]	An asynchronous event has occurred on this transport endpoint.
[TSYSERR]	A system error has occurred during execution of this function.

SEE ALSO
t_bind(3N).

UNIX System V Network Programmer's Guide.

DIAGNOSTICS
t_unbind returns 0 on success and −1 on failure and t_errno is set to indicate the error.

NAME

xdr – library routines for external data representation

DESCRIPTION

XDR routines allow C programmers to describe arbitrary data structures in a machine-independent fashion. Data for remote procedure calls (RPC) are transmitted using these routines.

Index to Routines

The following table lists XDR routines and the manual reference pages on which they are described:

XDR Routine	Manual Reference Page
xdr_array	xdr_complex(3N)
xdr_bool	xdr_simple(3N)
xdr_bytes	xdr_complex(3N)
xdr_char	xdr_simple(3N)
xdr_destroy	xdr_create(3N)
xdr_double	xdr_simple(3N)
xdr_enum	xdr_simple(3N)
xdr_float	xdr_simple(3N)
xdr_free	xdr_simple(3N)
xdr_getpos	xdr_admin(3N)
xdr_inline	xdr_admin(3N)
xdr_int	xdr_simple(3N)
xdr_long	xdr_simple(3N)
xdr_opaque	xdr_complex(3N)
xdr_pointer	xdr_complex(3N)
xdr_reference	xdr_complex(3N)
xdr_setpos	xdr_admin(3N)
xdr_short	xdr_simple(3N)
xdr_string	xdr_complex(3N)
xdr_u_char	xdr_simple(3N)
xdr_u_long	xdr_simple(3N)
xdr_u_short	xdr_simple(3N)
xdr_union	xdr_complex(3N)
xdr_vector	xdr_complex(3N)
xdr_void	xdr_simple(3N)
xdr_wrapstring	xdr_complex(3N)
xdrmem_create	xdr_create(3N)
xdrrec_create	xdr_create(3N)
xdrrec_eof	xdr_admin(3N)
xdrstdio_create	xdr_create(3N)

SEE ALSO

xdr_admin(3N), xdr_complex(3N), xdr_create(3N), xdr_simple(3N), rpc(3N).

NAME

xdr_admin: xdr_getpos, xdr_inline, xdrrec_eof, xdr_setpos – library routines for external data representation

DESCRIPTION

XDR library routines allow C programmers to describe arbitrary data structures
in a machine-independent fashion. Protocols such as remote procedure calls
(RPC) use these routines to describe the format of the data.

These routines deal specifically with the management of the XDR stream.

Routines

See rpc(3N) for the definition of the XDR data structure.

#include <rpc/xdr.h>

u_int
xdr_getpos(const XDR *xdrs);

> A macro that invokes the get-position routine associated with the XDR
> stream, *xdrs*. The routine returns an unsigned integer, which indicates the
> position of the XDR byte stream. A desirable feature of XDR streams is
> that simple arithmetic works with this number, although the XDR stream
> instances need not guarantee this. Therefore, applications written for por-
> tability should not depend on this feature.

long *
xdr_inline(XDR *xdrs; const int len);

> A macro that invokes the in-line routine associated with the XDR stream,
> *xdrs*. The routine returns a pointer to a contiguous piece of the stream's
> buffer; *len* is the byte length of the desired buffer. Note: pointer is cast to
> long *.

> Warning: xdr_inline may return NULL (0) if it cannot allocate a contigu-
> ous piece of a buffer. Therefore the behavior may vary among stream
> instances; it exists for the sake of efficiency, and applications written for
> portability should not depend on this feature.

bool_t
xdrrec_eof(XDR *xdrs);

> This routine can be invoked only on streams created by xdrrec_create.
> After consuming the rest of the current record in the stream, this routine
> returns 1 if the stream has no more input, 0 otherwise.

bool_t
xdr_setpos(XDR *xdrs, const u_int pos);

> A macro that invokes the set position routine associated with the XDR
> stream *xdrs*. The parameter *pos* is a position value obtained from
> xdr_getpos. This routine returns 1 if the XDR stream was repositioned,
> and 0 otherwise.

> Warning: it is difficult to reposition some types of XDR streams, so this
> routine may fail with one type of stream and succeed with another.
> Therefore, applications written for portability should not depend on this
> feature.

SEE ALSO
     rpc(3N), xdr_complex(3N), xdr_create(3N), xdr_simple(3N).

NAME
     xdr_complex: xdr_array, xdr_bytes, xdr_opaque, xdr_pointer,
     xdr_reference, xdr_string, xdr_union, xdr_vector, xdr_wrapstring –
     library routines for external data representation

DESCRIPTION
     XDR library routines allow C programmers to describe complex data structures in
     a machine-independent fashion. Protocols such as remote procedure calls (RPC)
     use these routines to describe the format of the data. These routines are the XDR
     library routines for complex data structures. They require the creation of XDR
     stream [see xdr_create(3N)].

Routines
     See rpc(3N) for the definition of the XDR data structure.

     #include <rpc/xdr.h>

     bool_t
     xdr_array(XDR *xdrs, caddr_t *arrp, u_int *sizep,
           const u_int maxsize, const u_int elsize,
           const xdrproc_t elproc);

           xdr_array translates between variable-length arrays and their correspond-
           ing external representations. The parameter *arrp* is the address of the
           pointer to the array, while *sizep* is the address of the element count of the
           array; this element count cannot exceed *maxsize*. The parameter *elsize* is
           the sizeof each of the array's elements, and *elproc* is an XDR routine that
           translates between the array elements' C form and their external represen-
           tation. This routine returns 1 if it succeeds, 0 otherwise.

     bool_t
     xdr_bytes(XDR *xdrs, char **sp, u_int *sizep,
           const u_int maxsize);

           xdr_bytes translates between counted byte strings and their external
           representations. The parameter *sp* is the address of the string pointer.
           The length of the string is located at address *sizep*; strings cannot be
           longer than *maxsize*. This routine returns 1 if it succeeds, 0 otherwise.

     bool_t
     xdr_opaque(XDR *xdrs, caddr_t cp, const u_int cnt);

           xdr_opaque translates between fixed size opaque data and its external
           representation. The parameter *cp* is the address of the opaque object, and
           cnt is its size in bytes. This routine returns 1 if it succeeds, 0 otherwise.

     bool_t
     xdr_pointer(XDR *xdrs, char **objpp, u_int objsize,
           const xdrproc_t xdrobj);

           Like xdr_reference except that it serializes NULL pointers, whereas
           xdr_reference does not. Thus, xdr_pointer can represent recursive
           data structures, such as binary trees or linked lists.

```
bool_t
xdr_reference(XDR *xdrs, caddr_t *pp, u_int size,
     const xdrproc_t proc);
```

> xdr_reference provides pointer chasing within structures. The parameter *pp* is the address of the pointer; *size* is the sizeof the structure that **pp* points to; and *proc* is an XDR procedure that translates the structure between its C form and its external representation. This routine returns 1 if it succeeds, 0 otherwise.

> Warning: this routine does not understand NULL pointers. Use xdr_pointer instead.

```
bool_t
xdr_string(XDR *xdrs, char **sp, const u_int maxsize);
```

> xdr_string translates between C strings and their corresponding external representations. Strings cannot be longer than *maxsize*. Note: *sp* is the address of the string's pointer. This routine returns 1 if it succeeds, 0 otherwise.

```
bool_t
xdr_union(XDR *xdrs, enum_t *dscmp, char *unp,
     const struct xdr_discrim *choices,
     const bool_t (*defaultarm)(const XDR *, const char *,
          const int));
```

> xdr_union translates between a discriminated C union and its corresponding external representation. It first translates the discriminant of the union located at *dscmp*. This discriminant is always an enum_t. Next the union located at *unp* is translated. The parameter *choices* is a pointer to an array of xdr_discrim structures. Each structure contains an ordered pair of [*value, proc*]. If the union's discriminant is equal to the associated *value*, then the *proc* is called to translate the union. The end of the xdr_discrim structure array is denoted by a routine of value NULL. If the discriminant is not found in the *choices* array, then the *defaultarm* procedure is called (if it is not NULL). Returns 1 if it succeeds, 0 otherwise.

```
bool_t
xdr_vector(XDR *xdrs, char *arrp, const u_int size,
     const u_int elsize, const xdrproc_t elproc);
```

> xdr_vector translates between fixed-length arrays and their corresponding external representations. The parameter *arrp* is the address of the pointer to the array, while *size* is is the element count of the array. The parameter *elsize* is the sizeof each of the array's elements, and *elproc* is an XDR routine that translates between the array elements' C form and their external representation. This routine returns 1 if it succeeds, 0 otherwise.

```
bool_t
xdr_wrapstring(XDR *xdrs, char **sp);
```

> A routine that calls `xdr_string`(*xdrs*, *sp*, *maxuint*); where *maxuint* is the maximum value of an unsigned integer.

> Many routines, such as `xdr_array`, `xdr_pointer` and `xdr_vector` take a function pointer of type `xdrproc_t`, which takes two arguments. `xdr_string`, one of the most frequently used routines, requires three arguments, while `xdr_wrapstring` only requires two. For these routines, `xdr_wrapstring` is desirable. This routine returns 1 if it succeeds, 0 otherwise.

SEE ALSO

> `rpc`(3N), `xdr_admin`(3N), `xdr_create`(3N), `xdr_simple`(3N).

NAME

xdr_create: xdr_destroy, xdrmem_create, xdrrec_create, xdrstdio_create − library routines for external data representation stream creation

DESCRIPTION

XDR library routines allow C programmers to describe arbitrary data structures in a machine-independent fashion. Protocols such as remote procedure calls (RPC) use these routines to describe the format of the data.

These routines deal with the creation of XDR streams. XDR streams have to be created before any data can be translated into XDR format.

Routines

See rpc(3N) for the definition of the XDR, CLIENT, and SVCXPRT data structures.

```
#include <rpc/xdr.h>
```

```
void
xdr_destroy(XDR *xdrs);
```

A macro that invokes the destroy routine associated with the XDR stream, *xdrs*. Destruction usually involves freeing private data structures associated with the stream. Using *xdrs* after invoking xdr_destroy is undefined.

```
void
xdrmem_create(XDR *xdrs, const caddr_t addr,
    const u_int size, const enum xdr_op op);
```

This routine initializes the XDR stream object pointed to by *xdrs*. The stream's data is written to, or read from, a chunk of memory at location *addr* whose length is no more than *size* bytes long. The *op* determines the direction of the XDR stream (either XDR_ENCODE, XDR_DECODE, or XDR_FREE).

```
void
xdrrec_create(XDR *xdrs, const u_int sendsz,
    const u_int recvsz, const caddr_t handle,
    const int (*readit)(const void *, char *, const int),
    const int (*writeit)(const void *, const char *, const int));
```

This routine initializes the XDR stream object pointed to by *xdrs*. The stream's data is written to a buffer of size *sendsz*; a value of 0 indicates the system should use a suitable default. The stream's data is read from a buffer of size *recvsz*; it too can be set to a suitable default by passing a 0 value. When a stream's output buffer is full, *writeit* is called. Similarly, when a stream's input buffer is empty, *readit* is called. The behavior of these two routines is similar to the system calls read and write [see read(2) and write(2), respectively], except that *handle* (CLIENT, or SVCXPRT) is passed to the former routines as the first parameter instead of a file descriptor. Note: the XDR stream's *op* field must be set by the caller.

Warning: this XDR stream implements an intermediate record stream. Therefore there are additional bytes in the stream to provide record boundary information.

```
void
xdrstdio_create(XDR *xdrs, FILE *file, const enum xdr_op op);
```

This routine initializes the XDR stream object pointed to by *xdrs*. The XDR stream data is written to, or read from, the standard I/O stream *file*. The parameter *op* determines the direction of the XDR stream (either XDR_ENCODE, XDR_DECODE, or XDR_FREE).

Warning: the destroy routine associated with such XDR streams calls fflush on the *file* stream, but never fclose [see fclose(3S)].

SEE ALSO

fclose(3S), read(2), rpc(3N), write(2), xdr_admin(3N), xdr_complex(3N), xdr_simple(3N).

NAME

xdr_simple: xdr_bool, xdr_char, xdr_double, xdr_enum, xdr_float,
xdr_free, xdr_int, xdr_long, xdr_short, xdr_u_char, xdr_u_long,
xdr_u_short, xdr_void — library routines for external data representation

DESCRIPTION

XDR library routines allow C programmers to describe simple data structures in a
machine-independent fashion. Protocols such as remote procedure calls (RPC)
use these routines to describe the format of the data.

These routines require the creation of XDR streams [see xdr_create(3N)].

Routines

See rpc(3N) for the definition of the XDR data structure.

```
#include <rpc/xdr.h>
```

```
bool_t
xdr_bool(XDR *xdrs, bool_t *bp);
```

xdr_bool translates between booleans (C integers) and their external
representations. When encoding data, this filter produces values of either
1 or 0. This routine returns 1 if it succeeds, 0 otherwise.

```
bool_t
xdr_char(XDR *xdrs, char *cp);
```

xdr_char translates between C characters and their external representations. This routine returns 1 if it succeeds, 0 otherwise. Note: encoded
characters are not packed, and occupy 4 bytes each. For arrays of characters, it is worthwhile to consider xdr_bytes, xdr_opaque or xdr_string
[see xdr_bytes, xdr_opaque and xdr_string in xdr_complex(3N)].

```
bool_t
xdr_double(XDR *xdrs, double *dp);
```

xdr_double translates between C double precision numbers and their
external representations. This routine returns 1 if it succeeds, 0 otherwise.

```
bool_t
xdr_enum(XDR *xdrs, enum_t *ep);
```

xdr_enum translates between C enums (actually integers) and their external
representations. This routine returns 1 if it succeeds, 0 otherwise.

```
bool_t
xdr_float(XDR *xdrs, float *fp);
```

xdr_float translates between C floats and their external representations. This routine returns 1 if it succeeds, 0 otherwise.

```
void
xdr_free(xdrproc_t proc, char *objp);
```

Generic freeing routine. The first argument is the XDR routine for the
object being freed. The second argument is a pointer to the object itself.
Note: the pointer passed to this routine is not freed, but what it points to
is freed (recursively).

```
bool_t
xdr_int(XDR *xdrs, int *ip);
```

> xdr_int translates between C integers and their external representations. This routine returns 1 if it succeeds, 0 otherwise.

```
bool_t
xdr_long(XDR *xdrs, long *lp);
```

> xdr_long translates between C long integers and their external representations. This routine returns 1 if it succeeds, 0 otherwise.

```
bool_t
xdr_short(XDR *xdrs, short *sp);
```

> xdr_short translates between C short integers and their external representations. This routine returns 1 if it succeeds, 0 otherwise.

```
bool_t
xdr_u_char(XDR *xdrs, char *ucp);
```

> xdr_u_char translates between unsigned C characters and their external representations. This routine returns 1 if it succeeds, 0 otherwise.

```
bool_t
xdr_u_long(XDR *xdrs, unsigned long *ulp);
```

> xdr_u_long translates between C unsigned long integers and their external representations. This routine returns 1 if it succeeds, 0 otherwise.

```
bool_t
xdr_u_short(XDR *xdrs, unsigned short *usp);
```

> xdr_u_short translates between C unsigned short integers and their external representations. This routine returns 1 if it succeeds, 0 otherwise.

```
bool_t
xdr_void(void);
```

> This routine always returns 1. It may be passed to RPC routines that require a function parameter, where nothing is to be done.

SEE ALSO

rpc(3N), xdr_admin(3N), xdr_complex(3N), xdr_create(3N).

NAME

ypclnt,   yp_get_default_domain,   yp_bind,   yp_unbind,   yp_match,
yp_first,   yp_next,   yp_all,   yp_order,   yp_master,   yperr_string,
ypprot_err – YP client interface

SYNOPSIS

#include <rpcsvc/ypclnt.h>
#include <rpcsvc/yp_prot.h>

DESCRIPTION

This package of functions provides an interface to the YP network lookup service.
The package can be loaded from the standard library, /usr/lib/libnsl.{so,a}.
Refer to ypfiles(4) and ypserv(1M) for an overview of the YP name services,
including the definitions of *map* and *domain*, and a description of the various
servers, databases, and commands that comprise the YP name service.

All input parameters names begin with *in*. Output parameters begin with *out*.
Output parameters of type char ** should be addresses of uninitialized character pointers. Memory is allocated by the YP client package using malloc(3), and
may be freed if the user code has no continuing need for it. For each *outkey* and
outval, two extra bytes of memory are allocated at the end that contain NEWLINE
and NULL, respectively, but these two bytes are not reflected in *outkeylen* or *out-
vallen*. *indomain* and *inmap* strings must be non-NULL and NULL-terminated.
String parameters which are accompanied by a count parameter may not be
NULL, but may point to NULL strings, with the count parameter indicating this.
Counted strings need not be NULL-terminated.

All functions in this package of type *int* return 0 if they succeed, and a failure
code (YPERR_*xxxx*) otherwise. Failure codes are described under DIAGNOSTICS
below.

Routines

yp_bind (indomain);
char *indomain;

> To use the YP name services, the client process must be bound to a YP
> server that serves the appropriate domain using yp_bind(). Binding
> need not be done explicitly by user code; this is done automatically when-
> ever a YP lookup function is called. yp_bind() can be called directly for
> processes that make use of a backup strategy (for example, a local file) in
> cases when YP services are not available.

void
yp_unbind (indomain)
char *indomain;

> Each binding allocates (uses up) one client process socket descriptor; each
> bound domain costs one socket descriptor. However, multiple requests to
> the same domain use that same descriptor. yp_unbind() is available at
> the client interface for processes that explicitly manage their socket
> descriptors while accessing multiple domains. The call to yp_unbind()
> make the domain *unbound*, and free all per-process and per-node resources
> used to bind it.

If an RPC failure results upon use of a binding, that domain will be unbound automatically. At that point, the ypclnt() layer will retry forever or until the operation succeeds, provided that ypbind is running, and either

- the client process cannot bind a server for the proper domain, or
- RPC requests to the server fail.

If an error is not RPC-related, or if ypbind is not running, or if a bound ypserv process returns any answer (success or failure), the ypclnt layer will return control to the user code, either with an error code, or a success code and any results.

```
yp_get_default_domain (outdomain);
char **outdomain;
```

The YP lookup calls require a map name and a domain name, at minimum. It is assumed that the client process knows the name of the map of interest. Client processes should fetch the node's default domain by calling yp_get_default_domain(), and use the returned *outdomain* as the *indomain* parameter to successive YP name service calls.

```
yp_match(indomain, inmap, inkey, inkeylen, outval, outvallen)
char *indomain;
char *inmap;
char *inkey;
int inkeylen;
char **outval;
int *outvallen;
```

yp_match() returns the value associated with a passed key. This key must be exact; no pattern matching is available.

```
yp_first(indomain, inmap, outkey, outkeylen, outval, outvallen)
char *indomain;
char *inmap;
char **outkey;
int *outkeylen;
char **outval;
int *outvallen;
```

yp_first() returns the first key-value pair from the named map in the named domain.

```
yp_next(indomain, inmap, inkey, inkeylen, outkey, outkeylen, outval, outval
char *indomain;
char *inmap;
char *inkey;
int inkeylen;
char **outkey;
int *outkeylen;
char **outval;
int *outvallen;
```

yp_next () returns the next key-value pair in a named map. The *inkey* parameter should be the *outkey* returned from an initial call to yp_first () (to get the second key-value pair) or the one returned from the *n*th call to yp_next () (to get the *n*th + second key-value pair).

The concept of first (and, for that matter, of next) is particular to the structure of the YP map being processing; there is no relation in retrieval order to either the lexical order within any original (non-YP name service) data base, or to any obvious numerical sorting order on the keys, values, or key-value pairs. The only ordering guarantee made is that if the yp_first () function is called on a particular map, and then the yp_next () function is repeatedly called on the same map at the same server until the call fails with a reason of YPERR_NOMORE, every entry in the data base will be seen exactly once. Further, if the same sequence of operations is performed on the same map at the same server, the entries will be seen in the same order.

Under conditions of heavy server load or server failure, it is possible for the domain to become unbound, then bound once again (perhaps to a different server) while a client is running. This can cause a break in one of the enumeration rules; specific entries may be seen twice by the client, or not at all. This approach protects the client from error messages that would otherwise be returned in the midst of the enumeration. The next paragraph describes a better solution to enumerating all entries in a map.

```
yp_all(indomain, inmap, incallback);
char *indomain;
char *inmap;
struct ypall_callback *incallback;
```

yp_all () provides a way to transfer an entire map from server to client in a single request using TCP (rather than UDP as with other functions in this package). The entire transaction take place as a single RPC request and response. yp_all () can be used just like any other YP name service procedure, identify the map in the normal manner, and supply the name of a function which will be called to process each key-value pair within the map. The call to yp_all () returns only when the transaction is completed (successfully or unsuccessfully), or the foreach function decides that it does not want to see any more key-value pairs.

The third parameter to yp_all () is
```
        struct ypall_callback *incallback {
        int (*foreach) ();
        char *data;
        };
```
The function foreach is called
```
        foreach(instatus, inkey, inkeylen, inval, invallen, indata);
        int instatus;
        char *inkey;
        int inkeylen;
        char *inval;
        int invallen;
```

```
        char *indata;
```

The *instatus* parameter will hold one of the return status values defined in
<rpcsvc/yp_prot.h — either YP_TRUE or an error code. (See
ypprot_err(), below, for a function which converts a YP name service
protocol error code to a ypclnt layer error code.)

The key and value parameters are somewhat different than defined in the
synopsis section above. First, the memory pointed to by the *inkey* and
inval parameters is private to the yp_all() function, and is overwritten
with the arrival of each new key-value pair. It is the responsibility of the
foreach function to do something useful with the contents of that
memory, but it does not own the memory itself. Key and value objects
presented to the foreach function look exactly as they do in the server's
map — if they were not NEWLINE-terminated or NULL-terminated in the
map, they will not be here either.

The *indata* parameter is the contents of the incallback->data element
passed to yp_all(). The data element of the callback structure may be
used to share state information between the foreach function and the
mainline code. Its use is optional, and no part of the YP client package
inspects its contents — cast it to something useful, or ignore it.

The foreach function is a Boolean. It should return zero to indicate that
it wants to be called again for further received key-value pairs, or non-
zero to stop the flow of key-value pairs. If foreach returns a non-zero
value, it is not called again; the functional value of yp_all() is then 0.

```
yp_order(indomain, inmap, outorder);
char *indomain;
char *inmap;
int *outorder;
```

> yp_order() returns the order number for a map.

```
yp_master(indomain, inmap, outname);
char *indomain;
char *inmap;
char **outname;
```

> yp_master() returns the machine name of the master YP server for a
> map.

```
char *yperr_string(incode)
int incode;
```

> yperr_string() returns a pointer to an error message string that is
> NULL-terminated but contains no period or NEWLINE.

```
ypprot_err (incode)
unsigned int incode;
```

> ypprot_err() takes a YP name service protocol error code as input, and
> returns a ypclnt layer error code, which may be used in turn as an input
> to yperr_string().

FILES
>   /usr/lib/libyp.a

SEE ALSO
>   ypserv(1M), malloc(3), ypupdate(3N), ypfiles(4)

DIAGNOSTICS
>   All integer functions return 0 if the requested operation is successful, or one of
>   the following errors if the operation fails.

```
    #define YPERR_BADARGS
             "1    /* args to function are bad */"

    #define YPERR_RPC
             "2    /* RPC failure - domain has been unbound */"

    #define YPERR_DOMAIN
             "3    /* can't bind to server on this domain */"

    #define YPERR_MAP
             "4    /* no such map in server's domain */"

    #define YPERR_KEY
             "5    /* no such key in map */"

    #define YPERR_YPERR
             "6    /* internal yp server or client error */"

    #define YPERR_RESRC
             "7    /* resource allocation failure */"

    #define YPERR_NOMORE
             "8    /* no more records in map database */"

    #define YPERR_PMAP
             "9    /* can't communicate with rpcbinder */"

    #define YPERR_YPBIND
             "10   /* can't communicate with ypbind */"

    #define YPERR_YPSERV
             "11   /* can't communicate with ypserv */"

    #define YPERR_NODOM
             "12   /* local domain name not set */"

    #define    YPERR_BADDBfR
             "13   /* yp database is bad */"

    #define    YPERR_VERSfR
             "14   /* yp version mismatch */"

    #define    YPERR_ACCESS
             "15   /* access violation */"

    #define    YPERR_BUSY
             "16   /* database busy */"
```

NAME
yp_update – changes yp information

SYNOPSIS
#include <rpcsvc/ypclnt.h>

yp_update(domain, map, ypop, key, keylen, data, datalen)
char *domain;
char *map;
unsigned ypop
char *key;
int keylen;
char *data;
int datalen;

DESCRIPTION
yp_update() is used to make changes to the YP database. The syntax is the same as that of yp_match() except for the extra parameter *ypop* which may take on one of four values. If it is YPOP_CHANGE then the data associated with the key will be changed to the new value. If the key is not found in the database, then yp_update() will return YPERR_KEY. If *ypop* has the value YPOP_INSERT then the key-value pair will be inserted into the database. The error YPERR_KEY is returned if the key already exists in the database. To store an item into the database without concern for whether it exists already or not, pass *ypop* as YPOP_STORE and no error will be returned if the key already or does not exist. To delete an entry, the value of *ypop* should be YPOP_DELETE.

This routine depends upon secure RPC, and will not work unless the network is running secure RPC.

SEE ALSO
secure_rpc(3N)

NAME
hosts – host name data base

SYNOPSIS
/etc/hosts

DESCRIPTION
The hosts file contains information regarding the known hosts on the DARPA Internet. For each host a single line should be present with the following information:

Internet-address official-host-name aliases

Items are separated by any number of SPACE and/or TAB characters. A '#' indicates the beginning of a comment; characters up to the end of the line are not interpreted by routines which search the file. This file is normally created from the official host data base maintained at the Network Information Control Center (NIC), though local changes may be required to bring it up to date regarding unofficial aliases and/or unknown hosts.

Network addresses are specified in the conventional '.' notation using the inet_addr routine from the Internet address manipulation library, inet(3N). Host names may contain any printable character other than a field delimiter, NEWLINE, or comment character.

EXAMPLE
Here is a typical line from the /etc/hosts file:

```
192.9.1.20          gaia                              # John Smith
```

FILES
/etc/hosts

SEE ALSO
gethostent(3N), inet(3N).

NAME

netconfig – network configuration database

SYNOPSIS

#include <netconfig.h>

DESCRIPTION

The network configuration database, /etc/netconfig, is a system file used to
store information about networks connected to the system and available for use.
The netconfig database and the routines that access it [see getnetconfig(3N)]
are part of the UNIX System V Network Selection component. The Network
Selection component also includes the environment variable NETPATH and a group
of routines that access the netconfig database using NETPATH components as
links to the netconfig entries. NETPATH is described in sh(1); the NETPATH access
routines are discussed in getnetpath(3N).

netconfig contains an entry for each network available on the system. Entries
are separated by newlines. Fields are separated by whitespace and occur in the
order in which they are described below. Whitespace can be embedded as
"*blank*" or "*tab*". Backslashes may be embedded as "\\". Each field
corresponds to an element in the struct netconfig structure. struct netconfig and the identifiers described on this manual page are defined in
/usr/include/netconfig.h.

network ID

A string used to uniquely identify a network. *network ID* consists of non-
null characters, and has a length of at least 1. No maximum length is
specified. This namespace is locally significant and the local system
administrator is the naming authority. All *network ID*s on a system must
be unique.

semantics

The *semantics* field is a string identifing the "semantics" of the network,
i.e., the set of services it supports, by identifying the service interface it
provides. The *semantics* field is mandatory. The following semantics are
recognized.

tpi_clts   Transport Provider Interface, connectionless

tpi_cots   Transport Provider Interface, connection oriented

tpi_cots_ord
            Transport Provider Interface, connection oriented, sup-
            ports orderly release.

flag   The *flag* field records certain two-valued ("true" and "false") attributes of
networks. *flag* is a string composed of a combination of characters, each of
which indicates the value of the corresponding attribute. If the character is
present, the attribute is "true." If the character is absent, the attribute is
"false." "–" indicates that none of the attributes is present. Only one
character is currently recognized:

v   Visible ("default") network. Used when the environment
                      variable NETPATH is unset.

protocol family

The *protocol family* and *protocol name* fields are provided for protocol-specific applications.

The *protocol family* field contains a string that identifies a protocol family. The *protocol family* identifier follows the same rules as those for *network IDs*, that is, the string consists of non-null characters; it has a length of at least 1; and there is no maximum length specified. A "−" in the *protocol family* field indicates that no protocol family identifier applies, that is, the network is experimental. The following are examples:

loopback	Loopback (local to host).
inet	Internetwork: UDP, TCP, etc.
implink	ARPANET imp addresses
pup	PUP protocols: e.g. BSP
chaos	MIT CHAOS protocols
ns	XEROX NS protocols
nbs	NBS protocols
ecma	European Computer Manufacturers Association
datakit	DATAKIT protocols
ccitt	CCITT protocols, X.25, etc.
sna	IBM SNA
decnet	DECNET
dli	Direct data link interface
lat	LAT
hylink	NSC Hyperchannel
appletalk	Apple Talk
nit	Network Interface Tap
ieee802	IEEE 802.2; also ISO 8802
osi	Umbrella for all families used by OSI (e.g., protosw lookup)
x25	CCITT X.25 in particular
osinet	AFI = 47, IDI = 4
gosip	U.S. Government OSI

protocol name

The *protocol name* field contains a string that identifies a protocol. The *protocol name* identifier follows the same rules as those for *network IDs*, that is, the string consists of non-NULL characters; it has a length of at least 1; and there is no maximum length specified. The following protocol names are recognized. A "−" indicates that none of the names listed applies.

tcp	Transmission Control Protocol
udp	User Datagram Protocol
icmp	Internet Control Message Protocol

network device
> The *network device* is the full pathname of the device used to connect to the transport provider. Typically, this device will be in the **/dev** directory. The *network device* must be specified.

directory lookup libraries
> The *directory lookup libraries* support a "directory service" (a name-to-address mapping service) for the network. This service is implemented by the UNIX System V Name-to-Address Mapping feature. If a network is not provided with such a library, the *netdir* feature will not work. A "–" in this field indicates the absence of any lookup libraries, in which case name-to-address mapping for the network is non-functional. The directory lookup library field consists of a comma-separated list of full pathnames to dynamically linked libraries. Commas may be embedded as "\,"; backslashs as "\\".

Lines in **/etc/netconfig** that begin with a sharp sign (#) in column 1 are treated as comments.

The **struct netconfig** structure includes the following members corresponding to the fields in in the **netconfig** database entries:

char * nc_netid	Network ID, including NULL terminator
unsigned long nc_semantics	Semantics
unsigned long nc_flag	Flags
char * nc_protofmly	Protocol family
char * nc_proto	Protocol name
char * nc_device	Full pathname of the network device
unsigned long nc_nlookups	Number of directory lookup libraries
char ** nc_lookups	Full pathnames of the directory lookup libraries themselves
unsigned long nc_unused[9]	Reserved for future expansion (not advertised to user level)

The **nc_semantics** field takes the following values, corresponding to the semantics identified above:

> NC_TPI_CLTS
> NC_TPI_COTS
> NC_TPI_COTS_ORD

The **nc_flag** field is a bitfield. The following bit, corresponding to the attribute identified above, is currently recognized. **NC_NOFLAG** indicates the absence of any attributes.

> NC_VISIBLE

FILES
> /etc/netconfig
> /usr/include/netconfig.h

SEE ALSO

netdir_getbyname(3N), getnetconfig(3N), getnetpath(3N), netconfig(4)
Network Programmer's Guide
System Administrator's Guide

NAME

publickey – public key database

SYNOPSIS

/etc/publickey

DESCRIPTION

/etc/publickey is the public key database used for secure RPC. Each entry in the database consists of a network user name (which may either refer to a user or a hostname), followed by the user's public key (in hex notation), a colon, and then the user's secret key encrypted with a password (also in hex notation).

This file is altered either by the user through the chkey(1) command or by the system administrator through the newkey(1) command.

SEE ALSO

chkey(1), newkey(1), publickey(3N).

NAME

rpc – rpc program number data base

SYNOPSIS

rpc

DESCRIPTION

The rpc program number database contains user readable names that can be used in place of RPC program numbers. Each line has the following information:

    name of server for the RPC program
    RPC program number
    aliases

Items are separated by any number of blanks and/or tab characters. A # indicates the beginning of a comment; characters up to the end of the line are not interpreted by routines which search the file.

Below is an example of an RPC database:

```
#
#              rpc
#

rpcbind       100000       portmap sunrpc portmapper
rusersd       100002       rusers
nfs           100003       nfsprog
mountd        100005       mount showmount
walld         100008       rwall shutdown
sprayd        100012       spray
llockmgr      100020
nlockmgr      100021
status        100024
bootparam     100026
keyserv       100029       keyserver
```

NAME
ttydefs − file contains terminal line settings information for `ttymon`

DESCRIPTION
`/etc/ttydefs` is an administrative file that contains information used by `ttymon` to set up the speed and terminal settings for a TTY port.

The `ttydefs` file contains the following fields:

ttylabel
: The string `ttymon` tries to match against the TTY port's *ttylabel* field in the port monitor administrative file. It often describes the speed at which the terminal is supposed to run, for example, 1200.

initial-flags
: Contains the initial `termio`(7) settings to which the terminal is to be set. For example, the system administrator will be able to specify what the default erase and kill characters will be. *initial-flags* must be specified in the syntax recognized by the `stty` command.

final-flags
: *final-flags* must be specified in the same format as *initial-flags*. `ttymon` sets these final settings after a connection request has been made and immediately prior to invoking a port's service.

autobaud
: If the autobaud field contains the character 'A', autobaud will be enabled. Otherwise, autobaud will be disabled. `ttymon` determines what line speed to set the TTY port to by analyzing the carriage returns entered. If autobaud has been disabled, the hunt sequence is used for baud rate determination.

nextlabel
: If the user indicates that the current terminal setting is not appropriate by sending a BREAK, `ttymon` searches for a `ttydefs` entry whose *ttylabel* field matches the *nextlabel* field. If a match is found, `ttymon` uses that field as its *ttylabel* field. A series of speeds is often linked together in this way into a closed set called a hunt sequence. For example, 4800 may be linked to 1200, which in turn is linked to 2400, which is finally linked to 4800.

SEE ALSO
`ttymon`(1M), `sttydefs`(1M)
System Administrator's Guide, "Service Access"

NAME

updaters – configuration file for YP updating

SYNOPSIS

/var/yp/updaters

DESCRIPTION

The file /var/yp/updaters is a makefile (see make(1)) which is used for updating YP databases. Databases can only be updated in a secure network, that is, one that has a publickey(4) database. Each entry in the file is a make target for a particular YP database. For example, if there is a YP database named publickey.byname that can be updated, there should be a make target named publickey.byname in the updaters file with the command to update the file.

The information necessary to make the update is passed to the update command through standard input. The information passed is described below (all items are followed by a NEWLINE, except for the actual bytes of key and actual bytes of date).

- Network name of client wishing to make the update (a string)
- Kind of update (an integer)
- Number of bytes in key (an integer)
- Actual bytes of key
- Number of bytes in data (an integer)
- Actual bytes of data

After getting this information through standard input, the command to update the particular database should decide whether the user is allowed to make the change. If not, it should exit with the status YPERR_ACCESS. If the user is allowed to make the change, the command should make the change and exit with a status of zero. If there are any errors that may prevent the updater from making the change, it should exit with the status that matches a valid YP error code described in <rpcsvc/ypclnt.h>.

FILES

/var/yp/updaters

SEE ALSO

make(1), ypupdated(1M), ypupdate(3), publickey(4)

NAME

ypfiles – the YP database and directory structure

DESCRIPTION

The YP network lookup service uses a distributed, replicated database of dbm files contained in the /var/yp directory hierarchy on each YP server. A dbm database consists of two files, one has the filename extension .pag and the other has the filename extension .dir. For instance, the database named publickey, is implemented by the pair of files publickey.pag and publickey.dir.

A dbm database served by the YP is called a YP *map*. A YP *ypdomain* is a subdirectory of /var/yp containing a set of YP maps. Any number of YP domains can exist. Each may contain any number of maps.

No maps are required by the YP lookup service itself, although they may be required for the normal operation of other parts of the system. There is no list of maps which YP serves — if the map exists in a given domain, and a client asks about it, the YP will serve it. For a map to be accessible consistently, it must exist on all YP servers that serve the domain. To provide data consistency between the replicated maps, an entry to run ypxfr periodically should be made in the privileged user's crontab file on each server. More information on this topic is in ypxfr(1M).

YP maps should contain two distinguished key-value pairs. The first is the key YP_LAST_MODIFIED, having as a value a ten-character ASCII order number. The order number should be the system time in seconds when the map was built. The second key is YP_MASTER_NAME, with the name of the YP master server as a value. makedbm(1M) generates both key-value pairs automatically. A map that does not contain both key-value pairs can be served by the YP, but the ypserv process will not be able to return values for "Get order number" or "Get master name" requests. See ypserv(1M). In addition, values of these two keys are used by ypxfr when it transfers a map from a master YP server to a slave. If ypxfr cannot figure out where to get the map, or if it is unable to determine whether the local copy is more recent than the copy at the master, extra command line switches must be set when it is run.

YP maps must be generated and modified only at the master server. They are copied to the slaves using ypxfr(1M) to avoid potential byte-ordering problems among YP servers running on machines with different architectures, and to minimize the amount of disk space required for the dbm files. The YP database can be initially set up for both masters and slaves by using ypinit(1M).

After the server databases are set up, it is probable that the contents of some maps will change. In general, some ASCII source version of the database exists on the master, and it is changed with a standard text editor. The update is incorporated into the YP map and is propagated from the master to the slaves by running /var/yp/Makefile, see ypmake(1M). All Sun-supplied maps have entries in /var/yp/Makefile; if a YP map is added, edit this file to support the new map. The makefile uses makedbm(1M) to generate the YP map on the master, and yppush(1M) to propagate the changed map to the slaves. yppush is a client of the map ypservers, which lists all the YP servers. For more information on this topic, see yppush(1M).

FILES

```
/var/yp
/var/yp/aliases
/var/yp/Makefile
```

SEE ALSO

makedbm(1M), ypinit(1M), ypmake(1M), yppoll(1M), yppush(1M), ypserv(1M), ypxfr(1M), dbm(3), publickey(4)

NAME

environ – user environment

DESCRIPTION

When a process begins execution, exec routines make available an array of strings called the environment [see exec(2)]. By convention, these strings have the form *variable=value*, for example, PATH=/sbin:/usr/sbin. These environmental variables provide a way to make information about a program's environment available to programs. The following environmental variables can be used by applications and are expected to be set in the target run-time environment.

HOME   The name of the user's login directory, set by login(1) from the password file (see passwd(4)).

LANG   The string used to specify localization information that allows users to work with different national conventions. The setlocale(3C) function looks for the LANG environment variable when it is called with "" as the *locale* argument. LANG is used as the default locale if the corresponding environment variable for a particular category is unset.

For example, when setlocale() is invoked as

         setlocale(LC_CTYPE, ""),

setlocale() will query the LC_CTYPE environment variable first to see if it is set and non-null. If LC_CTYPE is not set or null, then setlocale() will check the LANG environment variable to see if it is set and non-null. If both LANG and LC_CTYPE are unset or null, the default C locale will be used to set the LC_CTYPE category.

Most commands will invoke

         setlocale(LC_ALL, "")

prior to any other processing. This allows the command to be used with different national conventions by setting the appropriate environment variables.

The following environment variables are supported to correspond with each category of setlocale(3C):

LC_COLLATE   This category specifies the collation sequence being used. The information corresponding to this category is stored in a database created by the colltbl(1M) command. This environment variable affects strcoll(3C) and strxfrm(3C).

LC_CTYPE   This category specifies character classification, character conversion, and widths of multibyte characters. The information corresponding to this category is stored in a database created by the chrtbl(1M) command. The default C locale corresponds to the 7-bit ASCII character set. This environment variable is used by ctype(3C), mbchar(3C), and many commands; for example: cat(1), ed(1), ls(1), and vi(1).

LC_MESSAGES	This category specifies the language of the message database being used. For example, an application may have one message database with French messages, and another database with German messages. Message databases are created by the mkmsgs(1M) command. This environment variable is used by exstr(1), gettxt(1), gettxt(3C), and srchtxt(1).
LC_MONETARY	This category specifies the monetary symbols and delimiters used for a particular locale. The information corresponding to this category is stored in a database created by the montbl(1M) command. This environment variable is used by localeconv(3C).
LC_NUMERIC	This category specifies the decimal and thousands delimiters. The information corresponding to this category is stored in a database created by the chrtbl(1M) command. The default C locale corresponds to "." as the decimal delimiter and no thousands delimiter. This environment variable is used by localeconv(3C), printf(3C), and strtod(3C).
LC_TIME	This category specifies date and time formats. The information corresponding to this category is stored in a database specified in strftime(4). The default C locale corresponds to U.S. date and time formats. This environment variable is used by many commands and functions; for example: at(1), calendar(1), date(1), strftime(3C), and getdate(3C).

MSGVERB   Controls which standard format message components fmtmsg selects when messages are displayed to stderr [see fmtmsg(1) and fmtmsg(3C)].

SEV_LEVEL   Define severity levels and associate and print strings with them in standard format error messages [see addseverity(3C), fmtmsg(1), and fmtmsg(3C)].

NETPATH   A colon-separated list of network identifiers. A network identifier is a character string used by the Network Selection component of the system to provide application-specific default network search paths. A network identifier must consist of non-NULL characters and must have a length of at least 1. No maximum length is specified. Network identifiers are normally chosen by the system administrator. A network identifier is also the first field in any /etc/netconfig file entry. NETPATH thus provides a link into the /etc/netconfig file and the information about a network contained in that network's entry. /etc/netconfig is maintained by the system administrator. The library routines described in getnetpath(3N) access the NETPATH environment variable.

NLSPATH   Contains a sequence of templates which **catopen**(3C) uses when attempting to locate message catalogs. Each template consists of an optional prefix, one or more substitution fields, a filename and an optional suffix.

For example:

    NLSPATH="/system/nlslib/%N.cat"

defines that **catopen**() should look for all message catalogs in the directory **/system/nlslib**, where the catalog name should be constructed from the *name* parameter passed to **catopen**(), %N, with the suffix .cat.

Substitution fields consist of a % symbol, followed by a single-letter keyword. The following keywords are currently defined:

%N	The value of the *name* parameter passed to **catopen**().
%L	The value of LANG.
%l	The language element from LANG.
%t	The territory element from LANG.
%c	The codeset element from LANG.
%%	A single % character.

An empty string is substituted if the specified value is not currently defined. The separators "_" and "." are not included in %t and %c substitutions.

Templates defined in NLSPATH are separated by colons (:). A leading colon or two adjacent colons (::) is equivalent to specifying %N.

For example:

    NLSPATH=":%N.cat:/nlslib/%L/%N.cat"

indicates to **catopen**() that it should look for the requested message catalog in *name*, *name*.cat and /nlslib/$LANG/*name*.cat.

PATH   The sequence of directory prefixes that **sh**(1), **time**(1), **nice**(1), **nohup**(1), etc., apply in searching for a file known by an incomplete path name. The prefixes are separated by colons (:). **login**(1) sets PATH=/usr/bin. (For more detail, see **sh**(1).)

TERM   The kind of terminal for which output is to be prepared. This information is used by commands, such as **mm**(1) or **vi**(1), which may exploit special capabilities of that terminal.

TZ   Time zone information. The contents of the environment variable named TZ are used by the functions **ctime**(3C), **localtime**() (see **ctime**(3C)), **strftime**(3C) and **mktime**(3C) to override the default timezone. If the first character of TZ is a colon (:), the behavior is implementation defined, otherwise TZ has the form:

std offset [*dst* [*offset*], [*start* [/*time*], *end* [/*time*]]]

std and *dst*
>Three or more bytes that are the designation for the standard (*std*) and daylight savings time (*dst*) timezones. Only *std* is required, if *dst* is missing, then daylight savings time does not apply in this locale. Upper- and lower-case letters are allowed. Any characters except a leading colon (:), digits, a comma (,), a minus (–) or a plus (+) are allowed.

offset
>Indicates the value one must add to the local time to arrive at Coordinated Universal Time. The offset has the form:

>*hh* [: *mm* [: *ss*]]

>The minutes (*mm*) and seconds (*ss*) are optional. The hour (*hh*) is required and may be a single digit. The *offset* following *std* is required. If no *offset* follows *dst* , daylight savings time is assumed to be one hour ahead of standard time. One or more digits may be used; the value is always interpreted as a decimal number. The hour must be between 0 and 24, and the minutes (and seconds) if present between 0 and 59. Out of range values may cause unpredictable behavior. If preceded by a "–", the timezone is east of the Prime Meridian; otherwise it is west (which may be indicated by an optional preceding "+" sign).

start/time, end/time
>Indicates when to change to and back from daylight savings time, where *start/time* describes when the change from standard time to daylight savings time occurs, and *end/time* describes when the change back happens. Each *time* field describes when, in current local time, the change is made.

>The formats of *start* and *end* are one of the following:

>>*Jn*   The Julian day n ($1 \le n \le 365$). Leap days are not counted. That is, in all years, February 28 is day 59 and March 1 is day 60. It is impossible to refer to the occasional February 29.

>>*n*   The zero-based Julian day ($0 \le n \le 365$). Leap days are counted, and it is possible to refer to February 29.

>>*Mm.n.d*   The dth day, ($0 \le d \le 6$) of week n of month m of the year ($1 \le n \le 5$, $1 \le m \le 12$), where week 5 means "the last d-day in month m" which may occur in either the fourth or the fifth week). Week 1 is the first week in which the dth day occurs. Day zero is Sunday.

Implementation specific defaults are used for *start* and *end* if these optional fields are not given.

The *time* has the same format as *offset* except that no leading sign ("−" or "+") is allowed. The default, if *time* is not given is 02:00:00.

Further names may be placed in the environment by the **export** command and *name*=*value* arguments in **sh**(1), or by **exec**(2). It is unwise to conflict with certain shell variables that are frequently exported by .profile files: MAIL, PS1, PS2, IFS (see profile(4)).

SEE ALSO

chrtbl(1M), colltbl(1M), mkmsgs(1M), montbl(1M), netconfig(4), strftime(4), passwd(4), profile(4) in the *System Administrator's Reference Manual*.

exec(2), addseverity(3C), catopen(3C), ctime(3C), ctype(3C), fmtmsg(3C), getdate(3C), gettxt(3C), localeconv(3C), mbchar(3C), mktime(3C), printf(3C), strcoll(3C), strftime(3C), strtod(3C), strxfrm(3C), strftime(4), timezone(4).

cat(1), date(1), ed(1), fmtmsg(1), ls(1), login(1), nice(1), nohup(1), sh(1), sort(1), time(1), vi(1) in the *User's Reference Manual*.

getnetpath(3N), in the *Programmer's Guide: Networking Interfaces*.

mm(1) in the *DOCUMENTER'S WORKBENCH Software Technical Discussion and Reference Manual*.

NAME

ICMP – Internet Control Message Protocol

SYNOPSIS

```
#include <sys/socket.h>
#include <netinet/in.h>
#include <netinet/ip_icmp.h>

s = socket(AF_INET, SOCK_RAW, proto);

t = t_open("/dev/icmp", O_RDWR);
```

DESCRIPTION

ICMP is the error and control message protocol used by the Internet protocol family. It is used by the kernel to handle and report errors in protocol processing. It may also be accessed by programs using the socket interface or the Transport Level Interface (TLI) for network monitoring and diagnostic functions. When used with the socket interface, a raw socket type is used. The protocol number for ICMP, used in the *proto* parameter to the socket call, can be obtained from getprotobyname() [see getprotoent(3N)]. ICMP file descriptors and sockets are connectionless, and are normally used with the t_sndudata / t_rcvudata and the sendto() / recvfrom() calls.

Outgoing packets automatically have an Internet Protocol (IP) header prepended to them. Incoming packets are provided to the user with the IP header and options intact.

ICMP is an datagram protocol layered above IP. It is used internally by the protcol code for various purposes including routing, fault isolation, and congestion control. Receipt of an ICMP redirect message will add a new entry in the routing table, or modify an existing one. ICMP messages are routinely sent by the protocol code. Received ICMP messages may be reflected back to users of higher-level protocols such as TCP or UDP as error returns from system calls. A copy of all ICMP message received by the system is provided to every holder of an open ICMP socket or TLI descriptor.

SEE ALSO

send(2), getprotoent(3N), recvfrom(3N), t_rcvudata(3N), t_sndudata(3N), routing(4), inet(7), ip(7).

Postel, Jon, *Internet Control Message Protocol — DARPA Internet Program Protocol Specification*, RFC 792, Network Information Center, SRI International, Menlo Park, Calif., September 1981.

DIAGNOSTICS

A socket operation may fail with one of the following errors returned:

EISCONN   An attempt was made to establish a connection on a socket which already has one, or when trying to send a datagram with the destination address specified and the socket is already connected.

ENOTCONN   An attempt was made to send a datagram, but no destination address is specified, and the socket has not been connected.

ENOBUFS   The system ran out of memory for an internal data struc-
                           ture.

EADDRNOTAVAIL   An attempt was made to create a socket with a network
                           address for which no network interface exists.

NOTES

Replies to ICMP echo messages which are source routed are not sent back using
inverted source routes, but rather go back through the normal routing mechanisms.

NAME

IP – Internet Protocol

SYNOPSIS

#include <sys/socket.h>

#include <netinet/in.h>

s = socket(AF_INET, SOCK_RAW, proto);

t = t_open ("/dev/rawip", O_RDWR);

d = open ("/dev/ip", O_RDWR);

DESCRIPTION

IP is the internetwork datagram delivery protocol that is central to the Internet protocol family. Programs may use IP through higher-level protocols such as the Transmission Control Protocol (TCP) or the User Datagram Protocol (UDP), or may interface directly to IP. See tcp(7) and udp(7). Direct access may be via the socket interface (using a raw socket) or the Transport Level Interface (TLI). The protocol options defined in the IP specification may be set in outgoing datagrams.

The STREAMS driver /dev/rawip is the TLI transport provider that provides raw access to IP. The device /dev/ip is the multiplexing STREAMS driver that implements the protocol processing of IP. The latter connects below to datalink providers [interface drivers, see if(3N)], and above to tranport providers such as TCP and UDP.

Raw IP sockets are connectionless and are normally used with the sendto() and recvfrom() calls, [(see send(2) and recv(2)] although the connect(2) call may also be used to fix the destination for future datagrams [in which case the read(2) or recv(2) and write(2) or send(2) calls may be used]. If proto is zero, the default protocol, IPPROTO_RAW, is used. If proto is non-zero, that protocol number will be set in outgoing datagrams and will be used to filter incoming datagrams. An IP header will be generated and prepended to each outgoing datagram; received datagrams are returned with the IP header and options intact.

A single socket option, IP_OPTIONS, is supported at the IP level. This socket option may be used to set IP options to be included in each outgoing datagram. IP options to be sent are set with setsockopt() [see getsockopt(2)]. The get-sockopt(2) call returns the IP options set in the last setsockopt() call. IP options on received datagrams are visible to user programs only using raw IP sockets. The format of IP options given in setsockopt() matches those defined in the IP specification with one exception: the list of addresses for the source routing options must include the first-hop gateway at the beginning of the list of gateways. The first-hop gateway address will be extracted from the option list and the size adjusted accordingly before use. IP options may be used with any socket type in the Internet family.

At the socket level, the socket option SO_DONTROUTE may be applied. This option forces datagrams being sent to bypass the routing step in output. Normally, IP selects a network interface to send the datagram, and possibly an intermediate gateway, based on an entry in the routing table. See routing(4). When SO_DONTROUTE is set, the datagram will be sent using the interface whose network number or full IP address matches the destination address. If no interface matches, the error ENETUNRCH will be returned.

Raw IP datagrams can also be sent and received using the TLI connectionless primitives.

Datagrams flow through the IP layer in two directions: from the network *up* to user processes and from user processes *down* to the network. Using this orientation, IP is layered *above* the network interface drivers and *below* the transport protocols such as UDP and TCP. The Internet Control Message Protocol (ICMP) is logically a part of IP. See icmp(7).

IP provides for a checksum of the header part, but not the data part of the datagram. The checksum value is computed and set in the process of sending datagrams and checked when receiving datagrams. IP header checksumming may be disabled for debugging purposes by patching the kernel variable ipcksum to have the value zero.

IP options in received datagrams are processed in the IP layer according to the protocol specification. Currently recognized IP options include: security, loose source and record route (LSRR), strict source and record route (SSRR), record route, stream identifier, and internet timestamp.

The IP layer will normally forward received datagrams that are not addressed to it. Forwarding is under the control of the kernel variable *ipforwarding*: if *ipforwarding* is zero, IP datagrams will not be forwarded; if *ipforwarding* is one, IP datagrams will be forwarded. *ipforwarding* is usually set to one only in machines with more than one network interface (internetwork routers). This kernel variable can be patched to enable or disable forwarding.

The IP layer will send an ICMP message back to the source host in many cases when it receives a datagram that can not be handled. A time exceeded ICMP message will be sent if the time to live field in the IP header drops to zero in the process of forwarding a datagram. A destination unreachable message will be sent if a datagram can not be forwarded because there is no route to the final destination, or if it can not be fragmented. If the datagram is addressed to the local host but is destined for a protocol that is not supported or a port that is not in use, a destination unreachable message will also be sent. The IP layer may send an ICMP source quench message if it is receiving datagrams too quickly. ICMP messages are only sent for the first fragment of a fragmented datagram and are never returned in response to errors in other ICMP messages.

The IP layer supports fragmentation and reassembly. Datagrams are fragmented on output if the datagram is larger than the maximum transmission unit (MTU) of the network interface. Fragments of received datagrams are dropped from the reassembly queues if the complete datagram is not reconstructed within a short time period.

Errors in sending discovered at the network interface driver layer are passed by IP back up to the user process.

SEE ALSO

read(2), write(2), connect(3N), getsockopt(3N), recv(3N), send(3N), routing(4), icmp(7), inet(7) tcp(7), udp(7).

Postel, Jon, *Internet Protocol - DARPA Internet Program Protocol Specification*, RFC 791, Network Information Center, SRI International, Menlo Park, Calif., September 1981.

DIAGNOSTICS

A socket operation may fail with one of the following errors returned:

EACCESS
: A IP broadcast destination address was specified and the caller was not the privileged user.

EISCONN
: An attempt was made to establish a connection on a socket which already had one, or to send a datagram with the destination address specified and the socket was already connected.

EMSGSIZE
: An attempt was made to send a datagram that was too large for an interface, but was not allowed to be fragmented (such as broadcasts).

ENETUNREACH
: An attempt was made to establish a connection or send a datagram, where there was no matching entry in the routing table, or if an ICMP destination unreachable message was received.

ENOTCONN
: A datagrem was sent, but no destination address was specified, and the socket had not been connected.

ENOBUFS
: The system ran out of memory for fragmentation buffers or other internal data structure.

EADDRNOTAVAIL
: An attempt was made to create a socket with a local address that did not match any network interface, or an IP broadcast destination address was specified and the network interface does not support broadcast.

The following errors may occur when setting or getting IP options:

EINVAL
: An unknown socket option name was given.

EINVAL
: The IP option field was improperly formed; an option field was shorter than the minimum value or longer than the option buffer provided.

NOTES

Raw sockets should receive ICMP error packets relating to the protocol; currently such packets are simply discarded.

Users of higher-level protocols such as TCP and UDP should be able to see received IP options.

NAME
sockio – ioctls that operate directly on sockets

SYNOPSIS
#include <sys/sockio.h>

DESCRIPTION
The IOCTL's listed in this manual page apply directly to sockets, independent of any underlying protocol. The **setsockopt** call (see **getsockopt**(3N)) is the primary method for operating on sockets, rather than on the underlying protocol or network interface. ioctls for a specific network interface or protocol are documented in the manual page for that interface or protocol.

SIOCSPGRP   The argument is a pointer to an int. Set the process-group ID that will subsequently receive SIGIO or SIGURG signals for the socket referred to by the descriptor passed to ioctl to the value of that int.

SIOCGPGRP   The argument is a pointer to an int. Set the value of that int to the process-group ID that is receiving SIGIO or SIGURG signals for the socket referred to by the descriptor passed to ioctl.

SIOCCATMARK   The argument is a pointer to an int. Set the value of that int to 1 if the read pointer for the socket referred to by the descriptor passed to ioctl points to a mark in the data stream for an out-of-band message. Set the value of that int to 0 if the read pointer for the socket referred to by the descriptor passed to **ioctl** does not point to a mark in the data stream for an out-of-band message.

SEE ALSO
ioctl(2), getsockopt(2), filio(4)

NAME

TCP – Internet Transmission Control Protocol

SYNOPSIS

```
#include <sys/socket.h>
#include <netinet/in.h>

s = socket(AF_INET, SOCK_STREAM, 0);

t = t_open("/dev/tcp", O_RDWR);
```

DESCRIPTION

TCP is the virtual circuit protocol of the Internet protocol family. It provides reliable, flow-controlled, in order, two-way transmission of data. It is a byte-stream protocol layered above the Internet Protocol (IP), the Internet protocol family's internetwork datagram delivery protocol.

Programs can access TCP using the socket interface as a SOCK_STREAM socket type, or using the Transport Level Interface (TLI) where it supports the connection-oriented (T_COTS_ORD) service type.

TCP uses IP's host-level addressing and adds its own per-host collection of port addresses. The endpoints of a TCP connection are identified by the combination of an IP address and a TCP port number. Although other protocols, such as the User Datagram Protocol (UDP), may use the same host and port address format, the port space of these protocols is distinct. See inet(7) for details on the common aspects of addressing in the Internet protocol family.

Sockets utilizing TCP are either active or passive. Active sockets initiate connections to passive sockets. Both types of sockets must have their local IP address and TCP port number bound with the bind(2) system call after the socket is created. By default, TCP sockets are active. A passive socket is created by calling the listen(2) system call after binding the socket with bind(). This establishes a queueing parameter for the passive socket. After this, connections to the passive socket can be received with the accept(2) system call. Active sockets use the connect(2) call after binding to initiate connections.

By using the special value INADDR_ANY, the local IP address can be left unspecified in the bind() call by either active or passive TCP sockets. This feature is usually used if the local address is either unknown or irrelevant. If left unspecified, the local IP address will be bound at connection time to the address of the network interface used to service the connection.

Once a connection has been established, data can be exchanged using the read(2) and write(2) system calls.

TCP supports one socket option which is set with setsockopt() and tested with getsockopt(2). Under most circumstances, TCP sends data when it is presented. When outstanding data has not yet been acknowledged, it gathers small amounts of output to be sent in a single packet once an acknowledgement is received. For a small number of clients, such as window systems that send a stream of mouse events which receive no replies, this packetization may cause significant delays. Therefore, TCP provides a boolean option, TCP_NODELAY (defined in /usr/include/netinet/tcp.h), to defeat this algorithm. The option level for

the **setsockopt()** call is the protocol number for TCP, available from
getprotobyname() [see getprotoent(3N)].

Options at the IP level may be used with TCP; See ip(7).

TCP provides an urgent data mechanism, which may be invoked using the out-
of-band provisions of **send**(2). The caller may mark one byte as urgent with the
MSG_OOB flag to **send**(2). This sets an urgent pointer pointing to this byte in the
TCP stream. The receiver on the other side of the stream is notified of the urgent
data by a SIGURG signal. The SIOCATMARK ioctl() request returns a value indicating whether the stream is at the urgent mark. Because the system never
returns data across the urgent mark in a single read(2) call, it is possible to
advance to the urgent data in a simple loop which reads data, testing the socket
with the SIOCATMARK ioctl() request, until it reaches the mark.

Incoming connection requests that include an IP source route option are noted,
and the reverse source route is used in responding.

A checksum over all data helps TCP implement reliability. Using a window-based
flow control mechanism that makes use of positive acknowledgements, sequence
numbers, and a retransmission strategy, TCP can usually recover when datagrams
are damaged, delayed, duplicated or delivered out of order by the underlying
communication medium.

If the local TCP receives no acknowledgements from its peer for a period of time,
as would be the case if the remote machine crashed, the connection is closed and
an error is returned to the user. If the remote machine reboots or otherwise loses
state information about a TCP connection, the connection is aborted and an error
is returned to the user.

SEE ALSO

read(2), write(2), accept(3N), bind(3N), connect(3N), getprotoent(3N),
getsockopt(3N), listen(3N), send(3N), inet(7), ip(7).

Postel, Jon, *Transmission Control Protocol - DARPA Internet Program Protocol
Specification*, RFC 793, Network Information Center, SRI International, Menlo Park,
Calif., September 1981.

DIAGNOSTICS

A socket operation may fail if:

EISCONN	A connect() operation was attempted on a socket on which a connect() operation had already been performed.
ETIMEDOUT	A connection was dropped due to excessive retransmissions.
ECONNRESET	The remote peer forced the connection to be closed (usually because the remote machine has lost state information about the connection due to a crash).
ECONNREFUSED	The remote peer actively refused connection establishment (usually because no process is listening to the port).

EADDRINUSE	A bind() operation was attempted on a socket with a network address/port pair that has already been bound to another socket.
EADDRNOTAVAIL	A bind() operation was attempted on a socket with a network address for which no network interface exists.
EACCES	A bind() operation was attempted with a reserved port number and the effective user ID of the process was not the privileged user.
ENOBUFS	The system ran out of memory for internal data structures.

NAME
ticlts, ticots, ticotsord – loopback transport providers

SYNOPSIS
#include <ticlts.h>
#include <ticots.h>
#include <ticotsord.h>

DESCRIPTION
The devices known as ticlts, ticots, and ticotsord are "loopback transport providers," that is, stand-alone networks at the transport level. Loopback transport providers are transport providers in every sense except one: only one host (the local machine) is "connected to" a loopback network. Loopback transports present a TPI (STREAMS-level) interface to application processes and are intended to be accessed via the TLI (application-level) interface. They are implemented as clone devices and support address spaces consisting of "flex-addresses," i.e., arbitrary sequences of octets, of length > 0, represented by a netbuf structure.

ticlts is a datagram-mode transport provider. It offers (connectionless) service of type T_CLTS. Its default address size is TCL_DEFAULTADDRSZ. ticlts prints the following error messages (see t_rcvuderr(3N)):

TCL_BADADDR	bad address specification
TCL_BADOPT	bad option specification
TCL_NOPEER	bound
TCL_PEERBADSTATE	peer in wrong state

ticots is a virtual circuit-mode transport provider. It offers (connection-oriented) service of type T_COTS. Its default address size is TCO_DEFAULTADDRSZ. ticots prints the following disconnect messages (see t_rcvdis(3N)):

TCO_NOPEER	no listener on destination address
TCO_PEERNOROOMONQ	peer has no room on connect queue
TCO_PEERBADSTATE	peer in wrong state
TCO_PEERINITIATED	peer-initiated disconnect
TCO_PROVIDERINITIATED	provider-initiated disconnect

ticotsord is a virtual circuit-mode transport provider, offering service of type T_COTS_ORD (connection-oriented service with orderly release). Its default address size is TCOO_DEFAULTADDRSZ. ticotsord prints the following disconnect messages (see t_rcvdis(3N)):

TCOO_NOPEER	no listener on destination address
TCOO_PEERNOROOMONQ	peer has no room on connect queue
TCOO_PEERBADSTATE	peer in wrong state
TCOO_PEERINITIATED	peer-initiated disconnect
TCOO_PROVIDERINITIATED	provider-initiated disconnect

USAGE
Loopback transports support a local IPC mechanism through the TLI interface. Applications implemented in a transport provider-independent manner on a client-server model using this IPC are transparently transportable to networked environments.

Transport provider-independent applications must not include the header files listed in the synopsis section above. In particular, the options are (like all transport provider options) provider dependent.

ticlts and ticots support the same service types (T_CLTS and T_COTS) supported by the OSI transport-level model. The use of ticlts and ticots is encouraged.

ticotsord supports the same service type (T_COTSORD) supported by the TCP/IP model. The use of ticotsord is discouraged except for reasons of compatibility.

FILES

/dev/ticlts
/dev/ticots
/dev/ticotsord

NAME

UDP – Internet User Datagram Protocol

SYNOPSIS

```
#include <sys/socket.h>
#include <netinet/in.h>

s = socket(AF_INET, SOCK_DGRAM, 0);

t = t_open("/dev/udp", O_RDWR);
```

DESCRIPTION

UDP is a simple datagram protocol which is layered directly above the Internet Protocol (IP). Programs may access UDP using the socket interface, where it supports the SOCK_DGRAM socket type, or using the Transport Level Interface (TLI), where it supports the connectionless (T_CLTS) service type.

Within the socket interface, UDP is normally used with the sendto(), sendmsg(), recvfrom(), and recvmsg() calls [see send(2) and recv(2)]. If the connect(2) call is used to fix the destination for future packets, then the recv(2) or read(2) and send(2) or write(2) calls may be used.

UDP address formats are identical to those used by the Transmission Control Protocol (TCP). Like TCP, UDP uses a port number along with an IP address to identify the endpoint of communication. The UDP port number space is separate from the TCP port number space (that is, a UDP port may not be connected to a TCP port). The bind(2) call can be used to set the local address and port number of a UDP socket. The local IP address may be left unspecified in the bind() call by using the special value INADDR_ANY. If the bind() call is not done, a local IP address and port number will be assigned to the endpoint when the first packet is sent. Broadcast packets may be sent (assuming the underlying network supports this) by using a reserved broadcast address; This address is network interface dependent. Broadcasts may only be sent by the privileged user.

Options at the IP level may be used with UDP; see ip(7).

There are a variety of ways that a UDP packet can be lost or corrupted, including a failure of the underlying communication mechanism. UDP implements a checksum over the data portion of the packet. If the checksum of a received packet is in error, the packet will be dropped with no indication given to the user. A queue of received packets is provided for each UDP socket. This queue has a limited capacity. Arriving datagrams which will not fit within its *high-water* capacity are silently discarded.

UDP processes Internet Control Message Protocol (ICMP) error messages received in response to UDP packets it has sent. See icmp(7). ICMP source quench messages are ignored. ICMP destination unreachable, time exceeded and parameter problem messages disconnect the socket from its peer so that subsequent attempts to send packets using that socket will return an error. UDP will not guarantee that packets are delivered in the order they were sent. As well, duplicate packets may be generated in the communication process.

SEE ALSO

read(2), write(2), bind(3N), connect(3N), recv(3N), send(3N), icmp(7), inet(7), ip(7), tcp(7).

Postel, Jon, *User Datagram Protocol*, RFC 768, Network Information Center, SRI International, Menlo Park, Calif., August 1980.

DIAGNOSTICS

A socket operation may fail if:

EISCONN	A connect() operation was attempted on a socket on which a connect() operation had already been performed, and the socket could not be successfully disconnected before making the new connection.
EISCONN	A sendto() or sendmsg() operation specifying an address to which the message should be sent was attempted on a socket on which a connect() operation had already been performed.
ENOTCONN	A send() or write() operation, or a sendto() or sendmsg() operation not specifying an address to which the message should be sent, was attempted on a socket on which a connect() operation had not already been performed.
EADDRINUSE	A bind() operation was attempted on a socket with a network address/port pair that has already been bound to another socket.
EADDRNOTAVAIL	A bind() operation was attempted on a socket with a network address for which no network interface exists.
EINVAL	A sendmsg() operation with a non-NULL msg_accrights was attempted.
EACCES	A bind() operation was attempted with a reserved port number and the effective user ID of the process was not the privileged user.
ENOBUFS	The system ran out of memory for internal data structures.

Prentice Hall, the leading publisher of C and UNIX® System V reference books and documentation, is continuously expanding its channels of distribution in order to make book buying as easy as possible for professionals for whom access to timely information is crucial. Won't you help us to serve you more efficiently by completing this brief survey? Individuals completing this survey will be added to our C and UNIX® System bookbuyer list and will receive our new C and UNIX® System Catalog and other announcements on a regular basis.

Title Purchased:_____
Author:_____

I. How did you purchase the book?
_____ by mail _____ by phone _____ by fax
_____ in a bookstore _____ in a software store
_____ through a corporate book distribution service
_____ at a professional meeting or seminar

II. Was this purchase charged to your business?
_____ Yes _____ No

III. Are you involved in developing and/or instructing training courses? _____ Yes _____ No
If so, please provide the following information:

Course Title: _____
Number of Students Per Year: _____
Books in Use: _____

IV. Are you interested in packaging UNIX System V documentation with your product?
_____ Yes _____ No

V. Would you like to receive information about our custom documentation program?
_____ Yes _____ No

VI. Please list topics of importance to you and your colleagues on which you would like to see books published: _____
_____

VII. Are you interested in submitting a manuscript to Prentice Hall for possible publication? _____ Yes _____ No Area of Research _____

Name _____
Title_____
Name of Firm_____
Address _____
_____

NO POSTAGE
NECESSARY
IF MAILED IN THE
UNITED STATES

BUSINESS REPLY MAIL

FIRST CLASS   PERMIT NO. 365, ENGLEWOOD CLIFFS, NJ

POSTAGE WILL BE PAID BY ADDRESSEE

PRENTICE HALL
Attn: PTR Marketing Manager
College Marketing Department
Route 9W
Englewood Cliffs, NJ 07632-9940

What do YOU think?

AT&T values your opinion. Please indicate your opinions in each of the following areas. We'd like to know how well this document meets your needs.

Book Title:_____

	Excellent	Good	Fair	Poor
Accuracy - Is the information correct?	❑	❑	❑	❑
Completeness - Is information missing?	❑	❑	❑	❑
Organization - Is information easy to find?	❑	❑	❑	❑
Clarity - Do you understand the information?	❑	❑	❑	❑
Examples - Are there enough?	❑	❑	❑	❑
Illustrations - Are there enough?	❑	❑	❑	❑
Appearance - Do you like the page format?	❑	❑	❑	❑
Physical binding - Do you like the cover and binding?	❑	❑	❑	❑

Does the document meet your needs? Why or why not?

_____

_____

_____

What is the single most important improvement that we could make to this document?

_____

_____

_____

Please complete the following information.

Name (Optional): _____

Job Title or Function: _____

Organization: _____

Address: _____

_____

Phone: (   ) _____

If we need more information may we contact you? Yes ❑ No ❑   **Thank you.**

BUSINESS REPLY MAIL

FIRST CLASS MAIL   PERMIT NO. 199   SUMMIT, NJ

POSTAGE WILL BE PAID BY ADDRESSEE

AT&T
Department Head
UNIX System Documentation and Development Dept.
Room F-308
190 River Road
Summit, NJ 07901-9907